The Global Emergence
of Gay and Lesbian Politics

The Global Emergence of Gay and Lesbian Politics

National Imprints of a Worldwide Movement

Edited by

BARRY D ADAM, JAN WILLEM DUYVENDAK,
AND ANDRÉ KROUWEL

TEMPLE UNIVERSITY PRESS
Philadelphia

Temple University Press, Philadelphia 19122
Copyright © 1999 by Temple University
All rights reserved
Published 1999
Printed in the United States of America

⊗ The paper used in this publication meets the requirements of the
American National Standard for Information Sciences—Permanence
of Paper for Printed Library Materials, ANSI Z39.48-1984

Library of Congress Cataloging-in-Publication Data

The global emergence of gay and lesbian politics : national imprints
    of a worldwide movement / edited by Barry D Adam, Jan Willem
    Duyvendak, and André Krouwel.
         p.   cm.
    Includes bibliographical references and index.
    ISBN 1-56639-644-1 (cloth : alk. paper).—ISBN 1-56639-645-X
    (pbk. : alk. paper)
       1. Gay rights—History.   2. Gay men—Political activity.
    3. Lesbians—Political Activity.   I. Adam, Barry D.   II. Duyvendak,
    Jan Willem.   III. Krouwel, André.
    HQ76.5.G56   1999
    305.9′0664′09—DC21   98-17218

Contents

The Global Emergence
of Gay and Lesbian Politics

BARRY D ADAM,
JAN WILLEM DUYVENDAK,
AND ANDRÉ KROUWEL

1   Introduction

GAY AND lesbian movements have a century-long history since the founding of the Scientific-Humanitarian Committee in a Berlin apartment in 1897. Early initiatives to advance the citizenship rights of gay and lesbian people dissolved in the Holocaust, however, and the authoritarian forms of moral and sexual regulation that swept both the communist world and the Western democracies in the mid-twentieth century almost suffocated the attempts to start over after World War II (Adam 1995: chap. 3). Contemporary movements trace their origins to Amsterdam, Copenhagen, Paris, and Los Angeles, where a few brave individuals renewed efforts in the 1950s to carve out small gay-friendly spaces in the chilly climate of post-war reconstruction. The tidal change that transformed gay and lesbian movements from a handful of scattered, low-profile organizations to a worldwide phenomenon was catalyzed by the rise of the New Left in the 1960s and 1970s. The New Left grew out of the civil rights movement, which was struggling to advance African Americans in the United States at the same time that nationalist movements in Africa and Asia were throwing off colonialism. The New Left included student movements not only in North America, Western Europe, and Japan but also in Mexico and Czechoslovakia (Wallerstein 1989). Out of these transformations emerged environmental and feminist movements and a new critique of family, gender, and sexual repression in the form of gay liberation and lesbian feminism. By the 1990s virtually every urban center in North America, the European Union, Australia, and New Zealand and many major cities in Latin America, eastern Asia, and South Africa had a variety of gay and lesbian organizations.

The International Lesbian and Gay Association, founded in 1979, continues to receive inquiries from places that have never before had any form of organized gay or lesbian presence. With the fall of the Soviet government in 1991, groups quickly emerged in Moldova and Siberia. Letters arrived from the provinces in China, from sub-Saharan Africa, and from Bolivia, India, and Indonesia. Pioneering volumes edited by the International Lesbian and Gay Association (International Gay Association

1985; International Lesbian and Gay Association 1988; Hendriks, Tielman, and van der Veen, 1993) have gathered together participants' experiences from around the world. Journalists have documented international aspects of these experiences through impressionistic traveler's accounts (Miller 1992) or reprints from existing stories in the gay press (Likosky 1992), while Rex Wockner has built the most effective gay and lesbian news distribution system on current affairs from around the world. And scholars like Dennis Altman (1971, 1996) have consistently offered an international, comparative eye toward developments in gay and AIDS movement trends.

This collection, *The Global Emergence of Gay and Lesbian Politics*, seeks to provide not simply an account of the existence of gay and lesbian movements but also a systematic understanding of how and why they have come about. Although movements exist around the world, they vary tremendously in their form and objectives. Same-sex bonding in many cultures does not necessarily entail a sense of personal identity or an idea of a community of shared interests. The content and meaning of "gay" or "lesbian" are contested terrain, varying within and among societies. How homosexually interested people come together, organize, and identify group objectives, then, differs immensely from place to place; this volume seeks to sort out and make sense of many of these differences. One of the ways to do this is to employ the tools of social theory to determine how social analysis can improve the understanding of movement successes and failures, but the experiences of gay and lesbian movements can also test the viability of theories that claim to offer new insight into social movement development.

At the same time, the social conditions that have limited the development of movements affect the ability to carry out a comparative analysis. Because the growth of gay and lesbian studies has been possible in only a very few places in the world, basic research has yet to be done on gay and lesbian movements in many countries, and movements are only embryonic (or not yet existent) in several major cultural areas, including the Arab world.

SOCIAL MOVEMENT THEORIES

Although the study of social movements has expanded enormously in recent decades in both Europe and the United States (McAdam, McCarthy, and Zald, 1988; Klandermans, Kriesi, and Tarrow 1988; Koopmans 1995), there has been a surprising neglect of gay and lesbian movements among social movement theorists (Duyvendak 1995). Studies of gay and lesbian movements have been mostly restricted to particular geographical areas or historical periods, and comparative surveys and analyses are rare (Adam 1995).

Social movements have been studied from various perspectives: in particular, the resource mobilization approach (Oberschall 1973; W. Gamson 1975; McCarthy and Zald 1977; Aya 1990) and the political process or political opportunity structure approach (Tilly 1978; McAdam 1982; Kitschelt 1986; Tarrow 1989; Kriesi 1991; Kriesi et al. 1992). Both approaches tend to assume that actors behave rationally, maximize their benefits, and minimize their costs by responding instrumentally to opportunities in the environment. This sets them apart from the classical approach (Adorno et al. 1950; Smelser 1962; Gurr 1970) and the new social movement approach (Touraine 1978; Melucci 1980, 1989), in which psychological or cultural factors play a larger role.

As the emergence of emancipation movements shifted the boundaries of the political, blurring the demarcation of the political and private spheres, the lines between the state and civil society faded as well. Social movements put forward political demands in the moral sphere and moral demands in the political sphere (J. Gamson 1989). New social movements have forced the traditional political actors not simply to mediate interests but also to address the cultural construction of difference and issues around the "good life" (Offe 1985).

Still, new social movement theories are not without their problems (Adam 1993), especially when applied to gay and lesbian movements. A somewhat syncretic thesis on the origins of the new social movements, drawn from the work of Jürgen Habermas (1975), Henri Lefèbvre (1976), Claus Offe (1984), Carl Boggs (1986), and Samuel Bowles and Herbert Gintis (1986) might follow these lines: crises of advanced capitalist societies, which were "managed" in the postwar era by the modern Keynesian state, have been displaced onto crises of social reproduction. In other words, the ossification of electoral and party systems combined with the bureaucratization of trade unions have resulted in a displacement of political activity onto new sites. Habermas (1987: 392), in particular, asserts that the purpose of new social movement mobilization is "primarily one of . . . defending and restoring endangered ways of life," namely addressing issues of "quality of life, equal rights, individual self-realization, participation, and human rights." New social movement theory typically postulates that popular mobilization in the current era has been characterized by a shift toward

- attempts to decolonize the life-world of intrusions by the economic and political spheres,
- the mobilization of largely middle-class constituencies, and

- the rise of a new "cultural politics" oriented less to "bread-and-butter" issues than toward questions of identity, rights, and autonomy (Adam 1993, 1997)

Although the imagery of contemporary movement practice advanced by this version of new social movement theory describes the evolution of the gay and lesbian movement toward "networks composed of a multiplicity of groups that are dispersed, fragmented, and submerged in everyday life" with "short-term and reversible commitment, multiple leadership, temporary and ad hoc organizational structures" (Melucci 1989: 60), this theory is only partly applicable to gay and lesbian mobilization. Gay and lesbian organizations

- are not simply protective of existing lifestyles but also innovative of new ways of living,
- remain fully engaged with the state in order to change traditional moral regulation,
- are much more than middle-class or first-world mobilizations,
- vary widely in organizational form from the formal, federal model of Italy and Denmark to the spontaneity of OutRage and Queer Nation, and
- address virtually every sphere of life including the workplace and labor unions, street violence, housing and domestic relationships, delivery of health and social services, organized religion, and cultural representations in mass media and education (Adam 1995: 178).

And the gay and lesbian movement is not simply an example of "identity politics," a claim that applies, at most, to its "cultural" or nationalist face rather than to the whole of gay and lesbian movement practice.

MOVEMENTS AND MODERNITY

In the late twentieth century, lesbians, gay men, and their movements have tended to be cast by their allies as embodying a progressive social formation akin to other new social movement constituencies. Their adversaries have shared this conception by interpreting them as a leading sign of modernity, encoding them into an opposing antimodernist discourse that draws on a millennium of antihomosexual thought in the West. There is nothing "essential" or "necessary" about these identities. Manifestations of same-sex desire in societies studied by anthropologists and classicists show social characteristics that share few, if any, of the traits assigned by either contemporary sign system (Adam 1985a; Greenberg 1988). Discourse analysis might claim that the homosexual/heterosexual opposition and the constructions of these terms over time show how Western subjectivities continue to be reproduced through symbolic universes that make these distinctions real. At the same time, an approach that ignores social structure cannot account for the ways in which discourses of homosexuality evolve, shift, and reconstitute each other in history. Social conflicts over representation index structural processes where opposed social groups deploy, promote, or combat representations in struggles over economic, political, and cultural benefits. Moreover, it is only in the twentieth century that homosexual desire has acquired a historical subjectivity such that its adherents can themselves enter into the fray as sociohistorical actors able to affect the differentiation process.

To encapsulate a good deal of historical and sociological analysis into a few sentences, the development of a modern capitalist world system over the last half-millennium has reorganized both the public and private spheres in ways that have shaped the emergence of gay and lesbian peoples and movements around the world (D'Emilio 1983; Adam 1985b). The modern world system has reorganized and incorporated indigenous economies into wage/labor systems, thereby breaking the hold of traditional kinship codes as the primary productive and redistributive systems in societies. This reorganization has permitted greater personal autonomy, initially for men and eventually for women, in the choice of spouse or domestic partner. It has allowed the ascendancy of romantic love ideologies and of subjective feeling as a "ground" for personal bonding. It has moved vast majorities of people from rural to urban life. It has opened public spaces where men, and less often women, have been able to encounter each other outside existing community and kin ties. And on this new terrain have grown the social networks that have become gay and lesbian worlds functioning as "oases of refuge and intimacy in a depersonalized, atomized world" (Adam 1995: 13–14). Just as for nineteenth-century Jews, the comparatively recent historical visibility of lesbians and gay men has associated them with modernity in public discourse.

Changes in the modern world system have also contributed to the formation of reactionary social forces aimed at not only reinforcing the preeminence of traditional morality and culture but "disciplining" upstart and "undeserving" emergent social groups as well. As Philip Corrigan and Derek Sayer (1985) point out, the nation-state might usefully be thought of as the site where social groups defined variously by race, language, religion, gender, and sexuality forge a hegemony over a territory. Hegemonic social groups, in turn, institutionalize their own cultures as national cultures, thereby generating a range of subordinated and minority groups who must find a place in an alien world. The consolidation of an intense antisodomy orthodoxy at the apogee of the feudal period in the thirteenth and fourteenth centuries (Boswell 1980) solidified ecclesiastical doctrines into an official morality and culture that entered into the formation of nation-states of the eighteenth, nineteenth, and twentieth centuries. These doctrines also played no small role in differentiating and labeling a portion of the national citizenries as a people apart, marked by their (homo)sexuality.

Orthodox discourses, in cultures with Judeo-Christian or Islamic heritages, interpellate "homosexuals" as a sign of decadence and chaos; modernized reactionary discourses combine this meaning with its rejection of modernity. The adherents of antihomosexual world views have come from a range of social groups disturbed or threatened by modernity—usually traditional elites fearful of change and declining social classes resentful of groups on the rise. This kind of sociologic was already evident in the reaction of British elites to the French Revolution (Corrigan and Sayer 1985), where a general crackdown on dissenters encompassed homosexual men as well (Adam 1995:12). In the twentieth century, reactionary forces such as Nazism and McCarthyism have attacked gay men and lesbians along with such other symbols of the modern as Jews and socialists. And it is a symbolic logic that is drawn on by homophobic forces, from the Colorado human rights repeal campaign of 1992 to the death squads in Colombia and Brazil.

Little wonder, then, that early gay and lesbian movements aligned themselves with Enlightenment values of secularization, science, humanism, democracy, and personal autonomy in an effort to break free from the stifling orthodoxies of the medieval era. This discursive system has grounded the political orientation of much of the twentieth century, in which gay and lesbian movements have attempted to intervene in a field of contenders who wield constructions of homosexuality over the heads of gay, lesbian, bisexual, and transgendered people, often with baleful consequences. Within this general historical context, local conflicts play out within the "game plan" bequeathed by Western tradition.

MOVEMENTS AND POSTMODERNITY

In advanced, industrial societies in the 1980s and 1990s, the Keynesian welfare state has increasingly given way to neoliberal restructuring in a globalized marketplace (Adam forthcoming). The social dislocation accompanying these changes exerts a complex range of forces on gay/lesbian and other social movements. The initiatives taken by the Margaret Thatcher and Ronald Reagan governments spawned a generation of state imitators around the world (often with the coercive "encouragement" of the World Bank and International Monetary Fund). A rhetoric of "belt tightening" and "downsizing" has accompanied economic policies that have imposed a heavy burden of unemployment and have partially dismantled the "social safety net." A "family values" rhetoric has supplemented economic policies in order to privatize social responsibilities once assumed by the state and in order to target gay and lesbian people and single mothers as the lightning rods for the anxieties generated by this heightened economic insecurity. The emergence of AIDS in the 1980s created another site of contention over family, sexuality, and the provision of state services (Altman 1986, 1996; Patton 1990; Adam 1992; Kinsman 1992). In the post-Communist era, capitalist elites no longer feel the threat of socialism and test the limits of tolerance that citizens have for greater economic discipline and fewer payoffs. In the 1990s the rightward trend echoes in a resurgence of political movements that thrive on resentment and nostalgia for simpler and more prosperous times.

It is in this neoliberal, "restructured" era that a discourse on postmodernism has arisen. Queer theorists have sought to reconceptualize gay, lesbian, bisexual, and transgendered peoples and identities in a postmodern framework where the grand narratives of modern movements, focused on equality and emancipation, give way to a paradoxical affirmation and deconstruction of difference (Seidman 1996). At the same time that gay and lesbian people have been embracing the symbols of queer nationality to an unprecedented degree, the idea of queer ethnicity has met its strongest critics (J. Gamson 1995). It is not altogether surprising that gay and lesbian movements have encountered the greatest resistance to the realization of the rights and freedoms of full citizenship in the countries where that the modernist agenda has been subjected to thoroughgoing reconsideration—the United States and the United Kingdom—whereas in the Netherlands and Scandinavia, the "queer" challenge has found little resonance.

The essays in this collection show how gay and lesbian identities, cultures, and movements have flourished in (or been impeded by) various national environments. While full-fledged participation in the rights and freedoms of liberal democracy has been increasingly realized, especially in northern Europe, the struggle continues elsewhere against forces that continue to marshall premodern rhetoric. The proponents of postmodernism typically presume that liberal democratic pluralism is already fully realized, in order to read the fall of "grand narratives" as the sign of a new social field of personal freedom, irony, and playfulness. Yet in a neoliberal era, there are many classes and regions of people who react defensively against the changes around them, often by reaching for the comforting rhetoric of tradition and conservatism. This is clear enough in the New Right constituencies of the United States, as well as in the alliances among church, business, and often foreign (usually U.S.) corporate interests in Latin America. There is no guarantee of historical progress that inevitably consigns fascism, nationalism, or fundamentalism to the margins. Reactionary forces have triumphed at various times in the twentieth century with devastating consequences. With leftist alternatives beleaguered by the sorry history of Communism, reactionary discourses enjoy a particular prominence as citizens of the contemporary era seek to understand and resist the forces of globalization, class polarization, and social dislocation. It is in this context that gay and lesbian movements continue to act within a tradition of the advancement of democratic rights—in some societies relatively complacently, where liberal democracy seems inalterably entrenched, in others more vigorously, where rights must be continually reaffirmed and reconstructed. It is remarkable that as some queer theorists critique gay and lesbian identities as confining or dispensable, from the vantage point of the urban subcultures of the First World, groups are coming together under the gay, lesbian, and sometimes transgendered banner in such places as the Philippines, Korea, Ecuador, El Salvador, Bulgaria, and Turkey, even though homosexual interests have traditionally found quite different expression in these cultures.

Movements and National Cultures

This collection offers national portraits of sixteen countries, from each of the five inhabited continents, with histories of gay and lesbian political organization. As such, it is the most comprehensive and systematic overview of gay and lesbian movements around the globe that has appeared to date—but there is still much to be done. Because the growth of gay and lesbian studies has been possible in very few places in the world and movements are only nascent (or not yet existent) in a number of countries—especially in Asia and Africa—primary research has yet to be done on gay and lesbian movements in many countries. In addition, lesbian groups that have worked outside of gay and lesbian organizations, especially when they have been low-profile "tendencies" within women's movements, have been somewhat elusive to scholarly documentation. Our hope is that this volume will stimulate more work specifically (1) on movements in countries in Asia, Africa, Latin America, and eastern and southern Europe, (2) on lesbian, bisexual, and transgendered groups, (3) on organizations rooted in minority cultures in advanced industrial societies (such as Aboriginal, Africana, Arabic, Latino, and south Asian), and (4) by indigenous authors.

What the chapters herein reveal are the ways that national traditions shape discourses through which homosexually interested people come to understand themselves and their "rightful" place in the societies in which they live. These essays show that any sense of commonality that might be evoked by the widespread adoption of such terms as "gay," "lesbian," or "bisexual" must be tempered by the diversity within and among national cultures. And they demonstrate a Foucauldian point: that gay and lesbian movements are both *a part of* and *apart from* the societies around them, both resisting and participating in—even reproducing—dominant public discourses. The authors of these chapters contend that some societies, such as those in Japan and France, allow social movements only the rhetoric of sameness and inclusion, forcing the discontented to advance themselves in those terms to be credible at all. Some movements, such as those in the Netherlands and the Czech Republic (as well as those in Norway, Sweden, Denmark, and Iceland), have been so integrated into the institutional structures of the state that opposition has largely given way to a sense of participation, citizenship, and perhaps co-optation. Other movements—especially where the battle lines are strongly drawn, as in the United States and the United Kingdom—have a strong sense of almost "ethnic" separateness and an ambivalent oscillation between an affirming pride in a transgressive identity and a wish to deconstruct it (J. Gamson 1995). This paradox is lodged in the heart of the category "queer."

The conclusion to this collection picks up the comparative theme to explore questions of (de)mobilization and national identity in this movement with worldwide presence.

REFERENCES

Adam, Barry D. 1985a. "Age, Structure, and Sexuality." *Journal of Homosexuality* 11 (3–4):19.

———. 1985b. "Structural Foundations of the Gay World." *Comparative Studies in Society and History* 27 (4): 658–70. Reprinted in *Queer Theory/Sociology*. Ed. Steven Seidman. Cambridge, Mass.

———. 1992. "The State, Public Policy, and AIDS Discourse." In *Fluid Exchanges*. Ed. James Miller. Toronto: University of Toronto Press.

———. 1993. "Post-Marxism and the New Social Movements." *Canadian Review of Sociology and Anthropology* 30 (3): 316–36. Reprinted in *Organizing Dissent*. 2d ed., edited by William Carroll. Toronto: Garamond, 1997, pp. 39–56.

———. 1995. *The Rise of a Gay and Lesbian Movement*. Rev. ed. New York: Twayne.

———. 1997. "Mobilizing around AIDS." In *In Changing Times*. Ed. Martin Levine, Peter Nardi, and John Gagnon. Chicago: University of Chicago Press.

———. Forthcoming. "Globalization and the Mobilization of Gay and Lesbian

Communities." In *Global Flows*. Ed. Pierre Hamel, Henri Lustiger-Thaler, and Sasha Roseneil. London: Macmillan.

Adorno, Theodor, Else Frenkel-Brunswik, Daniel Levinson, and R Nevitt Sanford. 1950. *The Authoritarian Personality*. New York: Wiley.

Altman, Dennis. 1971. *Homosexual: Oppression and Liberation*. New York: Outerbridge and Dienstfrey.

———. 1986. *AIDS in the Mind of America*. Garden City, N.Y.: Doubleday.

———. 1996. *Power and Community*. London: Falmer.

Aya, Roderick. 1990. *Rethinking Revolutions and Collective Violence*. Amsterdam: Het Spinhuis.

Boggs, Carl. 1986. *Social Movements and Political Power*. Philadelphia: Temple University Press.

Boswell, John. 1980. *Christianity, Social Tolerance and Homosexuality*. Chicago: University of Chicago Press.

Bowles, Samuel, and Herbert Gintis. 1986. *Democracy and Capitalism*. New York: Basic.

Corrigan, Philip, and Derek Sayer. 1985. *The Great Arch*. Oxford: Basil Blackwell.

D'Emilio, John. 1983. "Capitalism and Gay Identity." In *Powers of Desire*. Ed. Ann Snitow, Christine Stansell, and Sharon Thompson. New York: Monthly Review.

Duyvendak, Jan Willem. 1995. *The Power of Politics: New Social Movements in France*. Boulder, Colo. Westview.

Gamson, Joshua. 1989. "Silence, Death and the Invisible Enemy: AIDS Activism and Social Movement 'Newness.'" *Social Problems* 36, no. 4 (October): 351–65.

———. 1995. "Must Identity Movements Self-destruct? A Queer Dilemma." *Social Problems* 42, no. 3 (August): 390–407.

Gamson, William. 1975. *The Strategy of Social Protest*. Homewood, Ill.: Dorsey.

Greenberg, David. 1988. *The Construction of Homosexuality*. Chicago: University of Chicago Press.

Gurr, Ted. 1970. *Why Men Rebel*. Princeton: Princeton University Press.

Habermas, Jürgen. 1975. *Legitimation Crisis*. Boston: Beacon.

———. 1987. *The Theory of Communicative Action*. Vol. 2. Boston: Beacon.

Hendriks, Aart, Rob Tielman, and Evert van der Veen. 1993. *The Third Pink Book: A Global View of Lesbian and Gay Liberation and Oppression*. Buffalo, N.Y.: Prometheus.

International Gay Association. 1985. *IGA Pink Book 1985*. Amsterdam: COC-magazijn.

International Lesbian and Gay Association. 1988. *The Second ILGA Pink Book*. Utrecht, Netherlands: Publicatiereeks Homostudies #12.

Kinsman, Gary. 1992. "Managing AIDS Organizing." In *Organizing Dissent*. Ed. William Carroll. Toronto: Garamond.

Kitschelt, Herbert P. 1986. "Political Opportunity Structures and Political Protest: Anti-nuclear Movements in Four Democracies." *British Journal of Political Science* 16:57–85.

Klandermans, Bert, Hanspieter Kriesi, and Sidney Tarrow, eds. 1988. *From Structure to Action: Social Movement Participation across Cultures*. Greenwich, Conn.: JAI.

Koopmans, Ruud. 1995. *Democracy from Below: New Social Movements and the Political System in West Germany*. Boulder, Colo.: Westview.

Kriesi, Hanspieter. 1991. *The Political Opportunity Structure of New Social Movements: Its Impact on Their Mobilization*. Berlin: WZB.

Kriesi, Hanspieter, Ruud Koopmans, Jan Willem Duyvendak, and Marco Giugni. 1992. "New Social Movements and Political Opportunities in Western Europe." *European Journal of Political Research* 22:219–44.

Lefèbvre, Henri. 1976. *The Survival of Capitalism*. London: Allison and Busby.

Likosky, Stephen. 1992. *Coming Out*. New York: Pantheon.

McAdam, Doug. 1982 *Political Process and the Development of Black Insurgency, 1930–1970*. Chicago: University of Chicago Press.

McAdam, Doug, John D. McCarthy, and Meyer N. Zald. 1988. "Social Movements." In *Handbook of Sociology*. Ed. Neil Smelser. Newbury Park, Calif.: Sage.

McCarthy, John D. and Meyer N. Zald. 1977. "Resource Mobilization and Social Movements: A Partial Theory." *American Journal of Sociology* 82 (6):1212–41.

Melucci, Alberto. 1980. "The New Social Movements: A Theoretical Approach." *Social Science Information* 19 (2): 220.

———. 1989. *Nomads of the Present: Social Movements and Individual Needs in Contemporary Society*. Philadelphia: Temple University Press.

Miller, Neil. 1992. *Out in the World*. New York: Random House.

Oberschall, Anthony. 1973. *Social Conflict and Social Movements*. Englewood-Cliffs, N.J.: Prentice Hall.

Offe, Claus. 1984. *Contradictions of the Welfare State*. Cambridge, Mass.: MIT Press.

———. 1985. "New Social Movements: Challenging the Boundaries of Institutional Politics." *Social Research,* 52 (Winter): 817–68.

Patton, Cindy. 1990. *Inventing AIDS*. New York: Routledge.

Seidman, Steven, ed. 1996. *Queer Theory/Sociology*. Oxford: Blackwell.

Smelser, Neil. 1962. *Theory of Collective Behavior*. New York: Free Press.

Tarrow, Sidney. 1989. *Democracy and Disorder: Protest and Politics in Italy 1965–1975*. Oxford: Clarendon.

Tilly, Charles. 1978. *From Mobilization to Revolution*. Reading, Mass.: Addison-Wesley.

Touraine, Alain. 1978. *La voix et le regard*. Paris: Editions du Seuil.

Wallerstein, Immanuel. 1989. "1968, Revolution in the World-System." *Theory and Society* 18:431–49.

Barry D Adam

2 Moral Regulation and the Disintegrating Canadian State

THE FIRST formal gay and lesbian movement organization in Canada emerged in 1964 in a historical context similar to that of gay and lesbian communities in the nations of Western Europe, the United States, Australia, and New Zealand. The post–World War II period in Canada was characterized by the legal prohibition of (male) homosexuality and a highly inhospitable social climate that included the repression of homosexual issues in "respectable" public discourse and an overt regime of persecution (Adam 1993a). Nevertheless, according to historical scholarship, from at least as early as the nineteenth century, there was a series of sites where men, and later women, came to recognize and meet one another in a manner that we today recognize as "gay" (Adam 1995: 7). From the 1960s, Canadian lesbian and gay communities developed through a period of militance and growth in the early 1970s, a period of self-defense against right-wing reaction in the late 1970s and 1980s, and renewed cultural and political growth in the 1990s. Much of this chapter takes up the question of prospects for the future. In an era characterized by globalization, neoconservative political agendas, and divisiveness between Canada's two largest national cultures, what challenges face gay and lesbian movement groups today? How will the changing constellation of social forces and struggles over national identity affect gay and lesbian people in Canada?

FROM DECRIMINALIZATION TO LIBERATION

The first homophile organization formed in Vancouver under the name the Association for Social Knowledge (ASK). Inspired by contemporary homophile groups in California, ASK founded a social center through the initiative of two former COC (Cultural and Recreational Center) members from the Netherlands who were cognizant of the success of the Amsterdam clubhouse (Kinsman 1996). Begun in 1964, it lasted until 1969.

In 1969 the federal Parliament amended the Criminal Code to exempt from prosecution two consenting adults engaged in private sexual activity. Two events in the 1960s precipitated law reform. The first was the

1966 conviction of Everett Klippert, a man from the Northwest Territories, as a habitual sexual offender simply because he had had sex with several consenting adult men. The 1967 Supreme Court confirmation of his indefinite sentence (essentially a life term) opened a public debate on the effects of the antihomosexual law. The second event was the 1967 British decision to decriminalize homosexual acts, following a decade of public discussion opened by the Wolfenden Report, the result of a royal commission to investigate prostitution and homosexuality. In the 1960s many governments in Western Europe and North America began liberalizing a series of laws concerning abortion, obscenity, and contraception at the behest of popular movements. In Canada, Pierre Trudeau, then Canada's justice minister, introduced decriminalization as part of a comprehensive reform of the Criminal Code, announcing that the "state has no place in the bedrooms of the nation." The law passed with the approval of the Liberal and New Democratic parties; many Conservatives and the rural Québécois Parti Créditiste voted against it (Sylvestre 1979; Adam 1995; Kinsman 1996).

Decriminalization came about in an era of social movement mobilization as the cautious, defensive strategies of oppressed groups in the 1950s were giving way to a renewed self-assertion and pride (Adam 1978, 1995). In 1967 a feminist group formed in Toronto, and between 1969 and 1971 gay and lesbian people mobilized across the country—at first in major cities and on college campuses but soon after in almost every city of more than 100,000 inhabitants.

In 1969 a small University of Toronto Homophile Association formed, in 1970 the Vancouver Gay Liberation Front met, and by 1971 Montréal and Ottawa groups had mounted the first march on Parliament Hill. Like the movement elsewhere, Canadian organizations debated and split over issues such as the adoption of militant tactics and forms of leadership and participation, with Toronto Gay Action taking the liberationist stance articulated in the journal *The Body Politic,* while the Community Homophile Association of Toronto organized a social center and pressed for civil rights. In Vancouver the more moderate Gay Alliance toward Equality rapidly succeeded the Gay Liberation Front. The 1971 march in Ottawa forwarded an agenda that set the course for gay and lesbian efforts for many years to come:

• abolition of the gross indecency law
• uniform age of consent
• protection through human rights codes
• equal rights for same-sex couples
• destruction of police files

- right to serve in the armed forces
- elimination of discrimination in immigration, employment, custody and adoption, and housing (Jackson and Persky 1982: 217–20; Adam 1995; Kinsman 1996)

Like its counterparts in other countries, the Canadian movement experienced tensions over the frequent subordination of the concerns of lesbians in organizations dominated by gay men. Such groups as Gays of Ottawa flourished through the 1970s by assuring parity in the representation of men and women and of Anglophones and Francophones in its leadership. Many lesbians left other gay groups to pursue issues from within the women's movement. The struggle for the recognition and integration of lesbian issues in the feminist program often proved difficult and disheartening, but by the mid-1970s most women's organizations had embraced lesbian demands (Creet 1990).

In 1977, movement work began to show results. The federal (Liberal Party) government dropped "homosexuals" from its list of persons banned from immigrating into Canada, following an incident in which a U.S. citizen was stopped at a land crossing but then flown into the country through movement sponsorship. The participation of many gay and lesbian activists in the nationalist movement in Québec resulted in the addition of "sexual orientation" to a provincial human rights code a year after the Parti Québécois came to power (Sylvestre 1979).

REACTION AND REPRESSION

In the late 1970s and 1980s, corporate and state elites moved to restabilize their control of economy and policy and to damp down the gains made by labor and new social movements (Adam 1993b, 1995). In the United States the reactionary shift took the form of a formidable alliance of corporate interests, evangelical churches, traditionally conservative rural, white Protestants, southerners, and groups that lobbied against gun control, women's rights, pornography, and abortion. This New Right alliance culminated in the Reagan/Bush presidency, which breathed new life into U.S. military and imperial traditions and renewed reactionary discourses in the mass media (Adam 1995: chap. 6). Never immune from the omnipresent U.S. media net, the rightward shift of public discourse in Canada emboldened two conservative governments, which had been in power for well over a generation, to attempt to push gay people back into the closet.

The Jean Drapeau administration in Montréal, which had come to power in the 1950s on a plank of Roman Catholic moral restoration, began with a "cleanup" campaign. In the months preceding the opening of the 1976 Olympic Games, the police descended on seven bars and a bathhouse in four raids. The repressive offensive stalled in 1977 with the mass mobilization of a new Association pour les Droits des Gai(e)s du Québec, which resisted in the streets and in the courts by fighting the cases of several hundred men who had been arrested. It is in this context that the new Parti Québécois provincial government, a left nationalist political formation with no political connections to the Drapeau old guard, introduced "sexual orientation" into the provincial human rights code.

In Toronto, media panic was generated over the 1977 murder of a fourteen-year-old shoeshine boy by four men, reviving public images of gay child molestation and setting the stage for the police seizure of the *Body Politic,* a newspaper that had addressed pedophilia in an article called "Men Loving Boys Loving Men." The *Body Politic's* 1979 acquittal on obscenity charges was appealed by the Conservative provincial administration through four more years of court appearances before the paper's ultimate acquittal. In 1981, Toronto police arrested 286 "found-ins" and 20 "keepers" of a common bawdy house in a massive raid on city bathhouses during a provincial election campaign. As in Montréal, police attacks stimulated new gay mobilization, this time in the form of The Right to Privacy Committee, in a movement that had been losing energy in the mid-1970s.

In the late 1970s and early 1980s, then, the gay and lesbian movement was forced to take defensive action against a series of assaults initiated by police and governments. Not until the mid-1980s did the movement begin again to make gains in the consolidation of civil rights for gay and lesbian people. In the 1990s "the movement" has proliferated from a handful of organizations in major cities to many hundreds of specialized task-oriented groups located in numerous sites across the country. The single comprehensive gay or gay/lesbian organization has given way to groups of people interested in recreation, religion, film, theater, radio programing, politics, workplace, ethnic culture, parenting, police relations, addiction recovery, counseling, schools, scholarship, transgenderism, youth, and so on. Largest among them are AIDS organizations, which have become institutionalized through state funding. AIDS organizations have, over time, become "mixed" organizations, outgrowing their gay community roots (see Adam 1997). Groups tend to be loosely networked and visible primarily on Pride days, which grow every year. In Toronto, Pride day is the third largest event of the year after the Santa Claus Parade and Caribana, the Afro-Caribbean Mardi Gras. This proliferation and decentralization of movement organizations has profoundly impacted the larger society, as many nongay Canadians, in various spheres of their lives, encounter openly lesbian and gay people who work with them, share their interests, and participate in their cultural activities.

MORAL REGULATION IN CANADA

Some fifteen years after the first march on Ottawa, as a series of law reforms began to realize several aspects of the 1971 program, the momentum of change shifted back in favor of the gay and lesbian movement. The Ontario government added "sexual orientation" to its human rights code in 1986, and Manitoba and the Yukon Territory followed in 1987. By the 1990s, Canada's situation had become comparable to that of most of the European Union, Australia, and New Zealand, with eight of ten provinces and one of two territories passing the requisite legislation between 1977 and 1997. Holdouts, such as the military and the police, were eventually forced by lawsuits to accede to human rights demands. In 1996 the federal government amended the Canadian Human Rights Act after a Supreme Court ruling that read "sexual orientation" into Section 15 of the Canadian constitution, and in 1998 the Supreme Court ordered that "sexual orientation" be included in the human rights code of a ninth province, Alberta.

A number of indicators highlight how the state of civil rights for lesbian and gay people differs from Canada to the United States and the United Kingdom. Much of the difference has come about since the mid-1970s, as Canada has effected incremental change toward affirming equal legal rights, while a series of obstacles has checkmated change in the United States and the United Kingdom. The U.S. Congress has failed to pass a human rights law, even moving to strike down similar legislation, as well as a domestic partners' benefits law, in the District of Columbia.[1] Although ten of the fifty states, almost all in the north, have human rights laws, almost half continue to criminalize homosexuality, and existing city and state human rights laws have been subjected to repeated repeal referenda. In 1986 the U.S. Supreme Court upheld state laws that criminalize their gay citizens. In 1992 the Republican Party chose as a central party plank "family values," a program directed against single mothers and gay and lesbian people. In the same year, Colorado voted by a 53 percent majority to prevent the passage of equality rights laws for lesbian and gay people, striking down existing city ordinances. In 1996 the U.S. Supreme Court overturned the Colorado ban on human rights laws, leaving gay and lesbian residents in the state with the status que ante—that is, no statewide human rights protection, and in 1998 voters in Maine repealed that state's gay rights law.

In the United Kingdom, Anna Marie Smith (1994) demonstrates how the figures of the "dangerous queer" and the black immigrant have been deployed as trump cards to panic people into identifying with Thatcherism. Despite the mobilization of gay and lesbian communities and the participation of community activists in Labour coalitions in local government, the equal rights struggle has come up against intransigence and containment by established political forces (Cooper 1994). British legislation was marked by the 1988 passage of Clause 28, a law intended to deny the use of taxes paid by gay and lesbian citizens for support of their community, and an assault on freedom of speech in educational institutions (Jeffery-Poulter 1991: 168–69).

It is not easy to account for the differences between Canada and the United States, but at least five factors stand out:

1. Relatively fewer Canadians (6 percent) than U.S. citizens (22 percent) identify themselves as evangelical Protestants. Evangelicals appear as one of the most consistent opponents of equality for lesbians and gay men in U.S. political coalitions (Adam 1995: chap. 6). Antifeminist and antigay organizations, such as Renaissance International and REAL Women, have had only limited effectiveness in Canada (Herman 1994).
2. Canada has a consistently higher rate of union membership, 29.7 percent of workers unionized, compared with 15.5 percent in the United States (Statistics Canada 1993: 192; U.S. Bureau of the Census 1995: 443). Unions have been important sites of human rights initiatives, as they have included sexual-orientation protection in labor contracts and advocated for human rights policies with the state.
3. Canada has a lengthy social democratic tradition in the form of the New Democratic Party, which has come to power from time to time at the provincial level.
4. Canada lacks the imperial and militarist traditions of the United States and the United Kingdom, which bind national identity with homophobic panic (Adam 1994).
5. The structure of the Canadian state differs from the stucture of the U.S. state, a situation that requires a more detailed explanation (see below).

Differences between Canada and the United Kingdom are fewer, in that evangelical Protestants make up only a small part of the British population (United Kingdom. Central Office of Information 1994: 436), union members account for 35 percent of employees (United Kingdom. Central Office of Information 1994: 186), and the British Labour Party has traditionally represented a social democratic alternative.

The fifth, and perhaps most fundamental, difference between Canada and the United States concerns the structure of the state. Canada does not lack a history of "social purity" reformers consistent with other Anglo-American societies (Valverde 1991), which has perhaps had its greatest effect in a regime of censorship enshrined in customs agency practices, obscenity laws, and provincial film classification boards (Lacombe 1994; Kinsman 1996; Adam 1996a). It does lack, however, a history of successful hegemonization of traditional white, Anglo-Saxon, Protestant culture because of the national deadlock between English and French that has characterized the country since its founding. Prohibition ruled over the United States in the 1920s as an assertion of rural Protestant culture over a heterogeneous population of Catholics, blacks, and immigrants (Gusfield 1963), but it turned out to be much more temporary and regional in Canada, as the enthusiasm for temperance never found a comparable response in Québec. The disaccord between Québécois and Anglo-Canadian cultures has resulted in a weak state system of tentative compromises, lacking the full consolidation of a singular national identity that comes when a single hegemonic social group acquires the power to define and regulate the "deviant" and the "treasonous." In that sense, Canada bears some resemblance to the Netherlands, where a national ethos of liberal tolerance emerged out of the "pillarization" of Dutch society among Protestant, Catholic, and humanist sectors, none of which was able to gain ascendancy over the other (Lijphart 1968). In Canada this has taken the form of official "multiculturalism," which claims to respect difference rather than insist on national conformity.

National differences depend not on any "essential" trait of national "character" but on transitory historical conjunctures of internal social elements. Typifications of difference, then, can never be stable, and certainly Canada contains within it reactionary forces that press for a new national culture and moral regulation. In the United States antigay referenda have been part of a much larger agenda of social conservatism supported and promoted primarily by declining social classes, small business owners, and semirural, rural, less educated, and low-income constituencies (Adam 1995: 133). The same sectors have been part of a politics of resentment in Canada, which, from the 1920s to the 1960s, was best expressed by the right-wing populist Social Credit Party. Now the rejuvenation of the populist Right has occurred in the form of Social Credit's successor, Reform, which relies especially on a white rural "nativist" and middle-class suburban base (Sigurdson 1994; Harrison and Krahn 1995) similar to the Republican revival in the United States.

Given the precariousness of the Canadian state in the wake of the 1995 referendum, which showed Québec society to be evenly divided on the question of secession, we might ask, How will these forces likely influence the formation of societies organized around a Québécois state and a reduced Canadian state?

Québec without Canada

Contemporary Québec nationalism, which came to power in the form of a Parti Québécois government in 1976, emerged out of the Quiet Revolution of the 1960s. It was, in many ways, a progressive modernizing movement in the sense that it sought to build a postwar welfare state complete with state-run health, education, and welfare sectors similar to those in other advanced capitalist nations. Because the Roman Catholic church had long functioned in Québec, as it has in Ireland, as a bulwark of indigenous culture in an English-language sea, it retained the loyalty of the Québécois longer than it had in comparable advanced capitalist societies. The movement, which was to coalesce into the Parti Québécois, defined a secular progressive nationalism against the theocratic and traditionalist nationalism of the past. Rather like the Catalonian nationalism of the 1970s, the Parti Québécois implemented an agenda of social reform, replacing the patronal rule of the Maurice Duplessis regime with liberal democratic principles, expanding a public school system apart from church control, and introducing a new family law that gave women equal legal status. It was also the first jurisdiction of its size in North America to introduce a human rights law that granted its citizens protection from discrimination on the basis of sexual orientation. And this liberal democratic ideology has been enshrined in official documents of the nationalist party ever since (National Executive Council 1994).

With the prospect of an independent Québec greater than it has ever been before, much turns on the question of the social composition of the coalition that supports nationalism and an analysis of the direction that nationalism is now taking. In the 1960s, Pierre Trudeau (1968) critiqued Québec nationalism as regressive and undemocratic. As a labor lawyer acting on behalf of asbestos workers during the Duplessis regime and as a leading intellectual of the Quiet Revolution, Trudeau identified nationalism with its traditional authoritarian form. The question now is not What is nationalism "essentially"? but What are the sociohistorical conditions that shape the form that nationalism takes? If the patronal, authoritarian, and ecclesiastical nationalism of the 1950s is overthrown and the liberal democratic nationalism of the 1980s is now predominant, the issue is How stable is the current formation? How might it change in the context of a globalizing world economy? The ascendancy of Québec nationalism may, like rising regionalism inside the European Union, be part of a new articulation of regions with the world economy in which nation-states are declining in importance and effectiveness. It may also be a seedbed for a revival of older nationalist traditions within a political context in which neoconservatism has acquired new vitality.

It is clear enough that Québec nationalists have chafed at the multi-cultural policies of the federal government, which have not assigned Québécois culture the preeminence they feel it deserves. Multiculturalism is to be cast off in favor of "interculturalism" in a new Québec where French hegemony is to be undisputed and assimilation to this new national standard is to be a prerequisite of citizenship (Juteau 1993: 99). Over the last twenty years a series of struggles concerning education, immigration, public signs, and Aboriginal rights has given a concrete historical record to this policy. Legislation through that period has required all children of immigrants to attend Francophone schools; Anglophone schools are closed to them. Only French is permitted on public signs; English and other languages are banned. Nationalists have long believed that Canadian federalism has impeded the realization of national aspirations as Philip Corrigan and Derek Sayer (1985) have defined them—namely, the attainment of "French" hegemony within "their own" territory.

Like all other nationalisms, however, Québec nationalism raises vexed questions about who is inside and who is outside the national category. No nation can refer to an unproblematic essence; nationhood is perhaps inevitably constructed out of (sometimes unintentional) binary oppositions. As Yuki Shiose and Louise Fontaine (1995) remark in their review of the textual evolution of Québec official documents, "In sum, this conceptual model of the ethnic fragmentation of Québec supposes neither an almost complete integration of individuals (the American melting pot) nor a supposedly egalitarian juxtaposition of groups (the Canadian mosaic), but a hierarchical structure constructed of two categories: the 'Québécois nation,' anchored in mythic foundations, and the 'cultural communities' confined to their 'anthropological' past."[2] The official 1995 Declaration of Sovereignty reaffirms the shift toward traditionalist discourse, as nation, soil, and people are fused together by an essentializing and naturalizing rhetoric (Desbiens-Magalios 1996).

Nationalist forces, recognizing that a great many people in Québec feared they were not being included in the national category, have attempted to offer an ecumenical definition. During the 1995 referendum campaign, the nationalist camp mounted placards on city buses proclaiming, "Almond eyes, Québécois heart" (*Les yeux amandes, le coeur québécois*) over a picture of a young Asian woman and "Curly hair, Québécois heart" (*Les cheveux bouclés, le coeur québécois*) over a picture of a preteen Afro-Caribbean girl. Appearing at a time when some voices of reactionary nationalism had reappeared to reassert the supremacy of the Québécois "de pure laine,"[3] the placards were intended as an appeal to "ethnic" voters. Yet the placards could not fail to speak race and racism as they attempted to deny race in an inclusive message.[4] The outcome has been that "ethnic" and Aboriginal voters have overwhelmingly chosen federalism in secessionist referenda, which has resulted in intemperate outbursts of recrimination from the Québec premier and cabinet ministers.

Nationalism has also evolved in issues of interest to feminists. Although feminists were a prominent part of the nationalist coalition in the 1970s, there was a slide toward traditional signifers in the 1980s as national survival became conceptualized in terms of the "demographic question." As the Québec birth rate plunged from the 1960s to the low rates common to most advanced capitalist societies, nationalists began to worry about a demographic threat. As Heather Maroney (1992:15) remarks, "The baby as produced by pronatalist discourse was left in the care of traditional nationalist, antifeminist and religious guardians. When the political 'father' returned, it was to discover that the number of babies had shrunk, that physical reproduction could no longer be left to ideological exhortation, women's natures, and the private realm of the family." In 1988 the Liberal government of the day introduced a payment of $4,500 per child to women having a third or subsequent child. The recrudescence of naturalist discourse around women's issues parallels a similar naturalization of ethnicity where "the boundary between the 'nation' and the 'others' has become 'natural' and thus impassible. One no longer becomes a member of the 'nation' through learning French; one is or is not from birth" (Shiose and Fontaine 1995: 106).[5]

A similar evolution of nationalist discourse can be discerned in regard to gay and lesbian people. When the Groupe Interdisciplinaire de Recherches et d'Études Homosexualité et Société at the Université du Québec à Montréal held a colloquium on the "national question" just two months before the 1995 referendum, a young generation of Francophone scholars expressed a "disquiet" about nationalist rhetoric vis-à-vis gay and lesbian rights (Gadoua 1995; Serra 1995). The exhaustive sovereignty commission consultations around the province had produced a report from which lesbians and gay men were entirely absent and in which "family" and "nation" were frequently invoked together. And despite separate sections devoted to environmentalist, feminist, antiracist, and Aboriginal issues in the 1994 official platform of the Parti Québécois, lesbians and gay men were once again absent. Instead the document announces, "Sovereignty will make it possible to recast programs . . . and centralize them in Quebec so that an effective, coherent family policy can be established" (National Executive Council 1994: 33). Although veterans of nationalist struggles of the 1960s and 1970s reminded the younger generation at the Montréal colloquium of the human rights legacy of the Parti Québécois, the younger generation wondered why the concerns of the gay and lesbian community had faded away in the 1980s and 1990s.

The gamble today is whether an ethnically purified Québec state outside of Canada would institutionalize a liberal democratic culture fully protective of minority rights. The premier of Québec, Lucien Bouchard, argued during the 1995 referendum campaign that Québec sovereignty was essential to avoid the "slash and burn" neoconservative economic agenda of Ontario and Alberta. Yet over time, Québec has proven to be no more resistant to the pressures of global capitalism than the other provinces have.

All Québec members of the federal Parliament, whether nationalist Bloc Québécois or federalist Liberal, voted in favor of adding sexual orientation to the Canadian Human Rights Act. And when openly gay Bloc Québécois Member of Parliament Réal Ménard presented Motion M-264 to the federal Parliament to recognize same-sex spouses, a majority of his party voted in favor of his bill, arguing that a sovereign Québec was necessary so that the Québécois would not be held back by the reactionaries in the federal Parliament who ultimately defeated it (Canada. House of Commons 1995). At the same time, the Parti Québécois, which was already in power in Québec, showed no sign of introducing a comparable bill in the Québec National Assembly, despite its prominence on the public agenda. The year before the Ménard bill was introduced, Ontario had been convulsed in a debate over the same issue when the New Democratic Party (NDP) government introduced a comprehensive bill to recognize gay and lesbian relationships. (It failed in a free vote, when twelve NDP members defected to vote against it.) Certainly much of the gay and lesbian community has found nationalism to be the more hospitable camp, as federalism has become identified with business and a politics of threat. Yet because nationalism contains no safeguard against authoritarian turns, Québec stands at a crossroad concerning not only political sovereignty but also its identity as a nation. Naturalist and "family" discourses have traditionally been wielded as weapons to restrict or suppress gay and lesbian participation in civil society; their revival does not bode well for the struggle for equality.

CANADA WITHOUT QUÉBEC

The long historical stalemate between francophone and anglophone cultures, federal multiculturalism, and the weak federal state has resulted in a Canadian "character" of endless compromise, tolerance, and politeness. The result has been a fractured elite hegemony that might otherwise have been more repressive toward many minorities, including lesbians and gay men. Québec nationalism has rendered the federal state particularly fragile in the 1990s; the potential reconfiguration of English-language Canada raises at least two possible scenarios.

In the 1960s and 1970s, there emerged a movement to define a progressive Canadian national identity, parallel to the Quiet Revolution in Québec. This left nationalist trend, associated with the so-called "Waffle" faction of the NDP, sought to defend Canadian autonomy in several spheres: (1) the economy, where U.S. capital had secured a dominant position in the postwar period, (2) foreign policy, where the United States often expected to conscript Canada into its Cold War and imperial adventures, and (3) culture, where nationalists tried to carve out a space for indigenous artistic, literary, and scholarly development. It was a project that foundered on several shoals: (1) the difficulty of drawing together a coherent sense of commonality based on a series of far-flung, loosely connected regions, (2) the difficulty of including Québec in a Canadian nationalist project when Québec was defining itself outside of it,[6] (3) the largely successful assimilation of Canadian English-language popular culture into the Hollywood empire, and (4) the decisive turn taken by Canadian political and corporate elites in embracing continental free trade, which accelerated Canadian integration with U.S. political, economic, and cultural priorities. With the demise of the left nationalist project, a Canada without Québec would, ironically, become a nation by default that so far exists more as a projection from the minds of Québec nationalists than a vision shared by Anglo-Canadians themselves.

Waiting in the wings is Reform. Reform appears eager for the nationalist Bloc Québécois (BQ) to withdraw from Parliament in order to leave Reform as the official opposition. The Reform constituency, which is negligible in Québec, would jump proportionately in an Anglo-Canada. The middle-aged male, high-income, English-language former Conservative core of Reform (Archer and Ellis 1994: 290) would become one of the best-organized political forces in the country. Evangelicals would make up 7.5 percent of the population in a Canada without Québec, up from the current 5.9 percent. Vociferously opposed to multiculturalism, immigration, and "special interest groups" (Harrison, Johnston, and Krahn 1996), Reform represents a faction of the authoritarian white Anglo-Saxon Protestant constituency, which has been unable to consolidate power throughout much of Canadian history. In 1995, while a majority of BQ members voted for Réal Ménard's same-sex relationship motion, Reform opposed it unanimously, containing lesbians and gay men within the reactionary discourses that identify them with the destruction of the family (Erwin 1993; Adam 1995: chap. 6). All but one Reform member of Parliament voted against inclusion of "sexual orientation" in the Canadian Human Rights Act in 1996.

GLOBALIZATION AND NEOCONSERVATISM

The outstanding question remains how a Canada without Québec would look in a globalized world system. Changes in the modern world system can contribute to the formation of reactionary social forces aimed at reinforcing the preeminence of traditional morality and culture and at "disciplining" upstart and "undeserving" emergent social groups. As Philip Corrigan and Derek Sayer (1985) point out, the nation-state might usefully be thought of as the site where social groups defined variously by race, language, religion, gender, and sexuality forge a hegemony over a territory. Hegemonic social groups, in turn, institutionalize their own cultures as national cultures, thereby generating a range of subordinated and minority groups, which must find a place in an alien world.

The response of the Canadian state to globalization took a decisive turn when, in its second term, the Conservative government abandoned a century of economic protectionism by signing the Free Trade Agreement with the United States. The Free Trade Agreement soon became the North American Free Trade Agreement with the inclusion of Mexico in 1993. The formation of large free-trade blocs has been part of a neoconservative approach to globalization characterized by a wide range of policy and social consequences familiar to many advanced capitalist nations of the 1990s: deficit reduction; corporate deregulation; privatization; downsizing of the public sector; and shrinkage of health, education, and welfare services. It is a response that accommodates national economic and social priorities to forces of an emerging "new world order" and that, at the same time, participates in and accelerates these processes. These changes have been accompanied by what Gary Teeple (1995) calls "the decline of social reform"—the undermining of labor unions, environmental regulation, and employment equity programs—along with investment in social control measures and concerted campaigns to lower popular expectations.

Canada has yet to develop the potent combination of neoconservative economic and social agendas that has become ascendant in the United States (Diamond 1995). In 1993, worried about the direction the Conservatives had taken the country, voters decisively defeated the Conservative government. Yet their successors in the Liberal Party have continued to carry out the neoconservative economic agenda and appear largely bereft of a program on social issues. In a recent analysis of the impacts of the neoconservative response to globalization on issues of concern to feminism, Janine Brodie (1995) observes how the shrinkage in state spending has differentially impacted women. Her book conveys a sense of foreboding as it spells out the gendered impact of restructuring, the sidelining of the National Action Committee on the Status of Women from the policy process, and the decline of social reform in public discourse. So far, an aggressive antifeminism that rolls back the gains of the women's movement has yet to emerge.

Stuart Hall (1988a) notes that Thatcherism involved not simply a rearticulation of structural forces in Britain but, perhaps more important, a new authoritative narrative that cemented elite hegemony in place and manufactured a new set of enemies to blame for the nation's ills. Thatcherism, like Reaganism, won a degree of popular acquiescence by cobbling together the neoconservative ideology of global capital with a program of social conservatism. In that way, the New Right has articulated the popular anxiety over the harm wrought by the advance of global capital into a punitive rhetoric directed against social groups associated with change (Adam 1995: chap. 6). The "great transformation," which totally reordered British society in the nineteenth century and which, over the long run, produced popular movements of self-defense to contain the ravages of capitalization, is so far being replayed in the twentieth century in a way that foils oppositional discourse. The laissez-faire market, which "would have physically destroyed man and transformed his surroundings into a wilderness" (Polanyi 1957: 5), now enjoys rejuvenation at a global level. Social Darwinism now dresses up as neoliberalism. Hall (1988b: 2) remarks:

> Thatcherism is seen as forging new discursive articulations between the liberal discourses of the "free market" and economic man and the organic conservative themes of tradition, family and nation, respectability, patriarchalism and order. Its reworking of these different repertoires of "Englishness" constantly repositions both individual subjects and "the people" as a whole—their needs, experiences, aspirations, pleasures and desires—contesting space in terms of shifting social, sexual and ethnic identities, against the background of a crisis of national identity and culture precipitated by the unresolved psychic trauma of the "end of empire."

Thatcherism succeeded largely in "re-defining local government socialism as tyranny, anti-racism as an attack on democratic freedoms, pro-lesbian and gay policies as the promotion of AIDS, [and] environmental controls as a surrender of national sovereignty to European bureaucrats" (Smith 1994: 121). Although this formula cannot be simply transplanted into Canada, Hall's analysis of the ways the ascendant neoliberal/neoconservative right wing reassembled national culture into a more repressive configuration is pertinent. A Canada without Québec would lack its primary traditional brake on this peculiarly Anglo-Protestant version of New Right hegemony. Just how social conservatism becomes welded onto economic conservatism remains at issue here. Though the connection is not inevitable, there appear to be historical conjunctures of social forces that made this kind of coalition particularly deadly for gay and lesbian people, as well as for many other marginalized and subordinated groups. The alternative scenario may come from New Zealand. Although New Zealand suffered a substantial economic restructuring along neoconservative lines, an intensive national debate over gay and lesbian issues resulted in defeat of attempts to mount a renewed regime of moral regulation. A nationalist showdown over gay and lesbian rights eventually resulted in the inclusion of homosexual people in the national polity. During the 1970s and 1980s, the status of lesbians and gay men figured centrally in conflicts between Anglo-Saxon traditionalists, led by evangelical Protestants, and supporters of a syncretic Anglo-Maori vision of the nation as Aotearoa (the aboriginal name for New Zealand). Eventually homosexuality was decriminalized, and sexual orientation was added into human rights legislation (Parkinson 1988).

The articulation of moral regulation with neoconservative trends in the 1980s and 1990s has varied, then, from nation to nation. Multinational corporate elites have favored the Thatcher/Reagan strategy for meeting the demands of globalization and have had some success in selling to the U.S. and British populations the "bad medicine" of supply-side economics, high unemployment policy, tax cuts for rich corporations and families, and reduction of social services. Reductions in state spending have had very little direct impact on gay and lesbian organizations in Canada, because they have been almost always excluded from state funding, even before cutbacks became state policy. But a significant part of the success of the neoconservative agenda has been due to their ability to harvest the votes of large numbers of social conservatives by combining the neoconservative economic "pill" with the promise of cultural hegemony for moralist authoritarianism. Employing the well-worn but frequently successful formula favored by traditional conservatism, the objectives of the capitalist class have been sustained by a long-term assault on a reorganized cast of enemies. As Communists have diminished as the conservative nemesis, nonwhites, immigrants, aboriginal people, single mothers, and gays and lesbians have been drawn in as unwilling villains in the moral dramas promoted by the hegemonic culture.

Should the mutual stalemate of English and French in Canada be removed through Québec separation, both cultures will quite likely move toward the assertion of distinctive, "purified" ethnic cultures. In Anglo-Canada, this comes at a time when the neoconservative Reform Party is ascendant and Liberalism shows little sign of resistance to the same trends. Québec separation could have looked very different in its consequences in another era. The English/French deadlock has also been often cited as a major barrier to the development of the labor movement in Canada and to the development of a social democratic party large enough to form a national government. Because labor organizations have traditionally aligned themselves with nationalist forces in Québec, the New Democratic Party has never developed a significant Québec base. Governing parties without a Québec base have very rarely been able to form a government in Canada. But the decline of the federal New Democratic Party and of the Left around the world has diminished this option in the near future. The disarray of the Left at the end of the twentieth century, in the face of the globalization of the modern world system, has increased the vulnerability of a wide range of populations and hindered the advance of antisystemic movements.

NOTES

Acknowledgments: This essay was presented at the International Sociological Association conference, "Globalization and Collective Action," at the University of California, Santa Cruz 1996. A revised version was presented at a joint session of the Canadian Sociology and Anthropology Association and the Canadian Lesbian and Gay Studies Association, St. Catharines, Ontario, 1996.

1. On a subsequent try the District of Columbia succeeded in adding "sexual orientation" to its human rights law when Congress failed to veto it within the requisite time period.

2. I have translated from the French: "En somme, ce modèle conceptual de la fragmentation ethnique au Québec ne suppose ni une intégration à part entière des individus (le melting pot américain) ni une juxtaposition prétendument égalitaire des groupes (la mosaïque canadienne), mais une structure hiérarchique construite à partier de deux catégories: la «nation québécoise», ancrée dans des fondements mythiques, et les «communautés culturelles», confinées à leur passé «anthropologique.»"

3. Translated literally as "pure wool," this phrase refers to those with "true" French ancestry, a concept fraught with exclusionary racial connotations.

4. One shudders to think what the gay equivalent of these placards might have been.

5. I have translated from the French: "La frontière entre la «nation» et les «autres» est devenue «naturelle», donc infranchissable. On ne devient plus membre de la «nation» par l'apprentissage du français, on l'est ou on ne l'est pas dès la naissance."

6. In 1995 the Parti Québécois premier of Québec described the Canadian experience of Québec as a "prolonged stay in the dentist's chair."

REFERENCES

Adam, Barry D. 1978. *The Survival of Domination.* New York: Elsevier.

———. 1993a. "Winning Rights and Freedoms in Canada." In *The Third Pink*

Book. Ed. Aart Hendriks, Rob Tielman, and Evert van der Veen. Buffalo: Prometheus.

————. 1993b. "Post-Marxism and the New Social Movements." *Canadian Review of Sociology and Anthropology* 30 (3): 316–36.

————. 1994. "Anatomy of a Panic: State Voyeurism, Gender Politics, and the Cult of Americanism." In *Gays and Lesbians in the Military,* Ed. Wilbur J. Scott and Sandra Carson Stanley. Hawthorne, N.Y.: Aldine de Gruyter.

————. 1995. *The Rise of a Gay and Lesbian Movement:* Rev. ed. New York: Twayne.

————. 1996a. "Constructing Sexuality in the AIDS Era." in *Social Control in Canada.* Ed. Bernard Schissel and Linda Mahood. Toronto: Oxford University Press.

————. 1997. "Mobilizing around AIDS." In *In Changing Times.* Ed. Martin Levine, Peter Nardi, and John Gagnon. Chicago: University of Chicago Press.

Archer, Keith, and Faron Ellis. 1994. "Opinion Structure of Party Activists." *Canadian Journal of Political Science* 27 (2): 277–308.

Brodie, Janine. 1995. *Politics on the Margins.* Halifax: Fernwood.

Canada. House of Commons. 1985. *Debates.* 18 September.

Cooper, Davina. 1994. *Sexing the City.* London: Rivers Oram.

Corrigan, Philip, and Derek Sayer. 1985. *The Great Arch.* Oxford: Basil Blackwell.

Creet, M. Julia. 1990. "A Test of Unity." In *Lesbians in Canada.* Ed. Sharon Stone. Toronto: Between the Lines.

Desbiens-Magalios, Caroline. 1996. "Body and Soil: Nature Metaphors and National Territory in the Quebec Declaration of Sovereignty." Paper presented to the Canadian Sociology and Anthropology Association, St Catharines, Ontario, Canada.

Diamond, Sara. 1995. *Roads to Dominion.* New York: Guilford.

Erwin, Lorna. 1993. "Neoconservatism and the Canadian Pro-family Movement." *Canadian Review of Sociology and Anthropology* 30 (3): 401–20.

Gadoua, Bernard. 1995. "Le contexte de l'exclusion." Paper presented to the Groupe Interdisciplinaire de Recherches et d'Études Homosexualité et Société, Montréal.

Gusfield, Joseph. 1963. *Symbolic Crusade.* Urbana: University of Illinois Press.

Hall, Stuart. 1988a. "The Toad in the Garden." In *Marxism and the Interpretation of Culture.* Ed. Cary Nelson and Lawrence Grossberg. Urbana: University of Illinois Press.

————. 1988b. *The Hard Road to Renewal.* London: Verso.

Harrison, Trevor, Bill Johnston, and Harvey Krahn. 1996. "Special Interests and/or New Right Economics?" *Canadian Review of Sociology and Anthropology* 33 (2): 159–79.

Harrison, Trevor, and Harvey Krahn. 1995. "Populism and the Rise of the Reform Party in Alberta." *Canadian Review of Sociology and Anthropology* 32 (2): 127–50.

Herman, Didi. 1994. "The Christian Right and the Politics of Morality in Canada." *Parliamentary Affairs* 47 (2): 268–79.

Jackson, Ed, and Stan Persky. 1982. *Flaunting It!* Vancouver: New Star.

Jeffery-Poulter, Stephen. 1991. *Peers, Queers, and Commons: The Struggle for Gay Law Reform from 1950 to the Present.* London: Routledge.

Juteau, Danielle. 1993. "The Production of the Québécois Nation." *Humboldt Journal of Social Relations* 19 (92):79–108.

Kinsman, Gary. 1996. *The Regulation of Desire.* Rev. ed. Montréal: Black Rose.

Lacombe, Dany. 1994. *Blue Politics.* Toronto: University of Toronto Press.

Lijphart, Arend. 1968. *The Politics of Accommodation.* Berkeley and Los Angeles: University of California Press.

Maroney, Heather. 1992. " 'Who Has the Baby?' Nationalism, Pronatalism and the Construction of 'a Demographic Crisis' in Quebec 1960–1988." *Studies in Political Economy* 39:7–36.

National Executive Council of the Parti Québécois. 1994. *Quebec in a New World.* Toronto: Lorimer.

Parkinson, Phil. 1988. "Strangers in Paradise." In *The Second ILGA Pink Book.* Utrecht, Netherlands: Publicatiereeks Homostudies #12.

Polanyi, Karl. 1957. *The Great Transformation.* Boston: Beacon.

Serra, Christine. 1995. "Le nationalisme et le lesbianisme." Paper presented to the Groupe Interdisciplinaire de Recherches et d'Études Homosexualité et Société, Montréal.

Shiose, Yuki, and Louise Fontaine. 1995. "La construction des figures de l'«autre»." *Revue canadienne de sociologie et d'anthropologie* 32 (1): 91–110.

Sigurdson, Richard. 1994. "Preston Manning and the Politics of Postmodernism in Canada." *Canadian Journal of Political Science* 27 (2): 249–76.

Smith, Anna Marie. 1994. *New Right Discourse on Race and Sexuality.* New York: Cambridge University Press.

Statistics Canada. 1993. *Canada Year Book 1994.* Ottawa: Ministry of Supply and Services.

Sylvestre, Paul François. 1979. *Les homosexuels s'organisent.* Ottawa: Éditions Homeureux.

Teeple, Gary. 1995. *Globalization and the Decline of Social Reform.* Toronto: Garamond.

Trudeau, Pierre. 1968. *Federalism and the French Canadians.* Toronto: Macmillan.

United Kingdom Central Office of Information. 1994. *Britain 1995.* London: HMSO.

U.S. Bureau of the Census. 1995. *Statistical Abstract of the United States 1995.* Washington, D.C.: GPO.

Valverde, Mariana. 1991. *The Age of Light, Soap, and Water.* Toronto: McClelland and Stewart.

STEVEN EPSTEIN

3 Gay and Lesbian Movements in the United States

Dilemmas of Identity, Diversity, and Political Strategy

FROM ITS modest and clandestine early forms in the 1950s, gay and lesbian activism has evolved into one of the most dynamic, controversial, and internally differentiated sets of social movements in the United States. My goal is to present an analytical history[1] that shows how the general characteristics and tendencies, and the successes and failures, of these movements can be understood in terms of both external and internal factors—aspects of U.S. politics and society, on one hand, and ideological and strategic tensions inside and among these movements, on the other.[2]

My starting point is the assumption that the characteristically modern social identities known as "lesbian," "gay," "bisexual," "transgender," "queer," and so on carry with them no single or obvious political agenda. Political strategies and visions have to be developed and argued for, and they exist emphatically in the plural. Although this is no doubt true of gay and lesbian politics everywhere, it is perhaps especially evident in the United States, both because of the extent of the development of lesbian and gay communities and because of the highly diverse and multicultural character of the society as a whole. Even at a single moment in time—say, for instance, at one of the annual Lesbian and Gay Freedom Day parades held in cities across the United States, where contingents of sober-looking gay Mormons, young queer radicals, and leather-clad practitioners of sadomasochism may triumphantly march down the same route—the notion of a shared and fully articulated politics is a convenient fiction. This chapter argues that one of the most noteworthy aspects of gay and lesbian movements in the United States is the *proliferation* of political beliefs, practices, and organizations that often *compete* with one another to be perceived as legitimate and preferred.

In fact, there is no such thing as "the U.S. gay and lesbian movement," except insofar as more particular movements claim to speak for it. While much of what I call mainstream lesbian and gay politics roots itself in the assertion that it *is* "the movement," upon inspection, each term in the phrase "the gay and lesbian movement" either dissolves into a fog of ambiguity or congeals into sharp contradictions. The word "the" suggests unity and coherence, when in fact there have been multiple movements over time—"homophile," "gay liberationist," "lesbian feminist," "gay rights," and "queer," to name only a few—with widely different self-understandings and political strategies.[3] The term "gay and lesbian" is also problematic, for part of what is at stake in the contest that I describe is the very question of the movement's collective identity: who is the "we" on behalf of whom activists speak?[4] Do gay men share with lesbians a cohesive identity that can generate a single political vision? If so, does it encompass the demands of bisexuals and transgendered people or of self-styled "queers" who reject the terms "gay and lesbian"? And if so many in the United States feel the tug of multiple and overlapping claims on their identities, forming organizations as black gay men, or Jewish lesbians, or south Asian queers, and rejecting the notion that these compound identities can be broken down into their constituent parts, then in what sense can we speak of a "gay and lesbian" movement? Finally, the word "movement" should not go unexamined. Though it typically refers to recognizably political projects that have as their end such tangible goals as gay rights legislation, it can also denote activities directed toward the redefinition of culture and selfhood—movements for "sexual freedom," for new family forms, for "gay spirituality."[5]

With the goal of highlighting diversification, this chapter charts the evolution of a complicated patchwork of overlapping movements that have interacted and contended for primacy in different parts of the United States at different times in recent decades. Of course, these movements do not develop in a vacuum. And so, I sketch the broad social, political, and cultural factors that have facilitated or impeded the emergence of these movements—what analysts refer to as a movement's "opportunity structure" (Kitschelt 1986). I identify the institutions that these movements have centrally engaged—including the state, the market, organized religion, the mass media, and science and medicine—and point out the various audiences that the movements have addressed and been influenced by, including allies, adversaries, elite decision makers, and countermovements. I also try to trace the consequences of these movements for U.S. society—not just the explicit successes claimed by activists but also the more subtle, cultural ripple effects of movement agitation. In situating these movements firmly in their broader context, I pay attention to how they are shaped by features of the society and polity that distinguish the United States from other countries around the world—such well-known characteristics as the two-party system, the decentralized form of political administration that gives power to state and local governments, the tendency toward political mobilization along ethnic (and not class) lines, the bitter history of racial divides, the emphasis on civil liberties and civil rights as guaranteed by legislation or judicial precedent, the strength of religion and religious fundamentalism, and the widespread emphasis on self-actualization and the belief in the perfectibility of the self.

These features of U.S. society are important to the story I tell, not only because they establish the terrain on which struggles are waged but also because they help to explain a fundamental tension in gay and lesbian movement politics. On one hand, particularities of the United States have tended to favor the development of, and grant visibility and legitimacy to, one kind of lesbian and gay politics in the very midst of diversity: the formation of durable organizations and community groups that promote a liberal agenda of equal rights and inclusion, premised on a conception of gay men and lesbians as a clearly demarcated social group with a fixed, ethniclike identity. This is the particular form of gay and lesbian politics that often presents itself as "the movement"—and has won many victories. On the other hand, however, the limitations of this approach in achieving social change and in speaking for the multiplicity of lesbian and gay voices results in periodic eruptions of a different kind of politics: radical groups that contest these premises by calling attention to internal difference, questioning whether political and sexual identities are as stable or coherent as they are sometimes portrayed, or challenging the logic of relying on these identities as the ground on which to organize. Typically, this radical, utopian, "nonidentitarian" politics of difference has been short-lived, just because it is so hard to sustain and institutionalize, but the tension between it and a more mainstream "identity politics" has remained.[6]

To analyze this tension as it has revealed itself over time and, more generally, to explore differences among various manifestations of lesbian and gay politics, I find it helpful to disentangle the strands of the opposing arguments. *Three overlapping sets of debates* crop up again and again within this constellation of movements. These debates, each of which has been more or less salient at different moments in time, are at the heart of the struggle to define what sort of politics gay people should promote in the United States. They are implicated in the movements' signifying practices as activists seek to frame reality, mobilize adherents, and influence target audiences, and they affect whether the explanatory frames put forward by social movement actors ring true to members of the movements and others in the society.[7]

1. *Debates of identity and difference.* Is sexual identity perceived as something stable and given (an "orientation") or as something mutable or even chosen (a "preference"), and how does this affect political strate-

gies?[8] Is sexual desire for members of one's own sex believed to be something that everyone in the society might potentially experience at some moment, or is it the unique and defining attribute of a distinct minority?[9] Are lesbians and gay men fundamentally the same as heterosexuals, or do they constitute a group apart, with their own cultural forms? Are gays and lesbians in any sense a homogeneous group with a distinct identity, or are the internal differences stronger than any meaningful similarities? Is it possible to put forward a vision of a collective identity without simultaneously silencing those within the movement who perceive themselves to differ from it, whether because of their class, race, ethnicity, nationality, gender, specific sexual practices or erotic roles, political affiliations, religion, or other salient aspects of personal identity?

2. *Debates of desire.* How should society organize the expression of sexuality (Rubin 1993: 3–44)? What visions of the good society are implicit in ideas about how people should "be sexual" (Weeks 1985; Seidman 1992)? Are sexual relationships also relations of power—as, for example, lesbian feminists have argued? Should questions of sex be central to gay politics—as they were in the debate over the closure of gay bathhouses in San Francisco in the 1980s? Or should sexual differences be treated as socially insignificant and politically irrelevant—as they have been in arguments supporting the right of gay men or lesbians to marry or adopt children?

3. *Public/private debates.*[10] To what degree should the personal be made political? Are gay politics reducible to a "right to privacy" and the demand for government to stay out of the bedroom, as civil libertarians contend? Or does gay politics require the redrawing of the boundaries between public and private (Gross 1993), as in the demand that gays, lesbians, bisexuals, and transgendered people come out of the closet en masse and as in defenses of the political strategy of outing? What role ought the state to play in securing or mandating gay rights? What kinds of demands should be placed upon the state?

We can understand the strategies and tactics of specific groups, organizations, and movements by analyzing how activists debate these questions of identity and difference, sexuality, and the public/private divide and by analyzing how they frame distinctive answers in response to the institutions and actors they confront and the accidents of history. But seen over time, the answers often fall into the two broad patterns that I have described: mainstream, liberal, identity politics; and radical, nonidentitarian politics of difference. Therefore, the larger trajectory of gay and lesbian movements in the United States and the achievements and limitations of these movements reflect the peculiar oscillation between these two patterns of politics in the context of unique features of U.S. society.

PROLOGUE: HOMOPHILE ORGANIZATIONS OF THE 1950S AND 1960S

Unlike the European countries that saw the first glimmerings of homosexual rights organizing in the late nineteenth or early twentieth centuries, the United States did not witness its first social movement organizations concerned with the status of homosexuals until the 1950s.[11] Although a decade committed to the vigorous pursuit of normalcy was an improbable time for the emergence of such an effort, this development was predicated on a prior series of social transformations and upheavals, including urbanization and war.[12] Growing cities offered new havens for young men and women who experienced erotic desires for members of the same sex, permitting them to find one another in public spaces and to congregate in bars and other social institutions (D'Emilio 1983: 10–13).[13] The social disruption occasioned by the Second World War encouraged sexual experimentation, brought many homosexuals into contact with one another, loosened the ties of individuals to their communities of origin, and inspired them to settle down in liberal cities such as San Francisco after the war (D'Emilio 1983: 23–31; Bérubé 1990).

Increasingly, then, individuals who experienced same-sex erotic desires were able to make sense of those sentiments by situating themselves within emergent subcultures of others who seemed to be "like them." At the same time, the diffusion of psychoanalytic models of sexuality and identity encouraged the belief that the world was divided into two types of beings, heterosexuals and homosexuals, whose different "object choices" marked them as distinct categories of people.[14] The notion of homosexuality as a fixed condition or disorder largely confined to a minority of the population was part of the "cultural opportunity structure" (J. Gamson 1996) for the emergence of a homosexual politics—even as it conflicted with the findings of sex researcher Alfred Kinsey (Kinsey, Pomeroy, and Martin 1948; Kinsey 1953) that homosexual sexual *behavior* was a component of the sexuality of large portions of the "heterosexual" population.[15]

Indeed, Kinsey's findings were deemed shocking by a postwar society that dedicated itself to eradicating the "homosexual menace" and preventing its infectious spread through the body politic. In the conspiratorial world view of the McCarthy era, at the dawn of the Cold War, hidden homosexuals effeminized U.S. society and made the nation "soft," thereby facilitating a Communist takeover. In 1952, Congress passed an immigration bill banning foreign "sex deviants" from entering the country, and the following year President Dwight Eisenhower signed an executive order making "sexual perversion" grounds for exclusion from federal employment. This attention at the level of the federal government mirrored escalating persecution of homosexuals in many domains of personal life, including police harassment, employment discrimination, and forcible confinement in psychiatric hospitals and subjection to invasive "curative" techniques, such as electroshock therapy and aversion therapy (Adam 1987; Kennedy and Davis 1993).

Significantly, the first example of gay political organizing that would make a mark on U.S. society was promoted by a man who was doubly marginalized by the postwar hysteria over subversion and already inclined toward political militancy: Harry Hay, a homosexual who was a member of the Communist Party (Hay 1996). In 1951, Hay and several fellow Communists founded the Mattachine Society, which took its obscure name from a group of jesters who performed political satire in medieval Europe (Blasius and Phelan 1997: 283). In an interesting use of the Marxist concept of "false consciousness," Mattachine hoped to foment among homosexuals a critical awareness of their oppression, as a group, at the hands of the majority society (D'Emilio 1983: 58, 64–65).

However, as Mattachine grew and became more internally diverse, it quickly made a dramatic shift in political orientation and in the conception of its identity and goals. By 1953, Communists, perceived as a dangerous liability, were forced out of the organization, which now took as its end the integration of the homosexual into mainstream U.S. society. Then in 1955 this new, politically moderate, assimilationist politics was adopted by Del Martin and Phyllis Lyon, the two principal founders of the San Francisco Daughters of Bilitis (DOB), which was named for a book of poetry about love between women in Sappho's school (Blasius and Phelan 1997: 327). Mattachine and DOB, along with One magazine, founded in Los Angeles in 1953, formed the center of what came to be known as "homophile" politics—the organizational form that lesbian and gay organizing took throughout the 1950s and 1960s, until the advent of gay liberation.

In seeking to recruit members and influence elites, homophile activists from the mid-1950s to the mid-1960s presented a more-or-less consistent set of answers to the questions recurring in lesbian and gay social movements in the United States—questions concerning sexuality, identity and difference, and the public/private divide. In terms of identity, homophiles conceived of homosexuality as a fixed or innate condition, beyond the individual's control or responsibility, and a stable aspect of the self (Weitz 1984: 233–48)—a position that made sense as a response to claims by medical authorities that homosexuals could be "cured." While homophiles tended to emphasize the extent to which homosexuals might readily be integrated into the mainstream culture, they also took early steps toward what would later become a dominant direction in lesbian and gay politics: framing homosexuals not as a deviant subculture but as a distinct minority group, akin to other recognized minorities in U.S. society.[16]

On the question of sexuality and its place in society, homophiles offered little real analysis, preferring to play down the importance of differences in the organization or expression of sexual desire and substantially adopting the dominant view of homosexuality as a condition or variation with psychological causes. Finally, homophiles conceived of sexuality as a quintessentially private domain, but to support this private right, they argued, public education was necessary. To this end, DOB and Mattachine sought out sympathetic experts—lawyers, doctors, and ministers, among others—who might be swayed to their perspective and then speak out on behalf of beleaguered homosexuals.

The strategic and tactical implication of these frames was a reformist and cautious politics that was nonetheless remarkable in a climate of fierce repression. Against the popular conception of homosexuality as freakish, activists stressed the common humanity of homosexual men and women. Because they could be harassed by the police or fired from their jobs if they made themselves too publicly visible, homophile leaders kept a low profile. Movement publications brought homophile perspectives to a limited group of readers—circulation figures were reported to be twenty-two hundred for *Mattachine Review*, five hundred for DOB's *The Ladder*, and over five thousand for *One* (D'Emilio 1983: 110)—and membership remained quite small, even as chapters were established in New York, Chicago, Detroit, Denver, and Boston. Perhaps the movement's greatest victory in the 1950s came from the struggle waged by *One* to disseminate its views through the U.S. mail, which culminated in a legal case that eventually landed before the United States Supreme Court and was decided in favor of the magazine (D'Emilio 1983: 115). Homophiles also challenged police entrapment of gay men and won legal battles against state liquor authorities in the fight to allow alcohol to be served at gay bars (Bernstein 1997a: 30). But little was accomplished in the 1950s in terms of changing public attitudes about homosexuality, let alone improving the position of homosexuals in society. Indeed, as of 1960, with sodomy laws on the books in all fifty states, homosexual sexual practices themselves were strictly illegal throughout the entire United States.

The politics of the homophile movement underwent an important change in the middle of the 1960s with the rise of a more militant faction. An activist named Frank Kameny, who formed a chapter of Mattachine in Washington, D.C., in 1961, criticized what he called the "genteel, debating society approach" that had characterized the homophile movement (quoted in D'Emilio 1983: 153). As the Negro civil rights movement came to serve as the "master frame" (Snow and Benford 1992: 133–55; McAdam 1994: 42) available to all movements in the United States pursuing their rights, activists like Kameny turned to that movement for examples of how—and how not—to proceed.[17] They organized a national confederation, the North American Conference of Homophile Organizations (NACHO), and, at their 1968 conference in Chicago, formally adopted Kameny's slogan that encapsulated the new movement orientation: "Gay is good" (D'Emilio 1983: 199). Just as "Black is beautiful" signaled a defiant reversal of dominant stereotypes and a rejection of a label ("Negro") associated with passivity and subservience, so "Gay is good" repudiated, once and for all, the connotations of illness and inferiority that seemed to accompany the medical term "homosexual."

The new philosophies were reflected in new styles of protest that emerged in the middle and later years of the decade. In 1965 a small group of neatly dressed men and women from Washington Mattachine appeared on national television, walking patiently in a circle in front of the White House, holding signs supporting equal rights for gay people. With actions of this kind, the homophile movement—despite its failure in constructing a significant mass base—helped lay the groundwork for the liberation movement that would succeed it and supersede it (D'Emilio 1983: 219, 249).

OUT OF THE CLOSETS AND INTO THE STREETS

By the end of the 1960s, as social attitudes about sexual expressiveness became more liberal, the idea of a radical challenge to the oppression of gay men and lesbians began to be more conceivable. At the same time, the tactics even of the more militant homophile activists, modeled after the nonviolent tradition of the Negro civil rights movement, seemed increasingly timid in contrast to the disruptive protests ever more visible on the streets of U.S. cities and on the evening news broadcasts—the confrontational tactics of the anti–Vietnam war protesters, the Black Power movement, and others dedicated to radical change or revolutionary upheaval in the United States (D'Emilio 1983: 223). Increasingly, conditions seemed right for a new politics of sexuality, but what was lacking was a transformation of consciousness, or "cognitive liberation" (McAdam 1982): gay men and lesbians needed not only to perceive the existing sexual and social order as unjust but to acquire "a new sense of efficacy," whereby those "who ordinarily consider themselves helpless come to believe that they have some capacity to alter their lot" (Piven and Cloward 1979).

Though the development of such efficacy is inevitably a gradual process, in historical retrospect it may appear as a shift of startling abruptness. Such is the story of the patrons of a gay bar called the Stonewall Inn, located in the Greenwich Village neighborhood of New York City, shortly after 1:00 A.M. on 28 July 1969. When police raided the bar, as they were in the habit of doing periodically, and began hauling the customers into paddy wagons for transport to jail, some of the bar's patrons, including black and Puerto Rican drag queens and lesbians, decided they had had enough. A melee erupted as the crowd began throwing coins, bottles, cans, and bricks, yelling, "Gay power," and shouting epithets at the police (Duberman 1993: 196–201). Disturbances continued in the streets outside the Stonewall for several nights running. To be sure, the Stonewall rebellion was not as unique or consequential an event at the time as it came to be portrayed later (Murray 1996: 59–65). "But if the Stonewall riots did not *begin* the gay revolution," acknowledges Martin Duberman, the historian who has chronicled the events in greatest detail, "it remains true that those riots became a symbolic event of international importance," one that "occupies a central place in the iconography of lesbian and gay awareness" (Duberman 1993: 224, xv).

Members of the New York Mattachine Society, who viewed these turbulent developments with alarm, put a sign outside the Stonewall Inn: "We homosexuals plead with our people to please help maintain peaceful and quiet conduct on the streets of the Village" (Duberman 1993: 207). But within weeks, young gay men and women had formed a new group, the Gay Liberation Front (GLF), which would become the prototypical organization of the gay liberation movement (Marotta 1981). In a telling example of how the frames and tactics of one social movement will very often spill over to influence other, contemporary or subsequent, movements (Meyer and Whittier 1994), gay liberation activists borrowed heavily from the movements that they, as individuals, were already active in: the antiwar movement lent a suspicion of the government; the New Left lent an "apocalyptic rhetoric and sense of impending revolution" (D'Emilio 1983: 233–34); the women's liberation movement lent a critique of sexism and the idea that "the personal"—even "the sexual"—is "political"; Third World liberation movements lent the prideful affirmation of a stigmatized identity and the notion of resistance to an imperial state; and the hippie movement and counterculture lent an injunction to "do your own thing," a distrust of authority and dismissal of the older generation (here including older, "closeted" gay men and lesbians), and a belief that protest tactics could be playful and celebratory while still being subversive (Altman 1971: 234; D'Emilio 1983: 224; Adam 1987: 76; Cruikshank 1992: 61, 76; Duberman 1993: 220).

Gay liberation–style activism quickly spread around the country—in particular, the "action technology" (Oliver and Marwell 1992: 251–72) known as the "zap," which called for the graphic and confrontational disruption of the day-to-day routines of opponents. In October 1969 a "suicide squadron" of GLF members in New York interrupted a meeting of mayoral candidates after waiting two hours for candidates to reply to questions submitted to them. That same month gay students at Berkeley staged guerrilla theater and gay power demonstrations during orientation week. The following May, members of GLF, chanting "Suck cock; beat the draft" and "Bring our boys home," participated in a Washington, D.C., antiwar protest and held a "nude-in" in the Lincoln Memorial reflecting pool (Thompson 1994: 22–35). On the first anniversary of the Stonewall riot, two thousand men and women held a commemorative march through the streets of New York, while hundreds of others marched in other U.S. cities. By the following year the Stonewall anniversary celebration had spread to Paris and London and become an official, international gay event (Duberman 1993: 279).

Liberationists challenged corporations over their hiring practices, continued the fight against police entrapment, and organized large dances in cities around the country where, in the past, men and women had been arrested for dancing with partners of the same sex. One noteworthy struggle—which was over the very definition and character of gayness, as well as the personal safety of lesbians and gay men seeking to live their lives free of fear of confinement and stigmatization—was the campaign waged against the "war criminals" of the American Psychiatric Association to remove homosexuality from the list of mental illnesses and halt the attempts to "cure" homosexuals. This battle was won in 1973, after many disruptive "zaps" both outside and inside the association's conventions (Bayer 1981; Marcus 1992).

Earlier, homophile activists had begun to consolidate a "minority group" identity that emphasized the stability of sexual identity and called for homosexuals to take their place in U.S. society. Radical gay liberationists repudiated this agenda and put forward claims about sexuality, identity and difference, and the public and private that differed in nearly every particular from those of homophile activists. Where homophiles had had little to say about sexuality as such, liberationists saw sexuality as a subversive and revolutionary force. Adopting philosopher Herbert Marcuse's (1966) hybrid "Freudo-Marxism," they called for the liberation of the "polymorphous-perverse" forms of sexuality believed to lie latent within every individual. Lesbians and gay men, in this conception, were the vanguard in a vast struggle to redefine the family, gender roles, and our erotic and relational capacities as human beings. As writer and activist Dennis Altman noted, "Liberation . . . would involve a break-down of the barriers between male and female homosexuals, and between gays and straights. Masculinity and femininity would cease to be sharply differentiated categories." (1971: 106). The appeal to a universal bisexual potential was widespread in early movement rhetoric.[18] By implication, the collective subject of the new movement was necessarily transitory: paradoxically, the victory of the movement would result in the withering away of both "the homosexual" and "the heterosexual," with each replaced by "a new human for whom such distinctions no longer are necessary for the establishment of identity" (Altman 1971: 237).

Where homophile activists had endorsed a strong separation between public and private realms, liberationists, arguing that "the personal is political," placed at the center of their politics the act of coming out—the public and defiant affirmation of identity. As D'Emilio notes, in the years before gay liberation, "coming out" meant revealing one's homosexuality to other homosexuals; after gay liberation the public avowal of one's sexual desires and identity became a strategy for movement building and heightening the commitment of recruits. Liberationists connected the collective action frame of visible confrontation—epitomized by the slogan, "Out of the closets and into the streets!"—to the "Gay is good" frame by arguing that a healthy, liberated gay person simply had nothing to hide (D'Emilio 1983: 235–36).[19] Liberationists "engaged in public displays of affection, violated gender conventions, and gloried in the discomfort they deliberately provoked in others" (D'Emilio 1992: 243).

These distinctive ways of framing sexuality, identity, and the relation between public and private resonated with young gay men and lesbians around the country and pulled them into activism. These frames also implied particular strategies and tactics for the gay liberation movement. Because homosexuality was too transgressive ever to be integrated into the existing society, and because radical gays and lesbians were committed to the broader social struggle against capitalism, imperialism, racism, and sexism, it followed that gay liberation was a revolutionary movement with the goal of social and cultural transformation. Perhaps more so in rhetoric than in reality, gay liberation emphasized the importance of forming coalitions with other oppressed groups. Thus at the 1970 NACHO meeting in San Francisco, radicals fought against old-line homophiles to pass resolutions supporting women's liberation and the Black Panthers and calling for the removal of U.S. forces from Vietnam (Adam 1987: 79).

Yet, for all its flash and dazzle, gay liberation, as an organized movement, was short-lived, and the utopian notion of challenging fixed categories of identity proved particularly difficult to sustain or institutionalize. Almost immediately, tensions arose concerning the comprehensive political vision of radical gay liberation. In November 1969 several New York activists who found GLF too anarchic, impractical, and preoccupied with rhetoric split off to found a new, more focused organization called the Gay Activists Alliance (GAA) (Adam 1987: 80). Though it engaged in actions similar to those of GLF and used many of the same tactics, GAA conceived of itself as "exclusively devoted to issues involving gay rights" (Evans 1973) and was less committed to overthrowing the categories of gender and sexuality.

Gay liberation impelled a rapid proliferation of gay organizations: at the time of Stonewall, there were only about fifty lesbian or gay groups in the entire United States; by the end of 1973, there were more than a thousand, ranging from gay newspapers to crisis hotlines to social clubs (D'Emilio 1992: 244). But the groups with a radical and comprehensive political agenda soon faded from the scene. By 1971, New York's GLF had splintered into factions, and within a few years GLF and GAA chapters had disbanded around the country. As the political climate became conservative, "the belief that a revolution was imminent and that gays should get on board, was losing whatever momentary plausibility it had" (D'Emilio 1992: 245). Furthermore, the liberation movement proved unable to unite its various members. It did not speak fully to the experiences of gays and lesbians of color, who created such organizations as Third World Gay Revolution; and it alienated many working-class drag queens, who formed groups such as Street Transvestite Action Revolutionaries because they felt marginalized by middle-class GLF members who saw drag culture as unfortunate mimicry of outdated gender roles (M. Johnson 1972: 114).

Even more tellingly, gay liberation was unable to cope effectively with the politics of gender. Activists such as Jill Johnson declared that "lesbians are feminists, not homosexuals" (quoted in Adam 1987: 94), as lesbians influenced by the women's liberation movement increasingly came to feel alienated by the political, sexual, and personal styles of gay men. "What is a lesbian"? asked "The Woman-Identified Woman," the famous manifesto of a women's collective called the Radicalesbians: "A lesbian is the rage of all women condensed to the point of explosion" (Radicalesbians 1972: 172). If male opponents of "women's libbers" typically derided them as "man-hating lesbians," radical lesbians turned the argument on its head by positioning lesbianism as the quintessential act of female political resistance (Faderman 1991: 205–6). Although radical gay men and lesbians typically were united in condemnations of sexism and patriarchy, this new conception of lesbian identity as a form of political solidarity among women sat uneasily alongside the liberationist ethic of freeing the bisexual potential of all.

LESBIAN AND GAY RIGHTS IN THE 1970S

The irony of radical gay liberation is that its most profound effect was to promote the development of forms of identity, community, and politics that were antithetical to the liberationist vision. Radical activists who foresaw the "end of the homosexual" and the transcendence of constraining categories of gender and sexuality discovered instead, that they were helping to build communities organized around the notion that gays and lesbians were a distinct class of people with unique political interests. Liberationists who had connected the freedom of gay men and lesbians to a socialist agenda found, to their chagrin, that the new gay male culture was organized substantially around profit-making businesses, such as bars and bathhouses, and that homosexuality, far from posing a revolutionary challenge to U.S. society through its radical incompatibility with it, in fact seemed to do fine—perhaps even to thrive—under capitalism. Those who had promoted an androgynous style of personal dress and expression in the hopes of challenging gender roles greeted with some ambivalence the rise, among gay men, of the pervasive, so-called "Castro clone" style of exaggerated masculinity: short hair, mustaches, denim, plaid shirts, leather, and boots (Altman 1982a: 20, 85, 104; Fitzgerald 1986: 54, 58; Adam 1987: 100).

The developing gay neighborhoods, such as San Francisco's Castro District, became "a kind of laboratory for experimentation with alternate ways to live. [They were] also a carnival where social conventions were turned upside down just for the pleasure of seeing what they looked like the wrong way up" (Fitzgerald 1986: 12). As Frances Fitzgerald has noted, the pioneering of these new communities reflected the "extraordinary" and "quintessentially American" notion that people could "start all over again from scratch"—that they could make "new lives, new families, even new societies" by, in effect, reinventing themselves (Fitzgerald 1986: 23). Indeed, the 1970s was the era of the consolidation of a new, quasi-ethnic form of gay identity, community, and politics (Murray 1979, 1996; Altman 1982a; S. Epstein 1987).[20] Within more-or-less defined territorial enclaves (Castells 1983; Davis 1995: 284–303), gay men and, to a lesser degree, lesbians established gay restaurants, gay choruses, gay newspapers, gay churches and synagogues, and (by the 1980s) gay savings and loan associations. The distinctive rainbow flag, designed in San Francisco in 1978 (Thompson 1994: 23) and soon flying outside residences and businesses in the gay ghettoes, would come to mark the territory and welcome the "immigrants" who poured in from smaller, less hospitable towns and rural areas around the country. Hundreds of thousands of people would turn out each year for the Lesbian and Gay Freedom Day parades held in commemoration of Stonewall in cities around the United States—simultaneously an official holiday and a political and cultural event for the lesbian and gay population. Although the parade crowds were extraordinarily diverse, the gay enclaves themselves were narrower in their social composition—largely white and, with the increasing gentrification of property within them, largely middle class.

As Dennis Altman has noted, the widespread acceptance, by both straights and gays, of the notion that gay men and lesbians constituted a sort of ethnic group, roughly analogous to Jewish Americans or Italian Americans, represented not only an extraordinary change from twenty years earlier (when homosexuality was widely understood as a form of deviance or pathology, like alcoholism) but also a very American response: the ethnic model made sense in a country where people tend to identify themselves by ethnicity rather by class and where interest-group politics typically reflects the jockeying among ethnic groups for their "piece of the pie" (Altman 1982a: viii–ix, 224). The combined reliance on a quasi-ethnic, essentialist identity and the political model of the civil rights movement would distinguish this new, more mainstream "lesbian and gay rights movement" from gay political formations elsewhere around the world—and from alternatives within the United States.[21]

The communal and middle-class character of the new gay enclaves made it easier for the lesbian and gay rights movement to mobilize resources.[22] People who are well integrated into community institutions and organizations are more readily drawn into social movements (McAdam 1982; Lo 1992: 224–47), and many within the gay, quasi-ethnic communities were prepared to make substantial commitments of time and money. In this sense the formation of quasi-ethnic communities proved central to the rise of the lesbian and gay rights movement. Increasingly, the mainstream lesbian and gay rights movement, despite its white, middle-class base and its particular conception of the political agenda, would seek to present itself in hegemonic fashion as "the movement"—as what all gay politics boiled down to in the end.

Questions of sexuality, identity and difference, and the relation between public and private were framed by the lesbian and gay rights movement in ways that fostered the goal of defining and defending the interests of a gay quasi-ethnicity. Consistent with the quasi-ethnic model, the lesbian and gay rights movement expressed the view that being gay was a fixed or immutable condition, and gay men and lesbians (sometimes together, more often separately) were portrayed as belonging to communities that had distinctive cultural forms.[23] Internal differences within the culture, such as racial or class differences, were overlooked in the dominant rhetoric. Often the lineage of this culture was traced in ways that paid little attention to the particularities of the organization of desire in other societies, as in the attempt to lay claim to Plato, Sappho, or Michelangelo as "famous homosexuals in history." For similar reasons, activists tended to trumpet scientific arguments suggesting that homosexuality was biologically based, since such claims seemed to undercut the position that homosexuality was a chosen, sinful lifestyle and seemed to support the view that lesbians and gay men deserved protection as a legitimate minority. Indeed, the political corollary of this essentialist conception was that the state should be pressured to ensure the formal legal equality of lesbians and gay men as a people, much as had been done for African Americans and for women.

This movement did not present a coherent or sustained analysis of the place of sexuality in modern society. It did, however, disseminate a widely influential conception of "homophobia," which reframed the "social problem" of homosexuality by arguing that the real problem was the irrational fear of homosexuality on the part of many ill-informed straight people.[24] This conception was distinctly Freudian—ironically so, since Freud and his followers were themselves often denounced as homophobes by members of the movement. It assumed that homophobic attitudes and behaviors often were defense mechanisms for warding off recognition of one's own repressed homoerotic impulses (what Freud would call a "re-action-formation" [Weinberg 1972: 12])—hence the folk wisdom that the most violent homophobes and gay bashers were themselves "closet cases."

Finally, in terms of the public/private distinction, the lesbian and gay rights movement retained the liberationist rhetoric of gay pride while also endorsing the notion of a right to privacy in the expression of sexuality. The right to privacy was seen as a cornerstone of the struggle to "get government out of the bedroom" by abolishing laws against sodomy. These conceptions of sexuality, identity, and privacy came together in the form of a single-issue politics, modeled loosely on the civil rights movement and put forward by organizations that had much more formal bureaucratic and leadership structures than those of the gay liberation era (D'Emilio 1992: 246). Indeed, where liberationist, nonidentitarian politics seemed by their nature to be evanescent and resistant to institutionalization, gay ethnicity lent itself easily to the construction of organizations (Armstrong 1998).

The lesbian and gay rights movement sought to bring about social change through a variety of approaches. First, over the course of the 1970s, the movement built national organizations, such as the National Gay Task Force (later renamed the National Gay and Lesbian Task Force, or NGLTF), an advocacy group founded in 1973, which by the end of the decade claimed ten thousand mostly white, male, and middle-class members (Altman 1982a: 123). Three years later the Gay Rights National Lobby (GRNL) was founded as a lobbying group to bring pressure to bear on the U.S. Congress, and in 1980 the Human Rights Campaign Fund (later shortened to Human Rights Campaign, or HRC) was created as a fund-raising tool to support candidates perceived to be "gay friendly." Compared with the size of the emergent gay and lesbian communities, these organizations were small, and compared with the diversity of lesbians and gay men in terms of race and class, their social composition was fairly monolithic. The first national organization formed by gay men and lesbians of color, the National Coalition of Black Lesbians and Gays, opened its doors in 1978 and held its first national convention in 1982 (Ridinger 1996: 188–89).

Second, in line with a familiarly American tendency to turn to the courts to ensure legal protection for minorities, activists created legal support organizations, such as the Lambda Legal Defense and Education Fund (LLDEF) founded in New York in 1972, and the Gay and Lesbian Advocates and Defenders (GLAD) founded in Boston in 1978. These organizations took on the legal cases of lesbians and gay men fighting discrimination and also filed many "friend of the court" briefs in the hope of influencing judicial decisions.

Third, activists sought to overturn sodomy laws and pass antidiscrimination laws. In California an activist lobbying effort proved successful in overturning the state's sodomy law, and in many other states—twenty-one of them by the end of 1978—sodomy statutes were removed as part of a general process of penal code reform (Bernstein 1997a: 44). The first federal civil rights bill for gay men and lesbians was introduced into Congress in 1974 by Bella Abzug and Ed Koch, both Democrats from New York. But the fierce opposition to legislation at the federal level meant that lesbians and gay men, in the interim, faced the time-consuming challenge of proceeding state by state or city by city in pursuit of antidiscrimination statutes within the decentralized governance structure of the United States.

Fourth, the movement sought to make inroads into the Democratic Party, which—given the absence of powerful leftist parties in the American two-party system—was perceived by many activists as the only game in town. At the local level, lesbians and gay men formed groups such as San Francisco's Alice B. Toklas Lesbian and Gay Democratic Club, expressing support for liberal candidates who were willing to call for equal rights for gays and lesbians (Faderman 1991: 199). At the national level, activists sought to convince the party to adopt a gay rights plank in its platform; this effort failed in 1976 after Democratic presidential nominee Jimmy Carter retracted his support (Thompson 1994: 132).

Fifth, the lesbian and gay rights movement sought to elect openly gay men and women to local office. In 1974, activist and former college teacher Elaine Nobel was elected by a six-hundred-vote margin to the Massachusetts House of Representatives, becoming the first openly gay legislator in the United States (Ridinger 1996: 212). In 1977, after several unsuccessful tries, Harvey Milk, owner of a camera shop in San Francisco's Castro District, was elected to the city's Board of Supervisors.[25] When Milk, along with San Francisco Mayor George Moscone, was shot dead by a conservative member of the Board of Supervisors in 1978, the new mayor quickly named another gay leader, Harry Britt, to take Milk's place on the board. The power of the gay community within the city was further demonstrated in the White Night riots, which broke out when Dan White, Milk's killer, was convicted of manslaughter rather than murder: thousands of protesters marched on City Hall and set fire to police cars to protest the verdict.

In addition to legislative, judicial, and electoral activism, the lesbian and gay rights movement of the 1970s pursued change on many other fronts. It pressured businesses to adopt nondiscrimination policies, achieving victories with companies such as AT&T, with more than one million employees nationwide. Activists sought acceptance within church congregations and also formed their own gay congregations. The Metropolitan Community Church, for example, founded in 1968 by a Los Angeles activist, the Reverend Troy Perry, soon spread around the country. Activists created new organizations to document and respond to antigay violence (Jenness and Broad 1994; Jenness 1995). They also used the arts to educate the public about the goals of the movement; one noteworthy example is the 1978 documentary *Word Is Out: Stories of Some of Our Lives,* by filmmakers Nancy Adair and Casey Adair, which was based on lengthy interviews with twenty-six gay men and lesbians.

Beginning in the mid-1970s, the terrain of political contention for the lesbian and gay rights movement was radically altered by the rise of an organized opponent, the New Right, a social movement concerned in large part with the defense of "traditional" family, gender, and sexual forms.[26] This is a clear case in which the particularities of the United States affected the trajectory of lesbian and gay movements: because the centrality of religion in general and fundamentalism in particular made such an opponent possible in the United States, gay men and lesbians here faced a set of challenges that their counterparts in most other countries escaped.

In June 1977, voters in Dade County, Florida, galvanized by former beauty pageant winner Anita Bryant and her Save Our Children organization, repealed a recently passed ordinance that would have protected gays and lesbians against discrimination. The news, which hit gay and lesbian communities like a bombshell, proved to be only the first in a series of repeal efforts that spread across the country. The emergent threat provided leaders of gay and lesbian movements with a new agenda and a clear rhetorical target; increasingly, activists pointed to the dangers posed by the New Right as the reason that gays and lesbians needed to get involved in political work. In this way, movement organizers painted a picture of the antagonist (see Hunt, Benford, and Snow 1994: 185–208) as means of recruitment and mobilization.

The response was a considerable upswing in attendance at lesbian and gay demonstrations and Gay Pride Day events, including a turnout of 250,000 for a highly politicized Gay Pride Day in San Francisco in 1978 (Adam 1987: 105). In California more than thirty organizations sprang up, as activists fought a successful grassroots organizing campaign against an antigay referendum sponsored by state senator John Briggs, which called for the dismissal of all gay and lesbian teachers from California public schools. Following the repeal of a lesbian and gay rights ordinance in St. Paul, Minnesota, in 1978, support began building for a national show of strength against the rising tide of conservatism. The first national March on Washington for Gay and Lesbian Rights, held in Washington, D.C., on 14 October 1979, drew a sizable crowd; estimates ranged from 25,000, according to the U.S. Park Police, to 125,000, according to conference organizers.

A conference of Third World lesbians and gays was held just before the march, in part in an effort to increase participation by lesbians and gay men of color in the event and in gay and lesbian politics more generally (Ridinger 1996: 192–97). But in the aftermath of the march, it was hard to discern many long-term consequences of the mobilization. If the energy did not dissipate entirely, it was redirected to local organizing that emphasized building durable community institutions and organizations but lacked a comprehensive or radical agenda for social change.

Less evident to the broader public was the fact that more radical gay men and lesbians sought, throughout the 1970s, to keep alive the political impulses of the gay liberation movement. For many of these activists, the political Left continued to be the natural home of lesbian and gay politics, even if the Left was often indifferent or even hostile to gay concerns (Altman 1971: 217–26). *Gay Community News,* a national newsweekly founded in 1973 and based in Boston, was an important voice for a gay Left perspective in the United States that sought to "make connections" between the issues confronting gays and lesbians and those affecting other oppressed people. Meanwhile, gay men influenced less by the New Left than by the 1960s counterculture constructed alternative communities at some remove from the mainstream culture of the urban gay ghettoes but equally or more essentialist in their conceptions of gay men as a people. For example, in 1979, Harry Hay, onetime Communist and Mattachine founder, helped create the Radical Fairies, which held gatherings in the woods to promote a mystical conception of a uniquely gay male spirituality and sensuality (Hay 1996).

FROM LESBIAN NATION TO THE "DECENTERING" OF LESBIAN FEMINISM

By far the most significant alternative to the mainstream lesbian and gay rights movement of the 1970s, however, was lesbian feminist politics and culture. In the 1970s, as lesbian feminists framed sexuality, identity, and the boundary between public and private in ways that led to the establishment of a distinct, politically sensitized community, they preserved many of the radical insights of the liberationists. But they also began to consolidate the sort of essentialist conceptions of gender and sexual identities that liberationists had disavowed.

Lesbian feminists' attitudes about sexuality and identity were neither simple nor uniform, eventually resulting, as Arlene Stein (1997) has argued, in stark internal tensions in the 1980s. On one side, many "cultural feminists" asserted the view that all women who opposed patriarchy, regardless of their specific sexual practices, existed at some point along a "lesbian continuum" (Rich 1983: 177–206). Feminists were encouraged to identify as lesbians, whether that meant experimenting with the expression of sexual desire for other women or becoming "political lesbians" whose affinity for women was not consummated sexually. In this sense, lesbianism was portrayed as a "choice," indeed a political commitment, although one in which "same-sex *desire* became secondary to same-sex *identification,*" with sexuality "collapsed" into gender (A. Stein 1997: 38, 121). As a result, as Lillian Faderman (1991: 207) has observed, "there were probably more lesbians in America during the 1970s than at any other time in history."

But if cultural feminism blurred the boundary between lesbians and other women by playing down the significance of sexuality, the parallel current of "lesbian separatism" sought to create strong boundaries around the "Lesbian Nation" by emphasizing essential differences between lesbians and heterosexuals, whether male or female (A. Stein 1997: 120). Furthermore, both cultural feminists and lesbian separatists (groups that in practice often overlapped) assumed the existence of essential differences between women and men, including their ways of being sexual (A. Stein 1997: 120). As one lesbian writer expressed it in 1975, "If we are to learn our own sexual natures we have to get rid of the male-model of penetration and orgasm as the culmination of love-making" (Barbara Lipschutz, quoted in Faderman 1991: 231).

Lesbian feminists dedicated themselves to building an alternative culture, or what Verta Taylor and Nancy Whittier (1992: 104–29) identify as a "social movement community": they formed collective households and cooperatively run small businesses, and they opened women's bookstores and coffeehouses (A. Stein 1997: 109). They played consequential roles in related social movements, including the women's health movement (Radicalesbians Health Collective 1972: 122–41) and the reproductive rights movement, while often holding leadership positions in other movements for peace and social justice. As recent analysts (Taylor and Whittier 1992: 104–29; Taylor and Rupp 1993) have argued, the building of lesbian feminist communities should be understood not as a "retreat" from the activist politics of the 1960s, but as a distinct "cycle of feminist activism" that made sense in a more conservative time, one organized around the elaboration of a culture that socialized women into a "collective oppositional consciousness."

However, to heighten the boundaries protecting the Lesbian Nation, lesbian feminists attempted in the most thoroughgoing terms to put into practice the maxim that feminism had pioneered: the personal is political (Taylor and Whittier 1992: 104–29; A. Stein 1997: 92). Minute details of private life, including choices of food, clothing, and language, were asserted to be public, politically consequential statements. This construal of the relation between public and private reflected a desire for a "totalizing" identity within an organic community (A. Stein 1997: 119–20). But the emphasis on uniformity and "political correctness" (Faderman 1991: 230) meant that differences had to be subsumed; this led to particular difficulties for a movement that had attracted a heterogeneous group of women, some of whom felt and acted upon a strong erotic attraction for other women and some of whom did not (A. Stein 1997: 119–20, 181–82). Thus, whereas the more mainstream lesbian and gay rights movement provided lesbians with inadequate space to articulate a feminist critique of gender inequality and the traditional family, lesbian feminism put such politics at the center but made it hard to analyze the place of sexuality itself within sexual politics (Whisman 1996: 116–23).

Over the course of the late 1970s and the 1980s, the unifying model of lesbian feminism gradually became less stable, as lesbian feminist communities were racked with disputes over racial and sexual diversity. If lesbian feminism was a quintessential example of identity politics, its trajectory also demonstrated that any "politics of identity" is simultaneously a "politics of difference" (Escoffier 1985: 148–49). Increasingly, the "organic community" seemed unable to accommodate the proliferation of identities, sexualities, and politics among lesbians, many of whom reacted against what they perceived to be a constraining insistence on uniformity and political correctness (A. Stein 1993, 1997).

In the 1970s, lesbians of color began to form political groups, such as the National Black Feminist Organization, founded in 1974 (Faderman 1991: 242), and in 1980 the first Black Lesbian Conference was held in San Francisco. The Combahee River Collective, a black feminist group that included many lesbians, argued that feminist theory was inadequate for conceptualizing the sources of women's oppression, which for many women included their oppression as people of color or as members of the working class. Increasingly, the broader lesbian feminist community was criticized for promoting a "false universalism" (A. Stein 1997: 15), and lesbians of color began to form autonomous organizations (Ramos 1987). As Gloria Anzaldúa described it, if the woman of color was typically made "invisible" in U.S. society, then "the *lesbian* of color is not only invisible, she doesn't even exist. Our speech, too, is inaudible. We speak in tongues like the outcast and the insane" (Anzaldúa 1981: 165; see also Moraga and Anzaldúa 1981; Smith 1983; Anzaldúa 1987). Some proposed additive models of oppression, in which those who were doubly, triply, or quadruply oppressed laid claim to unique political identities arising from the authenticity of lived experience; others insisted that different systems of oppression, such as race, class, gender, and sexuality, were not fully comparable and that they intersected in complicated ways that additive models did not capture. In either case the notion of lesbian feminists as a unitary collective subject became harder and harder to maintain.

The boundary-making project of lesbian feminism, which had preserved the political community by drawing sharp lines around a lesbian feminist identity, resulted in "border skirmishes" (A. Stein 1997: 119): should bisexuals, or pre- and postoperative transsexuals, be considered part of the women's community? To lesbian separatists who endorsed strongly essentialist conceptions of femaleness and lesbianism, male-to-female transsexuals were not "real women," and bisexuals were "traitors" who continued to enjoy "heterosexual privilege." Perhaps the most divisive debates, however, were those that came to be known collectively as the "sex wars." What range of sexual expression was permissible within, or appropriate to, lesbianism? On a broader and more important scale, what were the contingent or intrinsic relations between sexuality and power, and what forms of sex were compatible with a liberatory political vision that challenged social oppression (Vance 1984; Duggan and Hunter 1995)?

Early lesbian feminists, convinced that every personal choice carried political consequences, had criticized the butch/fem role playing of a previous generation of lesbians as a residue of patriarchal gender relations, and they had endorsed a vision of egalitarian sensuality that did not valorize a "male" model of penetration and the hegemony of the orgasm. In the late 1970s and early 1980s, a range of discontented lesbians criticized this as a limited, "vanilla" sexuality. Many insisted on the personal salience of erotic roles such as butch and fem; others who came out of the closet as sadomasochists insisted that the expression of dominance within a stylized erotic encounter was not to be equated with, or seen as reflecting or furthering, systems of oppression within the broader society—relations of power in sex were not, in any simple sense, continuous with relations of power in society (Rubin 1993: 3–44; Califia 1994). Similar debates erupted over the particularly explosive issue of pornography (Duggan and Hunter 1995). On one side, "antiporn" feminists organized groups such as Women against Violence against Women—which argued that pornography encouraged violence against women and violated their civil rights—and they pressed for antipornography legislation. On the other side, "pro-sex" feminists founded organizations such as the Feminist Anti-censorship Taskforce. These activists maintained that women, as producers and consumers of pornography, had a right to unfettered sexual pleasure. They also argued against the notion that "representation" could be equated with "reality"—that the objectification of women in sexual imagery had a direct causative effect on male violence toward women (Vance 1993: 29–49).

By the late 1980s, as the unitary identity of lesbian feminism was challenged in these multiple ways, there was no longer a working consensus on how to frame debates about identity, sexuality, and the relation between public and private. Lesbian identity, community, and politics had become "decentered" (A. Stein 1992, 1997: 152). "A multiplicity of lesbian groupings emerged, each representing a smaller subculture and special interest" (A. Stein 1997: 185). But at the same time, over the course of the 1980s, the radical impulses of lesbian feminism spread outward to infuse a variety of other social movements, partly by example and partly by the direct participation of lesbians in those movements. A feminist consciousness and a commitment to nonhierarchical forms of social movement organization became noteworthy features of radical AIDS activism, the antinuclear movement, the ecology movement, and the movements against U.S. intervention in Central America (B. Epstein 1991), and many pro-sex feminists became active in AIDS-prevention work. As Barbara Epstein (1988: 27) has noted, the particular role of lesbians in leadership positions in direct-action movements raises interesting questions about

"whether a minority subculture can provide the spark for political mobilization that transcends its own boundaries." In this sense, the decentering of lesbian feminism may signify the exchange of a well-defined political identity for a more diffuse political influence.

THE AIDS CRISIS AND THE AIDS MOVEMENT

The rightward shift in U.S. politics that marked the ascendance of the
New Right was confirmed by the election of Ronald Reagan to the presidency in 1980. His eight years in office, followed by the single-term presidency of his vice-president, George Bush, marked a drastically constrained political opportunity structure for gay and lesbian and other
progressive social movements in the United States. Particularly under
Reagan, as the power and influence of the New Right expanded, gays and
lesbians proved to be one of its most useful targets. But even as the gay
and lesbian struggle against the New Right continued in full swing, an entirely unforeseen challenge materialized out of nowhere in 1981: a deadly
epidemic disease, sexually transmitted, and linked epidemiologically and
in the popular imagination to gay men. In the United States, as elsewhere,
the AIDS epidemic demonstrated how the contingent occurrences of history can decisively shift the trajectories of social movements.[27]

Although, from the outset, AIDS affected heterosexuals as well as gay
men, in the United States, AIDS quickly became understood in the mass
media as a "gay disease," often viewed loosely as a product of gay
"promiscuity" or "the gay lifestyle." Members of New Right groups such
as Jerry Falwell's Moral Majority moved rapidly to claim AIDS as evidence that the practice of homosexuality was contrary to nature, and they
argued that the devastating illness was God's revenge for immorality. Pat
Buchanan, former speechwriter for Richard Nixon and future Republican
presidential candidate, gave these views broad currency in the pages of
the New York Post, in a column entitled "AIDS Disease: It's Nature Striking Back" (Altman 1986: 59).

Especially in the early years of the epidemic when its cause remained
mysterious, though even after the means of transmission became known,
the stigmatization of gay men as an AIDS threat to the so-called general
population was widespread. Public opinion surveys indicated that many
Americans were not only shunning people with AIDS but also seeking to
limit contact with anyone they suspected might be gay (Blake and Arkin
1988). In this environment, gay communities faced a nearly overwhelm-
ing set of political challenges. They had to respond when people with
AIDS, or those infected with the human immunodeficiency virus (HIV),
were subjected to discriminatory treatment—evicted from their apart-

ments, dismissed from their jobs, or ignored by hospital personnel. They had to make sure that those with the disease received adequate care, support, and social services. They had to push government to take the epidemic seriously and devote sufficient funds to medical and social services. And they had to educate their communities about how to reduce the risk of infection with HIV.

Unlike many other countries that confronted AIDS in the 1980s, the United States already had extensive large and highly mobilized gay communities, which gave AIDS organizing a solid base on which to begin— community organizations that could take on new tasks, wealthy donors whose contributions could bankroll new organizations, activists already committed to the defense of gay rights, newspapers that could keep people up to date on political and medical developments, and neighborhoods in which people could see, before their eyes, the ravages of the epidemic and recognize the urgency of action. In the early 1980s, gay and lesbian activists created two grassroots organizations that proved to be pivotal in confronting the epidemic: the Gay Men's Health Crisis (GMHC) in New York City and, across the country, the San Francisco AIDS Foundation. In one of the most sustained grassroots organizing efforts in recent decades, hundreds of additional organizations were soon established across the United States to confront the multiple threats of the disease by creating hot lines, food banks, speakers' bureaus, and disease-prevention campaigns. As Dennis Altman has noted, although local, volunteer responses to illness and other crises have a long history in the United States, the necessity for such organizing reflected, as well, the absence of a coordinated governmental response to a public health emergency by an indifferent Republican administration (1986: 90, 181).

Many lesbians became involved in the AIDS movement, thereby tightening, at least temporarily, the political and personal connections between lesbians and gay men (Schwartz 1993: 230–44). Dubious explanations have been proposed for the participation of lesbians, including notions of an essential female tendency toward care giving and a belief that women had to fill in for the many men who had died (for critiques see Vaid 1995: 293; Rofes 1996: 258). Better explanations have emphasized as determinants of lesbian mobilization "shared values, sympathy for political goals, and existing organizational membership" not only in gay and lesbian politics but also in the women's health movement (Stoller 1995: 270). While AIDS did indeed cause the deaths of many prominent gay male activists, raising fears of a "leadership vacuum," the epidemic also propelled many previously nonpolitical gay men into activism. For a generation of relatively privileged, middle-class gay men, government had been something to restrict, to keep out of their "private" lives. As the boundary between private illness and public health exploded, these same men sought active governmental involvement to fund AIDS research and care, and they threw their energies into building the grassroots organizations and transforming them into stable organizational forms (Altman 1988: 301–15; S. Epstein 1996: 187).

As the large AIDS service organizations established cooperative funding arrangements with local governments and federal agencies, raised millions of dollars from individuals and big corporations, and grew to employ hundreds of people, gay communities achieved "legitimation through disaster" (Altman 1988: 301–15)—but at the cost of a turn from grassroots organizing to professional bureaucratic management (Altman 1988: 301–15; Patton 1990). Once again, the trend in gay politics seemed to be the establishment of stable, quasi-ethnic organizations that surrendered radical political goals for immediate practical effectiveness. Though these organizations were heavily dependent on volunteer labor, complaints would grow that decision making within them was top-down rather than bottom-up. In a revealing episode, a bitter unionization drive at the San Francisco AIDS Foundation demonstrated the substantial gap in perceptions between "workers" and "management" at the agency. Often the large organizations competed for public funds with the smaller groups, in racial-minority communities, which were dedicated to fighting AIDS among African Americans, Latinos, Asian Americans, or Native Americans (Vaid 1995: 278). Such struggles furthered the tendency for the official identity of the gay community to be taken as white and for the work of lesbians and gay men of color to be ignored (C. Cohen 1993, forthcoming).

The challenge of AIDS also had complicated and contradictory effects on debates about the place of sexuality in gay politics. Many feared that gay male identity had been "derailed" by the epidemic: if the identity, at root, was tied to sexual behaviors, and if specific sexual behaviors could no longer safely be performed, then was it still possible to "be gay"? (Rofes 1996: 65–66) In the early years of the epidemic (and again more recently), some activists advanced the view that the rampant sexual experimentation of the 1970s had indeed been a mistake (Callen and Berkowitz 1982: 23). Many in the mass media and the gay press put forward the view that AIDS was, or ought to be, ushering in a new era of monogamy and fidelity among gay men—a "maturation," after the "adolescent" wildness of the 1970s (Seidman 1988). However, by 1985, with the near-universal acceptance of the evidence that AIDS was caused not by "the gay lifestyle" but by a virus, most activists had come to endorse a "sex-positive" conception of "safer-sex education," which affirmed the inherent value of sexuality as part of the liberatory ethic of gay politics and refused to yield ground to the advocates of sexual conventionalism. Activists battled with conservatives in the U.S. Congress, such as the homophobic Senator Jesse Helms, for the right to produce federally funded HIV-prevention materials that described in plain and effective language sexual acts and the associated risks of viral transmission.

Still, the question of how much to defend gay male sexuality remained unsettled throughout the 1980s, as the divisive controversy over the closure of San Francisco's bathhouses in 1984 amply demonstrated (Murray 1996: 110–25). Over the course of the previous decade, gay men and lesbians had achieved a measure of social acceptance in the United States, in part through a strategic decoupling of sexuality from identity in public discourse. They had come to be accepted as a people with civil rights, even in a society that officially condemned their sexual practices: hence the paradox that "for years the mayor of New York could proclaim an official Gay Pride Week while the very people being honored remained criminals under state law" (Altman 1982a: 9). Because AIDS seemed to restigmatize gay identity by linking it firmly to a "diseased" sexuality, many political moderates were uncomfortable with the revival of a liberationist rhetoric that seemed to valorize sexual abandon.

ACTING UP

Around 1987, with the growing fear that most or perhaps all of those infected with HIV—estimated to be about half the gay men in the most densely concentrated gay neighborhoods—would eventually progress to symptomatic illness, disquiet about the pace and politics of biomedical research swelled into mass unrest. As in the early 1980s, this upswing of grassroots AIDS activism originated in gay and lesbian communities and spread from there. In New York, activist and playwright Larry Kramer, cofounder of GMHC, helped create a radical activist organization, the AIDS Coalition to Unleash Power—better known by its acronym, ACT UP. Soon there were ACT UP chapters in San Francisco, Boston, Chicago, Houston, Los Angeles, New Orleans, Seattle, and other cities as ACT UP became, briefly, the most visible social movement organization in the United States.

A magnet for radical young gay men and lesbians, ACT UP practiced an in-your-face politics of "no business as usual." Adopting styles of political and cultural practice derived from the gay liberation movement of the early 1970s, the peace movement, and the punk subculture, ACT UP became famous for its imaginative street theater, its skill at attracting the news cameras, and its well-communicated sense of urgency. ACT UP chapters typically had no formal leaders; in many cities, meetings operated by the consensus process. As Joshua Gamson describes in a participant/observer study of the San Francisco chapter, ACT UP shared the basic characteristics of "new social movements"—"a (broadly) middle-class membership and a mix of instrumental, expressive, and identity-oriented activities" (1989: 354; Elbaz 1992).

On the national scene, the New York City chapter dominated—with upward of 150 members at regular weekly meetings and a $300,000 budget by the end of 1988—through chapters in San Francisco, Los Angeles, and Boston were also prominent in the movement. Ostensibly, since AIDS was not a "gay disease," ACT UP was not a "gay organization," but members in fact tended to be gay or lesbian, and many of the group's activities—and the pink-triangle background of its distinctive "Silence = Death" logo—suggested the centrality of gayness to its organizational identity (J. Gamson 1989). The history of gay challenges to medical authorities, as in the early-1970s campaign against the psychiatric profession, informed ACT UP's undeferential approach to scientists and medical experts.

The impetus for individuals to become involved varied considerably depending upon social identity. Men who were HIV-positive often had pragmatic goals, such as access to potentially life-prolonging medications. Many lesbians, and some heterosexual women, became active in ACT UP, in part to promote better research on the development of HIV infection in women and on the risk of infection in lesbian sex (ACT UP/New York Women and AIDS Book Group 1990; Corea 1992; Schneider and Stoller 1995). In some cities, African Americans and Latinos formed caucuses within ACT UP as well. Often gay men and lesbians of color, serving as bridges between predominantly gay and white groups such as ACT UP and predominantly heterosexual, community-based organizations in communities of color, helped build coalitions to work on such issues as clean-needle exchange and AIDS prevention in prisons (C. Cohen 1993, forthcoming).

During the late 1980s, ACT UP activists engaged in manifold projects directed at a variety of social institutions, including the state, the church, the mass media, and the health care sector (Crimp and Rolston 1990)—though at times, like the queer activist groups that sprang up in their wake, they seemed less concerned with achieving institutional change than with posing general challenges to cultural norms (J. Gamson 1989). Although some within gay communities were openly disgruntled with ACT UP's confrontational tactics and its tone of abrasive self-righteousness, others noted the creative ways in which the activists marshalled their moral outrage, retained an emphasis on sexual freedom as part of a political agenda, and challenged the conventional division between public and private. The deaths of prominent activists were often marked by loud and angry "political funerals" winding through city streets; in this way, traditionally private moments of death were transformed into public displays of defiance against an indifferent or hostile society and government.

ACT UP and other groups based in gay and lesbian communities were also central to the project of remaking biomedicine in the United States. Activists challenged the authority of experts and, by immersing themselves in technical details of virology and immunology, constituted themselves as grassroots experts who could debate scientists on research directions and priorities. They waged a successful campaign against the U.S. Food and Drug Administration for faster approval of experimental AIDS therapies. Subsequently, activists turned their attention to the National Institutes of Health, successfully demanding changes in the methods of testing AIDS drugs in order to speed up the process, get more patients into clinical trials, and ensure that trials were ethically conducted (S. Epstein 1995, 1996, 1997).

Once again in the trajectory of gay and lesbian activism, the radical grassroots challenge proved short-lived, but it provided the spark for more enduring, if more mainstream, organizational forms. By the early 1990s, activism focused on AIDS treatments had become more professionalized, and the more confrontational and controversial street activism of ACT UP had subsided. Many individual ACT UP chapters had been riven by ideological cleavages between single-issue pragmatic politics and multi-issue radical politics, leading to splits reminiscent of the split between the Gay Activists Alliance and the Gay Liberation Front in 1969. These strategic tensions were intensified by the clash of identities, as political divisions developed between men and women, between white people and people of color, and between HIV-positive and HIV-negative people within ACT UP (S. Epstein 1996: 288–94).

Such difficulties notwithstanding, the movement seemed likely to have an enduring influence, as the frames and tactical repertoires of AIDS activists were quickly adopted by participants in other health-related movements, such as breast cancer activists. In addition, ACT UP and the internal movement culture that it fostered provided the spark for a new, queer identity and politics that have important implications for gay and lesbian movements in the 1990s. Just as radical AIDS activism borrowed from the strengths of gay liberation, part of its legacy was a set of new cultural forms and tactical repertoires employed by subsequent queer activists.

Lesbian and Gay Rights in the 1980s

Although it often seemed that gay and lesbian politics in the 1980s were preoccupied with AIDS, the mainstream lesbian and gay rights movement maintained a diverse political agenda throughout the decade. The quasi-ethnic/

territorial model of organizing remained central, concretely symbolized by a 1984 vote for the incorporation of West Hollywood, which promptly elected a majority of openly gay or lesbian city council members. In San Francisco the institutionalization of the lesbian and gay rights movement was mirrored in an explosion of local civic and political organizations: only 93 lesbian and gay organizations existed between 1975 and 1979, but that number jumped to 255 between 1980 and 1983 and the numbers stayed roughly at that level through the mid-1990s (Armstrong 1998: chap. 1).

The emphasis on civil rights legislation and protection from discrimination also continued, though the 1980s saw a proliferation of new, nationwide organizations with different emphases—including Parents and Friends of Lesbians and Gays (PFLAG), which brought relatives of gay men and lesbians into the movement, and the Gay and Lesbian Alliance Against Defamation (GLAAD), which focused public attention on representations of gay men and lesbians in the mass media and the entertainment industry. The decade was also marked by new cultural and political movements, such as the lesbian "baby boom," the grassroots development of lesbian and gay history projects, the rise of gay and lesbian studies in universities (Escoffier 1990), and the birth of many lesbian and gay professional groups (Taylor and Raeburn 1995). Two members of Congress, Gerry Studds and Barney Frank, both from Massachusetts, came out of the closet; and gays and lesbians both expressed support for and sought to pressure the Democratic Party in a large demonstration outside the Democratic National Convention in San Francisco in 1984. In Oregon, however, voters repealed a ban on job discrimination in 1988, as skirmishes continued between lesbian and gay activists and the New Right.

In 1982, when Georgia police officers entered the home of a man named Michael Hardwick to serve a warrant for traffic violations, they found him having sex with another man. Hardwick was arrested and convicted under Georgia's sodomy law, and the verdict in *Bowers v. Hardwick* was appealed all the way to the United States Supreme Court. Rejecting the argument that gay sex was protected by a "right to privacy," the Court upheld the constitutionality of Georgia's sodomy law in a split (five-four) vote in 1986,[28] sparking angry demonstrations outside federal buildings across the United States. The NGLTF formed a Privacy Project, directed by Sue Hyde, designed to assist activists around the country in contesting state sodomy laws; but only one sodomy statute, in Washington, D.C., was overturned partly as a result of these efforts (Bernstein 1997a: 69).

Frustration with the court's ruling, along with mounting concern about AIDS, was a primary force behind a mass mobilization the following year: the second National March on Washington for Gay and Lesbian Rights, held on 15 October 1987. More than two hundred thousand people from around the United States poured into Washington for the five-hour demonstration, which called for legal recognition of gay relationships, passage of the federal gay rights bill, and a ban on discrimination based on HIV status, among other issues. Two days before the march, more than six hundred demonstrators were arrested in a large act of civil disobedience at the U.S. Supreme Court building in protest of the Hardwick decision. The week's events also included a display of 1,920 panels of the Names Project's AIDS Quilt and a public "commitment ceremony" attended by two thousand lesbian and gay male couples (Ridinger 1996: 198–201). Roughly coinciding with the advent of ACT UP, this national mobilization reflected a rare moment in which the mainstream lesbian and gay rights movement seemed to move in sync with more radical, grassroots activism. But it was indeed a moment, not an enduring political formation.

Outside the mainstream, radical gay and lesbian activists in the 1980s participated in Jesse Jackson's presidential campaigns and in the Rainbow Coalition, formed alliances with labor unions, and created organizations such as San Francisco's Lesbians and Gays against Intervention (LAGAI). Organizations of gay men and lesbians of color struggled simultaneously to counter racism in lesbian and gay organizations and homophobia in organizations promoting civil rights for racial minorities (C. Cohen 1996: 362–94). In 1983, for example—shortly after march organizer Walter Fauntroy, a member of Congress from Washington, D.C., publicly dismissed gay rights as a trivial concern on a par with "penguin rights" (Boykin 1996; Ridinger 1996: 167, 188–89)—the National Coalition of Black Lesbians and Gays successfully fought for the inclusion of black lesbian feminist poet Audre Lorde as a speaker at the twentieth-anniversary commemoration of the Reverend Martin Luther King Jr.'s March on Washington.

Sex radicals in the 1980s defended "public sex," argued that sex remained the "front line" of gay politics, and insisted that a "right to privacy" made sense only in the context of freedom in a public world (Altman 1982b). Marginalized groups such as the North American Man-Boy Love Association (NAMBLA), which promoted an end to age-of-consent laws, found themselves shunned by the broader movement and excluded from events such as Gay Pride Day parades (J. Gamson 1997). Cultural radicalism continued to thrive in cities like San Francisco, sometimes taking overtly political forms: for example, the Sisters of Perpetual Indulgence, wearing their trademark nuns' habits and heavy facial makeup, held such events as an "exorcism" of Jerry Falwell. Much as liberationists had made homophile activists uneasy at an earlier time, mainstream gay men and lesbians sometimes took the political and cultural radicals to task for giving the community a "bad name." Indeed, as lesbian and gay elites moved farther into the mainstream, they were increasingly inclined to police the public image of the community.[29] But in practice the practitioners of radical and liberal interest-group politics often mingled freely at the same demonstrations and political and cultural events.

QUEER NATIONS AND ANTINATIONS

The early 1990s saw the birth of a new queer style and social identity; a short-lived blossoming of chapters of a social movement organization named Queer Nation in cities around the United States; a queer sensibility within other activist groups such as the Lesbian Avengers, the Women's Action Coalition, and the Women's Health Action Mobilization; and the flourishing, of queer theory in university settings. Queer politics was an important phase in the historical oscillation between mainstream identity politics and utopian nonidentitarian politics. On one hand, queer politics arose in opposition to the forms and styles of identity politics that constituted the mainstream lesbian and gay rights movement and in response to the mainstream movement's inability to confront difference within gay and lesbian communities (Duggan 1992; Seidman 1993: 105–42, 1994, 1997). On the other hand, like the liberationists who had challenged fixed categories of identity two decades earlier, queer activists found it hard to sustain a nonidentitarian project—in fact, queer politics carried within it a tension between rejecting fixed identities and organizing around a new, "queer national" identity (Bérubé and Escoffier 1991).

Queer Nation was founded in 1990 in New York City, where it organized large demonstrations against recent gay bashings. At the 1990 New York Lesbian and Gay Pride Parade, members of Queer Nation circulated fifteen thousand copies of an anonymous flyer entitled "I Hate Straights": "I hate trying to convince straight people that lesbians and gays live in a war zone, that we're surrounded by bomb blasts only we seem to hear, that our bodies are heaped high, dead from fright or bashed or raped, dying of grief or disease, stripped of our personhood" (quoted in Gross 1993: 81). As Larry Gross notes, "This essay served as a spark on a pile of kindling," much as the Stonewall riot had done twenty-one years earlier, "and within days it seemed that groups calling themselves Queer Nation were springing up around the country" (Gross 1993: 82). Many present and former members of ACT UP, who had been mobilized by AIDS but wanted to work on other issues affecting their communities, flocked to Queer Nation meetings.

Despite the self-consciousness with which the term "queer" was employed, its usages were inconsistent, and a precise definition is nearly impossible. "Queer" was put forward by activists as a replacement for labels such as "gay" and "lesbian" and, indeed, for the modes of community and self-expression associated with them (Duggan 1992; Seidman 1993: 105–42, 1994, 1997). In part, the turn to "queer" was an act of linguistic reclamation, in which a pejorative term was reappropriated to negate its power to wound. More important, queerness connoted a provocative politics of difference—an assertion that those who embraced the identity did not "fit in" to the dominant culture or the mainstream gay and lesbian culture and had no interest in doing so (Williams 1994). Queerness therefore appealed to a range of people who felt shut out by the mainstream movement and its relative successes toward social integration, including young people, people of color, bisexuals and transgendered people, and sex radicals.

Queer activists framed issues of sexuality, identity and difference, and the public/private divide in ways that resembled radical gay liberation circa 1970, but with some important points of divergence. Queer conceptions of sexuality recalled the ideal of liberating the polymorphous-perverse forms of pleasure; but in the queer rendering of this notion, the emphasis was on the valorization of any and all sexuality that broke with the "heteronormative" and challenged conventional norms and schemas of classification. Therefore, at least some of the time, queer politics was an anti-identity politics (J. Gamson 1995). Queerness repudiated the notion that one's identity or sexuality should be fixed, stable, or nameable, and it embraced "a liminal position within the contingent sexual and gender frontiers of contemporary capitalist societies" (Phelan 1994: 154). Like the liberationists, queers wanted to smash the categories, but where liberationists located the "end of the homosexual" within the utopian project of creating a "new human," queers seemed motivated more by a suspicion of labels and a desire not to be pigeonholed—the difference, in short, between a Freudo-Marxian politics and a Foucauldian one.[30]

Bisexual and transgender politics fitted nicely into the queer agenda for just this reason: they seemed to challenge the binary divisions between gay and straight and between male and female (Seidman 1997: 230–31). For years, bisexuals and transgendered people had fought for a space within gay and lesbian politics, with mixed success—often overlooked or pushed aside by gay men and denounced as threats by lesbian feminists. But in many respects gay and lesbian politics had helped to make bisexual and transgender politics conceivable, since the very idea that one might form collective political identities around the sexual identities of individuals is one that, once advanced, has a self-perpetuating, perhaps endless, character (Weeks 1985: 244; Halberstam 1994). As bisexuals and transgendered people moved from forming support groups to organizing politically, they found that gay and lesbian politics provided the model; and they sought their place within gay and lesbian movements, even as they challenged the binary divide between gay/lesbian and straight that these earlier movements had reinforced (Hutchins and Kaahumanu 1991; Weise 1992; Bornstein 1995; Rust 1995). In the 1990s they seemed to find in queer politics not only acceptance but also valorization of their sexualities as "transgressive."[31]

Ironically, but perhaps predictably, the goal of challenging fixed categories of identity coexisted with the tendency to establish a new, self-consciously queer identity that could serve as a basis of political mobilization. Queerness was sometimes put forward as a new, unifying identity—a global replacement term that could substitute for the growing list of sexual minorities. As an editor of the New York City queer magazine *Outweek* put it, "When you're trying to describe the community, and you have to list gays, lesbians, bisexuals, drag queens, transsexuals (post-op and pre), it gets unwieldy. Queer says it all" (quoted in Duggan 1992: 21). More often, "queer" ended up describing the particular identity of subcultures of urban young people who felt estranged from their gay and lesbian elders. In fact, the mainstream lesbian and gay community served the same symbolic role for these young queers that timid, closeted homosexuals had served for an earlier generation of gay liberationists (Murray 1996: 207). Social movements often develop their own cultures and become "worlds unto themselves" (McAdam 1994: 45), so it is not surprising that, as activist and writer Urvashi Vaid notes, queers "quickly established a new and fairly orthodox tribal language. [Queer Nation] had a dress code (leather, shaved heads, Doc Martens, and T-shirts with big lettering), an anti-establishment stand . . . , and an attitude that spoke to the nineties (postmodern, in their faces, militant)" (1995: 296). In these moments, queer politics was just the latest incarnation of identity politics, indeed one that seemed to conceive of political subjectivity in rather fixed and nationalist terms—as the name Queer Nation suggested.

The latent tension in queer activism "between nationalism and its most thoroughgoing deconstruction" (Phelan 1994: 154) sometimes made for self-contradictory politics and in the end may have contributed to the short life of Queer Nation. But both senses of queer—the identity-stabilizing and the identity-destabilizing—suggested the same approach to the question of the public/private divide. More thoroughly than radical gay liberationists, queers sought to obliterate this boundary. Members of Queer Nation "saw themselves as militantly visible—wearing T-shirts

and stickers with blatant slogans in unavoidable Day-Glo colors: PRO-
MOTE HOMOSEXUALITY, GENERIC QUEER, FAGGOT, MILITANT DYKE"
(Gross 1993: 83). In events such as Queer Nights Out, where queers
would invade heterosexual singles' bars and begin kissing; or Queer Shopping, where young urban queers would flock to suburban shopping malls;
or Be-Ins held at popular tourist destinations such as San Francisco's Pier
39, members of Queer Nation claimed the public sphere as its own and
constructed a "counterpublic" out of "the traditional national icons, the
official and useful spaces of everyday life, [and] the ritual places of typical pleasure" (Berlant and Freeman 1993: 214). Against the gay and lesbian mainstream that had developed a territorially based, "ghetto" politics, queers promoted a movement of de-territorialization (Davis 1995:
284–303). "*Whose* fucking streets? *Our* fucking streets!" proclaimed
queer activists, as they altered demonstration routes at whim, to the con-
sternation of the police. Yet even as they spilled over the boundaries of
the heterosexual society, they defiantly proclaimed their marginalization
within it and insisted they could never be part of it.

A corollary of militant visibility was the assumption that it was legitimate and valuable to "out," or publicly disclose, the homosexuality of
prominent closeted men and women in the worlds of politics, business,
the media, and entertainment (Signorile 1993). Sometimes outing was a
tactic reserved for those who led closeted gay lives while harming lesbians
and gay men in their public lives, such as politicians who frequented gay
bars but voted against gay rights legislation. At other times, advocates of
outing claimed that even public figures or celebrities who did not hurt the
community should be outed so they could serve as role models in the community—whether they wanted to or not. Highly controversial in gay and
lesbian communities in the early 1990s, outing rested on the more essentialist conception of queer nationalism—it stressed "a rhetoric of alle-
giance and accountability to the One Community" and punished the
"traitors" whose identity and politics diverged from a "party line" (Gross
1993: 108–32; see also Duggan 1992).

Queers envisioned a sort of "cultural politics" directed at "regulative
norms" and "disciplinary mechanisms of power" (Blasius 1994: 129).
Queer groups adopted the tactic of the gay liberation "zap," pushing the
notion of politics as theater even farther. But as Joshua Gamson notes,
queer theatrical performance often had limited value in posing challenges
to powerful political institutions such as the state: "The overarching
strategy of cultural deconstruction, the attack on the idea of the normal,
does little to touch the institutions that make embracing normality . . .
both sensible and dangerous" (1995: 400). Furthermore, for all their attention to the performative aspects of their collective actions, queers

were sometimes criticized for being indifferent to whether their actions had measurable effects on any identifiable audiences (Murray 1996: 133). As in many forms of identity politics, queer dramaturgy sometimes seemed to be directed more at the affirmation of self than at genuine conversation with the other. As the queer movement's most popular slogan suggested, the goal was less to reason with the straight world than to inform it that its views had become irrelevant in the face of universal queer visibility: "We're here; we're queer! Get used to it!"

As a social movement organization, Queer Nation endured for less than two years. Although the members of Queer Nation chapters were not homogeneous with regard to age, the group was too heavily identified as a youth movement—and too committed to confrontational direct action and antiassimilationism—to mobilize a mass base. Even the very use of the term "queer" continued to provoke bitter disagreement within gay and lesbian communities, as in the debate that erupted in San Francisco in 1993 when the Freedom Day Parade organizers adopted the slogan "Year of the Queer" (J. Gamson 1995). Moreover, queers who struggled to avoid defining themselves in terms of any fixed identity found this hard to implement within an organizational form. And as Queer Nation chapters consolidated queer identities, they were beset with gender and racial disputes that helped to bring about their demise.[32]

Queer politics demonstrated both the promise and the limits of a nonidentitarian politics in the sharpest fashion since the days of radical gay liberation. If Queer Nation itself was short-lived, a queer sensibility survived and permeated other organizations—including universities, where queer theory[33] thrived, and activist groups like the Lesbian Avengers, which was founded in New York in 1993 and had twenty chapters by 1995 (Schulman 1994). The significant numbers of people who continued to insist that they were "queer" rather than "gay," "lesbian," "bisexual," or "transgendered," testified to the enduring significance of the queer movement—as a reminder that, for many, the goal of the politics of sexuality was not assimilation but confrontation and as evidence that the mainstream lesbian and gay rights movement, despite or because of its attempt to present itself as "the gay and lesbian movement," was incapable of aggregating the diverse interests of all those on behalf of whom it purported to speak.

SOCIAL MOVEMENT ORGANIZATIONS AND THEIR ANTAGONISTS IN THE 1990S

Even apart from the debates around queerness, politics in the 1990s was inflected by the tension between essentialist conceptions of gay identity and culture and challenges to that model. One side of this tension was manifest in the continued growth and cultural legitimation of the mainstream, quasi-ethnic form of gay identity and community. As many activists seized upon gay scientists' reports of the possible discovery of a "gay brain" or "gay gene" (LeVay 1993; Hamer and Copeland 1994), as direct marketers targeted the "gay consumer," and as pollsters sampled the opinions of the "gay voter," the mainstream lesbian and gay rights movement seemed tied to a homogeneous model of collective identity articulated substantially through consumption practices and the display of trinkets—gay-themed credit cards, "freedom rings," and rainbow flags. Quasi-ethnic territorialism also continued in full force. In 1997 the city of Chicago officially designated a stretch of North Halsted Street known familiarly as Boys' Town as one of the city's distinctive neighborhoods, along with Greektown and Chinatown, and constructed ceremonial towers along the street, ringed with the colors of the rainbow flag (D. Johnson 1997).

Yet at the same time, the extraordinary diversification of gay and lesbian movements in the 1990s belied this assumption of a uniform collective interest. This diversification was most clearly expressed in three respects: racial politics, a new debate over sexual expression and sexual mores, and the emergence of an overt Left/Right split within lesbian and gay communities.

A large number of gay, lesbian, or queer political organizations promoting the interests of people of color, including African Americans, Native Americans, Asian Americans, and Latinos, were born in the late 1980s and early 1990s. The Latino/a Lesbian and Gay Organization (LLEGO), dedicated to fighting homophobia, sexism, and discrimination, was founded in 1987 at the National March on Washington and brought hundreds of Latinas and Latinos from around the country to its annual meetings. The Black Lesbian and Gay Leadership Forum was established in 1988 with the goals of building alliances with black organizations, launching antiracism campaigns in the gay white community, and arranging conferences on the black church's attitudes toward homosexuality (Boykin 1996). Trikone (from the Sanskrit word for "triangle"), an organization of lesbian, gay, and bisexual south Asians, began marching in the San Francisco Lesbian and Gay Freedom Day Parade in 1986 and since 1993 has participated in India Day parades in the Bay Area. Activists in organizations like these were often inspired by writers, filmmakers, and artists who sought to articulate the particular dilemmas confronting gay men and lesbians of color (Beam 1986; Anzaldúa 1987; Roscoe 1988; Nelson 1993)—such as filmmaker Marlon Rigg's testimony, in his poignant and arresting 1991 film *Tongues Untied:* "In this great gay mecca, I was an invisible man."

Activists of color challenged the goals of the mainstream, pushed for the radicalization of the movement, and emphasized the importance of constructing coalitions between gay and lesbian communities and other constituencies promoting social change (Seidman 1993: 105–42). Some activists, such as those working with the Audre Lorde Project in Brooklyn, sought to construct a multiracial coalition of queers of color. Others noted the specific effects of gay and lesbian immigration to the United States from other countries: in the "queer diaspora," political strategizing had to recognize that not everyone had the same relationship to the state or to institutions of citizenship (Gopinath 1996: 119–27). Still others analyzed the social and political consequences of racial eroticization and the perpetuation, within gay and lesbian communities, of racially based stereotypes concerning sexual dominance and submissiveness (Fung 1996: 181–98).

Sexuality, another site of internal diversity, once again became an area of political contention in the mid-1990s. In San Francisco, community members who felt that the annual Freedom Day Parade had become "too sexual" and that "outrageous" behavior gave ammunition to political opponents in the New Right established an alternative, "family-oriented" street fair held the preceding day. In New York, bitter fights broke out when a gay group calling itself Gay and Lesbian HIV Prevention Activists called for the city's health department to crack down on sex clubs, which were portrayed as contributing to the spread of HIV. In highly publicized books and opinion pieces in the mass media, Gabriel Rotello and Michelangelo Signorile, two spokespersons of this movement who had migrated rightward from earlier involvements in queer politics, repudiated what Rotello called the "the orgiastic, Dionysian vision of liberation proclaimed in the immediate aftermath of Stonewall," and they advocated "the construction of a gay culture that validates sexual moderation and restraint" (Rotello 1997: 290, 243; Signorile 1997). Rotello pointed to lesbians as role models for gay men—ironically so, since by the 1990s the notion of lesbians as monogamous and sexually unadventurous was increasingly being rejected by lesbians themselves. In 1997 a number of activists and academics founded a new organization—Sex Panic!—to challenge these ideas as typical of the sex-negative and sex-phobic tendencies of U.S. society and to assert the centrality of sexual freedom to queer politics. Similar debates erupted in San Francisco, where activists fought calls to close the sex clubs that had sprung up after the closure of the bathhouses.

In part, the controversy over sexual blatancy revived the fights over sexuality that had marked the lesbian "sex wars" and the early years of the AIDS epidemic. But at root, the debate was not about just AIDS or sexuality but about broader conceptions of the community (Dangerous Bedfellows 1996; Crain 1997; Warner 1997). What were its norms? Who spoke for it? What was its present relation to its own past history? The debate also marked another episode in a familiar story: the split over whether the social legitimation of the lesbian and gay mainstream should be achieved by sacrificing those in the community who were deemed unrespectable (see Murray 1996: 93; J. Gamson 1997; see also C. Cohen forthcoming).

A further marker of the strategic and philosophical divides within the movement was the emergence of a visible gay Right. This included neoconservatives, who repudiated sexual radicalism and sought to reduce the gay movement's struggle to the establishment of equal rights in the public realm (Sullivan 1995), as well as traditional conservatives, who denounced the "puerile posturing" and "queerthink" promoted by the "queer establishment" (Bawer 1993, 1996: ix, xii). The Log Cabin Republican Club, a "home for mainstream gay and lesbian Americans who . . . care deeply about equality [and] hold Republican views on crime, fiscal responsibility and foreign policy," established more than fifty chapters around the country, with a national office in Washington, D.C. Though the organization proved capable of raising more than $100,000 per election cycle, it found itself in the embarrassing position of not being able to find many Republican candidates willing to accept the group's donations.

Other national lesbian and gay organizations, such as the Human Rights Campaign (with sixty full-time staff members and a budget of $2.5 million by 1997), pursued centrist strategies and relied heavily on wealthy, white male donors for their electoral fund-raising. The National Gay and Lesbian Task Force, by contrast (with twenty-two full-time staff members and a budget of $2.7 million), moved in a more leftward and populist direction. In 1990 its director, Urvashi Vaid, heckled President George Bush at his first major address on AIDS and denounced the president's lack of meaningful action on the issue. Vaid emphasized building an organized movement base at the grassroots and insisted that the political agenda move beyond civil rights to encompass a broader vision of a better society (Vaid 1995). In its position papers, NGLTF supported coalition politics and drew links between issues affecting gay men and lesbians and other hot topics of the 1990s, including welfare reform and immigration issues.

In the face of these various forms of political diversification, unity came primarily through organizing to fight the New Right, including mobilizing against its electoral and legislative initiatives. As the clash between lesbian and gay activists and the New Right unfolded, gay rights emerged, improbably, as one of the defining social issues of the 1990s (Bull and Gallagher 1996: xi). Opposition between the mainstream lesbian and gay rights movement and the New Right not only served to consolidate each group's identity but also encouraged each group to pursue the strategy of urging the broader public to "dis-identify" with the other (Patton 1993: 145). Gays and lesbians sought to convince racial and religious minorities that the New Right posed a general threat to freedom, while New Right groups tried to drive a wedge into this alliance by arguing that gay men and lesbians were a wealthy and privileged group that had inappropriately claimed for itself the mantle of the civil rights movement (Boykin 1996).

Unlike gay and lesbian movements in other countries, U.S. activists in the 1990s found themselves in the extraordinary and unenviable position of fighting not only the repeal of gay rights ordinances at the local level (Adam 1995: 133) but also the passage of citywide and statewide referenda that sought to make it legally impossible for gay rights laws ever to be established (Bernstein 1997a: 74). Activists in Oregon fought bitter but successful battles against such initiatives in 1992 and 1993, also dividing among themselves over whether to put forward a least-common-denominator antidiscrimination agenda or a more radical defense of queer sexualities (Bull and Gallagher 1996; Bernstein 1997b: 555). In Colorado 53 percent of voters supported a 1992 referendum that scrapped existing gay rights laws in the more liberal cities of Denver, Boulder, and Aspen and prohibited the establishment of any such laws in the future (Adam 1995: 133). National outrage on the part of lesbians and gay men prompted an organized boycott of travel to the state of Colorado, as well as a court challenge that eventually made its way to the United States Supreme Court. In 1996, in an important six-three decision for gays and lesbians from the Supreme Court, which was not known to favor them, the Court ruled that the state had no compelling interest in preemptively banning gays and lesbians from attempting to pass legislation securing their rights.

The creation of unity amid diversity was also the significant but transient result of two visible national mobilizations in the early 1990s: the third National March on Washington for Lesbian, Gay, and Bi Equal Rights and Liberation and New York City's Stonewall 25 which commemorated the twenty-fifth anniversary of the Stonewall riot. The National March drew as few as three hundred thousand and as many as one million participants, depending on who did the counting. Planners insisted on racial diversity and gender balance in all local delegations to the national steering committee that helped prepare for the march. And, as the name reflects, the march signaled a more complete inclusion of bisexuals in the political agenda, as well as a stated desire to accommodate both those who sought equal rights and those who insisted on a more radical politics of liberation. The following year, Stonewall Twenty-five put more than one million marchers, including many international contingents, on the streets of Manhattan, with participants marching past the United Nations building, demanding respect for the human rights of lesbians, gays, and bisexuals around the world. Unlike earlier national marches, these events attracted significant attention in the mass media, but like earlier marches, these national shows of strength seemed to have little lasting impact on movement mobilization either nationally or locally.

The failure to build on these national demonstrations in any significant way was accompanyied by another conspicuous lack: there were no widely recognized, charismatic leaders. As commentators had been noting for some time (Jernigan 1988), gay and lesbian movements in the United States seemed to produce remarkably few such leaders. There was no shortage of popular heroes, such as the gay men and lesbians who became public figures through their legal battles against dismissal from the military. And celebrities, such as Chastity Bono (the lesbian daughter of Sonny Bono and Cher) and Candace Gingrich (the sister of right-wing politician Newt Gingrich), had become a familiar presence at marches and parades. But—perhaps because of the proliferation and diversity of movements and organizations—gay and lesbian movements seemed to have difficulty generating or sustaining leaders with the imagination and personal qualities needed to mobilize or redirect collective sentiments in powerful ways, to generate solidarity across the divisions within the movements, or to construct coalitions with movements of other kinds.

As activists waged trench warfare against the New Right in local initiatives around the United States, many held out the hope that larger successes might be won at the national level. Particularly in contrast to the overt, antigay hate mongering that marked the 1992 Republican National Convention, the stated positions of Democratic presidential candidate Bill Clinton seemed to hold open the prospect of a new political opportunity structure for gay and lesbian movements. Clinton explicitly mentioned gay people in his nomination acceptance speech at the Democratic National Convention and included openly gay people in his campaign team and, later, in his administration. However, when his attempt to make good on a campaign promise to end the persecution of gay men and lesbians in the U.S. military met with energetic political opposition, Clinton quickly backed down and proposed a regressive "compromise" that, in practice, continued to lead to the dismissal of gay men and lesbians from the military. This and subsequent actions by Clinton—on issues such as gay marriage—demonstrated that there was no political party of consequence in the U.S. political system with which lesbian and gay activists could unproblematically ally and that the U.S. two-party system provided restricted opportunities for the advancement of a gay rights agenda.

These two issues—gays in the military and gay marriage—merit additional attention for the extraordinary amount of controversy that they provoked. Given that no other country that has openly considered the issue of military service by lesbians and gay men has greeted the prospect with any great degree of panic or preoccupation, the popular hysteria surrounding the issue in the United States testified to unique aspects of the U.S. political and cultural environment. As Barry Adam notes, an explanation that points to the power of the New Right alone seems insufficient to account for the psychological charge of the debate (Adam 1994: 103–18), which raised the specter of "vulnerable" heterosexual soldiers being eyed by predatory homosexuals in shower rooms and pointed, in rather Freudian terms, to the threat that overt homosexual desire posed to sublimated male bonding and esprit de corps.[34] Much like the targeting of homosexuals during the McCarthy era, the debate about gays in the military seemed wrapped up in concerns about the "feminization" of the state, in a country whose whole national identity in the period since the Second World War has centered on its global military might (Adam 1994: 113).

The debate over gay marriage was equally freighted with symbolic power for all concerned. In the 1980s and early 1990s, lesbians and gay men won substantial victories in obtaining domestic partner benefits such as health insurance for the lovers of gay men and lesbians employed by many businesses, city governments, and universities around the United States—no small matter in a country without national health care. A number of cities, such as San Francisco, had formal provisions for couples to register at City Hall as domestic partners. No one seemed quite prepared, however, when the Hawaii Supreme Court ruled in 1993, that a lower court had improperly dismissed a lawsuit challenging the state's policy of denying marriage licenses to gay or lesbian couples. The court suggested that it would most likely rule in favor of the lawsuit, and a lower court eventually did so in 1997. Meanwhile, conservatives around the country were shocked to realize that if Hawaii permitted gay marriages, then the U.S. Constitution might require every other state to recognize those marriages. Even as gay men and lesbians throughout the United States began imagining wedding-and-honeymoon trips to Hawaii, conservatives in many state legislatures began introducing measures to define marriage strictly as the union of a man and a woman. Such measures had become law in twenty-five states by mid-1997. At the same time, members of the U.S. Congress proposed a national Defense of Marriage Act, which Clinton announced in September 1996 that he would sign, effectively ensuring its passage.

The marriage debate was revealing for what it suggested about the limits of popular endorsement of the equality of gay men and lesbians. While substantial percentages of those surveyed in opinion polls disapproved of discrimination against gays and lesbians in the workplace, far fewer were able to conceive of gay marriage as anything other than an oxymoron.[35] More than a referendum on homosexuality, the debate encapsulated American confusion about the very nature of the family and its place in late-twentieth-century society (Pollitt 1996; Stacey 1996). At the same time, the marriage issue sparked passionate arguments among gay men and lesbians themselves. In the wake of the lesbian "baby boom" of the late 1980s and 1990s, the legal fights for custody and adoption of children by gay and lesbian parents, and well-publicized struggles by lesbians and gay men to be the acknowledged legal guardians of their partners in the event of medical incapacitation, many saw "family" issues as the cutting edge of movement politics (Weston 1991; Stacey 1996); for them, gay marriage was the single most important marker of progress. To others, however, the "aping" of heterosexual marital institutions was a betrayal of radical liberationist and feminist critiques of traditional models of gender, sexuality, and the family and reflected an unfortunate desire to assimilate into the mainstream.[36]

Somewhat similarly, debates within gay and lesbian communities about military service pitted those who saw inclusion in the military as the pivotal step in the march for equality and genuine citizenship against those who questioned gay support for a historically misogynistic, racist, and homophobic institution that acted in the interest of U.S. imperial ambition. Thus, viewed from one angle, the demand for inclusion in these two core institutions of the nation—marriage and the military—was a radical move; indeed it was more radical than queer antiassimilationism, which contented itself with denouncing those institutions from the sidelines. But from another angle, this conventional understanding of gay citizenship, which positioned sexual minorities as being "just like everyone else," surrendered the idea that lesbians, gay men, bisexuals, and transgendered people could promote meaningful political alternatives only insofar as they were *different* from the straight majority. In the debates over marriage and the military, "the U.S. lesbian and gay movement" once again was distinguished as much by its internal diversity and disagreement as it was by its ability to bring contentious social issues to center stage.

In November 1997, when President Clinton made his way to the podium at a fund-raising dinner for the Human Rights Campaign, it marked the first time that a U.S. president ever spoke at an event sponsored by a lesbian and gay civil rights organization. Given how unthinkable this would have been even twenty years earlier, it is clear that an impressive sea of change in public sentiment had occurred in the interim. At the same time, the fragility of gay rights in the United States is so apparent, the cultural climate surrounding sexuality is so repressive, and the strides toward equal citizenship are so limited in comparison to other Western countries that it becomes crucial to reflect both on the peculiarities of the United States and on the internal difficulties of U.S. gay and lesbian movements.

In 1960 no cities or states in the United States guaranteed equal rights to gay men and lesbians. Every state outlawed sodomy, and there were no openly gay elected officials anywhere in the United States. By 1997 thirty states and the District of Columbia had abolished their sodomy laws. Eleven states and dozens of cities and counties had passed laws protecting lesbians and gay men (and sometimes bisexuals and transgendered people) from various forms of discrimination based on sexual orientation, and elsewhere gubernatorial executive orders and mayoral proclamations officially banned discrimination. As a result, by the mid-1990s more than one-fifth of Americans lived in cities or counties providing legal protection (Wald, Button, and Rienzo 1996: 1153). In addition, five states, including New York, now offer domestic partner benefits to gay and lesbian state employees. With the exception of Wisconsin and Minnesota, however, every state that has banned discrimination (including Hawaii) is on the Atlantic or Pacific Coast, leaving the inhabitants of the vast interior without protection (Sherrill 1996: 469). Sodomy laws remain on the books in most of the South, several western states, Michigan, and even liberal Massachusetts. And, although in 1997 the U.S. Senate came surprisingly close to passing a bill banning employment discrimination, relief is not very likely to come soon at the federal level.

At this writing, three members of the U.S. House of Representatives are openly gay—though all were closeted when first elected to that office—as are eleven other men and women in state-level governments. In late 1997, Virginia Apuzzo, a former executive director of the NGLTF, became the highest-ranking openly gay or lesbian person in government in U.S. history when she was appointed assistant to the president for management and administration. Increasingly, large segments of the society appear ready to countenance the presence of lesbians and gay men in roles that were previously unthinkable—gay and lesbian ministers, gay and lesbian athletes, gay and lesbian characters in popular television shows and films. Newspapers that in the recent past covered homosexuality as a crime story or a titillating social problem now routinely present commentary and analysis on lesbian and gay politics, community, and identity. Television talk shows provide a forum, however constrained, for those with the most marginalized sexualities to tell their stories to a national audience (J. Gamson 1998). Even in the domain of organized religion, there have been significant changes. In 1997, for example, the Interfaith Alliance, a nationwide organization of more than fifty denominations, announced its support for a federal antidiscrimination law protecting lesbians and gay men in the workplace.

In more subtle respects, too, gay and lesbian movements have made their mark on the polity and the broader culture. As Alberto Melucci (1989: 73–76) has noted, social movements often have a "hidden efficacy" that becomes apparent only over time: by challenging cultural codes and conventions, they suggest to the broader society "that alternative frameworks of meaning are possible."[37] Thus, for example, the fight by gay men and lesbians to gain legal permission to adopt children may reflect a deeper challenge to ideas about what families ought to look like, while the struggle to use public funds to support sexually explicit and sex-positive AIDS educational campaigns marks the extent to which beliefs about the relation between sex, pleasure, and sin are currently subject to debate. Even the emergence of heterosexuality as an increasingly salient social identity marks the subtle influences of lesbian and gay movements on the broader culture (Katz 1995).

These indicators of social change are significant, and they speak, at least in part, to the power of political activism and the diffuse effects of the visibility of lesbian/gay/bisexual/transgender communities. At the same time, other measures suggest that the gains of U.S. gay and lesbian movements of recent decades coexist with strong antipathy toward gay men and lesbians that has varied little over time. For example, the General Social Survey, the most complete statistical survey of public attitudes on a range of social issues over the years, revealed no meaningful change in beliefs about the acceptability of gay sexuality between 1973 and 1991 (Smith 1994: 63–97). In 1973, 73 percent of those surveyed said that sex between members of the same sex was "always wrong"; in the 1991 survey, that figure was 77 percent. Another survey, the American National Election Study, asks respondents to rank different social groups using a "feeling thermometer." Responses over time reveal that feelings toward gays and lesbians are "colder" than feelings for many other oppressed groups, including blacks and people on welfare, and "warmer" only than feelings for illegal aliens (Sherrill 1996: 470). Findings such as these are consistent with Urvashi Vaid's contention that lesbians, gay men, bisexuals, and transgendered people in the United States have been granted "virtual equality"—"a state of conditional equality based more on the appearance of acceptance by straight America than on genuine civic parity" (Vaid 1995: xvi).

Such attitudes reflect not only the power of religious fundamentalism in the United States but also the deep undercurrents of anxiety about sexuality and the legacy of the "sexual revolution." Numerous episodes—from the public furor in 1989 and 1990 over the exhibition of sexually explicit and sadomasochistic work by acclaimed gay photographer Robert Mapplethorpe (Cruikshank 1992: 51) to recent laws in California and other states mandating the "chemical castration" of sex offenders—demonstrate that sexuality remains a fertile domain for staging moral panic. The most comprehensive recent survey of sexual behaviors and attitudes in the United States found that respondents could be clustered into seven distinct subsets based on their responses to questions about the acceptability of homosexuality, premarital sex, extramarital sex, abortion, and pornography. In five of the seven clusters, accounting for three-quarters of the entire population surveyed, "same-gender sex" was rated as "always wrong" by heavy majorities (between 65 percent and 98 percent). In the remaining two clusters, less than 10 percent of respondents agreed that same-gender sex was always wrong (Laumann et al. 1994: 509–40, esp. 514). The results suggest not only that discomfort with lesbian and gay sexuality in U.S. society extends far beyond the New Right but also that there is little middle ground between the attitudinal clusters that are heavily opposed and those that are quite supportive.

These findings also underscore the point that the ways in which gay and lesbian movements frame sexuality and identity matter. A substantial sector of the population is more inclined at present to accept the argument that gays, as a people, deserve protection from discrimination than to feel really comfortable with the idea of sex between men or sex between women (see Yang 1997). So, on one hand, social movements that play down questions of sexuality and emphasize issues of fairness would seem to have a short-term, tactical advantage. But, on the other hand, this approach may well jettison the possibility of long-term, fundamental improvement either in the social standing of gay men, lesbians, bisexuals, and transgendered people or in the overall political climate surrounding sexuality.

An analogous framing dispute (Benford 1993) is suggested by findings that people who believe that homosexuals are "born that way" are considerably more likely to support gay rights than those who believe that homosexuals have "chosen" their lifestyle ("Poll Finds Even Split" 1993). Awareness of such views prompts social movement organizations to promulgate a conception of gay people as a fixed, identifiable group in society and to latch onto biological research suggesting genetic causes of homosexuality—and this frame resonates with many gay men and lesbians. The difficulty, however, is that gay men and lesbians are constituted as involuntary victims; the movement is portrayed as internally homogeneous, and it has no language to discuss the fluid ways in which at least some people experience their sexuality; and the systems of sexual categorization in use in the society are simply taken for granted. Moreover, the essentialist model of identity lends itself to a single-issue, zero-sum model of politics that inhibits the formation of meaningful alliances with other constituencies for social change.

It would appear that this quasi-ethnic, rights-based, identity politics is overdetermined in the United States. In the absence of a political party that could promote a lesbian and gay political agenda, and in a society where political claims are so often advanced by mobilized ethnic identities, this strategy has an obvious appeal.[38] And the notion of gays as a people deserving equal protection under the law lends itself to judicial struggles in the U.S. legal context (Halley 1993: 82–102), while deflecting much of the hostility of those disquieted by unconventional forms of sexual expression. Furthermore, the strategy promotes the building of stable organizations and institutions. Yet the strategy is also highly problematic, given the proliferation of political forms and identities within gay and lesbian movements in the United States. As the historical record suggests, when the mainstream lesbian and gay rights movement advances these politics, it tends to present itself in hegemonic fashion as "the movement," almost insuring the periodic eruption of dissent from within lesbian and gay communities: hence the oscillation between the dominance of pragmatic, quasi-ethnic identity politics and the powerful surges of utopian alternatives that either insist on the instability of identities; or argue that it is dangerous to make identity the fundamental organizing principle; or assert the centrality of internal differences based on race, gender, or other characteristics that are suppressed by the hegemonic model; or reject the goal of assimilation and integration; or proclaim some combination of these views.

The multiplicity of voices and goals within U.S. gay and lesbian movements, in combination with specific features of U.S. society, therefore structures not only the familiar dilemmas of social movement politics—gradualism versus provocation, assimilationism versus separatism, single-issue groups versus coalitions, centralization versus grassroots localism—but also the less commonly found tension between the politics of stable identity and the politics of instability and difference. In the struggle between different conceptions of politics, various groups have competed to lay claim to "the movement" and say what it "really is," but none has entirely succeeded in doing so. Is there an alternative model—one that will "play" in the U.S. context; that will not suppress or deny difference; and that has the potential to improve the life conditions of lesbians, gay men, bisexuals, transgendered people, and queer people while also challenging the social organization of gender and sexuality and the culture of sexual repression? This politics would take "identity as a point of departure rather than a final destination" (Kauffman 1990: 79)—organizing less around identity than "sympathy and affinity," both within and between groups (Phelan 1994: 155). The goal would be to forge alliances across gay and other social movements, not on the basis of shared history or the congruence of experience but on the ground of similarities in their relations to the dominant constellations of power in the society (C. Cohen 1997: 458). But to succeed, this politics would need to promote a new vision of citizenship, articulating a model of belonging that neither embraced marginalization for its own sake nor surrendered the goal of social transformation.

NOTES

Acknowledgments: I am deeply indebted to the editors of this volume, as well as to Dennis Altman, Mary Bernstein, Héctor Carrillo, Jeff Escoffier, Josh Gamson, Joe Gusfield, Harry Hirsch, David Kirp, Steve Murray, Steve Seidman, Arlene Stein, Verta Taylor, Chris Waters, and Andy Williams, for providing essential feedback on a first draft of this chapter. Responsibility for the deficiencies that remain—and for my failure to follow the good advice of these friends and colleagues in all particulars—is mine alone.

1. Except insofar as this essay incorporates some of my empirical work on the AIDS movement (S. Epstein 1996)—and reflects, more generally and more loosely, my own experiences as participant/observer in gay communities and movements in the United States—it is not based on my own primary research. Instead, I have strived to synthesize the existing scholarly literature, organize it within a new analytical frame, and highlight it with concepts and tools that have been developed in the sociology of social movements. In completing this project, I drew from the existing, book-length analyses of gay and lesbian movements in the United States, including Altman 1971, 1982a; D'Emilio 1983, 1992; Adam 1987, 1995; Faderman 1991; Cruikshank 1992; Duberman 1993; Murray 1996; and A. Stein 1997. In addition the "historical sourcebook" recently compiled by Blasius and Phelan (1997) is an invaluable collection of documentary sources. Many specific facts presented in this essay but not otherwise referenced were obtained from Thompson 1994; National Museum and Archive 1996; and Ridinger 1996. Some of the information presented about individual movement organizations came from their Internet web pages.

2. Despite their visibility and distinctive characteristics, U.S. gay and lesbian movements have received relatively little notice from scholars who emphasize the sociological literature on social movements (see the critique in Warner 1993: ix–x). Exceptions (nearly all of them from the 1990s) include Adam 1987, 1995; J. Gamson 1989, 1995, 1996, 1997; A. Stein 1992, 1997; Taylor and Whittier

1992: 104–29; Taylor and Rupp 1993; Jenness and Broad 1994; Jenness 1995; Taylor and Raeburn 1995; Bernstein 1997a, 1997b; and Esterberg 1997. Only recently have the mainstream anthologies on social movements begun to include chapters on gay and lesbian movements, and only recently have sociological discussions of contemporary social movements in the United States routinely begun to point to gay and lesbian movements as examples (see, for instance, Johnston, Laraña, and Gusfield 1994): 3–35.

3. My goal here is not to obscure commonalities or reify complexity but to challenge problematic ways in which "the movement" has often been understood. That similarities among groups do nonetheless exist is a point I make throughout this essay.

4. My analysis draws upon recent work in the study of social movements that emphasizes the importance of the formation of collective identities—in particular, work that recognizes that collective identities are rarely stable and that shows how they may be as much the product as the prerequisite of movement activism. See, for example, the essays in Morris and Mueller 1992 and in Laraña, Johnston and Gusfield 1994, as well as Melucci 1989. On struggles to define and deploy collective identities in gay and lesbian movements in the United States—and on the policing of boundaries and the trajectory of internal divisions—see also A. Stein 1992, 1997; Taylor and Whittier 1992: 104–29; Seidman 1993: 105–42, 1994, 1997; J. Gamson 1995, 1996, 1997, 1998; Rust 1995; Whisman 1996; Bernstein 1997b; C. Cohen 1997; and Armstrong 1998. Though the issue of identity seems particularly problematic for gay and lesbian movements, my discussion resembles Cathy Cohen's (1996: 362–94, forthcoming) analysis of how monolithic conceptions of black identity obscure internal divisions and power struggles within African American communities.

5. A related issue concerns the relation and boundaries between "movement," "subculture," and "community" (Duyvendak 1995: 165–80). It is important to note that gay and lesbian movements in the United States are not strictly bounded by or encapsulated within formal movement organizations.

6. The tension I describe is similar to what Mary Bernstein (1997b) notes as the opposition between the "celebration" and "suppression" of differences in lesbian and gay "identity deployment." In her formal model, the tendency of the movement either to celebrate or suppress difference from the mainstream culture depends on specific structural factors in the organizational environment and the polity. Here—without necessarily disagreeing—I emphasize historical contingency, general aspects of U.S. society, and the problem of differences within lesbian and gay communities.

7. Throughout this chapter I rely upon the useful claim by recent analysts that social movements are not simply "carriers" or "transmitters" of ideology but are fundamentally and necessarily engaged in the "framing" of reality. Social movements seek to "frame, or assign meaning to and interpret, relevant events and conditions in ways that are intended to mobilize potential adherents and constituents, to garner bystander support, and to demobilize antagonists" (Snow and Benford 1988: 198). However, in order for frames to work, they must "resonate"—they must be empirically credible, consistent with personal experience, and congruent

with larger cultural heritages (Snow and Benford 1988: 207–10). See also Goffman 1974; Gitlin 1980; Snow et al. 1986; W. Gamson 1988; Snow and Benford 1992: 133–55; Benford 1993; and Hunt, Benford, and Snow 1994: 185–208.

8. In the field of lesbian and gay studies, the question of how to conceptualize sexual subjectivity in its social and historical specificity became known in the 1980s as the essentialist/constructionist debate (see the essays in E. Stein 1992): can categories of people such as "homosexuals" plausibly be said to exist in all societies throughout history, or are such categories radically contingent, with the possibilities of their existence determined by concrete social and cultural factors? Here I focus attention on the self-understandings of individual political actors and the collective understandings put forward by movement organizations and their interlocutors—in short, the political consequences of beliefs about the stability or mutability of identity. It should be clear that the "orientation versus preference" opposition does not precisely correspond to the opposition between essentialism and constructionism, though they have important points of convergence. (I failed to make this sufficiently clear in S. Epstein 1987, which was reprinted in E. Stein 1992.) On the political implications of beliefs about sexual identities, see also the citations in note 4 above.

9. Here I refer to what Eve Sedgwick (1990) has termed the distinction between "universalizing" and "minoritizing" discourses of sexual categorization.

10. As Jeff Weintraub (1997: 1–2) notes, the widespread employment of the distinction between public and private "often generates as much confusion as illumination, not least because different sets of people who employ these concepts mean very different things by them." Here I mean to invoke the distinction between a private sphere of eroticism, intimacy, and family and a public sphere of political and state action—the sense of the distinction that seems to be present in lesbian and gay activists' political philosophies, whether or not they believe that drawing such a dividing line is advisable. As Weintraub points out, such renderings of the public/private distinction cloud the issue of on which side of the divide to locate the market and the workplace.

11. Because this volume focuses on the post-1960s period, my discussion of gay activism in the 1950s and 1960s is cursory. The fullest treatment can be found in D'Emilio 1983.

12. More generally, the growth of manufacturing and the decline of farm labor had diminished the importance of the family as a productive unit, freeing individuals to pursue lives outside the bounds of traditional family forms and encouraging the belief that sex might serve the goals of pleasure and intimacy, rather than just the procreation of offspring whose economic labor was needed by the family (D'Emilio 1992: 6–7; Murray 1996: 52). On the broad "macroprocesses" that can lead to the emergence of social movements, see McAdam, McCarthy, and Zald 1988: 711.

13. Subcultures of both women and men desiring same-sex romantic and sexual contact were well developed in large U.S. cities by the 1920s and 1930s, especially in working-class neighborhoods, in European immigrant communities, and in African American communities (Faderman 1991; Kennedy and Davis 1993; Chauncey 1994; Mumford 1997).

14. On the role of sexologists and doctors in the elaboration of these categories, see Foucault 1980; Chauncey 1982–1983; and Weeks 1985.

15. Kinsey and his collaborators found that 37 percent of men and 13 percent of women in their sample had had at least one homosexual experience leading to orgasm. The representative character of Kinsey's sample has been much debated; see Laumann et al. 1994.

16. Perhaps the earliest popular work that conceptualized homosexuals as a distinct minority in U.S. society was Cory 1951.

17. "We would be foolish not to recognize what the Negro rights movement has shown us is sadly so," noted Kameny: "that mere persuasion, information and education are not going to gain for us in actual practice the rights and equality which are ours in principle" (quoted in Blasius and Phelan 1997: 335).

18. "We want to reach the homosexuals entombed in you, to liberate our brothers and sisters, locked in the prisons of your skulls," argued Martha Shelley, addressing the straight world. "We will never go straight until you go gay." (1972: 34).

19. Of course, as Gross (1993: 21) notes, young people of the sixties generation who had already located themselves outside the mainstream culture indeed had little to risk by coming out, whereas older gay men and lesbians had keener memories of persecution and police entrapment and much greater reason to fear the consequences of coming out.

20. This understanding of gayness as quasi-ethnic, which many analysts have remarked upon, appears to have been first described in these terms by Stephen Murray (1979).

21. Of course, the prior tendency to understand ethnic groups of any kind in essentialist terms is itself problematic; see S. Epstein 1987: 34–38.

22. On the importance of "resource mobilization" to the sustenance of social movements, see, for example, Oberschall 1973; McCarthy and Zald 1977; and W. Gamson 1990.

23. In S. Epstein 1987 I argued that the ethnic model of gayness, while essentialist, was less rigidly so than biological models of homosexuality, particularly when gay "ethnicity" was understood in a loose or metaphorical way. I still think this is true, but I am less certain now that the difference between these varieties of essentialism matters much in the political domain, especially when it comes to recognizing internal differences within lesbian and gay communities. For an "admittedly nitpicking" critique of my earlier article's treatment of identity and difference, see E. Cohen 1991: 73–76.

24. Actual use of the term "homophobia" appears to date from Weinberg 1972. (I thank Jeff Escoffier for pointing this out to me.) A psychotherapist, Weinberg defined homophobia as "the dread of being in close quarters with homosexuals—and in the case of homosexuals themselves, self-loathing" (1972: 4). Although it tended to imply the liberal view that homophobia might be cured by a good dose of education, the concept of homophobia had latent affinities with radical feminism when it recognized how deeply rooted antigay sentiment often was: it suggested that the greater inclination of straight men toward homophobic violence reflected their perception that gay men and lesbians posed symbolic threats to the conventional gender order.

25. Local electoral victories reflected the utility of an ethnic/territorial model of political organizing (Davis 1995: 284–303). Milk's election, for example, was made possible by a change in the political opportunity structure that gave power to the city's distinct "ethnic" neighborhoods: the voting laws had been amended so that supervisors were elected by district, rather than at large.

26. Though it is beyond the scope of this essay, the New Right (or Radical Right, or Christian Right) merits analysis as a social movement in its own right. As Didi Herman has argued, the New Right is "a paradigmatic movement for social change, and no more (nor less) a backlash impulse than feminism, gay rights, and others" (1997: 195). See also Adam 1987: 108–17; Diamond 1989.

27. An adequate assessment of the impact of AIDS on gay communities and movements in the United States is well beyond the scope of this chapter. As a start see Patton 1985, 1990; Altman 1986; Shilts 1987; Crimp and Rolston 1990; Schneider and Stoller 1995; Epstein 1996; Murray 1996; Kirp 1997; Levine, Nardi, and Gagnon 1997; and C. Cohen forthcoming. This chapter is also not the place for a full assessment of the AIDS movement, a constellation of groups and organizations whose boundaries extend well beyond gay and lesbian communities.

28. In 1990, after retiring from the Supreme Court, Justice Lewis Powell acknowledged that his vote to uphold Georgia's sodomy law had been a mistake (Cruikshank 1992: 194).

29. This is analogous to Cathy Cohen's (1996: 362–94, forthcoming) discussion of the role of black elites in policing the image of the African American community and marginalizing some of the most vulnerable within that community.

30. As Joshua Gamson (1995: 413) has noted, this deconstructive impulse within queer politics demands attention from scholars of social movements who have become used to studying how movements construct collective identities: for some movements, the goal of activism may be the *destabilization* of collective identity rather than its elaboration.

31. To be sure, while bisexuality and transgender seemed at times to challenge existing categories and binary divides, they are themselves categories, and thus at other moments they seemed to provide opportunities for the consolidation of new, more particular but equally fixed, identities.

32. For a range of views on the inclusion of gender and racial concerns in queer politics, see Maggenti 1991; Walters 1996; and C. Cohen 1997.

33. On queer theory, see Sedgwick 1990; de Lauretis 1991; Butler 1993; and Seidman 1996.

34. In this regard it was noteworthy that the public debate about gays in the military seemed preoccupied with the threat posed by *male* homosexuality. On the debate over gay men and lesbians in the military, see also Shilts 1993; Herek, Jobe, and Carney 1996; and Katzenstein 1996:229–47.

35. In a survey conducted in the spring of 1993 and reported in *U.S. News and World Report,* 65 percent favored ensuring equal rights for gay people, but only 35 percent supported recognizing "legal partnerships" for homosexuals (National Museum and Archive 1996: 104).

36. This divide over marriage was not entirely new; see Nardi 1996.

37. However, Melucci himself is disparaging and dismissive in reference to gay culture. See Melucci 1989: 159, and see the critique in Warner 1993: ix–x.

38. In Weberian terms, "status," rather than "class" or "party," becomes the logical organizing principle in this case (Gerth and Mills 1946: 180–95).

References

ACT UP/New York Women and AIDS Book Group. 1990. *Women, AIDS, and Activism*. Boston: South End.

Adam, Barry D. 1987. *The Rise of a Gay and Lesbian Movement*. Boston: Twayne.

———. 1994. "Anatomy of a Panic: State Voyeurism, Gender Politics, and the Cult of Americanism." In *Gays and Lesbians in the Military: Issues, Concerns, and Contrasts*. Ed. Wilbur J. Scott and Sandra Carson Stanley. Hawthorne, N.Y.: Aldine de Gruyter.

———. 1995. *The Rise of a Gay and Lesbian Movement*. Rev. ed. New York: Twayne.

Altman, Dennis. 1971. *Homosexual: Oppression and Liberation*. New York: Avon.

———. 1982a. *The Homosexualization of America*. Boston: Beacon.

———. 1982b. "Sex: The New Front Line for Gay Politics." *Socialist Review* 12 (5): 76–84.

———. 1986. *AIDS in the Mind of America*. Garden City: Anchor.

———. 1988. "Legitimation through Disaster: AIDS and the Gay Movement." In *AIDS: The Burdens of History*. Ed. Elizabeth Fee and Daniel M. Fox. Berkeley and Los Angeles: University of California Press.

Anzaldúa, Gloria. 1981. "Speaking in Tongues: A Letter to Third World Women Writers." In *This Bridge Called My Back: Writings by Radical Women of Color*. Ed. Cherríe Moraga and Gloria Anzaldúa. Watertown, Mass.: Persephone.

———. 1987. *Borderlands/La Frontera: The New Mestiza*. San Francisco: Spinsters.

Armstrong, Elizabeth. 1998. "Multiplying Identities: Identity Elaboration in San Francisco's Lesbian/Gay Organizations." Ph.D. diss., Department of Sociology, University of California, Berkeley.

Bawer, Bruce. 1993. *A Place at the Table: The Gay Individual in American Society*. New York: Simon and Schuster.

———. 1996. "Introduction." In *Beyond Queer: Challenging Gay Left Orthodoxy*. Ed. Bruce Bawer. New York: Free Press.

Bayer, Ronald. 1981. *Homosexuality and American Psychiatry: The Politics of Diagnosis*. New York: Basic.

Beam, Joseph, ed. 1986. *In the Life: A Black Gay Anthology*. Boston: Alyson.

Benford, Robert D. 1993. "Frame Disputes within the Nuclear Disarmament Movement." *Social Forces* 71:677–701.

Berlant, Lauren, and Elizabeth Freeman. 1993. "Queer Nationality." In *Fear of a*

Queer Planet: Queer Politics and Social Theory. Ed. Michael Warner. Minneapolis: University of Minnesota Press.

Bernstein, Mary. 1997a. "Sexual Orientation Policy, Protest, and the State." Ph.D. diss., Department of Sociology, New York University.

———. 1997b. "Celebration and Suppression: The Strategic Uses of Identity by the Lesbian and Gay Movement." *American Journal of Sociology* 103, no. 3 (November): 531–65.

Bérubé, Allan. 1990. *Coming Out Under Fire: The History of Gay Men and Women in World War Two.* New York: Free Press.

Bérubé, Alan, and Jeffrey Escoffier. 1991. "Queer/Nation." *Out/Look,* no. 11 (Winter): 14–16.

Blake, Susan, M., and Elaine Bratic Arkin. 1988. *AIDS Information Monitor: A Summary of National Public Opinion Surveys on AIDS: 1983 through 1986.* Washington, D.C.: American Red Cross.

Blasius, Mark. 1994. *Gay and Lesbian Politics: Sexuality and the Emergence of a New Ethic.* Philadelphia: Temple University Press.

Blasius, Mark, and Shane Phelan, eds. 1997. *We Are Everywhere: A Historical Sourcebook of Gay and Lesbian Politics.* New York: Routledge.

Bornstein, Kate. 1995. *Gender Outlaw: On Men, Women, and the Rest of Us.* New York: Vintage.

Boykin, Keith. 1996. *One More River to Cross: Black and Gay in America.* New York: Anchor.

Bull, Chris, and John Gallagher. 1996. *Perfect Enemies: The Religious Right, the Gay Movement, and the Politics of the 1990s.* New York: Crown.

Butler, Judith. 1993. *Bodies That Matter: On the Discursive Limits of "Sex."* New York: Routledge.

Califia, Pat. 1994. *Public Sex: The Culture of Radical Sex.* Pittsburgh: Cleis.

Callen, Michael, and Richard Berkowitz. 1982. "We Know Who We Are: Two Gay Men Declare War on Promiscuity." *New York Native,* 8 November, 23–29.

Castells, Manuel. 1983. *The City and the Grassroots.* Berkeley and Los Angeles: University of California Press.

Chauncey, George, Jr. 1982–1983. "From Sexual Inversion to Homosexuality: Medicine and the Changing Conceptualization of Female Deviance." *Salmagundi* 58–59:114–46.

———. 1994. *Gay New York: Gender, Urban Culture, and the Making of the Gay Male World, 1890–1940.* New York: Basic.

Cohen, Cathy J. 1993. "Power, Resistance and the Construction of Crisis: Marginalized Communities Respond to AIDS." Ph.D. diss., Department of Political Science, University of Michigan, Ann Arbor.

———. 1996. "Contested Membership: Black Gay Identities and the Politics of AIDS." In *Queer Theory/Sociology.* Ed. Steven Seidman. London: Blackwell.

———. 1997. "Punks, Bulldaggers, and Welfare Queens: The Radical Potential of Queer Politics?" *GLQ* 3 (4): 437–65.

———. Forthcoming. *The Costs of Community: AIDS, Marginalization and Black Politics in the Twenty-first Century.* Chicago: University of Chicago Press.

Cohen, Ed. 1991. "Who Are 'We'? Gay 'Identity' as Political (E)motion (A Theoretical Rumination)." In *Inside/Out: Lesbian Theories, Gay Theories*. Ed. Diana Fuss. New York: Routledge.

Corea, Gena. 1992. *The Invisible Epidemic: The Story of Women and AIDS*. New York: HarperCollins.

Cory, Donald Webster [Edward Sagarin]. 1951. *The Homosexual in America*. New York: Castle.

Crain, Caleb. 1997. "Pleasure Principles." *Lingua Franca* (October): 26–37.

Crimp, Douglas, and Adam Rolston. 1990. *AIDS Demographics*. Seattle: Bay.

Cruikshank, Margaret. 1992. *The Gay and Lesbian Liberation Movement*. New York: Routledge.

Dangerous Bedfellows, ed. 1996. *Policing Public Sex: Queer Politics and the Future of AIDS Activism*. Boston: South End.

Davis, Tim. 1995. "The Diversity of Queer Politics and the Redefinition of Sexual Identity and Community in Urban Space." In *Mapping Desire*. Ed. David Bell and Gill Valentine. London: Routledge.

De Lauretis, Teresa. 1991. "Queer Theory and Lesbian and Gay Sexualities: An Introduction." *differences: A Journal of Feminist Cultural Studies* iii–xviii.

D'Emilio, John. 1983. *Sexual Politics, Sexual Communities: The Making of a Homosexual Minority in the United States, 1940–1970*. Chicago: University of Chicago Press.

———. 1992. *Making Trouble: Essays on Gay History, Politics, and the University*. New York: Routledge.

Diamond, Sara. 1989. *Spiritual Warfare: The Politics of the Christian Right*. Boston: South End.

Duberman, Martin. 1993. *Stonewall*. New York: Dutton.

Duggan, Lisa. "Making It Perfectly Queer." 1992. *Socialist Review* 22, no. 1 (January–March): 11–31.

Duggan, Lisa, and Nan D. Hunter. 1995. *Sex Wars: Sexual Dissent and Political Culture*. New York: Routledge.

Duyvendak, Jan Willem. 1995. "Gay Subcultures between Movement and Market." In *New Social Movements in Western Europe: A Comparative Analysis*. Ed. Hanspeter Kriesi, Ruud Koopmans, Jan Willem Duyvendak, and Marco G. Guigni. Minneapolis: University of Minnesota Press.

Elbaz, Gilbert. 1992. "The Sociology of AIDS Activism: The Case of ACT UP/New York, 1987–1992." Ph.D. diss., City University of New York.

Epstein, Barbara. 1988. "Direct Action: Lesbians Lead the Movement." *Out/Look*, no. 2 (Summer): 27–32.

———. 1991. *Political Protest and Cultural Revolution: Nonviolent Direct Action in the 1970s and 1980s*. Berkeley and Los Angeles: University of California Press.

Epstein, Steven. 1987. "Gay Politics, Ethnic Identity: The Limits of Social Constructionism." *Socialist Review* 17, no. 3–4 (May–August): 9–54.

———. 1995. "The Construction of Lay Expertise: AIDS Activism and the Forging of Credibility in the Reform of Clinical Trials." *Science, Technology and Human Values* 20, no. 4 (Fall): 408–37.

———. 1996. *Impure Science: AIDS, Activism, and the Politics of Knowledge.* Berkeley and Los Angeles: University of California Press.

———. 1997. "AIDS Activism and the Retreat from the Genocide Frame." *Social Identities* 3, no. 3 (October): 415–38.

Escoffier, Jeffrey. 1985. "The Politics of Gay Identity." *Socialist Review,* 15, no. 4–5 (July-October): 119–53.

———. 1990. "Inside the Ivory Closet: The Challenges Facing Lesbian and Gay Studies." *Out/Look,* no. 10 (Fall): 40–48.

Esterberg, Kristin G. 1997. *Lesbian and Bisexual Identities: Consructing Communities, Constructing Selves.* Philadelphia: Temple University Press.

Evans, Arthur. 1973. "How to zap straights." In *The Gay Liberation Book.* Ed. Len Richmond and Gary Noguera. San Francisco: Ramparts Press.

Faderman, Lillian. 1991. *Odd Girls and Twilight Lovers: A History of Lesbian Life in Twentieth-Century America.* New York: Penguin.

Fitzgerald, Frances. 1986. *Cities on a Hill: A Journey through Contemporary American Cultures.* New York: Simon and Schuster.

Foucault, Michel. 1980. *The History of Sexuality. Volume 1: An Introduction.* Trans. Robert Hurley. New York: Vintage.

Fung, Richard. 1996. "Looking for My Penis: The Eroticized Asian in Gay Video Porn." in *Asian American Sexualities: Dimensions of the Gay and Lesbian Experience.* Ed. Russell Leong. New York: Routledge.

Gamson, Joshua. 1989. "Silence, Death, and the Invisible Enemy: AIDS Activism and Social Movement 'Newness.'" *Social Problems* 36, no. 4 (October): 351–65.

———. 1995. "Must Identity Movements Self-destruct? A Queer Dilemma." *Social Problems* 42, no. 3 (August): 390–407.

———. 1996. "The Organizational Shaping of Collective Identity: The Case of Lesbian and Gay Film Festivals in New York." *Sociological Forum* 11 (2): 231–61.

———. 1997. "Messages of Exclusion: Gender, Movements, and Symbolic Boundaries." *Gender and Society* 11, no. 2 (April): 178–99.

———. 1998. *Freaks Talk Back: Television Talk and Sexual Nonconformity.* Chicago: University of Chicago Press.

Gamson, William A. 1988. "Political Discourse and Collective Action." *International Social Movements Research* 1:219–44.

———. 1990. *The Strategy of Social Protest.* 2d ed. Belmont, Calif.: Wadsworth.

Gerth, H. H., and C. Wright Mills, eds. 1946. *From Max Weber.* New York: Oxford.

Gitlin, Todd. 1980. *The Whole World Is Watching: Mass Media in the Making and Unmaking of the New Left.* Berkeley and Los Angeles: University of California Press.

Goffman, Erving. 1974. *Frame Analysis: An Essay on the Organization of Experience.* New York: Harper and Row.

Gopinath, Gayatri. 1996. "Funny Boys and Girls: Notes on a Queer South Asian Planet." In *Asian American Sexualities: Dimensions of the Gay and Lesbian Experience.* Ed. Russell Leong. New York: Routledge.

Gross, Larry. 1993. *Contested Closets: The Politics and Ethics of Outing.* Minneapolis: University of Minnesota Press.

Halberstam, Judith. 1994. "F2M: The Making of Female Masculinity." In *The Lesbian Postmodern.* Ed. Laura Doan. New York: Columbia University Press.

Halley, Janet E. 1993. "The Construction of Heterosexuality." In *Fear of a Queer Planet: Queer Politics and Social Theory.* Ed. Michael Warner. Minneapolis: University of Minnesota Press.

Hamer, Dean, and Peter Copeland. 1994. *The Science of Desire: The Search for the Gay Gene and the Biology of Behavior.* New York: Simon and Schuster.

Hay, Harry. 1996. *Radically Gay: Gay Liberation in the Words of Its Founder.* Ed. Will Roscoe. Boston: Beacon.

Herek, Gregory M., Jared B. Jobe, and Ralph M. Carney, eds. 1996. *Out in Force: Sexual Orientation and the Military.* Chicago: University of Chicago Press.

Herman, Didi. 1997. *The Anti-gay Agenda: Orthodox Vision and the Christian Right.* Chicago: University of Chicago Press.

Hunt, Scott A., Robert D. Benford, and David A. Snow. 1994. "Identity Fields: Framing Processes and the Social Construction of Movement Identities." In *New Social Movements: From Ideology to Identity.* Ed. Enrique Laraña, Hank Johnston, and Joseph R. Gusfield. Philadelphia: Temple University Press.

Hutchins, Loraine, and Lani Kaahumanu, eds. 1991. *Bi Any Other Name: Bisexual People Speak Out.* Boston: Alyson.

Jenness, Valerie. 1995. "Social Movement Growth, Domain Expansion, and Framing Processes: The Case of Violence against Gays and Lesbians as a Social Problem." *Social Problems* 42, no. 1 (February): 145–70.

Jenness, Valerie, and Kendal Broad. 1994. "Antiviolence Activism and the (In)visibility of Gender in the Gay/Lesbian and Women's Movements." *Gender and Society* 8, no. 3 (September): 402–23.

Jernigan, David. 1988. "Why Gay Leaders Don't Last: The First Ten Years After Stonewall." *Out/Look,* no. 2 (Summer 1988): 33–49.

Johnson, Dirk. 1997. "Chicago Hails District as Symbol of Gay Life." *New York Times,* 27 August, A-8.

Johnson, Marcia P. 1972. "Rapping with a Street Transvestite Revolutionary: An Interview with Marcia Johnson." In *Out of the Closets: Voices of Gay Liberation.* Ed. Karla Jay and Allen Young. New York: Douglas.

Johnston, Hank, Enrique Laraña, and Joseph R. Gusfield. 1994. "Identities, Grievances, and New Social Movements." In *New Social Movements: From Ideology to Identity.* Ed. Enrique Laraña, Hank Johnston, and Joseph R. Gusfield. Philadelphia: Temple University Press.

Katz, Jonathan Ned. 1995. *The Invention of Heterosexuality.* New York: Dutton.

Katzenstein, Mary Fainsod. 1996. "The Spectacle of Life and Death: Feminist and Lesbian/Gay Politics in the Military." In *Gay Rights, Military Wrongs: Political Perspectives on Lesbians and Gays in the Military.* Ed. Craig A. Rimmerman. New York: Garland.

Kauffman, L. A. 1990. "The Anti-politics of Identity." *Socialist Review* 20, no. 1 (January–March): 67–80.

Kennedy, Elizabeth Lapovsky, and Madeline D. Davis. 1993. *Boots of Leather, Slippers of Gold: The History of a Lesbian Community.* New York: Routledge.

Kinsey, Alfred C. 1953. *Sexual Behavior in the Human Female.* Philadelphia: Saunders.

Kinsey, Alfred C., Wardell B. Pomeroy, and Clyde E. Martin. 1948. *Sexual Behavior in the Human Male.* Philadelphia: Saunders.

Kirp, David L. Forthcoming. "The Politics of Blood: Hemophilia Activism in the AIDS Crisis." In *Blood Feuds: AIDS, Blood, and the Politics of Medical Disasters.* Ed. Ronald Bayer and Eric Feldman. Berkeley and Los Angeles: University of California Press.

Kitschelt, Herbert P. 1986. "Political Opportunity Structures and Political Protest: Anti-nuclear Movements in Four Democracies." *British Journal of Political Science* 16, no. 1 (January): 57–85.

Laraña, Enrique, Hank Johnston, and Joseph R. Gusfield, eds. 1994. *New Social Movements: From Ideology to Identity.* Philadelphia: Temple University Press.

Laumann, Edward O., John H. Gagnon, Robert T. Michael, and Stuart Michaels. 1994. *The Social Organization of Sexuality: Sexual Practices in the United States.* Chicago: University of Chicago Press.

LeVay, Simon. 1993. *The Sexual Brain.* Cambridge, Mass.: MIT Press.

Levine, Martin P., Peter M. Nardi, and John H. Gagnon, eds. 1997. *In Changing Times: Gay Men and Lesbians Encounter HIV/AIDS.* Chicago: University of Chicago Press.

Lo, Clarence Y. H. 1992. "Communities of Challengers in Social Movement Theory." In *Frontiers in Social Movement Theory.* Ed. Aldon D. Morris and Carol McClurg Mueller. New Haven: Yale University Press.

Maggenti, Maria. 1991. "Women as Queer Nationals." *Out/Look* (Winter): 20–23.

Marcus, Eric. 1992. *Making History: The Struggle for Gay and Lesbian Equal Rights, 1945–1990: An Oral History.* New York: HarperCollins.

Marcuse, Herbert. 1966. *Eros and Civilization.* Boston: Beacon.

Marotta, Toby. 1981. *The Politics of Homosexuality.* Boston: Houghton-Mifflin.

McAdam, Doug. 1982. *Political Process and the Development of Black Insurgency, 1930–1970.* Chicago: University of Chicago Press.

———. 1994. "Culture and Social Movements." In *New Social Movements: From Ideology to Identity.* Ed. Enrique Laraña, Hank Johnston, and Joseph R. Gusfield. Philadelphia: Temple University Press.

McAdam, Doug, John D. McCarthy, and Meyer N. Zald. 1988. "Social Movements." In *Handbook of Sociology.* Ed. Neil Smelser. Newbury Park, Calif.: Sage.

McCarthy, John D., and Meyer N. Zald. 1977. "Resource Mobilization and Social Movements: A Partial Theory." *American Journal of Sociology* 82 (6): 1212–41.

Melucci, Alberto. 1989. *Nomads of the Present: Social Movements and Individual Needs in Contemporary Society.* Philadelphia: Temple University Press.

Meyer, David S, and Nancy Whittier. 1994. "Social Movement Spillover." *Social Problems* 41 (May): 277–98.

Moraga, Cherríe, and Gloria Anzaldúa, eds. 1981. *This Bridge Called My Back: Writings by Radical Women of Color.* Watertown, Mass.: Persephone.

Morris, Aldon D., and Carol McClurg Mueller, eds. 1992. *Frontiers in Social Movement Theory.* New Haven: Yale University Press.

Mumford, Kevin J. 1997. *Interzones: Black/White Sex Districts in Chicago and New York in the Early Twentieth Century.* New York: Columbia University Press.

Murray, Stephen O. 1979. "Institutional Elaboration of a Quasi-Ethnic Community." *International Review of Modern Sociology* 9:165–78.

———. *American Gay.* 1996. Chicago: University of Chicago Press.

Nardi, Peter M. 1996. "Saying 'I Do' to Broadening the Debate." *Los Angeles Times,* 5 February, op-ed, B-5.

National Museum and Archive of Lesbian and Gay History. 1996. *The Gay Almanac.* New York: Berkley.

Nelson, Emmanuel S., ed. 1993. *Critical Essays: Gay and Lesbian Writers of Color.* New York: Harrington Park.

Oberschall, Anthony. 1973. *Social Conflict and Social Movements.* Englewood Cliffs, N.J.: Prentice-Hall.

Oliver, Pamela, and Gerald Marwell. 1992. "Mobilizing Technologies for Collective Action." In *Frontiers in Social Movement Theory.* Ed. Aldon D. Morris and Carol McClurg Mueller, New Haven: Yale University Press.

Patton, Cindy. 1985. *Sex and Germs: The Politics of AIDS.* Boston: South End.

———. 1990. *Inventing AIDS.* New York: Routledge.

———. 1993. "Tremble, Hetero Swine!" In *Fear of a Queer Planet: Queer Politics and Social Theory.* Ed. Michael Warner. Minneapolis: University of Minnesota Press.

Phelan, Shane. 1994. *Getting Specific: Postmodern Lesbian Politics.* Minneapolis: University of Minnesota Press.

Piven, Frances Fox, and Richard A. Cloward. 1979. *Poor People's Movements.* New York: Vintage. Quoted in Doug McAdam, *Political Process and the Development of Black Insurgency, 1930–1970.* (Chicago: University of Chicago Press, 1982), 49–50.

"Poll Finds Even Split on Homosexuality's Cause." 1993. *New York Times,* 5 March, A-14.

Pollitt, Katha. 1996. "Gay Marriage? Don't Say I Didn't Warn You," *The Nation,* 29 April, 9.

Radicalesbians. 1972. "The Woman-Identified Woman." In *Out of the Closets: Voices of Gay Liberation.* Ed. Karla Jay and Allen Young. New York: Douglas.

Radicalesbians Health Collective. 1972. "Lesbians and the Health Care System." In *Out of the Closets: Voices of Gay Liberation.* Ed. Karla Jay and Allen Young. New York: Douglas.

Ramos, Juanita, ed. 1987. *Compañeras: Latina Lesbians (An Anthology).* New York: Latina Lesbian History Project.

Rich, Adrienne. 1983. "Compulsory Heterosexuality and Lesbian Existence." In *Powers of Desire: The Politics of Sexuality.* Ed. Ann Snitow, Christine Stansell, and Sharon Thompson. New York: Monthly Review.

Ridinger, Robert B. Marks. 1996. *The Gay and Lesbian Movement: References and Resources*. New York: Hall.

Rofes, Eric. 1996. *Reviving the Tribe: Regenerating Gay Men's Sexuality and Culture in the Ongoing Epidemic*. New York: Haworth.

Roscoe, Will, ed. 1988. *Living the Spirit: A Gay American Indian Anthology*. New York: St. Martin's.

Rotello, Gabriel. 1997. *Sexual Ecology: AIDS and the Destiny of Gay Men*. New York: Dutton.

Rubin, Gayle S. 1993. "Thinking Sex: Notes for a Radical Theory of the Politics of Sexuality." In *The Lesbian and Gay Studies Reader*. Ed. Henry Abelove, Michèle Aina Barale, and David M. Halperin. New York: Routledge.

Rust, Paula C. 1995. *Bisexuality and the Challenge to Lesbian Politics: Sex, Loyalty, and Revolution*. New York: New York University Press.

Schneider, Beth E., and Nancy E. Stoller, eds. 1995. *Women Resisting AIDS: Feminist Strategies of Empowerment*. Philadelphia: Temple University Press.

Schulman, Sarah. 1994. *My American History: Lesbian and Gay Life during the Reagan/Bush Years*. New York: Routledge.

Schwartz, Ruth L. 1993. "New Alliances, Strange Bedfellows: Lesbians, Gay Men, and AIDS." In *Sisters, Sexperts, Queers: Beyond the Lesbian Nation*. Ed. Arlene Stein. New York: Plume.

Sedgwick, Eve Kosofsky. 1990. *Epistemology of the Closet*. Berkeley and Los Angeles: University of California Press.

Seidman, Steven. 1988. "Transfiguring Sexual Identity: AIDS and the Contemporary Construction of Homosexuality." *Social Text* 19–20 (Fall): 187–205.

———. 1992. *Embattled Eros: Sexual Politics and Ethics in Contemporary America*. New York: Routledge.

———. 1993. "Identity and Politics in 'Postmodern' Gay Culture: Some Historical and Conceptual Notes." In *Fear of a Queer Planet: Queer Politics and Social Theory*. Ed. Michael Warner. Minneapolis: University of Minnesota Press.

———. 1994. "Symposium: Queer Theory/Sociology. A Dialogue." *Sociological Theory* 12 (July): 166–77

———. 1997. *Difference Troubles: Queering Social Theory and Sexual Politics*. Cambridge: Cambridge University Press.

———, ed. 1996. *Queer Theory/Sociology*. Oxford: Blackwell.

Shelley, Martha. 1972. "Gay Is Good." In *Out of the Closets: Voices of Gay Liberation*. Ed. Karla Jay and Allen Young. New York: Douglas.

Sherrill, Kenneth. 1996. "The Political Power of Lesbians, Gays, and Bisexuals." *PS: Political Science and Politics* 29, no. 3 (September): 469–73.

Shilts, Randy. 1987. *And the Band Played On: Politics, People, and the AIDS Epidemic*. New York: St. Martin's.

———. 1993. *Conduct Unbecoming: Lesbians and Gays in the U.S. Military*. New York: St. Martin's.

Signorile, Michelangelo. 1993. *Queer in America: Sex, the Media, and the Closets of Power*. New York: Anchor.

———. 1997. *Life Outside: The Signorile Report on Gay Men, Sex, Drugs, Muscles, and the Passages of Life*. New York: HarperCollins.

Smith, Barbara, ed. 1983. *Home Girls: A Black Feminist Anthology*. New York: Kitchen Table/Women of Color Press.

Smith, Tom W. 1994. "Attitudes toward Sexual Permissiveness: Trends, Correlates, and Behavioral Connections." In *Sexuality across the Life Course*. Ed. Alice S. Rossi, Chicago and London: University of Chicago Press.

Snow, David A., and Robert D. Benford. 1988. "Ideology, Frame Resonance, and Participant Mobilization." *International Social Movement Research* 1:197–217.

———. 1992. "Master Frames and Cycles of Protest." In *Frontiers in Social Movement Theory*. Ed. Aldon D. Morris and Carol McClurg Mueller. New Haven: Yale University Press.

Snow, David A., E. Burke Rochford Jr., Steven K. Worden, and Robert D. Benford. 1986. "Frame Alignment Processes: Micromobilization and Movement Participation." *American Sociological Review* 51, no. 4 (August): 464–81.

Stacey, Judith. 1996. *In the Name of the Family: Rethinking Family Values in the Postmodern Age*. Boston: Beacon.

Stein, Arlene. 1992. "Sisters and Queers: The Decentering of Lesbian Feminism." *Socialist Review* 22, no. 1 (January–March): 33–55.

———. 1997. *Sex and Sensibility: Stories of a Lesbian Generation*. Berkeley and Los Angeles: University of California Press.

———, ed. 1993. *Sisters, Sexperts, Queers: Beyond the Lesbian Nation*. New York: Plume.

Stein, Edward, ed. 1992. *Forms of Desire: Sexual Orientation and the Social Constructionist Controversy*. New York: Routledge.

Stoller, Nancy. 1995. "Lesbian Involvement in the AIDS Epidemic: Changing Roles and Generational Differences." In *Women Resisting AIDS: Feminist Strategies of Empowerment*. Ed. Beth E. Schneider and Nancy E. Stoller. Philadelphia: Temple University Press.

Sullivan, Andrew. 1995. *Virtually Normal: An Argument about Homosexuality*. New York: Knopf.

Taylor, Verta, and Nicole C. Raeburn. 1995. "Identity Politics as High-Risk Activism: Career Consequences for Lesbian, Gay, and Bisexual Sociologists." *Social Problems* 42, no. 2 (May): 252–73.

Taylor, Verta, and Leila J. Rupp. 1993. "Women's Culture and Lesbian Feminist Activism: A Reconsideration of Cultural Feminism." *Signs* 19, no. 1 (Fall): 32–61.

Taylor, Verta, and Nancy E. Whittier. 1992. "Collective Identity in Social Movement Communities: Lesbian Feminist Mobilization." In *Frontiers in Social Movement Theory*. Ed. Aldon D. Morris and Carol McClurg Mueller. New Haven: Yale University Press.

Thompson, Mark, ed. 1994. *Long Road to Freedom: The Advocate History of the Gay and Lesbian Movement*. New York: St. Martin's.

Vaid, Urvashi. 1995. *Virtual Equality: The Mainstreaming of Gay and Lesbian Liberation*. New York: Anchor.

Vance, Carole S. 1993. "Negotiating Sex and Gender in the Attorney General's Commission on Pornography." In *Sex Exposed: Sexuality and the Pornography Debate*. New Brunswick, N.J.: Rutgers University Press.

———, ed. 1984. *Pleasure and Danger: Exploring Female Sexuality.* Boston: Routledge and Kegan Paul.

Wald, Kenneth D., James W. Button, and Barbara A. Rienzo. 1996. "The Politics of Gay Rights in American Communities: Explaining Antidiscrimination Ordinances and Policies." *American Journal of Political Science* 40, no. 4 (November): 1152–78.

Walters, Suzanna Danuta. 1996. "From Here to Queer: Radical Feminism, Postmodernism, and the Lesbian Menace (Or, Why Can't a Woman Be More Like a Fag)." *Signs* 21, no. 4 (Summer): 830–69.

Warner, Michael. 1993. "Introduction." In *Fear of a Queer Planet: Queer Politics and Social Theory.* Ed. Michael Warner. Minneapolis: University of Minnesota Press.

———. 1997. "Media Gays: A New Stone Wall." *The Nation,* 14 July, 15–19.

Weeks, Jeffrey. 1985. *Sexuality and Its Discontents: Meanings, Myths and Modern Sexualities.* London: Routledge and Kegan Paul.

Weinberg, George. 1972. *Society and the Healthy Homosexual.* New York: St. Martin's.

Weintraub, Jeff. 1997. "The Theory and Politics of the Public-Private Distinction." In *Public and Private in Thought and Practice: Perspectives on a Grand Dichotomy.* Ed. Jeff Weintraub and Krishan Kumar. Chicago: University of Chicago Press.

Weise, Elizabeth Reba, ed. 1992. *Closer to Home: Bisexuality and Feminism.* Seattle: Seal.

Weitz, Rose. 1984. "From Accommodation to Rebellion: The Politicization of Lesbianism." In *Women-Identified Women.* Ed. Trudy Darty and Sandee Potter. Palo Alto, Calif.: Mayfield.

Weston, Kath. 1991. *Families We Choose: Lesbians, Gays, Kinship.* New York: Columbia University Press.

Whisman, Vera. 1996. *Queer by Choice: Lesbians, Gay Men, and the Politics of Identity.* New York: Routledge.

Williams, A. M. 1994. "In Your Face and Just Out of Reach: The 'Queer' Social Movement in San Francisco, California's 'Castro.'" Unpublished article. Department of Anthropology, Yale University, New Haven.

Yang, Alan S. 1997. "Trends: Attitudes toward Homosexuality." Public Opinion Quarterly 61, no. 3 (Fall): 477–507.

James N. Green

4   "More Love and More Desire"
     The Building of a Brazilian Movement

THE YEAR 1978 was a magical time in Brazil. After more than a decade of harsh military rule, the generals' demise seemed imminent.[1] Hundreds of thousands of metalworkers, silent for a decade, laid down their tools and struck against the government's regressive wage policies. Students filled the main streets of the states' capitals chanting, "Down with the dictatorship!" Radio stations played previously censored songs, and they hit the top of the charts. Blacks, women, and even homosexuals began organizing, demanding to be heard.

During the long, tropical summer that bridged 1978 and 1979, a dozen or so students, office workers, bank clerks, and intellectuals met weekly in the city of São Paulo, Brazil's largest metropolis. Rotating from apartment to apartment, sitting on the floor for lack of adequate furniture, they plotted the future of the first homosexual rights organization in Brazil. The meetings randomly alternated between consciousness-raising and discussion. The participants, mostly gay men with a few lesbians moving in and out of the group, debated the most recent antigay statements in *Notícias Populares,* a large-circulation, scandal-driven newspaper, and the appropriate responses for their newly founded organization, Núcleo de Ação pelos Direitos dos Homossexuais (Action Nucleus for Homosexuals' Rights). They closely followed every new issue of the recently launched gay monthly publication *Lampião da Esquina.* This tabloid-sized newspaper, produced by a collective of writers and intellectuals from Rio de Janeiro and São Paulo, declared itself to be a vehicle for the discussion of sexuality, racial discrimination, the arts, ecology, and machismo.

As the summer progressed, the group's name became a heated topic of debate. Did the name Action Nucleus for Homosexuals' Rights discourage new members from joining the group because it too boldly declared a political agenda? Perhaps the tone of activism in the group's name was the reason that only a dozen people at any given time came to the semisecret meetings. Some wanted to change the name of the group to Somos (We Are) to pay homage to the publication put out by the Argentine Homosexual Liberation Front, South America's first gay rights group, which had come to life in Buenos Aires in 1971 and disappeared in the long night of the military dictatorship in March 1976. Others proposed a name that would clearly express the purpose of the organization: Grupo de Afirmação Homossexual (Group of Homosexual Affirmation). Designations that included the word "gay" were roundly rejected because, participants argued, they imitated the movement in the United States.

The final compromise—Somos: Grupo de Afirmação Homossexual— was the name the group took to a debate held on 6 February 1979 at the Social Science Department of the University of São Paulo, Brazil's largest and most prestigious university. The debate, which was part of a four-day series of panel discussions on the topic of organizing Brazil's "minorities,"—a reference to women, blacks, indigenous people, and homosexuals—became the coming-out event for the Brazilian gay and lesbian movement. The program on homosexuality featured a panel of speakers that included editors of the journal *Lampião* and members of Somos. More than three hundred people packed the auditorium to attend the event. The discussion period that followed the panelists' presentations was electric, as charges and countercharges between representatives of leftist student groups and gay and lesbian speakers crisscrossed the assembly room. For the first time, lesbians spoke openly in public about the discrimination that they encountered. Gay students complained that the Brazilian Left was homophobic. Defenders of Fidel Castro and the Cuban Revolution argued that fighting against specific issues, such as sexism, racism, and homophobia, would divide the Left. Rather, they opined, people should unite in a general struggle against the dictatorship.

The first controversy in the emergent Brazilian gay rights movement was taking shape. The lines were drawn. The rhetoric was already being spun. Within a year, tactical questions about aligning with other social movements or maintaining political and organizational autonomy would split Somos, by then the country's largest gay rights group, leaving other organizations throughout the country demoralized and without direction.

Few who listened to this public debate, however, could imagine how quickly a gay and lesbian movement would explode onto the Brazilian political scene. In a little more than a year, a thousand lesbians and gay men packed the Ruth Escobar Theater near downtown São Paulo to attend an indoor rally at the closing ceremony of the First National Gathering of Organized Homosexual Groups. A month later, on 1 May 1980, with the city surrounded by the Second Army and the zone under state of siege, a contingent of fifty openly gay men and lesbians marched with hundreds of thousands of other Brazilians through the downtown working-class neighborhood of São Bernardo in the nation's industrial center to commemorate International Workers' Day during a general strike. When the contingent moved into the Villa Euclides soccer stadium to participate in the rally at the end of the march, thousands of bystanders welcomed them with applause.[2] Six weeks later, one thousand gay men, lesbians, transvestites, and prostitutes weaved through the center of São Paulo, protesting police abuse and chanting, "Abaixo a repressão—mais amor e mais tesão" (Down with repression—more love and more desire). A movement had been born.[3]

Fifteen years later, in June 1995, over three hundred delegates representing gay and lesbian groups in sixty countries of Asia, Europe, North America, Central America, the Caribbean, and South America gathered in Rio de Janeiro to attend the week-long Seventeenth Annual Conference of the International Lesbian and Gay Association (ILGA). At the opening ceremony a federal congresswoman from the Workers Party launched a national campaign for same-sex domestic partnerships and for a constitutional amendment to prohibit discrimination based on sexual orientation. At week's end, the delegates and two thousand gay and lesbian supporters ended the convention by celebrating the twenty-sixth anniversary of the Stonewall rebellion with a march along Atlantic Avenue, the boulevard that borders the shining white sands of Copacabana Beach. A 25-foot-wide yellow banner demanding "Full Citizenship for Gays, Lesbians, and Transvestites" led the parade. A contingent of women followed, carrying signs advocating "Lesbian Visibility," which drew applause from observers. Drag queens teased and flirted with onlookers from atop a pink-hued "Priscilla" school bus and two large sound trucks lent by the bank workers' union. Many participants dressed in Carnavalesque masks and costumes. A 125-meter-long rainbow flag billowed in the wind. At the end of the march, people tearfully sang the national anthem and lingered until a light rain dispersed the crowd. The movement had come of age.

Legal but Not Legal

Although Brazilian colonial law had considered sodomy a sin, punishable by burning at the stake, the 1830 Imperial Criminal Code eliminated all references to sodomy.[4] Late-nineteenth- and twentieth-century laws, however, restricted homosexual behavior. Adults engaging in sexual activities with other adults in a public setting could be charged with "public assault on decency" for "offending propriety with shameless exhibitions or obscene acts or gestures, practiced in public places or places frequented by the public, and which . . . assaults and scandalizes society."[5] This provision, a revised carryover from the earlier Criminal Code, provided the legal basis for controlling any public manifestations of homoerotic or homosocial behavior. With catchall wording, the police or a judge could define and punish "improper" or "indecent" actions that did not conform to heterocentric constructions. Another method for regulating public manifestations of homosexuality was to charge a person with vagrancy. The police could arrest anyone who could not prove a means of support and a fixed domicile or who "earned a living in an occupation prohibited by law or manifestly offensive to morality and propriety."[6]

These two legal provisions gave the police the power to arbitrarily incarcerate homosexuals who engaged in public displays of effeminacy, wore feminine clothing or makeup, earned a living through prostitution, or took advantage of a shadowed building to enjoy a nocturnal sexual liaison. Criminal codes with vaguely defined notions of proper morality and public decency and provisions that strictly controlled vagrancy provided a legal net that could readily entangle those who transgressed socially sanctioned sexual norms. Underpaid police extorted bribes from men caught in compromising situations or without proper identification or work papers. Homosexuality, then, although not explicitly illegal, was behavior that could be easily contained and controlled by Brazilian police and courts.

GAY AND LESBIAN LIFE PRIOR TO THE 1970S

Brazil went through dramatic changes in the 1950s and 1960s. Millions of rural peasants and workers flooded the country's cities, and industrial production expanded to provide employment and many new manufactured products for the domestic market. Cities such as Recife and Salvador in the impoverished northeast, and Rio de Janeiro and São Paulo in the industrializing southeast acted as magnets for homosexuals from rural areas who sought anonymity in large cities away from their families' control. There they mingled with the natives of Brazil's major cities and joined in urban homosexual subcultures.

At that time, Brazil's traditional gendered construction of homosexuality was (and, to a great extent, remains) hierarchical and role based. Men who engage in same-sex activities fall into two categories: the *homem* ("real" man) and the *bicha* (fairy). This binary opposition mirrors the dominant heterosexually defined gender categories of *homem* (man) and *mulher* (woman), in which the man is considered the "active" partner in a sexual encounter and the woman, in being penetrated, is the "passive" participant.[7] As anthropologist Richard G. Parker has pointed out:

> The physical reality of the body itself thus divides the sexual universe in two. Perceived anatomical differences begin to be transformed, through

language, into the hierarchically related categories of socially and culturally defined gender: into the classes of *masculino* (masculine) and *feminino* (feminine). . . . Building upon the perception of anatomical difference, it is this distinction between activity and passivity that most clearly structures Brazilian notions of masculinity and femininity and that has traditionally served as the organizing principle for a much wider world of sexual classifications in day-to-day Brazilian life.[8]

Thus, in same-sex activities, the *homem* takes the "active" role of anally penetrating his partner. The *bicha* takes the "passive" role of being anally penetrated; his sexual "passivity" ascribes to him the socially inferior status of the "woman." Whereas the sexually penetrated "passive" male is socially stigmatized, the male who assumes the public (and presumably private) role of the penetrating *homem* is not. As long as he maintains the sexual role attributed to a "real" man, he may engage in sex with other men without losing social status.[9]

Similarly, women who transgress traditional notions of femininity—manifesting masculine characteristics, expressing independence, or feeling sexual desire for other women—are marginalized. Many lesbians' rejection of traditional feminine roles, including "passivity," place them outside the boundaries of the dominant gender paradigm. A common pejorative expression for a lesbian, *sapatão*, literally "big shoe," reflects the social anxiety about strong, masculinized women.[10]

Until the late 1950s there were no exclusively gay or lesbian bars in Brazil. Public homosociability centered on parks, plazas, cinemas, public rest rooms, or the tenuous occupation of restaurants, sidewalk cafes, and slices of popular beaches. Because many single people lived with their families until they married, sexual encounters often took place in rooms rented by the hour or in the homes of friends. Small parties, discreet drag shows, and weekend excursions to the country or a beach house afforded space free from social censure.

Carnaval was the one time during the year when gay men could express themselves freely and openly. Lesbians, although much more constricted by social norms, also appropriated Carnaval to playfully express their desires in public. For four days, drag balls, cross-dressing in public, and campy behavior reigned. In the 1950s, Rio de Janeiro's Baile das Bonecas (Dolls' Ball) began to attract an international audience, as gay men from all over South America came to participate in the revelry and watch plumed and sequined men compete with each other to be crowned the most glamorous and beautiful goddesses of Carnaval celebrations. Carnaval was the unique moment during the year when *tudo é permitido* (everything is allowed).

HOMOSEXUALITY UNDER BRAZILIAN MILITARY RULE

In 1964 the Brazilian military overthrew the radical/populist government of President João Goulart and initiated twenty-one years of authoritarian rule. Backed by the United States, the Brazilian generals outlawed opposition political parties, arrested leftist leaders, purged radical unions, and imposed tight controls over the press. Except for closeted homosexual leftists who were arrested by the dictatorship, the gay and lesbian subculture of Brazil's largest cities was initially unaffected by the *coup d'état*. Recently opened bars with a predominantly gay or lesbian clientele continued to provide a venue for socializing. Drag shows, which originated in these bars, began to reach a wider public, and several cross-dressers became celebrities. Various social groups held private drag parties, and one group even published over one hundred issues of its newsletter, *O Snob*, between 1963 and 1969. The success of this mimeographed newsletter, with its gossip columns and glamorously drawn man in drag on the cover, inspired nearly thirty similar publications throughout Brazil, as well as the short-lived Associação Brasileira da Imprensa Gay (Brazilian Association of the Gay Press) founded in 1967 and dissolved a year later.[11]

By 1968, public opposition to military rule had become widespread. Workers occupied factories in two industrial centers, and over one hundred thousand students and their supporters marched through the streets of Rio de Janeiro demanding an end to the military dictatorship. In response, a group of generals carried out a coup within the coup, putting hard-liner General Emílio Garrastazú Médici in power as president. From 1968 to 1973 the government waged a campaign of state terrorism against the opposition, especially against leftist organizations. Thousands were arrested and tortured.[12]

News of the gay liberation movement that emerged after the 1969 Stonewall riots reached Latin America in the early 1970s and encouraged the formation of groups in Argentina, Mexico, and Puerto Rico. However, the military repression in Brazil dissuaded all thoughts of founding a radical gay and lesbian movement. The informal gay publication *O Snob* and its imitators soon ceased distributing their newsletters for fear of being mistakenly persecuted as members of a leftist underground organization.[13] Under the strict moralistic guidelines of military censorship, references to homosexuality and gay Carnaval balls were muted in the press. Although some alternative journals occasionally reported about "gay power" in the United States, the formation of a political movement seemed impossible.

While the hard-line generals controlled the government, social and cultural transformations were taking place in Brazil that would affect notions of gender and homosexuality. Pop singers such as Caetano Veloso, Maria Bethânia, and Ney Matogrosso presented androgynous personas, which blurred sexual boundaries and implied bisexual desire. Bohemian and countercultural values that emphasized individual sexual freedom began to influence intellectuals and students. A youth culture that challenged traditional notions of sexuality and gender permeated the urban middle class.

By 1974 the military dictatorship was facing serious problems. The economy, which had grown dramatically during the period of most severe repression at the expense of the poor and the working class, was faltering as a result of the international oil crisis. The official opposition political party was gaining electoral ground in regional elections. New forms of resistance began to develop. Students revived self-governing organizations in the universities and held protests against military rule. Rank-and-file trade unionists staged wildcat strikes. Women who had been involved in underground opposition organizations began to publicly criticize sexism in the Left and raise feminist issues.[14] The Black United Movement emerged to challenge the national ideology according to which Brazil was a racial democracy.[15] In 1978, faced with a massive strike wave against its economic policies, the military decided to accelerate a process of gradual liberalization that would eventually return the government to civil control and grant amnesty to those involved in human rights violations.

THE FIRST GAY AND LESBIAN RIGHTS MOVEMENT

It was within this political and social climate that first the journal *Lampião* and then Somos were founded. Somos sparked the formation of at least seven groups by the time of the First Gathering of Organized Homosexuals in April 1980. Most were small and led by lower-middle-class students, workers, and intellectuals, some of whom had been members or supporters of one of various clandestine leftist organizations that survived the worst years of the dictatorship. They brought with them both their experience as organizers and misgivings about the frequent leftist critique of homosexuality as a "product of bourgeois decadence."

In May 1980, Somos split over participation in working-class mobilizations and the role of leftists in the gay movement. The enthusiasm of activists who had managed to organize both a successful national gathering and a mobilization against police repression dissipated. Those opposed to building alliances with labor and Left-led movements formed a new group in São Paulo, Grupo Outra Coisa: Ação Homossexualista (Something Else: Homosexualist Action Group). Somos lesbians who had already formed an autonomous collective within the larger organization also left the group to form a separate entity, Grupo Lésbico-Feminista (Lesbian Feminist Group), where they could pursue their agenda without having to deal with the problems of sexism in a group dominated by gay men. Somos Rio de Janeiro, which had modeled itself after Somos-São Paulo, also divided over leadership disputes. The principal editors of *Lampião* attacked the activist organizations, as circulation of the monthly journal, which had been in the tens of thousands, plummeted. The journal folded in mid-1981, and over the next three years most of the initial gay rights groups followed suit. From a peak of twenty groups in 1981, only seven survived in 1984, and of these only five attended the Second Gathering of Organized Homosexuals held that same year in Salvador, Bahia.[16]

A variety of factors contributed to a decline in the movement. With certain exceptions, most organizations never grew beyond several dozen members at a given time. They lacked financial resources and infrastructure. Many of the initial leaders became demoralized and left after their groups failed to grow significantly. Other activists did not have the experience to sustain their groups during the 1980s—Latin America's "Lost Decade"—when burgeoning foreign debts sparked run away inflation and massive unemployment. Moreover, the end of the dictatorship in 1985 created a false sense that democracy had been restored and that individual rights of homosexuals and other sectors of the society would expand without effort. The press, radio, and television carried more positive coverage of homosexuality and provided a vehicle for the movement's few public leaders to articulate their viewpoints. In addition, visible gay consumerism, which included more nightclubs, saunas, bars, and discos, sustained an illusion that greater freedom had been achieved and that Brazil's gays and lesbians did not require political organization.[17]

During this lull in activism, the Grupo Ação Lésbica-Feminista (Lesbian Feminist Action Group), founded in 1981, successfully won the battle to participate fully in the feminist movement. The group also maintained a public profile by publishing a bulletin, *Chanacomchana,* and participating in international lesbian conferences.[18] Luiz Mott, anthropology professor and founder of Grupo Gay da Bahia (currently the oldest group in Brazil), also steered the floundering movement through important campaigns that set the stage for the movement to expand in the late 1980s. The first victory of Grupo Gay da Bahia, located in the northeastern capital of Salvador, was to obtain legal recognition for the group. The second campaign involved convincing the Federal Council of Health to abolish the classification that categorized homosexuality as a treatable form of "sexual deviance." Spearheaded by Mott, the campaign won the endorsement of the nation's leading professional organizations and several local and state legislative bodies. Prominent intellectuals and celebrities signed a national petition calling for a repeal of the classification. The council removed homosexuality from the category of treatable illnesses in February 1985.[19]

During 1987 and 1988 Brazil held a constituent assembly to rewrite the nation's constitution. With the support of the group Lambda in São Paulo and Grupo Gay da Bahia, João Antônio de S. Mascarenhas, a former editor of *Lampião* and founder of Triangulo Rosa (Pink Triangle) in Rio de Janeiro, organized a campaign to include a provision prohibiting discrimination based on sexual orientation. On 28 January 1988, 461 of 559 members of the Constituent Assembly voted on the measure. But with only 130 favoring a constitutional provision outlawing discrimination, the provision failed. Twenty-five of the thirty-three evangelical pastors in the Constituent Assembly voted against the measure. All of the leftist Workers Party representatives backed the prohibition of discrimination based on sexual orientation.[20] Similar laws against discrimination on the basis of sexual orientation have been included in the constitutions of two Brazilian states. Important metropolises such as São Paulo, Rio de Janeiro, and Salvador and eighty other municipalities also have local codes outlawing discrimination, but they lack any legal bite.[21] During the Seventeenth Annual Conference of the International Lesbian and Gay Association, for example, owners of two sidewalk cafes in Copacabana expelled conference participants for holding hands in public.

VIOLENCE AND AIDS

Although most gay men and lesbians thought political organizations unnecessary during the apparent liberalization that accompanied the return to democracy, the dramatic increase of HIV infection and a wave of violence against gay men, transvestites, and lesbians revealed how precarious their rights were under a democratic regime. The first case of AIDS was diagnosed in Brazil in 1982, and most Brazilians quickly began to associate HIV and AIDS with rich gay men who had the resources to travel to the United States and Europe.[22] Reality was quite different. According to Richard Parker, the director of the Brazilian Interdisciplinary AIDS Association:

> The rapid transition from predominantly homosexual and bisexual transmission to rapidly increasing heterosexual transmission after the first decade becomes even more striking when reported cases of AIDS are viewed across time. While homosexual males accounted for 46.7 percent, and bisexual males for 22.1 percent, heterosexual men and women accounted for

only 4.9 percent of the national total between 1980 and 1986. During 1991, on the other hand, cases reported among homosexual men had fallen to 22.9 percent and cases among bisexual men had dropped to 11.1 percent, while cases reported among heterosexual men had risen to 20.1 percent of the national total.[23]

In the early years of the epidemic, misinformation and homophobia caused a panic, as the scandal sheets reported the arrival of the "gay pestilence." One of the first organized responses was initiated by Grupo Outra Coisa: Ação Homossexualista, which had split from Somos because of the latter's links with the Left. Its members distributed leaflets in the gay bars and cruising areas of São Paulo, informing the "homosexual collectivity of São Paulo" how to obtain more information about the disease.[24] Activists also met in 1983 with representatives of the Health Department of the State of São Paulo to ensure that public health officials fighting the epidemic would not discriminate against homosexuals.[25]

Some of the activists from the first wave of the gay and lesbian rights movement of the late 1970s began working in AIDS-related organizations. In the mid-1980s when a second generation of gay rights organizations emerged, they integrated AIDS education into their political activity. Groups such as Grupo Gay da Bahia, which survived the 1980s lull in the movement, managed to do so in part because the group also took up the fight around AIDS issues.[26]

The mid-1980s also saw a marked increase in violence against gay men, transvestites, and lesbians. Luiz Mott has documented the murder of more than twelve hundred homosexual men and women and transvestites in Brazil from the mid-1980s to the mid-1990s.[27] Several cases involved women killed by relatives who had discovered that they were having a lesbian affair.[28] Many other murderers were young hustlers who picked up gay men, then robbed and killed them. In 1987 one youth killed over a dozen men whom he had met at a park near São Paulo's financial district.[29]

Most of these murders were committed by unidentified groups or individuals who were never convicted. According to Grupo Gay da Bahia, twelve different groups have been involved in the bashing and killing of homosexuals.[30] During the years of military rule (1964–1985), paramilitary units formed; these were attached to the armed forces and to federal, state, and local police departments. Known as death squads, these groups assisted the military in extralegal activities, including the kidnaping and torture of opponents of the dictatorship. Some of these groups also carried out campaigns to "clean up" what they deemed "immoral behavior," specifically homosexuality. One such unit, the Cruzada Anti-Homossexualista (Antihomosexualist Crusade) sent threatening letters to Somos in 1981.[31] The Brazilian dictatorship passed a law in 1979 granting amnesty to all those involved in the killing and torture that had taken place during the previous fifteen years of military rule. As a result, those guilty of violations of human rights were never punished, and violence against homosexuals and transvestites continues unchecked. Death squads and similar groups still operate with impunity in Brazil. Without "subversive elements" to target with their activities, they have chosen more and more to cleanse Brazilian society of "immorality."

Of all reported killings by groups or individuals only 10 percent lead to arrests. Toni Reis, the president of the Brazilian Association of Gays, Lesbians and Transvestites has reported that of the twenty documented murders of homosexuals and transvestites over the last ten years in his native city of Curitiba, there were only two convictions. Adauto Belarmino Alves, the 1994 winner of the Reebok Human Rights Award, documented the killing of twenty-three transvestites in Rio de Janeiro during October 1994.[32] In some Brazilian states, because murders of homosexuals and transvestites go unreported they are not included in dossiers documenting violence against homosexuals and transvestites.[33]

The judicial system backs up these arbitrary actions against transvestites. In October 1994, the Court of Military Justice reduced the sentence of Cirineu Carlos Letang da Silva, a former soldier of the Military Police, who was convicted of murdering a transvestite known as Vanessa. The judge who dropped the sentence from twelve to six years, explained that transvestites are "dangerous." Vanessa had been shot in the nose and in the back.[34]

Perhaps the most dramatic case involved the 1993 murder of Renildo José dos Santos, a local town councilor from Coqueiro Seco in the state of Alagoas. On 2 February 1993, the town council suspended dos Santos for thirty days after he declared on a radio program that he was bisexual. He was charged with "practicing acts incompatible with the decorum due his position and bringing the reputation of the Council into disrepute." When the period of his suspension expired and the council failed to reinstate him, dos Santos sought a court order to allow his return to the council. The next day he was kidnaped. His remains were discovered on 16 March. His head and limbs had been separated from his body and the corpse burned. Although five men, including the mayor of the town, were arrested in the case, they were acquitted of any involvement in the murder. To date, no one has been punished for this crime.[35]

THE SECOND WAVE

The Third National Gathering of Homosexuals, held in January 1989 in Rio de Janeiro, was attended by only six organizations. Nevertheless, there were new groups among the participants. One such organization,

Atobá, founded in 1985 after a young man was killed in a gay bashing, brought together lesbians and gay men in working-class suburbs of Rio de Janeiro, far from the middle-class gay bars and clubs of Copacabana and Ipanema. The following four yearly national gatherings attracted more and more groups, and during the Seventh National Gathering of Homosexuals, held in January 1995, representatives of thirty-one organizations founded the Brazilian Association of Gays, Lesbians and Transvestites. Although most groups are still small, the formation of a national organization with affiliates from all regions of the continent-sized country foreshadows a dynamic growth of the movement.

A few developments contributed to the resurgence of gay and lesbian activism after the establishment of a democratic regime in 1985. Many different social movements, and the Workers Party, which had emerged from the struggle against the military dictatorship, began raising the question of how to democratize participation in a nonmilitary, civil society. Activists from the women's movement, neighborhood organizations, labor unions, and leftist groups argued that true democracy meant respect for ordinary citizens. Moreover, in 1992, millions of Brazilians demonstrated for the impeachment of President Fernando Collar, reinforcing the importance of mobilization to achieve political ends.

These experiences politicized many gays and lesbians. They joined local groups to receive support through consciousness-raising and discussion sessions. They also sought to achieve full citizenship rights for gays, lesbians, and transvestites by fighting against homophobia, violence, and discrimination. Lesbians took a leadership role in formulating the direction of the movement, waging a battle in 1993 to increase their visibility by changing the name of the yearly national meetings to Brazilian Gathering of Lesbians and Homosexuals. In September 1997, lesbian activists gathered in Salvador, Bahia, for a four-day conference—the Second National Lesbian Seminar—which focused on health and citizenship. The event brought together women from throughout the country for a wide range of discussions with such titles as Lesbian Citizenship, Homoeroticism in the Press, Our Health, Our Pleasure, Black Lesbians in the Union Movement, and Lesbians and Family Relationships.

At the same time, the media's increased discussion of homosexuality and the activities of the international movement affected discussions within Brazil. All the major newspapers, magazines, and television stations covered international Pride marches, debates about gays in the U.S. military, and AIDS issues. Talk shows featured the few activists who were willing to come out publicly and discuss issues openly and frankly. Popular singers, such as Renato Russo, announced their homosexuality and supported the movement.

There was also a shift in the way people who engage in same-sex erotic relations identify themselves. Although many Brazilians still think in terms of "active" and "passive" sexual roles, gay and lesbian identities similar to those in the United States and Europe have taken hold, especially among middle-class residents of the large urban centers. Whereas in 1980, Somos rejected the word "gay" as too bound to the movement in the United States, the English term now has widespread use among homosexual men and women and the media. However, coming out to family and employers, especially among noneffeminate men and nonmasculine woman, is not as common as it is in Europe and the United States. Even so, more and more activists are coming out in newspaper, magazine, and television interviews in an attempt to break the cultural code that "you can do what you want, but don't tell anyone."[36]

Additionally, organizing around AIDS issues has not only attracted individuals seeking information and support but also provided new resources and infrastructure. Groups have learned how to apply for grants from state and national ministries of health for AIDS education and prevention. In some cases an office rented with financial support has also served as a meeting place for local gay and lesbian groups.

The growth of the Workers Party as an umbrella organization for most social movements and leftist groups also politicized gay activists. In recent years, the Workers Party has channeled most of the opposition to the political, economic, and social problems facing Brazil. Its elected representatives in local, state, and federal offices provided much of the support for the gay and lesbian movement's legislative and legal activities. Recall that the entire Workers Party bloc supported the provision to include a prohibition of discrimination based on sexual orientation in the 1988 Constituent Assembly.[37] During the 1980s the Workers Party was the only ballot-status political party that included gay and lesbian rights in its program. Gay and lesbian activists formed a group within the Workers Party to educate the membership about issues of the movement. However, the Workers Party alliance with activists in the ecclesiastical-base communities of the Catholic Church caused the party's presidential candidate and former trade union leader, Luiz "Lula" Ignácio da Silva, to withdraw his support for same-sex civil marriages (união civil) during the 1994 presidential elections.[38] Lula's reluctance to come out in favor of full rights for gays and lesbians has been attributed to his own desire to win support from the Catholic hierarchy. His efforts proved fruitless, since on the eve of the presidential elections his ratings in the polls dropped dramatically when the government introduced a monetary plan that stabilized the economy. As a result, Lula lost his second bid for the presidency.[39] Nevertheless, in 1995 Workers Party Congresswoman Marta

Suplicy once again introduced congressional legislation to prohibit discrimination based on sexual orientation and to establish *parceria civil* (domestic partnership).

The movement has expanded in other important areas in recent years. Leaders in the bank workers', teachers', and social security workers' unions have begun to demand domestic-partner benefits for gay and lesbian members. Students at the University of São Paulo have established a center for the study of homosexuality. Activists of the Group of Homosexuals of the Partido Socialista dos Trabalhadores Unificados (United Socialist Workers Party) presented resolutions in the 1995 and 1997 Congress of the National Union of Students to endorse the campaign for same-sex domestic partnership and the constitutional provision outlawing discrimination based on sexual orientation. The resolutions were approved by the Congress despite the opposition of some leftist students.

Transvestites have also become active participants in the Brazilian movement. Since the 1960s, cross-dressers, many working as prostitutes, have become more visible on the streets of Brazil's major urban centers. Hormones and silicone injections have made the creation of a traditional feminine body accessible to large numbers of men who identify as cross-dressers. Although transvestites have been a prime target of hate crimes and murders, for many years a gulf existed between transvestites and gay and lesbian activists. In May 1993, however, the Associação de Travestis e Liberados (Association of Transvestites and Liberated People) organized the First National Gathering in Rio de Janeiro. Over one hundred people from Rio de Janeiro, São Paulo, and other states attended the conference. Representatives from other newly formed groups of transvestites also converged on the Seventh Brazilian Gathering of Lesbians and Homosexuals in January 1995, insisting that the movement broaden its focus to included issues facing transvestites. As a result, the name of the national organization founded at the gathering, the Brazilian Association of Gays, Lesbians and Transvestites, reflected an expanded constituency.

Gay and lesbian guides to Brazil boast innumerable bars and clubs, popular gay beaches, openly gay Carnaval celebrations, and slick new publications. Yet visibility and festivity do not necessarily produce activists. Despite all of the new levels of organizations achieved over the last few years, including annual Pride parades in Rio de Janeiro and São Paulo, the movement still remains weak, involving only a fraction of the millions of Brazilian gays, lesbians, and transvestites. Currently, there are more than fifty gay and lesbian groups in Brazil and a comparable number of AIDS organizations that direct many of their efforts to gay clients, but most of them are small, numbering no more than thirty members. Only a dozen or so larger groups have accumulated enough resources and membership to sustain offices, maintain an infrastructure, and provide leadership to the national movement. Even the largest demonstration to date at the close of the ILGA Conference had only two thousand participants.

Moreover, a May 1993 poll, which interviewed a cross section of two thousand Brazilian men and women, revealed that anxiety over homosexuality remains rampant. While 50 percent of those polled confirmed that they had daily contact with homosexuals at work, in their neighborhoods, or in bars and clubs that they frequent, 56 percent admitted that they would change their behavior toward any colleague they discovered to be homosexual (one in five would drop all contact with the person). Thirty-six percent would not employ a homosexual, even if he or she were best qualified for the position. And, of those interviewed, 79 percent would not accept having a son go out with a gay friend.[40]

Dr. Arnaldo Dominguez carried out another revealing survey in São Paulo in 1991. He distributed two hundred questionnaires to clinics and psychologists and a further six hundred to homosexuals. Thirty percent of the doctors thought homosexuality deserved condemnation. Seventy percent of the doctors considered bisexuality an abnormality, and 50 percent said they would be unprepared to discuss the subject if a homosexual client came to their office.[41]

Dramatic changes in the movement have occurred since its early days in the late 1970s. It has become much more inclusive. Members of leftist currents, such as the Workers Party and the United Socialist Workers Party, are considered a legitimate part of a politically diverse movement. Although organizations did not endorse candidates, most activists supported Lula and the Workers Party in the last elections. This does not mean, however, that the movement has mechanically adopted left-wing rhetoric, analysis, or methods of organization. Colorfully painted banners and rainbow-hued bunches of balloons usually distinguish gay and lesbian participation in political demonstrations, and consciousness-raising sessions—a legacy of both the international feminist movement and Brazilian pedagogist Paulo Freire—remain a key organizing tool for most groups. Lesbians, while still a numerical minority within the movement, play an equal role in the leadership of the national association. A small number of transvestites, politicized through their experiences with the police, have also assumed a place in the movement.

Where once political activities were carried out by valiant individuals and isolated groups, now the movement has developed nationally coordinated campaigns around issues such as violence, same-sex domestic partnerships, and national antidiscrimination legislation. Moreover, the public discussion about homosexuality has increased, as the media gives more coverage to issues that concern gays, lesbians, and transvestites and popular soap operas portray them more positively. The international movement has had a strong impact on Brazil, with key leaders traveling to the United States, Europe, and other countries in Latin America to participate in conferences or attend Pride demonstrations. The ILGA Conference in Rio de Janeiro brought many activists in contact with international delegates, fostering a rich interchange.

In August 1964, Gigi Bryant, a member of the social group that edited the newsletter O Snob, concluded a six-part series on the "art of cruising." In her article, she described Maracanãzinho, a large arena where events such as Holiday on Ice and the Miss Brazil beauty pageant take place: after dishing members of the groups who had attended shows there, Gigi joked that "since the faggot top-set is converging on Maracanãzinho, it is likely to become the social center of various social classes in the future."[42] What's more, she teased, "Indeed, it is very possible that in better days the First Gay Festival will take place there with representatives from other nations converging on our country. That would generate lots of publicity and be a grand utopia."[43]

In 1964, Gigi's predictions were good for a laugh. Yet, remarkably, she was right.

NOTES

Acknowledgments: I wish to thank Daniel Hurewitz and Moshé Sluhovsky for their editorial assistance in preparing this essay.

1. Maria Helena Moreira Alves, *State and Opposition in Military Brazil* (Austin: University of Texas Press, 1985); James N. Green, "Liberalization on Trial: The Brazilian Workers' Movement," North American Congress on Latin America, *Report on the Americas,* 13, no. 3 (May–June 1979); and Thomas E. Skidmore, *The Politics of Military Rule in Brazil, 1964–85* (New York, Oxford University Press, 1988).

2. Just like the debate a year before, the issue of marching in the 1980 May Day rally divided Somos and was fiercely discussed in the pages of *Lampião.* Those who participated in the demonstration argued that the fight for gay and lesbian rights and the movement against the military dictatorship were intertwined. Without democracy, the goals of the gay and lesbian organizations would be difficult to obtain. Opponents of the group's participation in the May Day demonstration, who organized a picnic at the zoo that day and split from the group several weeks later, argued that the working class and many trade union leaders were homophobic. Instead of engaging in politics on international workers' day, they maintained, gay men and lesbians should enjoy the holiday with friends as did thousands of other working people who were not protesting the dictatorship's policies.

For a more complete account of the early gay rights movement in São Paulo, see James N. Green, "The Emergence of the Brazilian Gay Liberation Movement: 1977–81," *Latin American Perspectives* 21, no. 1, issue 80 (Winter 1994); Edward MacRae, "Homosexual Identities in Transitional Brazilian Politics," in *The Making of Social Movements in Latin America: Identity, Strategy and Democracy*, ed. Arturo Escobar and Sonia E. Alvarez (Boulder, Colo.: Westview, 1992); and João S. Trevisan, *Perverts in Paradise*, trans. Martin Foreman (London: GMP, 1986).

3. For another overview of the gay movement in Brazil, see Luiz Mott, "The Gay Movement and Human Rights in Brazil," in *Latin American Male Homosexualities*, ed. Stephen O. Murray (Albuquerque: University of New Mexico Press, 1995).

4. José Henrique Pierangelli, *Códigos penais do Brasil: Evolução histórica.* (Baurú, Brazil: Jalovi, 1980), 26.

5. Ibid., 301.

6. Ibid., 316.

7. Peter Fry, *Para inglês ver: Identidade e política na cultura brasileira* (Rio de Janeiro: Zahar, 1982).

8. Richard G. Parker, *Bodies, Pleasures, and Passions: Sexual Culture in Contemporary Brazil* (Boston: Beacon, 1991), 41.

9. See Michel Misse, *O estigma do passivo sexual: Um símbolo de estigma no discurso cotidiano* (Rio de Janeiro: Achiamé, 1979).

10. Peter Fry and Edward MacRae, *O que é homossexualidade* (São Paulo: Brasiliense, 1983).

11. Agildo Guimarães, interview by James N. Green, tape recording, Rio de Janeiro, 6 October 1994.

12. See Alves, *State and Opposition in Military Brazil*, and Skidmore, *The Politics of Military Rule in Brazil, 1964–85.*

13. Anhuar Farad, interview by James N. Green, tape recording, Rio de Janeiro, 25 July 1995.

14. See Sonia E. Alvarez, *Engendering Democracy in Brazil: Women's Movements in Transition Politics* (Princeton: Princeton University Press, 1990).

15. See *Orpheus and Power: The Movimento Negro of Rio de Janeiro and São Paulo, Brazil, 1945–1988* (Princeton: Princeton University Press, 1994).

16. "A história do 'EBHO': Encontro Brasileiro de Homosexuais (continuação II)," *Boletim do grupo gay da Bahia* 13, no. 27 (August 1993): 7.

17. Mario Blander, "Lucros do lazer gay: Os donos da noite descobrem novo filão," *Isto é* (São Paulo), (27 April 1983,) 76–77.

18. Miriam Martinho, "Brazil," in *Unspoken Rules: Sexual Orientation and Women's Human Rights*, ed. Rachel Rosenbloom (San Francisco: International Gay and Lesbian Human Rights Commission, 1985), 22.

19. The Brazilian campaign involved modifying Code 302.0 of the World Health Organization's International Classification of Diseases, which had been incorporated into the Brazilian code. The World Health Organization struck the category from its list eight years later. Mott, "The Gay Movement and Human Rights in Brazil," 222–23.

20. João Antônio de Souza Mascarenhas, *A tríplice conexão: Machismo, conservadorismo político e falso moralismo, um ativista guei versus noventa e seis parlamentares* (Rio de Janeiro: 2AB Editora, 1997).

21. Mott, "The Gay Movement and Human Rights in Brazil," 223–24.

22. Richard Parker, "AIDS in Brazil," in *Sexuality, Politics and AIDS in Brazil: In Another World?* ed. Herbert Daniel and Richard Parker (London: Falmer, 1993), 9.

23. Ibid., 12.

24. Grupo Outra Coisa (Ação Homossexualista), "Informe à coletividade homossexual de São Paulo," mimeographed leaflet, June 1983.

25. Paulo Roberto Teixeira, "Políticas públicas em AIDS," mimeographed leaflet, n.d., 2.

26. Veriano Terto Jr., interview by James N. Green, tape recording, Rio de Janeiro, 24 July 1995.

27. Luiz Roberto Mott, *Epidemic of Hate: Violations of the Human Rights of Gay Men, Lesbians, and Transvestites in Brazil* (San Francisco: Grupo Gay da Bahia, Brazil and the International Gay and Lesbian Human Rights Commission, 1996).

28. Martinho, "Brazil," 18.

29. "Casos se repetem em São Paulo," *Folha de São Paulo,* 17 April 1990.

30. Grupo Gay da Bahia, "Grupos de extermínio de homossexuais no Brasil," leaflet, n.d.

31. "Um pouco de nossa história," *O corpo* (São Paulo), no. 0 (November 1980): 8.

32. "Reclamando nossos direitos," *Jornal folha de parreira* (Curitiba) 3, no. 25 (May 1995): 2.

33. The U.S. Department of State 1993 human rights country report for Brazil includes the following statement: "There continue to be reports of murders of homosexuals. São Paulo newspapers reported that three transvestites were murdered on March 14; other reports claimed that 17 transvestites were killed in the first three months of 1993. One military policeman was charged in the March 14 killings and was awaiting trial at year's end. Homosexual rights groups claim, however, that the vast majority of perpetrators of crimes against homosexuals go unpunished." U.S. Department of State, *Country Reports on Human Rights Practices for 1993* (Washington, D.C.: GPO, 1994), 376.

34. Marcelo Godoy, "Justiça reduz pena de matador de travesti," *Folha de São Paulo,* 9 October 1994, 4.

35. Amnesty International, U.S.A., *Breaking the Silence: Human Rights Violations Based on Sexual Orientation* (New York: Amnesty International Publications, 1994), 13–14.

36. This saying, *"pode fazer o que você quiser, mas não diga nada a ninguém,"* usually uttered in a tone that expresses reluctant tolerance, reflects the fear of shame if friends or relatives discover that a family member is a gay man or a lesbian.

37. A similar constitutional revision introduced in 1993 and voted on in 1994 received the support of 25 percent of the legislators. João Antônio de Souza Mas-

carenhas, *A Tríplice Conexão: Machismo, Conservadorismo Político e Falso Moralismo* (Rio de Janeiro: 2AB Editoro, 1997), 117.

38. "Lula se reúne com presidente da CNBB e diz que reconhecimento dos direitos de homossexuais também não será tratado," *Folha de São Paulo,* 13 April 1994.

39. Wilson H. da Silva, interview by James N. Green, tape recording, São Paulo, 5 May 1995.

40. According to the poll, in the northeast the number of those refusing to accept having a son go out with a gay friend increased to 87 percent. "O mundo gay rasga as fantasias," *Veja,* 12 May 1993, 52–53.

41. Ibid., 53.

42. Gigi Bryant, "Da arte de caçar, capítulo VII 'Country Club Gay,'" *O Snob* 2, no. 10, 15 August 1964, 6.

43. Ibid.

STEPHEN BROWN

5   Democracy and Sexual Difference
The Lesbian and Gay Movement in Argentina

IN THE afternoon of 27 August 1996, about twenty Argentinean lesbian, gay, bisexual, and transgendered activists stormed into the Constituent Assembly (*Convención Estatuyente*) of Buenos Aires. They carried blown-up photos of Carlos Jáuregui, the country's most prominent and respected gay activist, who had died of AIDS one week earlier. Followed by members of the press and television crews, the activists tracked down the members of the commission responsible for writing the new municipal charter and shamed each one of them into signing a statement in support of the prohibition of discrimination on the basis of sexual orientation, alongside gender, age, ethnicity, religion, and political ideology. A few days later, on 30 August, the assembly unanimously approved the nondiscrimination clause, and Buenos Aires became the first city in Spanish-speaking Latin America to protect nonheterosexuals from being discriminated against on that basis (Sardá 1996b, 1996c).

It is clear in this narrative that lesbian, gay, bisexual, and transgender activism[1] not only exists in Argentina but is sometimes quite prominent and yields tangible political results as well. This chapter aims to explain the emergence, expansion, and timing of the Argentinean lesbian and gay movement, my central thesis being that Argentinean lesbian and gay activism emerged in the late 1960s and early 1970s as a combination of a global and local cycle of protest, resting on the prior diffusion of lesbian and gay identity. New domestic constraints alone, however, overrode the favorable conditions and led to the rapid disappearance of activism in the mid-1970s. During the 1980s, lesbian and gay activists capitalized on certain new political opportunities—principally the return to democracy, the human rights discourse, and some international support—to build a movement. As such, the "political opportunity structures" approach to social movements constitutes a valuable analytical tool. However, the literature tends to gloss over the importance of identity and identity formation. Indeed, the diffusion of lesbian and gay identity is a prerequisite to activism, albeit insufficient in itself to create a movement. Moreover, opportunities are not enough to explain actions. Though one cannot make definitive statements from a single case study, I suggest that it is impor-

110

tant for social movement theory to make greater efforts to refrain from accepting identity as given, especially when sexuality is concerned, and to consider both its origins and consequences. Doing so will help provide a richer analysis of social movements generally, as well as a greater indication of the future of the lesbian and gay movement in Argentina.

Lesbian and gay activism, especially in developing countries, is an understudied area. Of the major volumes on social movements in Latin America, only one considers mobilization around the issue of sexual orientation (see MacRae 1992). Even the most recent attempts at synthesizing contemporary social movement theory fail to address lesbian and gay movements in any significant way.[2] In addition, major works on "social theory" by the likes of Jürgen Habermas make no mention of sexuality, and works by Ernesto Laclau and Chantal Mouffe and by Pierre Bourdieu barely even acknowledge it (Warner 1993: ix). It is not for a lack of organizing: formal lesbian and gay organizations have existed in the United States since the 1950s and have become prominent in North America and Western Europe in the last quarter of the twentieth century. In Latin America, "Every . . . country except Panama and Paraguay," according to Peter Drucker, "now has an organized gay–lesbian movement, many of them active since the mid-1980s" (1996: 92). To my knowledge, no academic study of the lesbian and gay movement in Argentina has ever been published.

PAST AND PRESENT

The Grupo Nuestro Mundo was founded in November 1969, while Argentina was under a military dictatorship. Although informal gay and lesbian social groups had previously existed, this was the first gay political organization in Argentina—and, in fact, in Latin America. In 1971, the Grupo Nuestro Mundo merged with other groups to form the radical Frente de Liberación Homosexual (FLH), subsequently bringing in ten constituent groups, including left-wing university students, anarchists, and religious associations, most of whose members were men. Even after the 1973 democratic elections and the return to power of Juan Domingo Perón, the FLH remained an underground organization, allying itself closely with the struggles of workers and feminists both nationally and internationally. Following Perón's death in 1974 and during his wife Isabel's presidency, right-wing paramilitary activities explicitly targeting homosexuals rapidly increased. The FLH's membership quickly dropped from one hundred to only a dozen. After the March 1976 military coup, some FLH members were tortured or murdered, and some went into exile. The rest ceased their public activities, and in June the FLH dissolved.[3]

During the Proceso de Reorganización Nacional, as the brutal dictatorship benignly called itself, formal lesbian and gay activism ceased to exist. In 1982 a few groups began to organize once again, and by the end of the year they had formed a rather loose coordination committee (Coordinadora de Grupos Gays). Between January 1982 and November 1983, the dictatorship—on its last leg—led a new wave of murders, claiming the lives of at least eighteen gay men in Buenos Aires, including a former member of the FLH. Only two of the murders were solved. In June 1982, a paramilitary group called the Comando Cóndor issued a statement that it intended to "finish off" the homosexuals. One member of the commission later appointed to investigate disappearances—Comisión Nacional sobre la Desaparición de Personas (CONADEP)—estimates that at least four hundred lesbians and gay men had been "disappeared," though no mention of this is made in the commission's official report, *Nunca Más* (Gays por los Derechos Civiles 1995: 3–4).

With the collapse of the military regime and the return to democracy in 1983, the country witnessed a rapid resurgence of lesbian and gay life. In a new atmosphere of freedom, numerous bars and clubs opened. But it was not the end of repression that sparked the renewal of activism: in March 1984 the police raided the gay club Balvanera, detaining some two hundred people; the owners left the country after receiving a series of threats. The repression, far from having disappeared under democratization, launched the lesbian and gay movement. In April 1984, 150 activists—no doubt inspired by the mass demonstrations that took place toward the end of the dictatorship and the "thirst for new understanding" that followed the discrediting of the military, the state, the church (which had collaborated with the dictatorship), and traditional values (Ferreyra Interview)—met in the gay bar Contramano and founded the Comunidad Homosexual Argentina (CHA). The CHA brought together gay men and lesbians of diverse political beliefs, fourteen of whom were prepared to be publicly identified (Jáuregui 1987: 202). Throughout the rest of the 1980s, the CHA remained the most important group by far, opening chapters in several cities. In the 1990s it went into decline.

The early 1990s were marked by a new proliferation of groups—both mixed/gay male–dominated groups and lesbian groups—at a time when President Carlos Menem's policies were demobilizing popular movements. The feminist lesbian group Las Lunas y las Otras first met in July 1990. Then in 1991 the CHA was granted legal status (*personería jurídica*) after a long struggle, bringing homosexuality to the public's attention and facilitating the formation of new groups. But the CHA soon found itself in the midst of an identity crisis over its concrete goals and strategies. There was much in-fighting, both personal and ideological, and many activists left and formed their own (gay and mixed) groups, such as the Sociedad de Integración Gay-Lésbica Argentina (SIGLA) and the Grupo de Investigación en Sexualidad e Interacción Social (Grupo ISIS) in 1992. Gays y Lesbianas por los Derechos Civiles (Gays DC) was founded in October 1991, also by former members of the CHA. And in September 1991, Ilse Fuskova appeared on national television as an out lesbian, inspiring a new wave of lesbian visibility and activism, including the founding of the group Convocatoria Lesbiana. In May 1991 the first transgender group, Transexuales por el Derecho a la Vida y la Identidad (TRANSDEVI) was founded and held its first demonstration (followed by several other associations). And in July 1992 the first Lesbian and Gay Pride March took place.

Though there has been a clear proliferation of organizations since the early 1990s, these twenty-odd groups are all quite limited in size. Each has a very small core leadership (whether official or de facto) and some peripheral activists who do volunteer work and often participate in demonstrations without necessarily debating or setting policy. Well-publicized, large-scale demonstrations attract participants from a wider pool. Notably, the annual Pride marches attract over one thousand lesbians and gay men who are not otherwise, or at least not formally, involved in the movement. Nonetheless, very little is done to attract new recruits. Though the Pride demonstrations are among the largest in Latin America, the movement is still, as one member of the CHA pointed out (Rojas Interview 1996) a long way from filling the Plaza de Mayo with supporters—the litmus test of Argentinean social movements since Perón.

Nearly all the mixed/gay male–dominated groups split off from the CHA or, like Gays DC, were later founded by former CHA members. Only the youngest of gay activists did not start off in the CHA. Many lesbians who began their activism with the CHA, or at least had some contact with the organization, later left, often over the male members' sexism. Historically, though, the lesbian groups owe much to the feminist movement.

Although certain alliances among like-minded groups (for example, the Frente Lesbiana) were formed and dissolved over the years it was only in 1995 that members of the various groups (mixed/male–dominated groups and female groups) began to meet regularly and work together on short-term projects. As a first activity, they organized a national gathering of lesbian, gay, transvestite, and transsexual (LGTT) organizations, held in Rosario in March 1996. This is now an annual event. (At that point, transgendered people were accepted, at least as close allies, into the lesbian and gay movement.) Their second major task was to organize the fifth annual LGTT Pride March (under its expanded title, which included the transgendered). Held on 28 June 1996—with approximately fifteen hundred participants—it was larger than the previous four annual marches. The third undertaking was the (previously mentioned) campaign to include a clause in the new Buenos Aires municipal charter to prohibit discrimination on the basis of sexual orientation.

POLITICAL OPPORTUNITIES AND THE EMERGENCE OF THE MOVEMENT

Though certain social historical changes on a more structural level—in addition to international diffusion and contacts—had earlier provided the conditions for organization around sexual identity to emerge, it was the collapse of the arch-conservative dictatorship in 1983 that provided an opening for the emergence of a lesbian and gay movement. Redemocratization provided a new space and vocabulary for those seeking lesbian and gay rights.

Argentinean lesbians and gay men, like those in almost all other countries, have a difficult relationship with the state, especially the police, when it comes to their sexuality. The police continually raid bars and clubs and use various regulations to detain lesbians, gay men, and transgendered people without charging them. Transvestites and transsexuals suffer disproportionately from police harassment. For example, Gays DC's legal service intervened in 331 cases of arbitrary arrest of transgendered people from January to November 1995, and they estimate the actual number of such arrests to be ten times higher (Gays por los Derechos Civiles appendix 1 1995:). Many are verbally and physically abused while in custody. Some still disappear and are later found murdered, and the cases go uninvestigated.[4]

Some twenty countries have nondiscrimination laws, only one of which—postapartheid South Africa—is in the developing world. Even in liberal democracies, lesbians and gay men often are not accorded the same rights as other collective groups. In the United States, for example, private consensual gay sex between adults is still outlawed in nineteen states. Argentina never legally forbade sodomitical acts, but lesbians and gay men are not treated equally before the law. Until November 1990, for instance, the province of Buenos Aires legally prohibited lesbians and gay men from voting, though the provision was not enforced (or enforceable). Except in matters under the jurisdiction of the city of Buenos Aires, it is currently perfectly legal to fire employees for being lesbian or gay, refuse them housing for that reason, or otherwise discriminate against them. However, even formal laws are no guarantee of legal protection: an employer can use other reasons to fire an employee, and the police can use other means, including planting evidence, to arrest an individual. In a broader sense, repression is often moral/social and not just physical.

So-called sexual minorities are not historically recognized by the Argentine state as legitimate collective actors and members of civil society. For years, the government refused to grant legal status to the CHA, thus impeding representation and fund-raising. The Supreme Court upheld this decision, citing as justifications the position of the Catholic Church, protection of the family, and medical opinion (Robinson 1991: 43a, 46a). Political parties of the Left have sometimes supported lesbian and gay rights and placed openly lesbian and gay candidates on their lists, but not one has ever been elected. Much of the Left has refused to ally itself with gay politics, either out of prejudice or fear of losing popular support. There is no Argentinean counterpart to the Brazilian Workers Party, which works with a wide range of social movements, including the lesbian and gay movement. In any case, Argentina is historically a two-party system: the Radicals and *Justicilistas* (Peronists), neither of which has demonstrated much sympathy for homosexual causes, alternately hold the reins of power. Pluralism clearly has its limits when it comes to interest representation regarding sexuality, among other issues. Nonetheless, the rise of a third party provides hope for lesbian and gay Argentineans. A few members of the center-left front known as the FREPASO have supported nondiscrimination measures in recent years. They could well influence public policy on the national level if they form a coalition government with the Radicals after the 1999 presidential elections.

From the very beginning, the CHA's strategy was to build bridges with other social movements on such issues as human rights, violence, and later AIDS. The effort to join with other people and groups who had suffered under military rule is clear in the first paid advertisement promoting gay and lesbian rights, published by the CHA in the 28 May 1984 issue of *El Clarín*) under the headline "WITH DISCRIMINATION AND REPRESSION THERE IS NO DEMOCRACY" (reproduced in Jáuregui 1987: 225). The ad further states, "No true democracy can exist if society permits the continuance of marginalized sectors and the various means of repression that still prevail," and it speaks of more than 1.5 million homosexual citizens "who . . . are worried about the national situation and who, like you, went through the hard years of the dictatorship."[5] Readers, who at that point were highly likely to be opposed to military rule, were thus invited to relate to gay men and lesbians and support their right to be free of discrimination and repression under a democratic system, regardless of the readers' own personal views on homosexuality.

At first, the CHA deliberately used the human rights discourse—which had achieved much legitimacy in contributing to the collapse of the military dictatorship—to promote lesbian and gay rights and to create links with other human rights organizations. It chose as its motto: "Freedom to express one's sexuality is a human right."[6] Over the next three years, however, President Raúl Alfonsín's government repeatedly caved in to military demands, and the human rights discourse was severely discredited. As a consequence, in 1987 the CHA changed tactics almost overnight, deciding to concentrate on AIDS. Suddenly HIV/AIDS appeared as the main topic of its newsletter, *Vamos a Andar*, and the CHA launched its "Stop AIDS" program. To the detriment of activism around sexual orientation, it then concentrated much of its energy on obtaining legal status.

The international arena also provided key models and support for activism in Argentina. From the days of the FLH to the present, Argentinean lesbian and gay publications have reflected a great awareness of the lives of gay men and lesbians all over the world, especially in the United States and Western Europe—their activism, political struggles and victories, and cultural activities. Adopting as their own the international symbols and representations and reclaiming historical figures, Argentineans have reinforced the diffusion of a global, essentialized identity. Of course, the significance of being gay or lesbian differs in different contexts, just as culture and practices differ from place to place. But international opportunity structures have contributed to the Argentinean lesbian and gay movement. For example, transnational linkages were very important in the CHA's efforts to win its *personería jurídica*, obtained through a coordinated international campaign to raise the issue while Menem was on an official visit to the United States in November 1991.[7] Gay groups' AIDS programs have received funding from foreign organizations ranging from the Norwegian Red Cross to the American Foundation for AIDS Research. Funding virtually dried up around 1994, however, and there are currently no AIDS-awareness campaigns or safer-sex outreach programs in Argentina (Hourcade Interview 1996).

Several long-time Argentinean activists cite inspiration from their brothers and sisters abroad in their struggle, sometimes through extended firsthand contact. Ilse Fuskova claims that she would never have found the courage to be among the first nationally out lesbians had she not spent several years working with lesbians in Germany and San Francisco. The idea of lesbian and gay archives was also foreign derived. International connections, now often via the Internet, and regional and worldwide gatherings (such as the Beijing Women's Conference, periodic Latin American Feminist Meetings, or meetings sponsored by the International Lesbian and Gay Association) play an important part in further diffusing lesbian and gay culture and representations and creating a greater sense of community. Thus, above and beyond "political opportunities" provided by financial assistance, both the prior international diffusion of lesbian and gay identity and the international models of activism contributed to the emergence and expansion of activism in Argentina.

IDENTITY AND POLITICS

Much of the literature on social movements emphasizes "resource mobilization" and the achievement of policy results. It analyzes collective action "in terms of the logic of strategic interaction and cost benefit analysis," using "such 'objective' variables as organization, interests, resources, opportunities and strategies" (Cohen 1985: 674–75). Indeed, the mechanics and outcomes of protest movements are important and certainly an improvement over earlier grievance-based conceptions of social movements. More broadly speaking, the "political opportunity structures" approach provides a valuable model for using opportunities and constraints that the movement must face to better understand the dynamics of the case. For Argentina, this has meant relating the lesbian and gay movement to democratization, the human rights discourse that emerged in the early 1980s, and international support. Yet when studying the Argentinean lesbian and gay movement, these are analytically insufficient. This emphasis ignores motivation; differing understandings, beliefs, priorities, and visions; and dynamic and sometimes contradictory relationships between individuals and groups, so much of which hinges on identity.

Since "these 'political opportunities' are but a necessary prerequisite to action," the current consensus in comparative social movements is to consider as well the "framing process," defined as "the conscious strategic efforts by groups of people to fashion shared understandings of the world and of themselves that legitimate and motivate collective action" (McAdam, McCarthy, and Zald 1996: 6, 8). In practice, however, this is too often reduced to prevailing culture and ideas/ideology, without considering the nature of identity. While trying not to "reproduce the ideological self-understanding of actors or slip into a social-psychological analysis of struggle" that would characterize a "pure identity-oriented analysis of social movements" (Cohen 1985: 695), I now turn to identity formation and its relationship to lesbian and gay politics in Argentina.

Same-sex eroticism does not necessarily create a homosexual identity in societies any more than it does in individuals. Just as many people who engage in it do not inevitably see or define themselves as any different from anyone else, societies do not naturally have "homosexuals." In Argentina homosexuality as we understand it today was invented, or historically emerged, just as it did elsewhere over the past 120 years or less. Though homosexual acts (same-sex eroticism) have existed throughout history and across cultures, it is only over the last century that the behavior has been legally codified as pertaining to a certain type of person. The medical discourse contributed much to this epistemological transition—see, for example, the works of Michel Foucault (1990) and, as applied to Argentina, Jorge Salessi (1995).

Rapidly expanding capitalism and urbanization also contributed to the invention of homosexuality. Notably, freeing labor from the household by means of wage earning allowed individuals, especially men, to live in cities where they could separate their public (work) lives from their private (sexual) lives, a division that was next to impossible in preindustrial rural locales. Freed from the family unit, a person could hide his or her sexuality at work and "be gay" in his or her free time. One's circle of friends could then be determined less by kinship and geographical proximity than by common sexual orientation. Urban spatial and commercial factors have also been important. Places to meet other homosexuals—usually bars but also (for gay men) public "cruising" areas—presented the industrial-age homosexual with new possibilities for congregation and group identification. For many, so-called public spaces sometimes afforded more privacy than their places of abode: Argentineans typically lived with extended families, and day laborers, especially immigrants, often stayed in boardinghouses. As women entered the work force, a similar process of separation of work and leisure allowed them to organize their personal lives around their sexuality (D'Emilio 1993).

There was a gradual, simultaneous change in the sexual categories and their interpretations. In the past, sexuality was defined by gender role, so that only the *pasivo* man in anal intercourse (the insertee) or "active" woman was marked by deviance, whereas the *activo* male (the inserter) and "passive" woman retained their status as normal.[8] Increasingly, sexuality has depended on the (anatomical) sex of the object of one's desire; thus anyone having intercourse with a member of the same sex, regardless of gendered roles, is defined as a homosexual. In New York City, for example, this shift reportedly took place around the 1930s for middle-class white men and later among the working classes and ethnic minorities (Chauncey 1994). In Argentina, this new sexual "regime" arguably became dominant around the 1970s, though it is not completely hegemonic today and has increased the number of individuals who may identify as gay or lesbian.

The common use of the rather clinical term "homosexual" and the English word "gay" reflect the Euro-American influence on the formation and labeling of identity. The colloquial local terms *puto, maricón, torta,* and *trava* are more deprecatory but are being reclaimed (much as are "fag," "queer," "dyke," and "tranny" in parts of the English-speaking world).

They are also considered more traditional or working-class appellations than "bourgeois" monikers like "gay" and "homosexual." Both kinds of terms are commonly used by activists, one for official communication and the other in conversation.

Though it may explain the rise of a relatively widespread lesbian and gay identity, the industrialization argument is not sufficient to cause the emergence of a movement. If rapid industrialization/urbanization occurred in Argentina in the 1940s and 1950s, why did noticeable lesbian and gay activism not arise until around 1970 and emerge more definitively as a movement only after 1984? Clearly other factors came into play.

I surmise that the timing of the emergence of gay activism owes much to events that marked a high point in an international protest cycle, including the 1969 Stonewall riots in New York,[9] mass student demonstrations in France and Mexico in 1968, opposition in the United States to the Vietnam War, the growing women's liberation movement, and left-wing activism across Latin American (inspired by the Cuban revolution) and in Europe. Argentina—whose inhabitants have long looked abroad (especially to Europe) for a cultural model—was especially open to responding to these events. It also followed the growth of overt domestic opposition to the military regime, marked by the protests in Córdoba (known as the *Cordobazo*), burgeoning left-wing activism, and the prominent guerrilla movement. Thus, I share the "suspicion that spin-off movements owe less to expanding political opportunities than to complex diffusion processes by which the ideational, tactical, and organizational lessons of the early risers are made available to subsequent challengers" (McAdam, McCarthy, and Zald 1996: 33), at least in the case of the FLH in the early 1970s. In other words, it was not so much a change in domestic conditions that led to the birth of gay activism; activism arose instead as part of a national and international moment of contesting established social relations (inspired by and learned from other actors) and adapting to local conditions (presumably inspiring others in turn).

In the early 1970s, an FLH member group adopted the controversial slogan "We don't have to liberate homosexuals; we must liberate the homosexual in everyone,"[10] echoing an earlier call by the New York–based Gay Liberation Front to "liberate the homosexual in everyone." This implied that gay people were essentially no different from heterosexuals; they had merely opened themselves up to a potential that all people have. This does not mean that the group wanted everyone to be gay; quite the contrary, it aimed to eliminate categories of people based on sexual orientation.

A fundamental contradiction arises from organizing around identity: it actually reinforces the categories and the boundaries between them (Taylor and Whittier 1992: 111). In the case of Argentina, and presumably elsewhere, the growth of lesbian and gay visibility has had an effect on *hetero*sexual identity as well and has tightened the boundaries of what is acceptable for straight people. For example, one lesbian activist recounted (Marek Interview 1996) that a straight woman once complained to her that all the talk about lesbianism made her avoid physical affection with her female friends for fear that people might think she was a lesbian.

Consistently told in myriad ways that homosexuality is wrong, perverted, or evil, gay men and lesbians need to affirm that it is good, or at least acceptable. Thrown into a stigmatized collectivity, they rarely challenge the existence of the category; they reclaim it. Concomitantly, they will resist the heterosexualization of their space. An interesting illustrative event occurred when representatives of the Liga Marxista and the Liga Socialista Revolucionaria, two very small left-wing groups, attended a June 1996 coordination meeting for the Pride march. They offered their support for the march, even though they considered sexual orientation irrelevant, and requested that the groups lend their voices to defend two left-wing political prisoners being held in Neuquén. This dismissal of the importance of sexuality met with an angry response: "I am proud to be a faggot," asserted one activist, to much agreement. No one defended the idea that the lesbian and gay movement should collectively mobilize on behalf of heterosexuals, though it was understood that groups and individuals should feel free to do so if they so chose. "We have our own history, saints and martyrs," replied another activist.[11]

In Argentina, the first wave of activism was radical, as epitomized by the Frente de Liberación Homosexual (1969–76), followed—after a seven-year hiatus because of military repression—by the integrationist tendencies of the CHA (mid- to late 1980s). With the formation of many new groups in the 1990s, however, Argentinean lesbian and gay activists have adopted a wide range of approaches and strategies that are sometimes mutually exclusive. For heuristic purposes, I divide contemporary Argentinean lesbian and gay political organizations into three different categories: (1) assimilationist groups, which seek to integrate the lesbian and gay community into the "mainstream," arguing that they are separated only by prejudice, or homophobia, (2) civil rights-based organizations, which mainly seek state-based legal guarantees and protection for sexual minorities, and (3) radical groups, which tend to deconstruct sexual identity.[12]

Assimilationist Groups

Assimilationist organizations, such as the CHA of the 1990s and SIGLA, preach integration into mainstream Argentinean society. Whereas the FLH chose to present the effeminate gay man and the butch lesbian as the most radical figures, these groups seek to portray homosexuals as essentially the same as everyone else, properly dressed in clothing commonly considered appropriate to their sex and manifesting little or no outward sign of gender deviance. They periodically protest defamation and discrimination, including through legal challenges. However, unlike the clandestine FLH, they desire recognition rather than the promotion of sexual liberation and the creation of a new order. These activists tend not to question, as did the FLH, the construction of sexuality. For them, lesbian and gay rights are but part of a redefinition of the relationship between the state and civil society, according the latter greater autonomy. Because their strategy is to "normalize" homosexuality, they often prefer to work with various human rights organizations and sometimes even the government than to work with other lesbian and gay groups. Alejandro Zalazar, CHA president from 1986 to 1997, accepted a human rights position with the Ministry of the Interior, which in the eyes of many activists severely discredited both him and the CHA. Assimilationist groups are especially reluctant to accept bisexuality, because it puts in question the assumptions about people being either homo- or heterosexual (Udis-Kessler 1996), and are reluctant to work with transgendered people, because of their obvious difference in appearance and gender ambiguity, and even on the assumption that they do not have a politics.[13]

Civil Rights Groups

Civil rights–oriented groups try to "normalize" homosexuality using a different-but-equal argument, rather than one based on sameness. In 1991, Gays DC was founded to protect the civil (not human) rights of gays and lesbians, deliberately refocusing the arena of struggle on civil society rather than in opposition to the state. Its motto, "Our struggle originates in the desire for all types of freedom,"[14] indicated a desire to build bridges with other communities. Until its collapse at the end of 1996, Gays DC provided legal services to "sexual minorities" and HIV-positive individuals in the private and public sector, in case of discrimination or arrest. It worked actively for equal rights for homosexuals, such as the right to adopt or marry and the campaign (which it spearheaded) for protection under the new Buenos Aires municipal charter. Its strategy was thus to seek the repeal of discriminatory laws, the nondiscriminatory application of existing laws, and the enactment of legal instruments to protect the LGTT community from discrimination. This was done through a combination of casework, lobbying, and public demonstrations. Visibility, one of the main goals of Lesbianas a la Vista as well, is a means of justifying increased attention to the needs of the LGTT community, a strategy for putting and keeping the issue on the public agenda. Given the risks of coming out in Argentine society, only a small minority of gay men and lesbians are open about their sexuality. The visibility strategy is thus also focused on civil society as a means to change attitudes and end discrimination.

The use of a discourse of "sexual minorities" implies treatment as a quasi-ethnic group, a tactic that echoes and updates the early CHA technique for linking groups and individuals that suffered from repression under the dictatorship. However, these activists carefully avoid mention of "human rights," as the term has lost the power it had in Argentina between 1983 and 1987. They encourage people, instead, to make connections between various positions of disadvantage, often stigmatized (though none more than homosexuality), and focus on discrimination rather than the nature of difference. For example, Gays DC cosponsored a campaign entitled "There is a cure for discrimination,"[15] distributing twenty-thousand pamphlets on rights for sexual minorities and plastering fifteen thousand posters across the city.

The civil rights activist groups, whose members often work in an ad hoc coalition, simultaneously resist the intrusion of the state into the private sphere and seek new state-sponsored legal guarantees and tools to protect equality. Indeed, state recognition is very important to some gay organizations (recall the CHA's struggle for legal status), and the movement seeks to ensure its members' access to equal protection under the law, as befits a liberal democratic system. It is nonetheless very much opposed to the state's repressive apparatus, as well as to the church's position on homosexuality and other social issues. In fact, the theme of the 1995 Pride march was "Discrimination condemns us; the police kill us; we're still standing."[16] This ambiguous relationship between the movement and the state (reflecting a position that is also both defensive and offensive) belies the tendency in much of the literature to present social movements as a clear-cut case of society vs. the state. These actors insert themselves into the existing political and economic structures and adopt what Jean Cohen refers to as "self-limiting radicalism" (1985: 664, 670). Pursuing "the path of civil rights" implies consciously choosing "legal reform, political access, visibility, and legitimation over the long-term goals of cultural acceptance, social transformation, understanding, and liberation"; as American lesbian activist Urvashi Vaid points out (1995: 106, 179), "civil rights can be won without displacing the moral and sexual hierarchy that enforces antigay stigmatization: you do not have to recognize the fundamental humanity of gay people in order to agree that they should be treated equally and fairly under the law."

A key ally in any visibility-oriented strategy is the news media. Without coverage, the impact of a demonstration is strictly limited. The media can diffuse the images and ideas to millions of readers and viewers and thus "play a central role in the construction of meaning and the reproduction of culture" (McAdam, McCarthy, and Zald 1996: 287). Argentinean activists are very successful at garnering media coverage for their events. They do so by combining good personal relations with journalists and the design of innovative images that attract media attention, without necessarily closing off channels of institutional influence, as they would if they used violence. Indeed, as McAdam, McCarthy, and Zald state, the most effective strategy involves "master[ing] the art of simultaneously playing to a variety of publics, threatening opponents, and pressuring the state, all the while appearing nonthreatening and sympathetic to the media and other publics" (1996: 344).

Radical Groups

I would characterize radical groups, such as the University of Buenos Aires–based Colectivo Eros and the Grupo de Jóvenes Gays y Lesbianas "Construyendo Nuestra Sexualidad," primarily by their rejection of the system. They tend to be mixed and function mainly internally. Both groups participate in wider political actions, but the Colectivo Eros works mainly on university-based issues and activities, and the principal function of the Grupo de Jóvenes Gays y Lesbianas is to provide an arena for young people struggling with their sexuality. Though the latter began as a closed discussion group, it is now advertising its meetings and trying to attract new members. Members are particularly visible at demonstrations.

These groups have apparently adopted a more social constructivist approach to sexuality, rejecting the prevalent essentialized notions about fixed "either/or" sexuality. Instead, they prefer to see sexual orientation as a continuum, in which all people have varying degrees of proclivities (which can also vary over time), and to avoid rigidly dividing the world into homo and hetero, even with a residual "bi" category. They attach value to gay and sexual liberation, often reclaiming the heritage of the FLH and likewise valuing their marginality, pointing out that rights discourse places no value on difference. These activists openly criticize the mainstream movement for failing to adopt a longer-term view and analysis, as well as for making concessions in exchange for tolerance. They are particularly vehement in their disagreement with the tactics of some of the assimilationist groups, in at least one case considering them worse enemies than the police "because at least the police don't pretend to be our friends." (Talavera Interview 1996) The radical groups are also a lot more likely to link not just oppressed groups (like the previous categories in my typology) but also causes of oppression under capitalism. They trace links between neoliberal policies, high unemployment, poverty, alienation, anomie, discrimination, and so forth. For example, they argue that the question of AIDS cannot be divorced from the health care and education systems, both of which are under attack from current economic policies. Their ultimate goal is not just equality for lesbians and gays but a transformation of society, not just in terms of sexuality but in terms of liberation of the human spirit. In spite (or perhaps because) of their more radical outlook, these groups find it difficult to define a concrete strategy, partly because their goals are so abstract. In addition, multiple goals tend to spread resources thin and promote internal divisions over prioritization (McAdam, McCarthy, and Zald 1996: 15). The collective's main achievement in 1997 was the establishment of a queer studies center at the university. As far as I am aware, these groups do not translate their analysis into activities that differ radically from those of other groups.

Cooperation and Identity

In spite of their differences, collaboration between these diverse groups is possible, for it is true that "Movements may largely be born of environmental opportunities, but their fate is heavily shaped by their own actions" (McAdam, McCarthy, and Zald 1996: 15). During the 1990s, encouraged by increased lesbian and gay visibility, many groups were formed to fill the gaps that initially the CHA and later others did not fill, some the result of factionalism, others the result of separate lesbian organizing. Rather suddenly, these groups began to work together in 1995, owing to a combination of several factors, among them the inclusion of transgender issues, personal contacts, group self-confidence, willingness to compromise, and international examples. However, although AIDS may have been an underlying motivating factor it played little or no direct role in coalition building, despite the fact that an estimated 70–80 percent of HIV transmission is through homosexual contact. Nevertheless, the dreams of ever closer cooperation dissipated by the end of 1996, as ideological cleavages resurfaced, rooted in contradictory conceptions of identity and strategies.

As Joshua Gamson points out (1995: 391), "Fixed identity categories are both the basis for oppression and the basis of political power." To eliminate the categories of sexual orientation would end oppression yet also destroy the identity of the activists, which is unimaginable to most, if not all. Yet accepting transgendered people into a common movement was a first step to dismantling the restricted essentialized identity of "lesbian or gay." Surprisingly, contrary to the

situation in North America, Australia, and Western Europe, this occurred in Argentina before the inclusion of bisexuals. In fact, it is only
since June 1996 that bisexuality has been addressed at all in the LGTT
movement in Argentina. At that time a male and a female activist
openly entered into a romantic relationship, creating much uproar in
the community. The woman was told that she had forfeited the right to
speak on behalf of lesbians. Now it seems that bisexuality is being progressively integrated into the movement's discourse, a second step to
dismantling the homo/hetero binary. In November 1996 a number of
groups formally agreed to henceforth include bisexuals as a separate
category when naming "sexual minorities" in public documents and
events (Sardá 1996a).

In Argentina, with the exception of the assimilationists, it appears that
the multiplicity of categories is being embraced, albeit somewhat reluctantly at times (though the categories are not being collapsed into an
equivalent of "queer"). Nonetheless, "the postmodern celebration of diversity" is insufficient (B. Epstein 1990: 58). It must be made desirable; it
must be made into a strength. As Steven Epstein writes (1987: 99),
"Rather than reifying difference into a defensive separatism or dissolving
it into a false vision of homogeneity, we need to acquire an appreciation
for difference as harmless, perhaps synergistic."[17] There has to be a middle ground between assimilation and isolation, where diversity is seen as
an asset. Otherwise, any social movement will waste its potential for
broader social change.

The idea of a "global community" of lesbians and gays is a misleading
one, for it erases other power differentials. As Vaid writes (1995: 286),
"A false assumption underlies all gay and lesbian organizing: that there is
something at once singular and universal that can be called gay or lesbian
or bisexual or even transgendered identity." Argentinean lesbians and gay
men cannot be detached from local conditions and other subject posi-
tionings, such as class, gender, and race/ethnicity. At some point, individual activists and the movement in general have to acknowledge that
"identities cannot be frozen or lived outside of interaction with other
identities. Individuals occupy multiple social positions, and no interpretation of those positions could long endure that dissolved all of them into
a single, totalizing identity" (Plotke 1990: 94).

Identity politics is thus eventually bound to reach an impasse by isolating one defining variable. The integrationist/assimilationist organizations have already rejected identity politics to a certain degree, by
seeking to collaborate with other (nonsexually-defined) groups. But
they do so more by abandoning than by embracing their difference. The
alternative would be to move beyond, rather than to deny, the basis for

differentiation according to sexual orientation, perhaps along the lines of a right to "sexual dissent" (Duggan, 1995).

Lesbian and gay movements are an excellent example of the "new paradigm of politics": social movement actors valuing "personal autonomy and identity" and seeking civil equality rather than organizing as a socioeconomic group seeking the redistribution of wealth or the conquest of political power. Furthermore, these organizations tend to be informal, spontaneous, with a low degree of horizontal and vertical differentiation, unlike formal, large-scale, representative organizations partaking in pluralist or corporatist interest intermediation under the "old paradigm" (Offe 1985: 832). Perhaps it would be preferable to speak, therefore, not of "new social movements" but of "new democratic struggles," as Chantal Mouffe suggests (quoted in Slater 1991: 32).

In summary, I argue that the emergence of lesbian and gay activism depended on the prior creation and diffusion (through national and international opportunity structures) of lesbian and gay identities, which in turn rested on certain social/historical conditions that came into being in the 1940s and 1950s. The foundation of the FLH occurred decades later, owing more to a global and local protest cycle and the diffusion of ideas than to an actual change in local conditions. Its demise, however, was due to domestic factors alone: new, insurmountable constraints in the form of a sudden increase in violent repression and the military coup of 1976. The emergence of the movement and the foundation of the CHA in 1984 were the direct result of a democratic opening, which gave activists (1) new opportunities (such as access to the media and the possibility of holding peaceful demonstrations) to oppose the violence and discrimination that, contrary to their expectations, they continued to experience under democratic rule, (2) a new human rights discourse with which to link their struggle with others who had opposed military rule, and (3) greater access to international models of political organizing and support. The expansion of the movement after 1990 was due to a combination of increased visibility, a narrow focus and incompatible views within the CHA, and the emergence of separate lesbian organizations. The lesbian and gay groups, in their various ways, have taken advantage of these new opportunities and, through their actions, have created additional opportunities.

However, this analysis is incomplete without a deeper look at identity. Without considering their visions of identity, we cannot fully understand the differences among lesbian and gay groups, how they can or cannot work together, what the dynamics are, and what the future may hold. When examining lesbian and gay movements, it is insufficient to consider them as one does other so-called new social movements. For race- and ethnicity-based movements, for example, identity is acquired in the home, the family, the neighborhood, based on physical and cultural differences. For lesbians and gay men, identity is a result of a historically constructed, transgressive sexual desire that sometimes becomes a fundamental point of personal definition. It would be naive to treat lesbians and gay men as merely a subculture or as one would, for example, treat members of the peace movement. For the lesbian and gay movement, looking at identity provides a valuable tool for understanding a complex and dynamic situation that political opportunity structures alone cannot fully explain.

Given the never ending conflicts within a very diverse community and the often contradictory strategies and goals, it is my impression that, for the time being, the different groups will continue to cooperate around specific short-term issues and actions but will not become any more unified. Yet they are taking steps to erode rigid boundary systems, notably in their recent inclusion of bisexuals and transgendered people under the same banner as lesbians and gay men. This could eventually lead to a lesser emphasis on issues geared toward a discrete community and a greater emphasis on issues that affect a wider and less-defined group of people who lack equal opportunities.

How can the lesbian, gay, bisexual, and transgender movement best achieve its goals? Much depends on the very identification of goals. The macrogoal of assimilationists—the integration of gay men and lesbians into the "mainstream"—would require the end of any discourse of difference, which their strategies and activities do not do much to promote. In any case, given the strength of identity and prejudice, this does not seem possible.

Current civil rights strategies are reasonably effective in Buenos Aires, but change on the national level is proving much more limited. To achieve more radical change, including in the cultural sphere, could require moving beyond identity politics in tandem with other (nonsexually-defined) actors. This would imply a further limitation of collaboration with accommodationist lesbian and gay activists, who value acceptance over challenges to broader issues of social change.

Drucker (1996: 101) concludes:

> The vision of gay–lesbian liberation in each country will be developed out of its movement's own experiences, and through dialogue among different currents. But the most fruitful approaches to gay–lesbian liberation will probably be those that combine sexual radicalism with coalition-building, link gay–lesbian demands with strategies for broader social transformation, and build unitary left organizations alongside independent lesbian and gay groups. Left opposition to repression and discrimination, and left support for self-organization by oppressed people are the keys.

Faith in the Left, however, may be misplaced, given its limited strength in Argentina in the 1990s and its weak commitment to lesbian and gay rights. Other social movements may constitute better allies as agents of change, ones that share a more holistic analysis of current socioeconomic problems. Trade unions, for example, which have a long activist history in Argentina, would theoretically make good partners for change. But given the current difficult economic and political situation in Argentina, social movements in general tend to be increasingly on the defensive, trying to maintain what they have achieved since democratization rather than demanding new concessions. For those who seek it, social transformation therefore remains a very long-term project.

NOTES

Acknowledgments: Previous versions of this chapter were presented at the Latin American Studies Association conference in Guadalajara, Mexico, on 19 April 1997 and at the Ninety-second Annual Meeting of the American Sociological Association in Toronto, Canada, on 10 August 1997. This essay is based on twenty-odd in-depth interviews that I held with activists belonging to a dozen lesbian, gay, and transgender organizations in Buenos Aires in May and June 1996 and in February 1997. During my visits, I attended numerous planning meetings, demonstrations, fund-raisers, and social events. I also interviewed several members of human rights and AIDS organizations that undertake relevant activities.

I am grateful to all those who commented on earlier drafts of this essay, especially Elisabeth J. Wood, whose support was invaluable from the very beginning. I also thank Christopher Mitchell and New York University's Center for Latin American and Caribbean Studies for providing an initial research grant, without which this project would never have been possible. Finally, I am grateful to the numerous Argentineans (and one Uruguayan) whose generous assistance made the research process both fascinating and enjoyable.

1. As the title of this chapter indicates, I focus primarily on lesbian and gay activism; however, I also sometimes include transgender issues. I use "transgendered" to denote individuals who are called *travestis* and *transexuales* in Argentina. Here, terminology is confusing, because a *travesti* in Argentina is not a transvestite, cross-dresser, or drag queen (referred to as *transformista* in Argentina); *travesti* refers instead to what is often called in North America a "pre-op" transsexual. In Argentina, *transexual* refers solely to someone having undergone genital reassignment surgery. Bisexuality is only beginning to be addressed in the movement. I avoid using the term "queer," now in vogue in North American scholarship, because it is rarely used in Argentina and, in fact, is often deliberately resisted for its erasure of difference among a diverse community of non-heterosexuals.

2. See McAdam, McCarthy, and Zald 1996. Only one chapter—Hanspieter Kriesi's "The Organizational Structure of New Social Movements in a Political

Context"—discusses the existence of a gay "collective identity," and yet the chapter treats it as merely an unproblematized "subcultural movement" not unlike many others (158).

3. It is not clear whether FLH members were persecuted as members of the organization, as gays or lesbians, as left-wing activists, or as a combination of these. For more information on the FLH, see Perlongher 1985; and Green 1994.

4. For example, Mocha Celis, a thirty-four-year old *travesti* prostitute whose life had been repeatedly threatened by the police, was seen getting into a police car on 18 August 1996. Later that night, she was found bleeding on the street, shot twice in the penis. She was immediately hospitalized but died soon after. The police maintain that they have found no leads (Sardá 1996d).

5. All translations are my own. The original text reads, "CON DISCRIMINACION Y REPRESION NO HAY DEMOCRACIA. . . . No existirá democracia verdadera si la sociedad permite la subsistencia de los sectores marginados y de los diversos métodos de represión aún vigentes," and it speaks of "personas que . . . nos preocupamos por la realidad nacional y transitamos junto a Ud. los duros años de la dictadura."

6. The Spanish reads, "El libre ejercicio de la sexualidad es un derecho humano."

7. Menem was essentially shamed into issuing a decree recognizing the CHA. Among the groups that participated were the International Lesbian and Gay Association, the (U.S.) National Gay and Lesbian Task Force, the AIDS Coalition to Unleash Power (ACT UP), and the World Congress of Gay and Lesbian Jewish Organizations (Julian 1991: 50–51). For more information on the role of the transnational assistance and local actors in Argentina, see Brysk 1993.

8. For further discussion of differing sexual models among Latin Americans and Latinos, see Almaguer 1993; and Murray 1995.

9. Stonewall symbolically marks the beginning of the gay liberation movement in the United States.

10. The original slogan is "No hay que liberar al homosexual; hay que liberar lo homosexual de cada persona."

11. The original quotes are "Soy orgulloso de ser puto" and "Tenemos nuestra propia historia, santos y mártires."

12. I have omitted from my typology of political groups: archival organizations (such as the Biblioteca Gay-Lésbica and Escrita en el Cuerpo), whose primary function is to collect documentation for public access; religious groups (like the Iglesia de la Comunidad Metropolitana), which provide for the spiritual needs of the community; and research organizations (for example, Grupo ISIS), which are more interested in scientific and social scientific issues surrounding homosexuality. Membership in these types of groups does not preclude membership in more politically oriented groups; in fact, members of these groups often support political work and participate in political demonstrations. Moreover, I do not discuss lesbian separatist groups, such as Las Lunas y las Otras and the recently dissolved Madres Lesbianas. These groups provide a women-only space for discussion and analysis, personal growth, and cultural expression. Their strategies involve reaching greater self-awareness, raised consciousness, and empowerment

through women- and lesbian-only activities, outside the reach of patriarchy. The closeted nature of their activities precludes political activism in the public sphere. Finally, I have excluded the various transgender organizations—such as the Asociación de Travestis Argentinas, Travestis Unidas, the Organización de Travestis y Transexuales Argentinas, and the Asociación por la Lucha de la Identidad de las Travestis—because I do not have sufficient information to distinguish them conceptually and analytically. Moreover, the struggle of transgendered people is somewhat different from that of gay men and lesbians: they seek a recognition of their personal gender identity rather than their sexual orientation, a demand considered more radical by most. Nonetheless, transgender militancy is strong and visible. Since the lesbian and gay movement itself is concentrated in the Buenos Aires area, that is where I focus my attention, though some groups—notably the Colectivo Arco-Iris in Rosario—have formed outside the capital, including, most recently, groups in Jujuy, Lobos, Neuquén, and Mar del Plata (where the church is more influential and people tend to be more socially conservative).

13. Freda Interview 1996: 28. Rafael Freda was the former CHA vice-president and is the current president of SIGLA. Nonetheless, the CHA appointed a transsexual to its executive in April 1996. She resigned in frustration before the end of the year (Berkins Interview, 1997).

14. The Spanish reads, "En el origen de nuestra lucha está el deseo de todas las libertades."

15. "La discriminación tiene cura" is the original slogan.

16. In Spanish it's "La discriminación nos condena; la policía nos mata; seguimos de pie."

17. In a footnote to this sentence, he observes, "This implies a greater degree of acceptance among the gay community of those who stand at the 'boundary,' namely bisexuals."

REFERENCES

Almaguer, Tomás. 1993. "Chicano Men: A Cartography of Homosexual Identity and Behavior." In *The Lesbian and Gay Studies Reader*. Ed. Henry Abelove, Michèle Aina Barale, and David M. Halperin. New York: Routledge.

Berkins, Lohanna. 1997. Interview by Stephen Brown. Buenos Aires, 6 February.

Brysk, Alison. 1993. "From Above and Below: Social Movements, the International System, and Human Rights in Argentina." *Comparative Political Studies* 26 (October): 259–85.

Chauncey, George. 1994. *Gay New York: Gender, Urban Culture, and the Making of the Gay Male World, 1890–1940*. New York: Basic.

Cohen, Jean L. 1985. "'Strategy or Identity': New Theoretical Paradigms and Contemporary Social Movements." *Social Research* 59, no. 4 (Winter): 663–717.

D'Emilio, John. 1993. "Capitalism and Gay Identity." In *The Lesbian and Gay Studies Reader*. Ed. Henry Abelove, Michèle Aina Barale, and David M. Halperin. New York: Routledge.

Drucker, Peter. 1996. "'In the Tropics There Is No Sin': Sexuality and Gay–Lesbian Movements in the Third World." *New Left Review* 218 (July–August): 75–101.

Duggan, Lisa. 1995. "Queering the State." In *Sex Wars: Sexual Dissent and Political Culture.* Ed. Lisa Duggan and Nan D. Hunter. New York: Routledge.

Epstein, Barbara. 1990. "Rethinking Social Movement Theory." *Socialist Review* 20 (90/91): 35–65.

Epstein, Steven. 1987. "Gay Politics, Ethnic Identity: The Limits of Social Constructionism." *Socialist Review* 17 (93–94): 9–54.

Ferreyra, Marcelo. 1996. Interview by Stephen Brown, Buenos Aires, 23 May.

Freda, Rafael. 1996. Interview. "Al Enemigo no lo vamos a vencer nunca." *NX* 3 (June).

Foucault, Michel. 1990. *The History of Sexuality, Volume I: An Introduction.* Trans. Robert Hurley. New York: Vintage.

Gamson, Joshua. 1995. "Must Identity Movements Self-destruct? A Queer Dilemma." *Social Problems* 42 no. 3 (August): 390–407.

Gays por los Derechos Civiles. 1995. "Violaciones de derechos humanos y civiles en la República Argentina basadas en la orientación sexual de las personas y de las personas viviendo con VIH/SIDA." 3d ed. (December).

Green, James N. 1994. "Feathers and Fists: A Comparative Analysis of the Argentine and Brazilian Gay Rights Movements of the 1970s." Paper presented at the Seventeenth International Congress of the Latin American Studies Association, Atlanta, 10 March.

Hourcade, Javier. 1996. Interview by Stephen Brown. Buenos Aires, 4 June.

Jáuregui, Carlos Luis. 1987. *La homosexualidad en la Argentina.* Buenos Aires: Ediciones Tarso.

Julian, Robert. 1991. "A Decisive Time for Argentina Gays." *The Advocate,* 17 (December): 50–51.

MacRae, Edward. 1992. "Homosexual Identities in Transitional Brazilian Politics." In *The Making of Social Movements in Latin America: Identity, Strategy and Democracy.* Ed. Arturo Escobar and Sonia E. Álvarez. Boulder, Colo.: Westview.

Marek, Claudina. 1996. Interview by Stephen Brown. Buenos Aire, 3 June.

McAdam, Doug, John D. McCarthy, and Meyer N. Zald, eds. 1996. *Comparative Perspectives on Social Movements: Political Opportunities, Mobilizing Structures, and Cultural Framings.* Cambridge: Cambridge University Press.

Murray, Stephen O. 1995. *Latin American Male Homosexualities.* Albuquerque: University of New Mexico Press.

Offe, Claus. 1985. "New Social Movements: Challenging the Boundaries of International Politics." *Social Research* 52 (Winter):817–68.

Perlongher, Néstor. 1985. "Una historia del FLH." In *Homosexualidad: Hacia la destrucción de los mitos.* Ed. Zelmar Acevedo. Buenos Aires: Ediciones del Sur.

Plotke, David. 1990. "What's So New about New Social Movements?" *Socialist Review* 20 (90/91): 81–102.

Robinson, Eugene. 1991. "Argentina's Gays Battle Attitudes." *Washington Post,* 12 December, 43A, 46A.

Rojas, Enrique J. 1996. Interview by Stephen Brown. Buenos Aires, 3 June.

Salessi, Jorge. 1995. *Médicos maleantes y maricas*. Buenos Aires: Beatriz Viterro.

Sardá, Alejandra. 1996a. "Argentina: 1996 Report." *Escrita en el Cuerpo, servicio electrónico de noticias*, 18 December.

———. 1996b. La invasión de la otra ciudadanía." *Escrita en el Cuerpo, servicio electrónico de noticias*, 28 August.

———. 1996c. "Prohibido discriminar en Buenos Aires." *Escrita en el Cuerpo, servicio electrónico de noticias*, 31 August.

———. 1996d. "Travesti asesinada por la policía." *Escrita en el Cuerpo, servicio electrónico de noticias*, 24 August.

Slater, David. 1991. "New Social Movements and Old Political Questions: Rethinking State–Society Relations in Latin American Development." *International Journal of Political Economy* 21 (Spring): 32–65.

Talavera, Julio. 1996. Interview by Stephen Brown. Buenos Aires, 14 June.

Taylor, Verta, and Nancy E. Whittier. 1992. "Collective Identity in Social Movement Communities: Lesbian Feminist Mobilization." In *Frontiers in Social Movement Theory*. Ed. Aldon Morris and Carol McClurg Mueller. New Haven: Yale University Press.

Udis-Kessler, Amanda. 1996. "Present Tense: Biphobia as a Crisis of Meaning." In *The Material Queer: A LesBiGay Cultural Studies Reader*. Ed. Donald Morton. Boulder: Westview.

Vaid, Urvashi. 1995. *Virtual Equality: The Mainstreaming of Gay and Lesbian Liberation*. New York: Anchor.

Warner, Michael. 1993. "Introduction." In *Fear of a Queer Planet: Queer Politics and Social Theory*. Ed. Michael Warner. Minneapolis: University of Minnesota Press.

6   The Lesbian and Gay Movement
    in Britain
    Schisms, Solidarities, and Social Worlds

Social movements may be viewed as collective enterprises to establish new
orders of life.

                        Herbert Blumer, "Collective Behaviour"

A SHORT history of lesbian and gay life in Britain in the
post–World War II period can be depicted as six sedimented layers. Each
emerges anew but leaves its continuing traces. The foundation layer—the
1950s and the 1960s—included some press scandals and notorious spy
and court cases involving homosexuals such as Guy Burgess, Donald
Maclean, Peter Wildeblood, Lord Montagu of Beaulieu, and John Giel-
gud (Hyde 1970); a major government commission recommending (limited) decriminalization of male homosexuality (*Wolfenden Report* 1957);
a campaigning pressure group (the Homosexual Law Reform Society set
up in 1958); a law to enact the proposed changes (the 1967 Sexual Offences Act); and a proliferation of gay and a few lesbian bars (Gray 1992).
The year 1970 marked the arrival of the next layer: the much more radical Gay Liberation Front (GLF). This increased gay visibility, as many
people came out of their closets, and political debates moved from liberal
and apologetic to radical and critical. But the GLF was short-lived. It was
paralleled by the emergence of second-wave feminism, and by 1973 most
of the lesbians had left the Gay Movement. A third layer thus appeared
around this time: the growth of a lesbian feminist movement and, along
with it, the quiet expansion of a host of new gay and lesbian institutions—
self-help groups like Friend and Switchboard, media forms like the *Gay
News*, larger and more extravagant clubs like Heaven and Bang's, and
campaigning organizations like the Campaign for Homosexual Equality
(CHE). It also marked the emergence of a more masculinist look among
gay men—the clone zone—which coincided with a period generally
sensed as marking a decline in the good fortune of the Movement (Palmer
1995: 34). A fourth layer was ushered in with AIDS circa 1983. Less concerned with gay politics per se, it heralded a proliferation of new and more

professional groupings, often with government backing—the Terrence Higgins Trust in the forefront. For a short while other matters of gay and lesbian life settled into the background. But in 1987 a fifth layer appeared: with the introduction of the Conservative government's internationally notorious Clause (later Section) 28 to outlaw the "promotion of homosexuality" in local government, a renewed activism returned. Seen by some as the British equivalent of Stonewall in a period commonly sensed to be a backlash, men and women started to work together, and briefly there was a very clear repoliticization of the movement (Annetts and Thompson 1992: chap. 18). A sixth sediment appeared in the late 1980s: the simultaneous queering of the younger gay and lesbian world along with a significant commercialization of the "scene." More or less corresponding to a new generation of gays and lesbians, this continues today. Significant widespread acceptance was symbolized in 1997 by out gay MPs (members of Parliament), an out gay cabinet minister, and an out Elton John singing at Princess Diana's funeral.

Because this description of layers is clearly oversimplified, what follows is an attempt to highlight some of the critical developments in more detail. My aim is to chart the workings of a movement (hereafter Movement) in Britain during this period. Centrally, I have two images to help me see this Movement, both drawn from a symbolic interactionist theory:[1] *social worlds* and *schisms*.[2] The Movement must be seen as a highly fluid, emergent series of overlapping social worlds[3] that make competing claims for change and employ diverse dramatic strategies to accomplish their goals. These worlds have differing styles, agendas, political rationales, goals, and organizational forms. And they are characterized centrally by schism, change, fluidity, weak hierarchical structures, little formal organization, minimal resources, ambiguous frames, and claims-making activities.[4]

WOLFENDEN, THATCHERISM, AND THE WIDER CONTEXT OF THE MOVEMENT

Lesbian and gay social movements ebb, flow, and mesh with the ongoing political, religious, economic, and cultural institutions. To trace the ongoing emergence of the Movement in Britain within the sociocultural history of modern Britain would take several books. Some have already started this task (Durham 1991; Jeffery-Poulter 1991) but two key themes need clarifying: the *Wolfenden Report* of 1957, which has proceeded throughout the second half of the twentieth century to redefine the relation between public and private moralities in the United Kingdom; and Thatcherism, which may be seen as the defining ideology of Britain in the late twentieth century, providing a laissez-faire approach to economics that fostered consumerism, while creating a moral climate of traditional family values against which all was to be judged.

The *Wolfenden Enquiry* was set up by the Conservative Party in the aftermath of several "homosexual scandals" and is linked to the Butler Reforms of the 1950s, which addressed (liberally) the death penalty, prostitution, obscenity, gambling, and suicide (Hall 1980; NDC 1980). It is the key to understanding the creation of moral discourse in postwar Britain—the backdrop to both early legal changes and later social activism—for the *Wolfenden Report* laid out a framework of regulation yet tolerance, a public space controlled by the law and a private space that is not the law's business. Thus, while condemning any public flaunting of the law, it was to permit a private world of consensual homosexual acts permitted by Parliament (though its arguments were largely based on a model of homosexuality that sees it as a fixed "condition," a position generally known as "essentialism," which has continued to dominate all debates).[5] *Wolfenden* was concerned with defining the role of the law in relation to sexuality "to preserve public order and decency, to protect the citizen from what is offensive and injurious, and to provide safeguards against the exploitation and corruption of others," while recognizing that "it is not the function of the law to interfere in the private lives of citizens, or to seek to enforce any particular patterns of behaviour." (Wolfenden, cited in Mort 1980: 39). Turning *Wolfenden* into law was a project for much of the 1960s, culminating in legislation during Labour Home Secretary Roy Jenkins's period of office. A renowned liberal democrat, Jenkins wanted a clear limit to the state's intervention in personal life, seeking to "create a climate of opinion which is favourable to gaiety, tolerance and beauty and unfavourable to puritan . . . . to petty minded disapproval, to hypocrisy and to a dreary ugly pattern of life" (from *The Labour Case*, quoted in Hall, 1980). In a strategy formulated by *Wolfenden* and largely carried through by Jenkins, homosexuality became decriminalized in major respects in 1967. It was a process that Hall has called the legislation of morality or "Wolfenden's double taxonomy": "toward stricter penalty and control, toward greater freedom and leniency: together the two elements in a single strategy" (Hall 1980: 14). In many respects it might be seen as one precondition for the emergence of a more widespread Movement.

The second major shaping influence, from the late 1970s onward, was the Conservative Thatcher government. As a major right-wing government, it dominated the background of the gay Movement between the years 1979 and 1997 and was marked by economic conservatism, religious moralism, and a very strong profamily agenda (Abbott and Wallace

1992). The government of this period ceaselessly attacked the so-called permissive period of legislation linked to Jenkins and the Labour government of 1967 and attempted to return to "basic, family, traditional values." Although it did not have an explicit policy of sexual regulation (Durham 1991) this "familism" pervaded all. The initiatives on sexual politics passed, largely, to the political right. Thatcherism led an assault on the "valueless values of the permissive society," with Margaret Thatcher herself famously remarking that "children who need to be taught to respect traditional moral values are being taught that they have an inalienable right to be gay" (Jeffery-Poulter 1991: 218). As Stuart Hall—the foremost sociological analyst of this period—remarked, "Thatchersim . . . has used its moral agenda as one of the principal areas where . . . identities are defined—the respectable normal folk who people the fantasies of the new right in relation to current debates around abortion, child abuse, sex education, gay rights and AIDS. It is above all through this moral agenda that the new right has become a cultural force" (1988: 282). This agenda continued when the subsequent prime minister, John Major launched the (now infamous)[6] Back to Basics campaign in 1993.

Wolfenden and Thatcherism are the prime backgrounds to the lesbian and gay Movement, but there are several other features of this period worth very briefly noting. First, as elsewhere in the Western world, the late sixties was a time of countercultural movements and student activism in Britain. And the Gay Liberation Front, along with the Women's Movement, must be seen as directly linked to that time. Many GLF activists were linked with university life—in fact, the first GLF meeting was organized by two sociology students at the London School of Economics (LSE), where the group's first meetings were also held. The LSE was itself seen as one of the key locations of the student struggles in the United Kingdom.

Second, from the 1980s this was also a time when the Conservative Party attempted to undo the power of local governments (many of which had been controlled by the Labour Party). Under Thatcher, the central state grew, but local authorities were under threat. Hence, for a good while, much of the activist work of the Lesbian and Gay Movement took place against an assault on local authority government and the so-called Loony Left, which was associated with it. With this background, the politics of the gay Movement started to change direction in the 1980s. In her important study of these "local state changes," Davina Cooper summarizes a key aspect of this shift, "By the early 1980's, the Lesbian and Gay Movement had undergone a substantial shift in emphasis. While the 1970's witnessed an emphasis on 'revolutionary strategies: separatism, political lesbianism and sexual deconstruction, the 1980's saw a renewed interest in affirming gay identity, developing political alliances, particularly between men and women and working within the state" (1994: 23). Thus, throughout the 1980s, activism switched largely to urban, Labour-controlled councils across Britain. Against a national backdrop of increasing conservatism and the ideology of the family, successful campaigns were launched at the level of the local state, setting up initiatives for change in local government—most especially in the Greater London Council (GLC), Manchester, Nottingham, and Southampton City councils, and the London Boroughs of Camden, Haringey, Islington, and Lambeth. Lampooned as the Loony Left, these groupings can be credited with many achievements: setting up centers (such as the London Lesbian and Gay Centre), establishing equal opportunity posts, and supporting campaigns around "positive images." It was at this local government level where, for a while, successes became possible.

The later period—from the mid 1980s onward—was also a time of consumer growth. The power of the market, which Thatcher advocated, generated—perhaps ironically—a network of new economic institutions around lesbian and gay life: the rise of the so-called Pink Pound. Criticized as they are by some wings of the Movement (for example, Edge 1995 and Field 1995), these new economic forms give a cohesion and unity to much of the lesbian and gay world, fostering a lifestyle rather than a lifestyle politics.

THE LESBIAN AND GAY MOVEMENT AS SOCIAL WORLDS

Having set the scene, just what is the Lesbian and Gay Movement in Britain? Rather than seeing it narrowly as a specific named political movement, it is more helpful to see it as a broadly based overlapping cluster of arenas of collective activity lodged in social worlds in which change is accomplished: some of it is overtly political, and some of it is economic (the Pink Economy), but much of it is cultural. Not wholly united and sometimes deeply schismatic, the modern Movement is composed of explicitly political groups alongside broader self-help organizations, subcultures and "scenes," media networks, rallies, and intellectual workers. Increasingly, it is also becoming connected to the Internet. While the main focus of this chapter is the political groupings, it helps to situate this discussion in a wider framework of social worlds.

First is the explicitly political social world, which may be roughly divided into two. There are the liberal and assimilationist voluntary pressure groups: often formally structured; usually middle class, male, and even elitist; and primarily concerned with claims over rights and legal change (the Homosexual Law Reform Society, the Albany Trust, the Campaign for Homosexual Equality, and Stonewall, as well as groups affiliated with the three major political parties and organized religions, such as the Gay Christian Movement). And there are the less formal, grassroots-based, and challenging radical activist collectives: the Gay Liberation Front, Radical Feminism, Outrage, and AIDS Coalition to Unleash Power (ACT UP). This is the classic divide of all gay movements—between those who seek legal change through lobbying and those who believe in a much more radical stance (Marotta 1981). But the radicalism comes in many forms, and these groupings are a prime focus later in this chapter.

Second is the much more amorphous world of communities and scenes. Unlike many social movements that cannot be said to constitute communities, the Movement cannot really be comprehended without being seen as a cultural form, a social world in which members sense an affinity with each other through sexuality, language, values, and common institutions such as bars and the media. There was certainly quite a widespread bar scene in Britain throughout the 1960s and even earlier (Westwood 1960; Hauser 1962), but a growth in alternatives to the bar scene began during the 1970s, along with rapid commercialization from the 1980s onward. Although it may seem odd to view as a social movement the development of mass discos such as Bangs in the 1970s and Heaven in the 1980s, or the 1990s street life in Soho around Compton Street or in Manchester's "village," they are certainly large-scale collective behaviors that have constituted social change in quite dramatic ways (Whittle 1994). Initially, they were largely male centered, but a growth in both the lesbian and bisexual scenes followed. Some might even argue that the "scene" has done more to liberate lesbian and gay lives than any of the more overt political movements. Alongside an elaborate bar scene, there also exists a network of organizations: in 1996 in London, for instance, you could find gay groups for the Welsh, Cypriots, black people, Asians, and Jewish people (Kosher Gays); gay groups for badminton, squash, Lycra cycling, windsurfing, football, bridge, swimming, and sailing; gay groups for artists, accountants and businesspeople, chamber choirs members, pagans and occultists, teenagers, those under twenty-five (Forbidden Fruits), and those over forty and fifty. And in the midst of all this were the cyberqueers![7]

Closely allied is the spread of gay and lesbian media. From virtual invisibility in all media save a few sensational and negative tabloid presentations in the 1960s (Pearce 1981) and a small array of early, largely unsuccessful, magazines (the staid *Man and Society* of the Albany Trust, the

CHE news magazine, *Lunch,* and the glossy but short-lived bisexual periodical *Jeremy*), came a period of experimentation (*Gay News* started publishing as a radical collective in June 1972 but became increasingly "professional" with a circulation of twenty thousand by 1976; *Gay Scotland* started in 1973 and had a circulation of two thousand by 1983). By the 1980s there was a well-established market for gay readers (*Gay News* merged with *Gay Times* in 1983 when it had a readership of around fifty thousand), and a "free press" distributed through bars and meeting places became available in most large cities (initially *Capital Gay,* followed by the *Pink Paper* and *Boyz*). By the 1990s a very confident journalistic world existed: glossy, glitzy, and nowhere near as directly political as its predecessors: *Diva, Attitude, Phase* became mouthpieces of a new-style Movement.[8] And closely allied was the development of a broader lesbian and gay media culture. For instance, gay publishing houses such as Gay Men's Press start to appear in the late 1970s. And there is now significant greater presence in other media, including television: Channel 4 started the first gay film series, *In the Pink,* for eight weeks in September 1986; *Out on Tuesday* started in 1989, gaining an audience of over a million. *Gay Times* is the current TV journal for lesbian and gays found on the British Broadcasting Corporation's (BBC) Channel 2 (Burston and Richardson 1995). Likewise, the popular culture and film industries have become more and more visibly gay. Many people get involved in the production of these media events, and a lot more are consumers of them. There are large celebratory gay entertainment gatherings—such as the Annual Stonewall Equality Pride held in the large Albert Hall and attracting upward of six thousand people—along with celebrities and political support. All this media work is crucial to the public life of the Movement—it gives it a visibility, a liveliness, and a mode of communication that many less successful movements simply do not have. And it has changed out of all recognition in the past twenty years (Howes 1993).

There are also self-help social worlds. From small counseling agencies—such as the Albany Trust, staffed by one professional counselor—which were formed in the late 1960s and early 1970s, a web of support systems has grown: FRIEND (Fellowship for the Relief of the Isolated and Emotionally in Need and Distress, CHE's counseling arm) was formed in 1971; Icebreakers (a more radical support group, which rejected professional counselors) was formed in 1973; and the London Gay Switchboard, which was founded in 1974 (receiving some twenty thousand calls in its first year and over a million calls in the next ten years), led to the establishment of a nationwide service of help lines. By the 1990s there were over a hundred such lines, many sponsored by local authorities and employing professional support. Since the advent of AIDS, there has also been a proliferation of HIV supports and scores of specialist support groups—some twenty-five HIV groups in London alone in 1996. This voluntary sector has become increasingly professionalized (Babuscio 1976), establishing, for instance, police liaison committees (something that the early Gay Liberation Movement would scarcely have believed, or wished to be, possible).

Then there is the more academic wing of the Movement—the ivory closet of lesbian and gay studies, a social world that has gathered its own momentum through books and conferences. From the earliest days of the Albany Trust, leaflets and books that put forward an analysis of the lesbian and gay experience have been produced alongside analyses of the homophobia and heterosexism that challenge the Movement. Such intellectual work is crucial to the claims-making activities of any social movement. And although there were relatively few people doing this work in the 1970s (often in small groups, such as those that produced *With Downcast Gays,* the *Gay Left* journal, and *Homosexuality and Anti-Psychiatry*), by the 1980s, a steady stream of gay and lesbian academics started to appear, holding their own conferences, writing their own library of books, and teaching their own courses (Plummer 1992; Wilton 1995; Medhurst and Munt 1997).

Yet another crucial world in the Movement consists of the Gay Pride Marches, the huge symbolic rallying events of the Movement. Although they generally occur only once a year, they play an enormously significant and powerful symbolic role. When the marches commenced in London in 1972, they attracted only a small devoted political crowd of about two thousand people. Throughout the 1980s, they grew exponentially. (The 1988 Section 28 march is regarded as a landmark event in size and political involvement.) In the 1990s the attendance at annual marches, combined with a festival, now has become enormous—estimates of a quarter of a million are not uncommon. But the nature of the rally has also changed: what was essentially a political and campaign-oriented rally is now largely expressive of a lifestyle commitment. It is much more commercialized. The rallies also perform a global function, uniting cultures, as in the 1992 EuroPride. There are many allied symbolic events, such as the Brighton Pride, Pride West, Pride Scotland, Pride Arts Festivals, the Gay Film Festivals, SM Pride, It's Queer Up North, and Candlelight Memorials.[9]

Finally, a new social movement world is emerging around the Internet. There are signs, especially among the young, that the web has become an increasingly important way of communicating and that some of this communication is focused on political issues. A 1995 issue of *Gay Times* listed a wide variety of web sites, many linked to the scene but quite a few linked to political activity (Digital Diversity, Europride 96, Gay Men Fighting AIDS; L and G Lawyers, Pride, Stonewall, the Pink Practice—and many other groups were listed as having web sites).[10]

CONTESTED CLAIMS IN THE LESBIAN AND GAY MOVEMENT: ARENAS OF SCHISM AND SOLIDARITY

It is my argument that to maintain vitality, all successful social movements must remain in conflict and struggle. Once conflict ceases, movements are prone to co-optation by the dominant order, becoming institutionalized or even ceasing to function. They need to be moved on through contestation, schism, and conflict: without these, they become static, wither, and often die.

The strength of the Lesbian and Gay Movement in Britain can usefully be seen through the eyes of these schisms. One cluster of schisms is external: there has to be a powerful sense of something being wrong, of change that is needed, and of adversaries. There is a public drama in which certain marker events become symbolic of potential (and actual) change. In general, the last three decades of the twentieth century have seen an increasing mainstreaming of the issues here. But other schisms (and this is sometimes also neglected) are internal to the Movement: they establish contrasting arenas of action between people within gay worlds, help mark out boundaries between them, give the Movement an inner dynamic for change, and perpetually remind the participants that the Movement is far from homogeneous or consensual. It is actually inappropriate to see one Lesbian and Gay Movement: it never has been a single entity. From its earliest days, the U.K. Movement has been involved in endless schisms and conflicts.

The Enemy Out There: Outer Schisms

The Movement may be depicted as engaging in a ceaseless stream of small episodic conflicts, organized campaigns that generally focus on rights and civil liberties, and much longer-term struggles whereby heterosexuality and heterosexism, the gender roles they endorse, and the families they sustain become the major symbolic enemy. I deal with only the first two here.

Episodic conflicts include such things as the Law Lords finding *International Times* guilty of "conspiracy to corrupt public morals" for publishing contact ads for gay men (1972) and the *Gay News* Blasphemy Trial, which led to the Gay News Defence Fund (1977). These are quite short-lived conflicts: they galvanize and are important symbolically, especially in quiet times, but they fade. Campaigns mobilize for longer periods of time. They include the long-running campaigns to correct the many weaknesses of the *Wolfenden* legislation—changing the law in Scotland and Northern Ireland (the 1967 Sexual Offences Act was extended to Scotland in 1980 and to Northern Ireland in 1982) and changing the age of consent (in 1981 the Criminal Law Revision Committee recommended reduction to age eighteen, an amendment that was made in 1994, by which time the favored age for campaigners was sixteen rather than eighteen; Stonewall played a key role, and there were mass demonstrations)—as well as the positive images campaigns, sex education debates (Epstein 1994), and the like. The list is long.

There were, however, two galvanizing campaigns during the 1980s that require special attention. The first dominated the earlier years of this period and centered on AIDS. The campaigns around HIV and AIDS rescued a slumbering gay Movement from the late 1970s and—in the midst of great tragedy—served to revitalize and reactivate the Movement. Significantly, this happened initially through the Terrence Higgins Trust, which was established in 1982 (by friends of the first British gay man to die of AIDS) and received its first government grant of thirty-five thousand pounds in 1985. (A brief account can be found in King 1993: 208–16). It became a leading campaign body, but it also signposted a different style of gay politics—one that moved from the informal radical styles of the past to a style that was more professional, more informed, certainly angry but always responsible, and very capable of working with government and other professionals as part of the AIDS industry. The gay Movement was becoming professional: people wore suits and ties, started being trained, and even got paid for their work! Although Terrence Higgins was to become the leading movement, many others were spawned: Scottish AIDS Monitor, National AIDS Trust, Crusaid, Body Positive, Positively Women, Blacklines, Frontliners, Mainliners, Project Sigma, London Lighthouse.

All of this mirrors the development of AIDS generally. A leading historian of HIV, Virginia Berridge, suggests that AIDS policy in Britain has moved through four main phases. Between 1981 and 1986 there was a policy from below, heavily shaped by the gay community's own response. The period from 1986 to 1987 brought a type of wartime emergency, when very considerable activity (not least the five-million-pound leaflet blitz on all households in Britain and the notorious iceberg imagery of the slogan Don't Die of Ignorance). The years 1987 to 1989 brought "normalization" and "professionalization," leading to the 1990s, when "AIDS is potentially at one and the same time being mainstreamed and marginalized" (Berridge 1996: 8) Progressively, AIDS work moved out into the statutory bodies and the voluntary bodies: sometimes this meant an active support for local lesbian and gay organizations, switchboards, and the like (often it did not). A central concern here becomes just how marginal gays can become to AIDS/HIV work: in many bodies the work gets taken over as a wider heterosexual issue. And this, in turn, has led to a frequent struggle between those who seek to highlight the centrality of AIDS to gay life and those who see it as a much broader problem) what has sometimes been called the degaying and regaying of AIDS debates (King 1993: 5).

The second key campaigning issue was against Section 28 of the Local Government Act (1988). Initially proposed by Dame Jill Knight and the Earl of Hawksbury, and lost because of a general election, Clause 28 was finally introduced by David Wiltshire and became Section 28 of the Local Government Act on 24 May 1988.[11] Its key provisions stipulated that a Local authority shall not intentionally promote homosexuality or teach the acceptability of homosexuality as a pretended family relationship. But it recognized the need for education that might prevent the spread of disease. It is generally seen as a very poor law: the language is highly ambiguous; it is directed at local authorities only; and the third clause, which is linked to HIV and sex education, leaves many possibilities open. To date it has not been put into effect (although it has encouraged self-censorship and fear). Yet it also had a remarkable symbolic value, signposting a "moral civil war" (Weeks 1995:9). Not just an attack on homosexuals, Section 28 provided a rallying cry over many issues, uniting the liberal humanist lobby in opposition. As David Evans notes, it links to "local authority power; the teaching profession; sex education; childhood innocence and suggestibility; the sanctity of the family and illness of plague dimensions; all galvanised under the banner threat of permissiveness" (1993: 125). But it was also a rallying cry for the gay Movement, and movements need symbolic marker events or they lose their momentum. Apart from several major public demonstrations against the bill (in Manchester a crowd of thirteen to twenty thousand; in London, some thirty thousand protested), there were some significant shifts in tactical style. Most notably, there were irate abseiling lesbians on ropes in the House of Lords, shouting, "Lesbians are angry" and the invasion of the Six O'Clock News (Carter 1992: chap. 17). The battle over Clause 28 is yet to be fully documented (but see Colvin and Hawksley 1989; Thomas and Costigan 1990; and Carabine 1995: chap. 4). It is generally seen as a "watershed in the struggle for gay equality" (Jeffery-Poulter 1991: 234) and as "the coming of age of the gay and lesbian movement."[12] It must surely be one of the ironies of lesbian and gay politics in Britain, as elsewhere, that the very moment when lesbians and gays were seemingly most under attack, a revitalized and strengthened Movement emerges. Section 28 was simultaneously one of the most severe attacks on gay rights since the founding of GLF in 1970 and the precipitator of the next activist generation. The newly elected Labour government of 1997 seems committed to its abolition (as well as to the lowering of the age of consent to sixteen).

The Enemy Within: Internal Schisms

A feature of social movement analysis that is often ignored but that, at least in the lesbian and gay case in Britain, seems crucially important is internal schisms. Maybe because in actuality there is little to hold lesbians and gays together—the category is an invented one mobilized through a collective-identity politics—differences did, do, and will always abound. These differences generate considerable internal conflict, but they keep the Movement alive and give it the dynamism for it to sustain growth and change. Schisms, as I try to capture below, may lead to solidarity.

"We're just like you" / "Fuck you in the face!" : Assimilationists and Transgressors

As we have seen, the classic split is between liberals and radicals.[13] The liberal wing of the Movement has a clear focus on rights and "respectability." There have been changes in these groups—the first ones were small and closeted; the more recent ones are, like Stonewall, much more visible, more out, and bigger. But their central strategy has been that of pressure groups campaigning for change. Usually small, always middle class and "respectable," they have worked within a framework of minority rights, their central claim being "equality before the law."

The old law reform movement—the Homosexual Law Reform Society (HLRS)—embodied this position initially. It continued throughout the 1970s as the Campaign for Homosexual Equality. Formed in 1969 in the north of England as the surviving group from the law reform lobby, it changed its name in 1971 and maintained a central commitment to law reform (launching a new draft bill in 1975). In 1970 there were five hundred members in fifteen local groups; by 1972 twenty-eight hundred members in sixty groups (Weeks 1990: 210). For much of the 1970s, its annual conference was a major symbolic rally. By 1980 it had over four thousand individual members and over a hundred groups (Marshall 1980: 77–84). In the same year, it split into two groups—one for campaigning and grassroots change (see Grass Roots 1982) and one for social needs and counseling.

Another lobbying group, Stonewall, appeared in the mid-1980s and became the major organization for the 1990s. After the campaigns around the notorious Clause 28, the slick, well-organized, and much more professional campaign group of Stonewall (and the associated Iris Trust Charity) was set up in May 1989. It is characterized by assimilation, a focus on law, the use of celebrities (Ian McKellen, Michael Cashman), professional lobbying, drafting equality bills, and the like. Ian McKellen states, "Our aim will be to identify in what ways the law should be changed . . . and to provide people who can function well in the media, people who can argue for the changes that need to happen. We are keen to get people who are gay and lesbian in the mainstream of society, who are not out, to come out. If they know there's an organisation like this that is well respected . . . they are far more likely to come out and help in raising money and offering expertise" (quoted in Jeffery-Poulter 1991: 246). Stonewall produced a draft Homosexual Equality Bill in 1990,[14] and it played a major role in the campaigns to lower the age of consent. Its 1993 leaflet, "The Case for Change: Arguments for an Equal Age of Consent," helped establish the terms of this debate: equality before the law, equal rights, the right to privacy, and gayness assumed to be a condition established in the early years of life and hence no threat. Reformist movements have inevitably taken the essentialist side of the constructionist/essentialist debate.[15] Hence they both believe and argue that homosexuals are born not made and that since no one can help their sexual orientation, the law has no place in its regulation. (In contrast, constructionists usually see homosexuality as much more linked to a choice—often political—and make different arguments that put them on the more radical edge of the Movement.) And along with Stonewall came a string of important pressure groups working for change: the Lesbian and Gay Police Association, the Lesbian and Gay Lawyer's Association, the Lesbian and Gay Christian movement, and Rank Outsiders (the gays in the military group). Even the Conservative Party developed a more active campaigning group: TORCHE (Tory Campaign for Homosexual Equality).[16]

By contrast, the radical revolutionary wing of the Movement has little concern for "respectability" and assimilation. Its foundation in Britain was the (relatively) short-lived Gay Liberation Front, which Simon Watney (1980: 65) has called "the most important movement for homosexuals that Britain has known," and more recently it has seen groups like ACT UP, Outrage, and various queer groups develop. The radical wing has little interest in being "respectable" or "professional," or even in prioritizing legal changes. Instead, it adopts a much more militantly confrontational approach: seeking widespread revolutionary social change—a restructuring of gender, family, and the whole society, not simply acceptance or equality before the law.

The GLF was the first radical group in Britain. From a meeting in the basement of the LSE on 13 October 1970, which nineteen people attended—one woman, the rest gay men—it led rapidly to larger and larger meetings, marches, and protests. In these earliest days it was a Movement largely about personal liberation and consciousness-raising. It had no formal leadership, and indeed any attempt to impose structure or leadership on its growing amorphous mass was swiftly rejected. Perhaps because of this, along with the proliferation of schisms and conflicts, it was to be very short-lived. But it was nevertheless overwhelmingly important: it was the founding of the Movement in Britain, and it was significant in making gayness "come out." It was never to go back in again. GLF was the first and most triumphal of the radical wings of the social movements. It achieved many things: a manifesto (summer 1971), original critiques, the first demonstration (against the film *Boys in the Band*) and a torchlight demonstration in Highbury Fields), the first noncommercial dances (initially at the LSE in December 1970 and then at Kensington Town Hall), a proliferation of such publications as *With Downcast Gays* and *Homosexuality and Anti-Psychiatry*,) a film (John Shane's *Come Together*), and a broadsheet (*Come Together*). Slogans and badges were everywhere (eight thousand badges were sold by GLF in the first year). But, above all, it raised public awareness of homosexuality in a way that simply had not happened before, and it brought "coming out" as a major political process to the forefront. It was largely middle class and overwhelmingly male (Weeks [1990: 191] suggests a ratio of five men to each woman). Despite its many successes, it was to be short-lived. As the scale of the meetings grew and grew, so did the scale of the conflicts from within. There were many: reformers versus radicals, women versus men, socialists versus libertarians. In Watney's account (1980: 67), possibly the major early split to occur was between the "actionists" (the organized Leninist members) and the "lifestylers" linked to the alternative society of the time; it was not long before this blossomed into the other full-scale conflict of the history of the gay Movement—a split between the radical drag queens and the "straights." As Watney says, "The situation was extremely confusing. Half the leadership of GLF appeared to be Maoists at one meeting and Radical Drag Queens at the next" (1980: 70; see also Power 1995).

Since the arrival of the Gay Liberation Front in 1970, there have always been small groupings making radically transgressive claims through dramatic performances. Their agendas seek total societal change, and the Movement uses slogans, street marches, and street theater as its central tools. It is directly confrontational—in your face. These worlds have never been especially large (even in the early meetings of GLF in London, numbers probably never topped five hundred), and its existence has often been precarious: because it is always antihierarchical and rejects organization, it lacks the resources to mobilize consistently and for long periods. It has to keep rediscovering itself.

By the late 1980s, however, radical gay politics was back on the agenda in a big way. Shepherd and Wallis, writing at the time, comment, "Whereas GLF politics adopted the stance of a romantic Big Refusal, the new generation is marked by an angry and radical/revolutionary desire for change. GLF burst forth in a period of relative economic stability and social and political liberalism: present struggles grapple within a period of intense political reaction" (1989: 19). This was written seconds away from the arrival of Queer Politics, which entered around 1988—almost the same time as in the United States. A leaflet circulating in 1991 put it bluntly, "Queer means to fuck with gender. There are straight queers, bi queers, tranny queers, lez queers, SM queers, fisting queers in every single street in this apathetic country of ours. . . . Each time the word 'queer' is used it defines a strategy, an attitude, a reference to other identities and a new self understanding. (And queer can be qualified as 'more queer', 'queer', or 'queerest' as the naming develops into a more complex process of identification") (quoted in Smyth 1991: 17, 20). ACT UP was to hold its first meetings in January 1989 (modeled on U.S. meetings after two U.S. activists, Rae Bos and Rob Archer, came to speak of their experiences); Outrage would have its first public meeting at the London Lesbian and Gay Centre in May 1990; and a range of smaller, often short-lived, groups appeared with names like PUSSY (Perverts Undermining State Scrutiny), Subversive, Street Queers, Queer Power Now, and Homocult, an anonymous group of dykes and faggots who produced their own manifesto and ran a club called Scum. There were new clubs, such as Queer Nation in London and Flesh in Manchester, and new magazines (and zines) like the Brighton-based *A Queer Tribe*. Queer Internetworks appeared. And with all this came queer theory too: a Lesbian and Gay Studies Conference at Essex University in December 1990 gave it prominence, and another conference was held at York University in 1992 (Bristow and Wilson 1993). A Manchester-based cell captures the new imagery (from Alan Sinfield, "What's in a Name?" quoted in Mort 1994: 210):

> HOMOSEXULTURE
> Our language is perversion
> Corruption Reclaiming Acting
> Changing Surviving subverting
> Evolving Life
> HETEROTRASH
> Their language is conserving
> Stagnating Lingering Death
> QUEER
> Love Yourself

Even though the term "queer" arrived early in Britain, it has never been as widespread and visible as it has been in the United States.

Gender Wars: Radical Lesbian Feminists and Their Enemies.
Absolutely crucial to any understanding of the Gay Movement in Britain is the schism over gender: from the very outset the relationships between the women's movement, the lesbian movement, and the gay male movement have been hotly contested. In 1972, for instance, lesbians split away from the GLF, accusing it of "gender fucking" and a misogynistic gay ghetto sexuality. But throughout its short history, there has been an ongoing series of rifts. At the 1980 Women's Liberation Movement and Men conference in London, one lesbian remarked, "I will no longer work with gay men. There is no way, absolutely no way, in which our interest can be said to be the same. Gay men, perhaps more than any other men, ally themselves with the activities and products of sexism. More than any other men they choose to act and construe themselves, and each other, in ways dominated by phallocentric ideologies and activities" (quoted in Stanley 1982: 211–12). Her arguments highlight the deeply misogynist attitude of gay men, causing women's issues to be ignored, erased, and marginalized. The most prominent spokesperson in Britain for this position was Sheila Jeffreys (1990), who now lives in Australia. She advocated a very distinctive separatist lesbian feminist identity based on radical feminist lesbianism, which was both angry at and despairing of the male patriarchal preoccupation with sex, fucking, sadomasochism (SM), pornography, and cruising. The splits are a recurrent feature of the politics of the British Movement. In 1985 a symbolic marker event was the attempt by Lesbians against Sado-Masochism (LASM) to ban SM supporters from the newly established London Lesbian and Gay Centre. A vitriolic battle ensued—and LASM lost. One lesbian feminist describes the vote:

> The Centre was packed with several hundred people, 40 per cent of whom were women. The s-m dykes sat in the front row of the hall, completely surrounded by gay men, whilst the feminists clustered in the middle. The s-m contingent said nothing. They didn't have to given that at every opportunity liberal apologists and gay men sprang to their defence, to roars of approval. Whenever a lesbian feminist managed to get a word in she was met with jeers and verbal abuse. After the vote was taken, the men and s-m dykes had won, even though the majority of the women present voted against the motion. It was devastating. The Centre ended up a men's club, to which women were admitted if they toed the line. (Reeves and Wingfield 1996: 62–63)

Like the other schisms, such feminist splits regularly repeat themselves. This is not surprising, since feminists' very analysis of the nature of lesbianism and women's oppression is at odds with that of most gay men, proponents of other shades of feminism, and many lesbians. Most recently, in a telling collection (Harne and Miller 1996), radical lesbian feminists have suggested that virtually every recent development in Britain—from prosex groups, such as Women against Censorship and lesbian SM groups, through bisexualities, lipstick lesbians, lesbian and gay studies, media representation, and all the queer representations—has been part of a backlash against lesbian feminist analyses. But for still other lesbians, these very developments may be seen as progressive and liberating.

Class Wars: The Ideal (Pomo) Homo and the Working Class

Many of the Movement founders had a strong connection to a Marxist-style politics that has been abhorrent to numerous others. As in many other countries, the radical wing of gay politics was clearly Left inspired—just as much feminist politics was. Gay Marxist discussion groups were common in the early days of the GLF, often Leninist with a strong base in class politics. By 1974 Gay Left had been formed to consistently pose socialist questions of the gay Movement. And by Autumn 1975 it was producing its own journal, *Gay Left,* whose mission statement described it as seeking to "contribute towards a Marxist analysis of homosexual oppression . . . to encourage . . . an understanding of the links between the struggle against sexual oppression and the struggle for socialism."[17] Its success was relatively short-lived, but other groups continued in its wake. Most notable has been the strong presence of the Socialist Worker's Party (SWP)[18] at most rallies and campaigns throughout the entire period under discussion.

But all of this has been decidedly on the fringe. For, in distinct contrast, a much stronger trend has been pushing in the opposite direction: a trend that completely accepts the capitalist market ethos, a preoccupation with gay consumerism and a massive commercialization of the entire gay and lesbian scene. Left critics remain, but they are swamped in a world of Gay Lifestyle Events (the Ideal Homo), Gay Business Organisations, Boyz Culture, and Lipstick Lesbians. To look at the 150-page, glossy, full-color catalogue of Gay Pride '96 is to enter an apolitical world of clubbing, Calvin Kleins, Mr Gay Britain, designer beers, body piercing, kitchen styles, dream houses, gay holidays, gay marriages, theme parties, suntan products, gyms for the body beautiful, antiques, flash cars, Internet, financial services, dance, video and media of all forms—and all this sandwiched between ads for Beneton, Eyeworks, Virgin Vodka, Mercury, Buffalo Boots, and American Express. Later in the year, the megastore Virgin produced its own 50-page designer catalogue for gays: *Crash, Bang, Wallop!*

The social movement that was once the Gay Liberation Front has indeed changed. But the critical voices still shout out in condemnation, and not just the Left but also lesbian feminists. As Chris Woods remarks in his analysis, "The politically active in the community have been marginalised in the interest of profit" (1995: 45; see also Field 1995). It has led—currently as I write this—to the antigay movement within the Movement (Simpson 1996). A schismatic paradox indeed!

The March of Differences

There were many other splits and schisms in the Lesbian and Gay Movement, too many for me to deal with them all. For instance, in 1972 the "radical faeries" helped foster a split, putting transgender conflict firmly on the agenda. In 1975, pedophiles were roundly condemned in CHE and *Gay News,* leading them to create their own controversial and excluded organizations, such as PAL (Paedophile Action for Liberation) and PIE (Paedophile Information Exchange). This was a shrewd action on the part of the Movement, because these groups subsequently became a major target of public attack (Plummer 1981: 113–32). Likewise, differences centered on SM were commonly discussed, like the one (raised above) at the London Lesbian and Gay Centre in 1985. Operation Spanner in 1992 involved police arrest of a group of gay sadomasochists, who were subsequently found guilty and imprisoned (an appeal made to the European Court of Human Rights was lost). Ironically this increased the visibility of sadomasochism, and possibly its practice, and deepened a further schism (Thompson 1994; Healy 1996) . And then there has been the pornography schism—a constant symbol of dispute (the London lesbian and gay bookstore, Gay's the Word, refused to stock gay pornography until recently). Bisexuality has become a challenging issue of late (Eadie 1993; Wilkinson 1996: 75–89). The Lesbian and Gay Movement in Britain—as elsewhere—is the umbrella movement for a myriad of sex wars.

Another split occurred in the early 1980s when race became an increasingly recognized issue. Starting notably within the lesbian and women's movement, the Gay Movement slowly started to take these concerns seriously. Yet although a black gay group first appeared in London in 1981 (Weeks 1990: 236), gay photographer Sunil Gupta noted in 1987 that you could walk into Gay's the Word bookstore and not find a general black section, never mind a specific awareness of culture and ethnicity. Gupta complained, "There is no specifically Black/Brown gay space" (1989: 164).

Closely allied were generational splits: even in the early days of GLF, there was always a noticeable tendency for the younger and older not to get on well. But taking root from the late 1980s onward, several issues served to clarify generational boundaries. Despised largely by older gay men and women, the word "queer" from 1988 on became a marker for "transgressive youth." It captured a new generation's energy and provided a strategy for radically transcending categories. It was a key symbolic marker event. As Frank Mort says, "Gay politics has been cast as flabby and reformist; the period of comfortable, middle aged men holding to a tired 1970's sexual agenda which has now lost its way. It is queer which now signifies youth, style and vibrancy and expresses the strongest dissatisfactions with an equal rights politics of inclusion, obsessed with piecemeal gains" (1994: 204). But it was more than just "queer." The changing nature of the scene was quite pronounced: more commercialism for sure but also a youthful world that appeared more at ease with itself. Noticeably, some lesbians and gays seemed to be coming together more: "Sex between gay men and lesbians is also coming out of the closet. . . . Now people talk openly of their opposite-sex-same-sexuality lovers and at the party after the s-m Pride March a gay man and a lesbian had sex on the dance floor, but it wasn't heterosexuality. You can tell" (Graham McKerrow, quoted in Eadie 1993: 150). Such were the emerging internal schismatic tendencies in the middle of the 1990s (Sinfield 1998).

Using the imagery of worlds and schisms, this chapter has tried to capture something of the dynamism of the Lesbian and Gay Movement in Britain since the late 1960s against the moral background of *Wolfenden* and Thatcherism. More than anything else, my goal has been to show that there is no one Movement; rather, there are many social worlds in tension with each other. Differences and conflicts actually serve to animate the Movement.

Implicitly, I also suggest that the Movement has been a success story. The changes that have occurred over some thirty years have helped homosexual life in Britain move from a crime, a sickness, and something deeply enshrouded in stigma to a phenomenon that, in some forms at least, is well on the way to being integrated and accepted. There have even been arguments that now, with a new Labour government, there is little left for the Movement to do, that most of the battles have been won. Of course, this may well be overly optimistic—and not least to those radical, transgressive queers who see no victory in integration. For them, the battles have only started. But that is only part of the continuing schism. Without it, the political wings of the Lesbian and Gay Movement may well collapse, leaving the Movement as communities, as media, as self-help, as cyberworlds, but not as overt politics.

NOTES

1. Throughout the account that follows, I draw heavily from a symbolic interactionist frame of social movement analysis, which has recently been clearly discussed as harboring five themes: emergence, symbolization, cognitive and

affective transformation, interactive determination, and fluidity (Snow and Davis 1995: 188–220). For a statement and review of symbolic interactionism in general, see Plummer 1996: 223–50, and for its earlier application to lesbian and gay movements, see Plummer 1995: chaps. 4 and 6.

2. Throughout my analysis I employ Herbert Blumer's (1939) very broad definition of a social movement (cited in the epigraph), in which many sectors—pressure groups, self-help groups, communities and social worlds, media—may all be seen as part of the Lesbian and Gay Social Movement. For others, a more narrow political focus may be central, but to me this just does not do justice to the workings of the movement.

3. On social world theory see especially Strauss 1979. I discuss it more fully in Plummer 1995: Chap. 9.

4. All of these terms have been carefully chosen because they reflect large bodies of writing that deal with social movements. Thus, resource mobilization theory is suggested by McAdam, McCarthy, and Zald (1988), claims making is suggested by Spector and Kitsuse (1987), and frame is suggested by Snow and Davis (1995). I do not follow any one of these theories but find merit in each. I have also found useful the idea that "social movements can be described as dramas in which protagonists and antagonists compete to affect audiences' different interpretations of power in a variety of domains, including those pertaining to religious, political, economic or life style arrangements" (Benford and Hunt 1992: 86).

5. The so-called essentialist/constructionist debate has been an intellectual backdrop to many of the struggles in the United Kingdom. See the early statements in Plummer 1981a.

6. Infamous might better describe the campaign, which backfired. Many in Major's government were subsequently exposed as living morally dubious private lives, and the accusation of a "sleaze" government was then made.

7. See the listings in any issue of *Gay Times*, from which these examples were culled.

8. For a brief discussion of the history of the early gay magazines, see Weeks 1990: 218–23.

9. The following are estimates of Gay Pride attendance:

First (?) Lesbian and Gay March in London,   1972   2,000
1984   1,000   (*Gay Times*, no. 72 [August 1994]: 18)
1985   7,500   (*Capital Gay*, 11 July 1986, 12)
Lesbian Strength March, 1988   4,000   (*Gay Times* [July 1988]: 22)
1988   29,000   (*Gay Times*, no. 119 [August 1988]: 12)
1989   20,000   (*Gay Times*, no. 131 [August 1989]: 10)
1990   38,000   (*Gay Times*, no. 143 [August 1990]: 8)
Manchester Liberation, 1991   10,000   (*Gay Times*, no. 152 [May 1991]: 17)
1991   45,000   (*Gay Times*, no. 155 [August 1991]: 13)
EuroPride, 1992   100,000   (*Gay Times*, no. 167 [August 1992]: 12)
1995   200,000   (*Gay Times* [February 1996]: 22)

10. See *The Internet Gay Times*, no. 207 (December 1995): 12–18. In the same issue a *Gay Times* CyberQueer Directory is announced.

11. Its key provisions stipulated:

28–1 A Local authority shall not

(a) intentionally promote homosexuality or publish material with the intention of promoting homosexuality

(b) promote the teaching in a maintained school of the acceptability of homosexuality as a pretended family relationship

(3) Nothing in subsection (1) above shall be taken to prohibit the doing of anything for the purpose of treating or preventing the spread of disease. (Colvin and Hawksley 1989, 1)

12. *Capital Gay,* 18 March 1988.

13. Important early U.S. studies (Marotta 1981; Echols 1989), which are very sensitive to these early schisms and conflicts, are worth a careful review.

14. See the summary by Peter Ashman, *Gay Times* (July 1990): 18–19.

15. As the Sunday *Times* observed, "The remarkable aspect of the debate is that no senior figure has come forward to rally these dissident views" (29 January 1994, 7). The *Telegraph, Express, Mail, Star,* and *Sun* all opposed equality but favored age eighteen (the *Telegraph* went for age twenty-one). A National Opinion Poll of 751 electors showed that 44 percent favored age twenty-one, 35 percent favored age eighteen, and only 13 percent favored age sixteen (Sunday *Times,* 20 February 1994, 1). See Wilson 1995 for some accounts of all this, and see Waites 1995 for an important analysis of essentialism /constructionism in this debate.

16. A note on political parties may be helpful: Formally, the British political system is dominated by three major political parties and a cluster of alternative political groupings. The Liberal Party, always a distinct minority, has for its entire thirty-year existence been the least problematic grouping: always at each stage in support of lesbian and gay rights and consistently voting for progay legislation. It has had its own scandals (not least surrounding Jeremy Thorpe, its leader in 1976), but it has consistently provided a backdrop of support for the gay movement. By contrast, the Conservative Party—which has been the ruling party from 1970 to 1974 and from 1979 to 1997—has overwhelmingly been the antigay party: it has generally fostered a climate of homonegativity, discrimination, and heterosexism. It has been the prime framer of the context in which the Movement has worked and has often established the very struggles to which the Movement has had to respond. It is the party that championed Section 28; it is the party that resisted changes in the age of consent; it was the party of law and order; and it was the party of the family and of a concern with "back to basics." But that said, there have been interesting exceptions: Conservatives who have come out as gay and left the party (Matthew Parrish), conservatives who have overtly championed gay causes (Edwina Currie, who was a leading figure in the 1994 age of consent debate, favoring age sixteen), gay Conservatives who have developed a Conservative Campaign for Homosexual Equality), and many Conservatives who have voted for gay rights in Parliament. It is quite wrong to posit, therefore, as some writers do, a Conservative Party conspiracy against gays, although the general hostility of the party certainly serves as a major mover of activism (Smith 1994; Woods 1995).

The Labour Party has had possibly the most mixed response. It was the party that facilitated the passage of the Sexual Offences Act in 1967—with Roy Jenkins as home secretary in a period of rapid liberalizing leglisation—and it is the party that came to develop a quite radical approach to same-sex relations during the 1980s, notably in a number of local authorities that set up gay units, education programs, equal opportunities, and nondiscrimination policies. The most famous of these was the campaign by the Greater London Council (run down and closed by the Tory Party in 1986), which donated around three-quarters of a million pounds in 1983 to set up a London Lesbian and Gay Centre and produced a major document in 1985 (just before its demise) called "Changing the World: A London Charter for Gay and Lesbian Rights" (Greater London Council 1985). Here is a far-reaching document that goes though many issues—media images, queer bashing, youth problems, education, religion, work, leisure, domestic relations, health, disability, aging, adoption and fostering, law, and immigration. It produced, in the end, no less than 142 recommendations for change. And then it went out of business.

17. The journal culminated in a book, *Homosexuality: Power and Politics* (Gay Left Collective 1980). Then the group drifted apart.

18. See Noel Halifax 1988 for the SWP position.

REFERENCES

Abbott, Pamela, and Claire Wallace. 1992. *The Family and the New Right*. London: Pluto.

Annetts, Jason, and Bill Thompson. 1992. "Dangerous Activism?" In *Modern Homosexualities: Fragments of Lesbians and Gay Experience*. Ed. Ken Plummer. London: Routledge.

Babuscio, Jack, ed. 1976. *We Speak for Ourselves: Experiences in Homosexual Counselling*. London: SPCK.

Benford, Robert and Scott Hunt. 1992. "Dramaturgy and Social Movements: The Social Construction and Communication of Power." *Sociological Inquiry* 62 (1):

Berridge, Virginia. 1996. *AIDS in Britain: The Making of Policy 1981–1994*. Oxford: Oxford University Press.

Blumer, Herbert. 1939. "Collective Behaviour." In *An Outline of the Principles of Sociology*. Ed. Robert E. Park. New York: Barnes and Noble.

Bristow, Joseph, and Angelia R. Wilson, eds. 1993. *Activating Theory: Lesbian, Gay, Bisexual Politics*. London: Lawrence and Wishart.

Burston, Paul, and Colin Richardson. 1995. *A Queer Romance: Lesbians, Gay Men and Popular Culture*. London: Routledge.

Carabine, Jean. 1995. "Invisible Sexualities: Sexuality, Politics and Influencing Policy Making." In *A Simple Matter of Justice: Theorising Lesbian and Gay Politics*. Ed. Angelia R. Wilson. London: Cassell.

Carter, Vicki. 1992. "Abseil Makes the Heart Grow Fonder: Lesbian and Gay Campaigning Tactics and Section 28." In *Modern Homosexualities: Fragments of Lesbian and Gay Experience*. Ed. Ken Plummer. London: Routledge.

Colvin, Madeleine, and Jane Hawksley. 1989. *Section 28: A Practical Guide to the Law and Its Implications*. London: National Council for Civil Liberties.

Cooper, Davina. 1994. *Sexing the City*. London: Rivers Oram.

Durham, Martin. 1991. *Sex and Politics: The Family and Morality in the Thatcher Years*. London : Macmillan.

Eadie, Jo. 1993. "Activating Bisexuality: Towards a Bi/Sexual Politics." In *Activating Theory*. Eds. Joseph Bristow and Angelia Wilson. London: Lawrence and Wishart

Echols, Alice. 1989. *Daring to Be Bad: Radical Feminism in America, 1967–1975*. Minneapolis: University of Minnesota Press.

Edge, Simon. 1995. *With Friends Like These: Marxism and Gay Politics*. London: Cassell.

Epstein, Debbie, ed. 1994. *Challenging Lesbian and Gay Inequalities in Education*. Buckingham, England: Open University Press.

Evans, David. 1993. *Sexual Citizenship*. London: Routledge.

Field, Nicolas. 1995. *Over the Rainbow: Money, Class and Homophobia*. London: Pluto.

Gay Left Collective. 1980. *Homosexuality: Power and Politics*. London: Allison and Busby.

Grass Roots. 1982. *A Campaign Manual for Gay People*. London. Pamphlet.

Gray, Anthony. 1992. *Quest for Justice*. London: Sinclair- Stevenson.

Greater London Council. 1985. "Changing the World: A London Charter For Gay and Lesbian Rights." London.

Gupta, Sunil. 1989. "Black, Brown and White." In *Coming on Strong: Gay Politics and Culture*. Ed. Simon Shepherd and Mick Wallis. London: Unwin Hyman.

Halifax, Noel. 1988. *Out, Proud and Fighting*. London: Socialist Worker's Party.

Hall, Stuart. 1980. "Reformism and the Legislation of Consent." In *Permissiveness and Control: The Fate of the Sixties Legislation*. Ed. National Deviancy Conference. London: Macmillan.

Harne, Lynne, and Elaine Miller, eds. 1996. *All the Rage: Reasserting Radical Lesbian Feminism*. London: Women's Press.

Hauser, Richard. 1962. *The Homosexual Society*. London: Bodley Head.

Healy, Murray. 1996. *Gay Skins: Class, Masculinity and Queer Appropriation*. London: Cassell.

Howes, Keith. 1993. *Broadcasting It*. London: Cassell.

Hyde, H. Montgomery. 1970. *The Other Love*. London: Heinemann.

Jeffery-Poulter, Stephen. 1992. *Peers, Queers and Commons: The Struggle for Gay Law Reform from 1950 to the Present*. London: Routledge.

Jeffreys, Sheila. 1990. *Anticlimax: A Feminist Perspective on the Sexual Liberation*. London: Women's Press.

King, Edward. 1993. *Safety in Numbers*. London: Cassell.

Marotta, Toby. 1981. *The Politics of Homosexuality*. Boston: Houghton Mifflin.

Marshall, John. 1980. "The Politics of Tea and Sympathy." In *Homosexuality: Power and Politics*. Ed. Gay Left Collective. London: Allison and Busby.

McAdam, Doug, John McCarthy, and Mayer Zald. 1988. "Social Movements." In *Handbook of Sociology*. Ed. Neil Smelser. Newbury Park, Calif.: Sage.

Medhurst, Andy, and Sally Munt. 1997. *Lesbian and Gay Studies: A Critical Introduction.* London: Cassell.

Mort, Frank. 1980. "Sexuality: Regulation and Contestation" In *Homosexuality: Power and Politics.* Ed. Gay Left Collective. London: Allison and Busby.

Mort. Frank. 1994. "Essentialism Revisited? Identity Politics and Late Twentieth Century Discourse of Homosexuality." In *The Lesser Evil and the Greater Good: The Theory and Politics of Sexual Diversity.* Ed. Jeffrey Weeks. London: Rivers Oram.

National Deviance Conference (NDC). 1980. *Permissiveness and Control.* London: Macmillan.

Palmer, Anye. 1995. "Lesbian and Gay Rights Campaigning: A Report From the Cool Face" In *A Simple Matter of Justice.* Ed. Angelia Wilson. London: Cassell.

Pearce, Frank. 1981. "How to Be Pathetic and Dangerous at the Same Time." In *The Manufacture of News.* Ed. Stan Cohen and Jock Young. 2d ed. London: Constable.

Plummer, Ken. 1981. "The Paedophile's Progress: A View from Below." In *Perspectives on Paedophilia.* Ed. Brian Taylor. London: Batsford.

———. 1995. *Telling Sexual Stories: Power, Change and Social Worlds.* London: Routledge.

———. 1996. "Symbolic Interactionism in the Twentieth Century: The Rise of Empirical Social Theory." In *The Blackwell Companion to Social Theory.* Ed. Bryan S. Turner. Oxford: Blackwell.

———, ed. 1981a. *The Making of the Modern Homosexual.* London: Hutchinson.

———, ed. 1992. *Modern Homosexualities: Fragments of Lesbian and Gay Experience.* London: Routledge.

Power, Lisa. 1995. *No Bath but Plenty of Bubbles.* London: Cassell.

Reeves, Carole, and Rachel Wingfield. 1996. "Serious Porn, Serious Protest." In *All the Rage: Reasserting Radical Lesbian Feminism.* Ed. Lynne Harne and Elaine Miller. London: Women's Press.

Shepherd, Simon and Mick Wallis. 1989. *Coming on Strong: Gay Politics and Culture.* London: Unwin Hyman.

Simpson, Mark. 1996. *Anti-Gay.* London: Cassell.

Sinfield, Alan, 1998. *Gay and After.* London: Serpent's Press.

Smith, Anna Marie. 1994. *New Right Discourse on Race and Sexuality, Britain 1968–1990.* Cambridge: Cambridge University Press.

Smyth, Cherry. 1991. *Lesbians Talk Queer Notions.* London: Scarlett.

Snow, David A. and Phillip W. Davis. 1995. "The Chicago Approach to Collective Behaviour." In *A Second Chicago School?* Ed. Gary Alan Fine. Chicago: University of Chicago Press.

Spector, Malcolm, and John Kitsuse. 1987. *Constructing Social Problems.* New York: Aldine de Gruyter.

Stanley, Liz. 1982. "'Male Needs': The Problems and Problems of Working with Gay Men." In *On the Problem of Men: Two Feminist Conferences.* Ed. Scarlet Friedman and Elizabeth Sara. London: Women's Press.

Strauss, Anselm. 1979. "A Social World Perspective." *Studies in Symbolic Interaction*. Vol. 1. Ed. Norman Denzin. London: JAI Press.

Thomas, Philip, and Ruth Costigan. 1990. *Promoting Homosexuality: Section 28 of the Local Government Act*. Cardiff, Wales: Cardiff Law School.

Thompson, Bill. 1994. *Sadomasochism*. London: Cassell.

Waites, Matthew. 1995. "The Age of Consent Debate: A Critical Analysis." Master's thesis, University of Essex, England.

Watney, Simon. 1980. "The Ideology of GLF." In *Homosexuality: Power and Politics*. Ed. Gay Left Collective. London: Allison and Busby.

Weeks, Jeffrey. 1990. *Coming Out: Homosexual Politics in Britain from the Nineteenth Century to the Present*. 2d ed. London: Quartet.

Weeks, Jeffrey. 1995. *Invented Moralities*. Oxford: Polity Press.

Westwood, Gordon. 1960. *A Minority: A Report on the Life of the Male Homosexual in Britain*. London: Longmans.

Whittle, Stephen, ed. 1994. *The Margins of the City: Gay Men's Urban Lives*. Aldershot, England: Ashgate.

Wilkinson, Sue. 1996. "Bisexuality as Backlash." In *All the Rage: Reasserting Radical Lesbian Feminism*. Ed. Lynne Harne and Elaine Miller. London: Women's Press.

Wilson, Angelia R., ed. 1995. *A Simple Matter of Justice: Theorising Lesbian and Gay Politics*. London: Cassell.

Wilton, Tamsin. 1995. *Lesbian Studies: Setting an Agenda*. London: Routledge.

Wolfenden Report of the Departmental Committee on Homosexual Offences and Prostitution. 1957. London: HMSO.

Woods, Chris. 1995. *State of the Queer Nation: A Critique of Gay and Lesbian Politics in 1990's Britain*. London: Cassell.

JUDITH SCHUYF AND ANDRÉ KROUWEL

7 The Dutch Lesbian and Gay Movement
The Politics of Accommodation

THE EVOLUTION of the Dutch homosexual emancipation movement is paradoxical. Since the early twentieth century, Christian Democrats have continuously controlled the executive branch of government,
yet lesbians and gay men seem to enjoy substantial social freedom and legal protection. Moreover, Dutch society is often referred to as permissive
and tolerant toward homosexual lifestyles. How can this paradox be explained? The answer must be sought in the structural characteristics that
underpin the political culture in the Netherlands. Usually referred to as the
"politics of accommodation" or "consociational politics" (Lijphart 1968),
this political culture and its institutions are geared toward achieving *consensus* between the various social groups, all of which are minorities.

The initial deep divisions within Dutch society, at the political level as
well as in other domains of social life, were institutionalized by the various political parties in a dense network of societal organizations, bound
together by religion or ideology. These networks are usually characterized
as "pillars" (*zuilen*). Although Dutch society was deeply divided at its
roots, the Catholic, Protestant, liberal, and socialist political elites—despite their vast ideological differences—cooperated pragmatically at the
political level. This political culture of consociational politics derives its
name from the "historical compromise" of 1917. In that year the confessional parties (in favor of equal state funding for religious schools) and
the secular parties (in favor of universal suffrage) reached an agreement
on both issues; male universal suffrage was introduced, and religious
schools received financial support from the state. Although broad cooperation existed at the elite level, the mass population was characterized by
political passivity and apathy (Daalder 1995). Secrecy and summit diplo-
macy were used in conflict resolution, and only a few political or ideological conflicts were discussed in the open. Politically sensitive issues
were kept out of the public debate or depoliticized. Because of the relative electoral strengths of the parties, no party could ever hope to gain a
majority by itself. Hence, government was and is only possible in coalition with other parties. And as another indicator of the inclusive political
culture of consensus democracy, Dutch coalition governments tend to ex-

pand beyond the necessary 50 percent threshold of parliamentary seats (De Swaan 1973; Andeweg, Tak, and Thomassen 1980; Daalder 1987).

CHRISTIAN DEMOCRATIC DOMINANCE

Despite their division into Catholic, Reformed, and Protestant segments, religious parties have dominated Dutch politics in the twentieth century. In the elections of 1909 the confessional parties jointly gained a majority in Dutch Parliament, which they maintained until 1967. Their electoral strength allowed the Roman Catholic State Party (RKSP), later renamed the Catholic People's Party (KVP), to participate in all coalition governments from 1918 until 1994. Moreover, the Catholic party preferred to coalesce with the right-wing, liberal Party for Freedom and Democracy (VVD). The dominant practice for the confessionals is to form a cabinet with the more progressive Social Democrats only in the case of utter necessity. The stable structure of the parties' electoral strength in the Netherlands allowed this Christian Democratic dominance to continue for over seventy years (Daudt 1982); however, this dominance is not only the result of confessional electoral strength (Kersbergen 1995, 1997). Also important is the Left/Right or socioeconomic dimension in Dutch politics. Christian Democratic parties, with their deliberate strategy of reconciliation and appeasement of class conflict, often occupy the center position on this dimension. Additionally, the fact that, between 1952 and 1994, the right-wing VVD and the left-wing Partij van de Arbeid (PvdA, or Party of Labor) seemed unwilling to cooperate in a coalition enabled the Catholic party to participate in every government since 1918 (see Krouwel 1993, 1998).

The dominance of Christian Democratic parties in electoral terms as well as their pivotal positions in coalition terms and the relative weakness of left-wing parties compelled the lesbian and gay movement to take into account the Christian Democratic parties' stance on homosexuality. Catholic and other confessional parties have always favored repressive policies on homosexuality (Oosterhuis 1992; Koenders 1996). In 1950, for example, the Catholic Center for Education in Statecraft (the scientific foundation of the KVP) published a report that proposed a total ban on homosexuality. Although the KVP officially distanced itself from this report, the party adopted a conservative position on the issue. The conservative position of all religious parties—KVP, Christian Historical Union (CHU), Anti Revolutionary Party (ARP), and the three small confessional parties—on moral issues like abortion and homosexuality remained relatively stable over time (Laver 1995). Left-wing and liberal parties (Green Left, D66, PvdA, and VVD) are more in favor of permissive policies on abortion and homosexuality.[1] This finding is corroborated in Budge, Robertson, and Hearl (1989), which analyzed the relative saliency of issues by measuring the proportion of the party platform devoted to them. With the addition of categories that are related to a positive attitude toward rights and freedoms of lesbians and gays,[2] it emerges that the secular parties are consistently more progressive than the confessional parties. During the 1960s and 1970s the PvdA showed a clear radicalization toward the Left, while the other secular parties put very little emphasis on progressive policies. In these decades, however, the Social Democrats occupied primarily the opposition benches. Although the saliency of homosexuality as a political issue declined considerably over time for the latter secular political parties,[3] the issue remained important for the confessional parties, who saw themselves as defenders of home and family.

Until 1963 the confessional parties obtained (more than) half of the parliamentary seats, allowing them to easily block progressive policies on moral issues. In addition, confessional parties consistently claimed the Ministries of Education, Justice, and Interior Affairs through which they could control policies on social order and moral issues. This pattern was well understood by the leadership of the Dutch gay and lesbian movement, who contacted the department at the ministerial level only when Social Democratic or liberal ministers controlled the Justice portfolio.

From the mid-1960s onward, however, the confessional parties lost a significant portion of their popular support in a process that has become known as depillarization. Religious affiliation and class position lost most of their explanatory power in the behavior of Dutch voters (Irwin and Holsteyn 1989). The percentage of the population adhering to a religious group declined from 80 percent in 1967 to 46 percent in 1989, and church attendance dropped dramatically from 90 percent in 1960 to 26 percent in 1986. In 1967 the three Christian Democratic parties together no longer polled 50 percent of the votes, and, what is more important in coalition terms, the Catholic People's Party was no longer the largest party. Forced by this weakened electoral and coalition position, the confessional parties merged into one interconfessional party, much like the Christian Democratic Union (CDU) in Germany. This Christian Democratic Appeal (CDA)[4] has held a similar pivotal position in the Dutch party system. However, since the formation of the CDA in 1980, the Christian Democrats have not been as dominant in electoral terms as were the three individual confessional parties. During the mid-1980s the party sustained its support at around 35 percent of the popular vote, but by 1994 the CDA had clearly lost its long-established political dominance. Liberal parties (VVD and D66), both with a more permissive attitude toward homosexuality, have gained in political strength in recent elections.

For the first time since 1918, the Netherlands is governed by a coalition cabinet without participation of a confessional party. After the election of 1994, liberals (D66 and VVD) and Social Democrats (PvdA) formed an unprecedented coalition cabinet.

The Dutch gay and lesbian movement has accommodated itself to the parameters of the political culture and power balance. Ever since its inception, the Dutch homosexual emancipation movement has been characterized by a strong orientation toward official authorities. This distinguishing feature—which was already apparent in the prewar Nederlands Wetenschappelijk-Humanitair Komitee, or NWHK (Dutch Scientific Humanitarian Committee)—also characterized the emancipation movement that emerged after World War II. The relation toward the state is primarily framed in the ideologically more neutral human rights discourse. Strong emphasis is placed on human rights (which have to be earned by homosexuals by being even more deserving than heterosexuals) as well as on the use of academic "evidence" to convince those with political and societal influence that homosexuality is a natural and normal phenomenon. The motto of the Dutch NWHK, *per scientiam ad justitiam* (through science to justice), highlights its policy of providing information about the nature and origins of homosexuality as a biological variety. After 1948 this policy became officially based on the Universal Declaration of Human Rights.

THE HOMOSEXUAL EMANCIPATION MOVEMENT AND THE STATE

After a century of liberal legislation under the influence of the French Napoleonic Code, the early twentieth century marked a new era of oppression of homosexuality in the Netherlands, primarily because of the advance of Christian-inspired political parties. These confessional parties, in particular the RKSP, used their political power to introduce restrictive legislation on pornography, prostitution, homosexuality, abortion, and gambling. In 1904, homosexuality was placed on the political agenda; this culminated in the 1911 introduction of Article 248 bis into the Penal Code by the conservative Catholic minister Regout. Article 248 bis, which prohibited homosexual contact between adults and minors (below the age of twenty-one) applied to both men and women. In response to the introduction of this article, J. A. Schorer founded the NWHK in 1911 after the German model,[5] and the Netherlands has known a continuous homosexual emancipation movement ever since.

The postwar emancipation movement COC (Cultural and Recreational Center) was founded as early as 1946 under the name Shakespeare

Club. This organization restricted itself to the same political/judicial strategy as the NWHK: lobbying key social and political figures to achieve equal rights for homosexuals. In the 1940s and 1950s the social and political climate remained too repressive for the COC to pursue a more visible strategy. A conspiracy of silence reigned over the daily lives of gays and lesbians, many of whom were forced to remain invisible for fear of losing their jobs (Schuyf 1994). Most of the COC's activities were directed internally toward entertainment and community building. Only its leaders communicated and negotiated with the external world: the authorities, the church, and the media (Tielman 1982). Early in 1947 the chairman of the Shakespeare Club, Nico Engelschman, initiated a dialogue with the chief of police of Amsterdam about the continuation of community meetings. The exchange of information was also useful to the authorities as a means of control and surveillance. This strategy of the early days was geared toward the dominant Dutch political culture. Of course, there never was a real "gay pillar" like the religious or socialist pillars, since the movement was always very small and fragmented and lacked an overarching ideology.

Nevertheless, the political and social repression united the movement until the late 1960s. During the 1950s, the Catholic elite became divided on the issue of homosexuality. The COC took advantage of this development by contacting some of the dissident Catholics to further their emancipatory case. Additional opportunities for a more progressive policy on homosexuality emerged, as mentioned earlier, when the confessional parties lost substantial popular support between 1963 and 1972. Hans Wansink (1985) has argued that the emancipation of homosexuals is closely related to this erosion of the pillarized structures during the 1960s. Under this more positive political constellation, the COC enlarged its membership.[6] Additionally, during the early 1950s, support came from the (heterosexual) Dutch Society for Sexual Reform (NVSH), which established close contacts and numerous cross-cutting memberships at the elite level. From 1956 onward the NVSH and the COC even organized joint activities on a small scale.

The development of the Dutch lesbian and gay movement is also characterized by a process of international diffusion. As early as 1951, when an international conference for sexual equal rights was held in Amsterdam, the COC was instrumental in initiating international cooperation among the European reform movements. This conference and the one organized the year after were such a success that the participants founded the International Committee for Sexual Equality (ICSE). International cooperation and exchange was primarily with three local groups from Germany, the Danish Forbundet af 1948, and Der Kreis from Switzerland.

There were also connections with Swedish, Norwegian, French, Belgian, and British organizations and individuals.

Immediately following World War II, the authorities used social work and psychiatry with the stated purpose of enhancing the mental health of society in general. Within the pillar system, psychiatrists and pastors had great moral authority, and despite their conservative opinions on homosexuality, what they saw as their duty toward society could be regarded as quite modern. The homosexual emancipation movement sought the help of some of these "enlightened" clergy and professional social workers to introduce more progressive attitudes. As early as 1952 the COC established contacts with probation workers, who were responsible for the reintegration of formerly imprisoned homosexuals. From 1954 onward a dialogue was begun with religious health care organizations and with the police vice squad. In particular, the cooperation with the director of the national Catholic Foundation for Mental Health, Cees Trimbos, proved vital for opening confessional minds to tolerance and acceptance of homosexuals. Reformative sermons given by Trimbos on national radio influenced thousands of people. The creation of an ecumenical group of influential health care specialists even led to a 1965 report pledging the abolition of Article 248 bis. And with the same objective of getting Article 248 bis abolished and obtaining legal status for the COC, the group maintained tenuous contact with representatives of political parties and the state bureaucracy during the fifties and sixties. Almost ten years before Stonewall in the United States, the bud of Dutch tolerance toward homosexuality had opened (Oosterhuis 1992; Schuyf 1994). In the late 1960s there was contact with Social Democratic Minister of Justice Samkalden and his liberal successor, Polak, on both issues. Thus, members from the homosexual movement managed to engage the clergy and the nonconfessional political parties in a discussion about equal rights. A climate of openness about homosexuality emerged, based on central values of humanity and self-acceptance. Ensuring a decent life for homosexuals according to bourgeois standards and curbing promiscuity were important goals. A number of publications promoted the belief that homosexuality was not intrinsically bad.

The late 1960s and early 1970s marked a turning point for the Dutch movement, as a more radical element came to the fore. From 1966 onward, several student work groups emerged. In the vision of these more radical gay rights activists, the problem was not homosexuality itself but the intolerance caused by societal reaction toward homosexuality. They concluded that society itself, not the homosexuals, had to be changed. Within the gay and lesbian movement, but primarily outside the COC, people used confrontational action to demand the "integration" of homosexuality in Dutch society (Stolk 1991). Together with other radical (political) groups, they no longer fought for acceptance and normality; they demanded the right to be different.[7] Attempts by the COC to gain control over these unruly organizations largely failed. Radicals organized the first public homosexual demonstration in January 1969 near the seat of the Dutch Parliament in The Hague during parliamentary discussions on the abolition of Article 248 bis. Soon after, on World War II Memorial Day (4 May) 1970, two gay men were arrested in an attempt to place a wreath especially for homosexual casualties at the official commemoration of World War II victims. At first, the COC distanced itself from these confrontational politics and public manifestations of homosexuality. Its leaders thought it wise not to oppose the authorities; instead, they sought (financial) support and facilitation from local and national governments. Under pressure from these more radical elements, however, the COC moved in a more left-wing direction from 1974 on. With the publication of the magazine *Dialoog* (Dialogue), the COC reluctantly entered the public domain.

In April 1971 the increasingly positive political and social climate resulted in the abolition of Article 248 bis from the Penal Code, equalizing the age of consent for homosexual and heterosexual sex to sixteen.[8] Typical for the politics of accommodation is that the Dutch Parliament itself initiated this move without any significant visible social pressure. Similarly, without any clear reason, the left-wing Den Uyl administration granted the COC legal status in 1973 and stipulated that homosexuality was no longer to be a ground for expelling someone from the armed forces. Although the COC had applied for legal status as early as 1961, it was refused on numerous occasions because the group allowed married people to become members, which, in principle, meant that it encouraged adultery (a criminal offense at the time).

From the late 1960s onward, the Dutch government started to facilitate the Dutch lesbian and gay movement financially. At the initiative of the COC, which without official legal status could not be subsidized directly, the Ministry of Welfare was persuaded to fund the Schorer Foundation in 1968 to provide social counseling for homosexuals. This initiative was executed in close cooperation with Christian health organizations. During the seventies, more and more government money went into social work for homosexuals, and the COC received government subsidies for its social work. Consequently, the COC's position as "Holy Mother Church" went practically unchallenged until the late 1980s.

As a result of declining repression and increasing state facilitation, homosexuality became more visible. During the late 1970s left-wing political parties founded gay (discussion) groups.[9] The merger of the Roman

Catholic trade union and the socialist union into one federation Federatie Nederlandse Vakverenigingen (FNV) also showed that the religious cleavage had lost much of its importance in Dutch society. This merger reduced the ideological profile of both trade unions, enabling gay and lesbian groups to appear within organized labor as well.[10]

Remarkably, it was a foreign event, rather than domestic developments, that triggered the first large public manifestation of the Dutch gay and lesbian movement. In 1977 former beauty queen Anita Bryant forced the city of Miami, Florida, to hold a referendum on its antidiscrimination law. As a result, Miami's gay rights law was struck down by a seventy percent majority. In reaction to these events, gays and lesbians took to the streets of Amsterdam on 25 June 1977. On 24 June 1978, around three thousand people celebrated a second International Day of Solidarity in Amsterdam, and in April 1979 lesbian and gay activists organized a demonstration against conservative Roman Catholic bishop Gijsen of Roermond.

Soon after, some gay and lesbian groups decided that the Netherlands should also have an annual Pride parade. In the United States this tradition had existed since the 1969 Stonewall incident (Duberman 1993). For this purpose, several of the political gay groups and other lesbian and gay organizations joined forces in Het Roze Front (the Pink Front) in 1979 to organize the largest visible expression of homosexuality, Roze Zaterdag (Pink Saturday). The history of Pink Saturday can be divided into three periods. In the first period, which spanned the years from 1977 to 1983, lesbian and gay activists constructed a broad movement. The second period of the Pink Front, from 1984 until 1989, is characterized by internal conflict, organizational breakdown, and ideological vagueness. The third period, which started in 1990, is one of increasing commercial involvement and decentralized control. During the 1990s, clear political goals and strategies have been almost completely absent. Participants of Pink Saturdays have not seemed very interested in influencing "official politics." The partylike festivities that came to characterize Pink Saturday indicated that community (Seidman 1993) dominated over political interests. Pink Saturday depoliticized most noticeably after the 1985 demonstration (Burgers and Franssen 1992; Krouwel 1994). However, even the earliest versions of the event were festive rather than purely political. In the earlier period the expression of gay aspirations was explicitly seen as a political and even subversive action. During the 1980s a more parliamentary strategy became more dominant. The right to be "different" and the expression of a gay "identity" combined and later even overshadowed by an emphasis on the human rights aspects of being gay. The parliamentary road led to the accentuation of a gay lifestyle as equal to all other lifestyles. The most striking observation is that, despite the collapse of the Pink Front and the organizational and ideological decline, the number of participants in Gay Pride Parades increased sharply over the years (Krouwel 1994). The first parades attracted between four thousand and six thousand people. In 1981, the year Parliament discussed a preliminary Equal Treatment Law for the first time, the Pink Front decided to organize the parade in a provincial town in the Catholic south of the country. During the parade there were some skirmishes with local youths. The following year's demonstration, which was held in the provincial town of Amersfoort, will be remembered as the most violent. Local youths attacked some of the participants, fifteen people were wounded, and the police stood by and did nothing. Amersfoort led to a new dialogue between the emancipation movement and the government, which resulted in a list of practical demands that each ministry could carry out under the aegis of the Ministry of Welfare. After the repeal of the antihomosexual Article 248 bis, the next step was to obtain equal treatment under the law.[11] With the introduction of plans for the Equal Treatment Law, it seemed that the aims of homosexual emancipation in the Netherlands had been completed and the movement had lost its mobilizing enemy for good. However, Christian control of government and crucial portfolios delayed the introduction of the bill for fifteen years. For Christian Democrats the most salient issue was the position of teachers at religious schools. Only in 1992, did an antidiscrimination provision in the Penal Code come into force, which amended most of the antidiscriminatory provisions to cover discrimination on the basis of "heterosexual or homosexual orientation" (Article 137c-f, 429 quater). It is now a criminal offense to use defamation or incitement to hatred against homosexuals or to discriminate against persons "in the performance of a public office, a profession or a business" on account of "their heterosexual or homosexual orientation." Finally in March 1994 the "real" Equal Treatment Law (Algemene Wet Gelijke Behandeling, or AWGB) came into existence. This law forbids making any distinction in labor contracts, in the professions, in the provision of goods and services, and in advice on education or occupation, although it does not stipulate any sanctions to violators. The main opposition to the Equal Treatment Law, as mentioned, came from religious groups. In the end, religious organizations formed an exception within the law, although as Minister of the Interior Ien Dales explicitly stated during the parliamentary discussion, the "single fact" of homosexuality may not count as a ground for dismissal.[12] The Equal Treatment Law recognizes indirect discrimination; individuals can file a complaint to the Committee for Equal Treatment, which then organizes a hearing and gives a (nonbinding) verdict. Although it seems that with the introduction of the AWGB homosexuals are protected against discrimination, there are, in fact, provisions in several laws that forbid practices carried out mainly by homosexuals: articles in local ordinances that prohibit transvestism and cruising in public toilets have not all been removed. Although the article is seldom enforced, it is still a criminal offense to have sex in public. Because there is a wide gap between the letter of the law and that which is deemed suitable for enforcement, many of these activities are *gedoogd* (tolerated) as long as they do not harm others. It is not uncommon for the Dutch to refrain from enforcing regulations that do not enjoy widespread public support.

By and large, Dutch law does protect homosexuals, and over the last few years increasing attention has been given to combatting antigay and antilesbian violence. There has been cooperation with the police in the prevention of violence and in the facilitation of investigation when violence does occur; within the judicial system antigay and antilesbian violence has been upgraded to consitute "a severe form of violence," thereby making it possible for suspects to be held on remand. Protection of individual rights is further guaranteed by the ratification of two international treaties.[13]

Nevertheless, the final step in the legal battle for lesbian and gay rights has not yet been taken. Despite the fact that virtually no distinction is made in law between heterosexual and homosexual cohabitation, heterosexual relationships and lifestyles are treated differently from homosexual relationships. Registered partnership is now possible in the Netherlands. In light of the parliamentary majority in favor of legal marriage for same-sex couples, the social democratic and liberal government parties have agreed to draft a law during the current term of parliament. Religious groups and some right-wing liberals oppose same-sex marriages on the ground that many countries would not offer their children for adoption if the children could be placed with a same-sex couple. Many lesbians and gays are confronted by the question of the position of children present in same-sex relationships, whether they originated from a prior heterosexual relationship or—as is increasingly the case—through artificial insemination. Various models of parenthood are being developed, including incorporating gay men as donors of semen and as role models as well as creating alternative family configurations among lesbians and gays. Yet, at present, because Dutch family law is based on biological relationships, no legal parenthood relationship can be established between a child and the lesbian partner of his or her mother or the gay partner of his or her father. Same-sex couples have not been granted the right to adopt children. The government of social democrats and liberals that came to power in 1994 has decided that this issue needs further discussion, despite positve advice from a national advisory committee.

Despite these lacunae in civil law, heterosexual and homosexual cohabitation are treated equally in reference to social security, income tax, and rent protection. However, the cohabitation contracts provided by Dutch government do not give contract couples equal rights to a joint pension (except in the case of some progressive pension funds) or equal inheritance taxes. Although it is not a formal legal recognition of cohabitation, official bodies have increasingly recognized the "living-together contract", which is, in fact, a declaration of joint household with the obligation for both partners to provide for each other. A person in a committed relationship loses his or her right to an independent income in the case of long-lasting unemployment. This provision is crucial within the Dutch welfare state regime, which has always been oriented toward the position of husband as caretaker/breadwinner and which aims to safeguard the family against disruptive forces of the labor market (Bussemaker and Kersbergen 1994: 8–25). Under the influence of Christian Democrats, social security benefits are primarily regarded as replacements for lost family income, and the welfare system provides few stimuli to reintegrate the unemployed back into the workforce. This high level of decommodification (making income independent of participation in the labor market) of caretaker/breadwinners, leading to long-term maintenance of socioeconomic status, is typical of conservative/corporatist welfare state regimes found in countries with strong Christian Democratic suport (Esping-Andersen 1987, 1990).

The mid-1980s marked a period of convergence in the relationship between the COC and national and local government. In 1986, Engelschman, the founder of the COC, received an official Royal decoration, and one year later a gay monument was established in the center of Amsterdam. Despite the primarily right-wing CDA and VVD governments, the 1980s were the golden years of government subsidies for lesbian and gay activity (although most of the grants were initiated by the short-lived coalition of PvdA, CDA, and D66 in 1982). The COC was funded with about one and a half million guilders a year (about $750,000); there was additional money for research and antidiscrimination activities. Gay and lesbian studies at several universities became subsidized to research the position of homosexuality in a number of social fields—including the police, the army, and the education system—and to research antilesbian violence and the specific position of lesbians and homosexuality within ethnic minorities. During 1983 and 1984 the Ministry of Welfare also subsidized the first national inventory of discrimination against lesbians and gays (Dobbeling and Koenders 1984) and the national Center for Anti-Homosexual Discrimination. The Ministry of Welfare also had a full-time policymaker for lesbian and gay emancipation until the early 1990s. Local councils followed suit. The larger towns employed policy-makers, and about 25 percent of the city councils with an active emancipation movement provided financial means for lesbian and gay emancipation. However, funding was made available only when the movement succeeded in putting a political issue on the agenda. Most of the stipulations for government grants force the applicants into a social and political straightjacket; cultural diversity is not encouraged, and political passivity is rewarded. The Ministry of Welfare is unable to give the exact amount spent on the emancipation movement in the 1980s and early 1990s, but it is estimated between eighteen and twenty-four million guilders ($9,000,000 to $15,000,000). After 1991, repeated cutbacks brought the total amount down to about seven hundred thousand guilders a year ($370,000). This decline in government grants was accelerated by the fact that social permissiveness toward homosexuality made it more difficult for lesbian and gay organizations to prove the need for cultural change through government support. This process was accompanied by a more liberal ideology of minimal state intervention and increased self-reliance.

The fact that money was pumped into the emancipation movement does not mean that there was direct representation of the movement in official government bodies. As a result of Dutch pillarization and a dense civil society, the government usually operates indirectly, with funding going primarily through secondary organizations. The COC is rarely represented as such in official government bodies, yet some professionals take part in advisory boards in a private capacity. This practice changed drastically with the advent of AIDS, following which the COC participated officially in the national Commission on AIDS Policy (NCAB). By officially involving the movement, the government created a legitimization of its AIDS policies with the groups most involved. AIDS brought an increasing flow of funds into the movement for AIDS-related activities; these were supplied by the Ministry of Welfare and Health Care, partly through secondary institutions such as the Schorer Foundation.

Unlike some countries where AIDS has generated widespread homophobia, the Netherlands has had a very moderate social reaction to AIDS. Again, this results from consociational practices typical for the Dutch polity. The emancipation movement was immediately given a voice in the campaigns to prevent AIDS. The main prevention strategies stressed the risk of certain forms of contact, thereby distracting attention from homosexuality as a lifestyle. Although many specific campaigns were directed toward gay men through their own media, prevention campaigns directed to the general public stressed the fact that condoms should always be used and made use of many heterosexual examples (see also Duyvendak 1995). This led to a certain degaying of AIDS, which was, in fact, not consistent with the actual situation (85 percent of people with AIDS in the Netherlands are gay men, although the number of heterosexuals with AIDS is increasing more rapidly). Close cooperation with the (local) authorities and health organizations also deradicalized AIDS activism in the Netherlands.

THE EMANCIPATION MOVEMENT AND SOCIETY AT LARGE

Next to the relatively permissive and facilitating posture of Dutch authorities, who have traditionally come from liberal, upper middle-class backgrounds the general liberal social attitude toward homosexuality in the Netherlands is puzzling. The dominant moral values, traditions, and religions in most societies are highly biased against a homosexual lifestyle. But people in the Netherlands are typically more tolerant toward homosexuality than are those in most other countries, and tolerance toward homosexuality has slowly risen since the late 1960s (Inglehart 1990: 194; Ester and de Moor 1993: 113).

This permissiveness is usually explained by the significant changes in the social and economic structure of the Netherlands during the 1950s and 1960s. Before 1945 most people received only primary education, but postwar generations have far higher levels of education. Substantial economic growth since the 1950s and the expansion of the welfare state have also increased the standards of living of many to an unprecedented level. Agricultural employment declined rapidly, replaced by jobs in the service sector. By the late 1970s more than 65 percent of the working population was employed in the nonmanual service and government sectors. As these jobs were often found in urban areas, many moved away from their traditional rural environment. The increase in income, education, and geographic mobility resulted in a more secular and permissive society. Within this increasingly tolerant political climate of the 1990s, homosexual groups in political parties are no longer able to find party political activists to maintain intraparty homosexual pressure groups. The increasing permissiveness was tapped in a number of surveys conducted by the national Social Cultural Plan Bureau, which asked the question Do you think that homosexuals should be free to live their own lives, or should this lifestyle be opposed? The responses are shown in Table 1.

In the early 1960s, age, urbanism, level of education, and religious affiliation were prime indicators of the degree of permissiveness toward homosexuality. And women, on the whole, were less tolerant toward homosexuality than were men. Although young Dutch citizens are far more tolerant than the older cohorts, by 1981 age and degree of urban-

TABLE I. *Social Tolerance toward Homosexuality, 1968–81*

Response	1968	1970	1974	1981
Homosexuals should live as they wish	56.4%	69.1%	83.8%	87%
Homosexuality should be opposed	30.7%	22.8%	16.2%	8.5%
No opinion	12.9%	8.1%	—	4.5%

ism had lost some of their explanatory power, and women and the less-educated had become much more tolerant. In fact, since 1981 religion has been the most important antihomosexual indicator. Apparently, a small part of the population, found in conservative Christian environments, continues to oppose homosexuality. In 1990 only 12 percent of the Dutch population was opposed to having homosexuals as neighbors, and only 22 percent opined that homosexuality could never be justified (European and World Value Surveys 1981, 1990). A survey conducted in 1991 showed that over 90 percent of the Dutch population agreed that lesbians and gay men should be allowed as much freedom as possible to run their own lives. Still, when more specific questions were asked, tolerance declined significantly. More than 15 percent of the population in 1991 was opposed to homosexual cohabitation. Half of the population was in favor of a civil marriage between same-sex couples, yet more than 50 percent objected to authenticating such a marriage with a church ceremony. More than 50 percent had no objection to having a female couple raise children, yet under 40 percent of the Dutch population deemed it acceptable for a male couple to raise children (SCP 1995; Dagevos 1996).

Despite this relatively tolerant social climate, in practice, discrimination against homosexuality still occurs at a number of levels in society: from downright physical violence (gay bashing and violation of property) to verbal abuse. For a number of years, complaints of antihomosexual violence were tabulated. The most frequent complaints were antigay bashing, violence, and discrimination in the immediate living environment. In fact, there are signs that the level of tolerance is diminishing again, especially among young people. Recent data suggest that within the secondary school system tolerance is scarce. From 50 to 70 percent of students think that it is best to hide homosexuality in school, 10 percent have extremely negative stereotypical ideas about gays and lesbians, and 20 percent agree that homosexuals should be discriminated against. Girls are more tolerant toward homosexuality than are boys; 53 percent of the boys (against 24 percent of the girls) would reject a fellow student who revealed in confidence that he or she was homosexual. Young males, especially young males from Islamic backgrounds, are less tolerant than are other groups in society (Akker 1996).

Dutch tolerance has often been described as "tolerance from a distance": it is easy to be tolerant if it does not touch your own immediate life. This is clear in the fact that fewer people completely oppose homosexuality than object to having homosexuals as neighbors. At the same time, homosexuals are tolerated as long as they do not differ too much from the rest of society. The old adage "You can be homosexual as long as you don't act homosexual" still holds. Well-adapted, prim and proper homosexuals—perhaps even those with registered partnerships—are welcomed as valued citizens, whereas promiscuous cross-dressing males and diesel dykes are still shunned by society. For lesbians the situation is worse than for gay men, as Dutch society is still characterized by remnants of a patriarchal structure. For a long time, men succeeded in marginalizing women by stigmatizing independent women as lesbians. Time and again surveys have shown that the Netherlands has one of the worst records of female emancipation among the industrialized nations, especially concerning labor market participation (Schmidt 1991; OECD 1994, 1995). Until the 1960s, female participation in the workforce was among the lowest in Europe (less than 20 percent), and the Netherlands has been repeatedly condemned by the European Court for failure to adhere to general European directives for equal treatment and payment of women in the workplace. Next to Botswana, for example, the Netherlands has the lowest percentage of female university professors in the whole world (a very high-status job in both countries). In addition to the restrictions of the conservative welfare state regime, the relatively scarce facilities for child care and maternity leave further hamper female labor participation. The picture of the Netherlands as an emancipated and tolerant society must be qualified on the basis of these facts.

THE DEVELOPMENT OF A GAY INFRASTRUCTURE AND SUBCULTURE

Before and during the Second World War, there were but a few locales catering to gay men (and almost none for lesbians). These places usually catered to prostitutes and petty criminals but also took gay men in the bargain. To meet others like them, many men were forced back into public places, such as public toilets and parks. The COC helped create an increasing number of clubhouses and cafes where people could meet outside of the "dangers and perversity" of the subculture. In the early fifties the only gay bars could be found in the larger cities: The Hague (which always had a rather well-developed gay and lesbian subculture), Rotterdam, Eindhoven, and Amsterdam. A commercial subculture started to blossom first in Amsterdam in the early 1960s (Hekma 1992). At the same time, leather bars started to attract numbers of foreign visitors. Van Hall, the mayor of Amsterdam, tried to curb the increasing number of bars by setting the maximum limit to twenty-five. This reactionary move did not sit well with the Dutch, and attempts to limit the number of bars were soon abandoned.

During the 1980s the number of meeting places (COC societies, bars, coffee shops, saunas, and hotels) rose enormously. Between 1982 and 1984 the number jumped from 230 to 358 (Veen 1985). Thereafter, the number of places stabilized and even slowly decreased. In 1984 almost half of the meeting places could be found in four cities: Amsterdam (25 percent of the total), The Hague, Rotterdam, and Eindhoven. In 1995, there were some 278 meeting places for gay men and 46 for lesbians (note that because there are few exclusively lesbian meeting places in the Netherlands, this number includes locales that have nights exclusively for lesbians on a regular basis). Amsterdam's contribution to the total has remained stable, but in the other three cities the number of meeting places has risen, so that 64 percent of the total number can now be found in only four cities. Outside these cities diversification has occurred: smaller towns or villages now often boast at least one gay bar. Within the larger cities the supply has diversified, now catering to every taste.

Similar developments over time can also be seen in the gay and lesbian press. The first homosexual magazine, *NWHK-Jaarverslag,* was published sporadically between 1918 and 1940. Its aim was to give the nonhomosexual public information about the nature of homosexuality, so that people could better form an opinion on the matter. A single issue of a magazine called *We,* the first magazine to be published for a homosexual public, appeared in 1932. Just before World War II the magazine *Levensrecht* (Right for Life) was issued. Printing was resumed immediately after the war, and in December 1946 readers of the magazine came together to found the Shakespeare Club, the predecessor of the COC. The magazine of the COC (albeit under different names and with different aims) has survived to this day. Until 1971 the publications of the COC were the only homosexual publications in the country. Circulation ran more or less parallel with the membership of the COC (about one thousand in 1949, three thousand in 1960, and five thousand in 1963). Outside of these publications little information on homosexuality was available. The national press was completely monopolized by the official papers of the different pillars and was placed under the strict ideological control of the political parties. Party chairmen or parliamentary leaders often held key editing positions on these newspapers. Nevertheless, there was little negative stereo-typing in the press. Rather, lesbians and gay men were made invisible, a segment of the population that was not addressed. It was only at the end of the 1950s that the first reports on incidents involving gay men appeared in the newspapers. In 1960 a mainstream book[14] discussed the gay subculture in a neutral manner. At the fifteenth anniversary of the COC, three main Liberal and Social Democratic newspapers gave an unbiased account of the festivities. In addition, the radio sermons broadcast by Trimbos showed an increasingly unprejudiced attitude in the media. In 1963 there was, nevertheless, a countermovement under the banner of Moral Rearmament (Morele Herbewapening), partly financed by the Philips family. It triggered such indignation among journalists and other members of Dutch society, however, that it backfired into positive reports on homosexuality.

In this media battle the COC used its new periodical, *Dialoog* (Dialogue), which addressed heterosexuals as part of the new strategy of the COC, though this did not lead to a significantly increased circulation. Only between 1978 and 1980 did the diversity and circulation of the gay and lesbian press rise exponentially. At least nineteen new magazines were published. Many were short-lived, but some, such as the *Gay-Krant* (a popular magazine), still exist today. In 1985 there were twenty national magazines, the most important of which were the COC magazine *SEK*, *Homologie* (an academic/cultural magazine), and the lesbian magazine *Diva*. Other magazines catered to smaller groups, such as Jewish homosexuals, those fond of browsing through lesbian archives, and gay and lesbian trade unionists. *Diva* proved to be economically unviable and soon disappeared. The total circulation of these magazines ran to 47,500 copies, of which 23,000 were subscriptions.[15] In 1996, the gay and lesbian press had a total output of 54,000 copies.[16] The total circulation of the lesbian press remained at 7,500 from the mid-1980s to the mid-1990s (*Diva* was replaced by the more homely *Zij-aan-Zij*, which started as a magazine for contact ads). *Gay-Krant* has shown impressive growth, especially considering that it is now a biweekly magazine. The diversity of the gay and mixed press has diminished considerably, however. Most smaller magazines have ceased to exist. There is increasing concentration into larger units. In 1985 the majority of readers of these magazines lived in the Randstad (the urbanized area in the western Netherlands), mainly in Amsterdam. Although the *Gay-Krant* was and still is read mainly in the province, recently there has been an increase in the number of readers in Amsterdam who—as intellectuals—at first scorned the popular paper. The new trend seems to be commercial magazines, which are distributed freely in the subcultural venues. The general picture of the subculture is one of increasing diversification; the press, on the contrary, seems to be undergoing a process of concentration.

The Subculture
and the Emancipation Movement

Until recently, the Dutch gay subculture was always closely intertwined with the emancipation movement. In the commercial subculture, the leaflets of the emancipation movement are usually very visible, and visitors of the commercial subculture also frequent the COC. Although the COC declared itself against the commercial subculture in principle, a love/hate relationship has existed between the COC and the gay subculture. A very moralist streak within the enlightened and well-educated COC board resulted in official condemnation of what they saw as the depravity of the subculture, with its promiscuity, superficiality, and gender bending. To many Dutch Protestants, regardless of their sexual preference, dancing was something wicked at worst and something useless at best. The increasing number of people who became members only in order to have the opportunity to dance was a thorn in the flesh of the morally minded. Nevertheless, there remained a deep division on the issue within the COC, and to this day the so-called recreation debate has never been resolved. From its founding onward, the COC had both an external and internal goal: recognition in society and the provision of a safe haven, where people could dance and, in general, be themselves. A piquant detail of the situation was the fact that in most smaller towns, the COC provided the only means of contact (apart from parks and public toilets).

With the ascension to power of a new chairman (Benno Premsela) in 1962, the COC adopted a more lenient attitude toward freedom of expression. The leadership officially changed its policies to a more external orientation and visibility and for the first time placed the word "homophile" in its official name. A television appearance by Premsela in 1964, in which he openly discussed his homosexuality, became a beacon for media accounts on the issue.

Initially the COC was a male-dominated club, although about one-fifth of its members were women. The advent of feminism in the seventies finally led to more visibility for lesbians. There were attempts at separate lesbian organization, but on the whole the ideas and theories of feminism (especially "the personal is political" with its wide consequences for gay identity politics and the norm of forced heterosexuality) have been more influential than have feminist organizations themselves. Lesbians within the COC started to realize that existing differences between men and women were not unrelated to their inferior position. Lesbian feminists within the movement found their paths blocked by the ideology of integration from the (male-dominated) COC board. The board's view was that lesbians should work together with gay men and should in no case organize separately.

Several groups of women then left the COC to found radical feminist groups such as Lavender September or socially oriented groups such as 7152. The COC reacted by intensifying its emphasis on integration. The struggle of feminists and gays was seen as one and the same because they both opposed traditional norms and values about masculinity and femininity. However, lesbians were recognized by neither the feminist movement (which feared being stigmatized as lesbian) nor the gay movement. This could lead only to a break within the COC. The circumstance was trivial—Amsterdam lesbians wanted their own coffee machine—nonetheless, in 1975 the separatists won the day when a special group for women within the COC was founded; it became autonomous in 1981 (Slob 1996).

The first lesbians-only bar was created in 1969, and there have been few commercially successful lesbian initiatives since. The vanguard of the lesbian movement pronounced lesbianism the epitome of feminism, under the slogan "Don't sleep with your oppressor." Lesbians were seen as superwomen, and have ever since consciously emphasized the social factors in their identity more than have gay men, who have tended to see themselves along rather more essentialist lines. Many women's cafes and centers became known as lesbian hideouts. But there remained an uneasy relationship between lesbians and heterosexual feminists in the women's movement. At the same time, the problems between men and women in the COC continued, as women battled to obtain the week's main evening out—Saturday—for themselves. In many COC local chapters, a separate women's committee was formed alongside mixed committees (which led to the odd but common expression "mixed woman" for a woman who continued to work with men); this created an uneasy form of organization. Nowhere did differences in organizational skills and issues of power between men and women become so clear as in these COC chapters. Yet separatism was never very strong in the Netherlands. In the eighties more radical lesbians joined the squatter's movement, adding an aversion to capitalist society in general to the problem of getting housing in the city centers, especially in Amsterdam. Other lesbians joined together to formulate specific political lesbian demands and put through formal political platforms. The encapsulating power of the state and the growing tendency to dissolve the elements in the welfare state that had made separatism possible in the first place finally ended separatism. The end of separatist lesbian feminism made differences between lesbians more visible. With the increasing emphasis on lifestyles in the early nineties, women started to experiment with gender styles: from masculine dildo-wearing, sadomasochistic dykes and gender benders to more feminine lipstick lesbians and lesbian mothers. The ubiquitous "pink dungaree dyke" has finally been replaced by a bewildering sample of sexual and other preferences. The women's committees within the COC chapters have all dissolved as a sign of the times.

As we have seen, the lesbian and gay movement grew significantly in the first half of the 1980s, only to stagnate in the late 1980s, when the first signs of division within the broad Pink Front became noticeable. This demise of the Pink Front is exemplary of the deep crisis that has taken hold in the lesbian and gay movement. The politicized identities so characteristic of the late seventies and eighties have all but disappeared as a result of decreased discrimination against younger middle-class gays, the granting of equal rights, commercialization, and a weariness over the struggle. At the time of this writing, the organized emancipation movement has a membership of about fourteen to fifteen thousand, most of whom are members of the COC. The seven main organizations are organized into one cluster by the Ministry of Welfare, which opted for listing a single post office box instead of seven nebulous clubs. The church-based organization Kringen has the fastest-growing membership, as its discussion-group method is more appealing to many gays and lesbians than is the promotion of interests (to which the COC now limits itself). This depoliticization can also be seen in the disappearance of women-only nights and women's caucuses within the COC, where the more radical and separatist activities were the first to vanish.

EMANCIPATION THROUGH ACCOMMODATION

The Dutch postwar gay and lesbian movement was largely a continuation of the prewar NWHK in terms of ideology, strategy, and elite recruitment. In fact, elite behavior is the main explanatory variable for the development and relative success of the movement. Key elements of the Dutch consociational democracy characterized the emancipation movement after World War II: at the elite level there is close cooperation and negotiation, whereas at the mass level passivity and apathy are promoted (Lijphart 1968). Consociational practices enabled the elite of the postwar gay emancipation movement to establish contacts and an exchange of information with elites from the dominant political parties. Dutch pillarization also established a political culture in which delegation of a substantial share of the practical daily policy implementation is left to intermediary organizations. This has resulted in a dense civil society with a large number of organized sectoral interest groups with whom the central government shares responsibility in policy formulation and which have a significant level of autonomy in the implementation of policy.

In the consensual Dutch political culture, the action pattern was intentionally limited to "civilized" information exchange at the elite level and paternalistic education to the wider public. This led to moderate demands for social change and high stability in leadership. In this political culture it is to be expected that the gay and lesbian movement in the Netherlands primarily oriented itself toward national and local political institutions and has always chosen a largely instrumental orientation (Burgers and Franssen 1992). Even during the years of radicalization and polarization (1969–77), the leadership negotiated with the authorities and attempted to moderate its constituency. The activities of the movement were increasingly subsidized and facilitated by the authorities, in reward for moderation in demands and external tranquility.

Despite the invisibility and social isolation of homosexuals in the 1940s and 1950s, the Netherlands, compared to neighboring countries, has had a relatively tolerant attitude toward lesbians and gay men. The attitude of the authorities has been far from repressive, and social acceptance of homosexuality increased consistently throughout the postwar period. In particular, the political parties of the Left—PvdA, D66, and the Communist Party of the Netherlands (CPN)—and the liberals within the right-wing VVD adopted more progressive policy positions toward lesbian and gay self-organization and public manifestation. Christian Democratic parties, on the other hand, have been far more reluctant to grant equal status to homosexual citizens. The strong position of the Christian Democrats has largely determined the room to maneuver for the leadership of the Dutch lesbian and gay movement.

Facilitation by central and local governments had a positive effect on the organization and mobilization potential of gay and lesbian organizations in the 1970s and 1980s and enabled the elite to mobilize substantial human and financial resources as well as to unite behind one political program. In addition, gay and lesbian groups of political parties, in or outside the Pink Front, mostly supported public manifestations of homosexuality. To get the attention of the media, politicians, and the general public, the Pink Front focused on the most salient political issues of the time. However, coherence and unity are not characteristic of the Dutch lesbian and gay movement. A long-term political agenda or platform existed only in the early days and even then was the subject of fierce debate. The connotation of the word "politics" has changed enormously over the years. These factors are all part of a wide process of depoliticization that continues to symbolize political and social relations in the Netherlands.

In addition to the generally high level of social and political tolerance, the pillar system seemed to guarantee a certain level of pluralism and autonomy for different social groups, including sexual minorities. This leads to an apparently contradictory conclusion. Although the improvement of the status of gays and lesbians is clearly associated with the decline of the rigid pillarization of Dutch society and in particular the decline of the (political) dominance of the Christian organizations, the pillar system also contributed to a tolerant social climate that allowed the emergence of alternative (sub)cultures. Political and social repression, which since the 1960s was never severe, has decreased even more in recent years. Wide popular tolerance of the homosexual lifestyle and its expressions has resulted in an almost complete loss of its political meaning and an almost overnight disappearance of the annual Gay Pride. Public manifestations of difference clearly contradict the dominant strategy of cooperation and mutual accommodation at the elite level. In a political culture where identities are important, it is quite acceptable to organize and mobilize adherents in order to reassert this identity. What does not seem appropriate in the Dutch context, however, is to impute certain characteristics to this identity and organize against the dominant culture. The very superficial liberal ideology that characterizes the public debate in the Netherlands allows people to distinguish between groups of a specific ethnic, cultural, social, and sexual character, yet the egalitarian culture prohibits a different treatment of these minorities. Government policies and financial grants to organized interests are allocated for the integration of minorities into mainstream society. Dutch lesbians and gays have been successful in taking advantage of the opportunities that arose in the political and social sphere as a result of consensual practices. In fact, their strategy was so successful that the movement(s) are now seeking new goals and ideals to justify their continuation.

Notes

Acknowledgments: We thank Donny Brandon (VWS), Joop van der Linden (COC), and Henk Krol (de GAY-KRANT).

1. On the basis of its left-wing attitude, the small proletarian Socialist Party seems to have the reputation of being in favor of homosexuality, whereas, in fact, it has always expressed a negative attitude toward what is sees as a form of "capitalist decadence."

2. In this study party manifestos are coded into fifty-two issue categories. Categories concerning a positive attitude toward (sexual) minorities are the following: favorable mention of the importance of personal freedom and civil rights (201); references to fair treatment of all people and an end to discrimination on the basis of racial, sexual, and other characteristics (503); opposition to traditional moral values (604); and favorable references to underprivileged minorities who are defined in neither economic nor demographic terms (for example, homosexuals, the disabled, and immigrants).

3. Green Left is a merger of the former Communist Party (CPN), the Pacifist Socialist Party (PSP), the Radical Political Party (PPR), the Evangelical People's Party (EVP), and some independents.

4. The CDA was formed in 1980 out of a merger of three parties: the KVP, the liberal Protestant CHU, and the orthodox Protestant ARP.

5. In Germany, unified under the Prussian regime and its legal system, homosexuality was recriminalized under paragraph 175 in 1871. In response, Magnus Hirschfeld founded the Wissenschaftlich-Humanitäres Komitee (Scientific Humanitarian Committee) in 1897, which influenced emancipation movements throughout Europe (Steakley 1975).

6. In 1949 the organization had 792 members, and it had doubled the number three years later. During the 1950s the membership rose to over 2000. In 1960 over 3000 people had joined the organization; by 1963 the number had risen to 5000.

7. Among these, the most influential were the Student Workgroups on Homosexuality, founded in 1967; Foundation for Free Relation Rights; New Lavender (1969); Red Queers (1974); and Lesbian Nation and Lavender September (1971).

8. Since 1991, any person who has sex with a minor between the ages of twelve and sixteen can be prosecuted only on the basis of a formal complaint made by the child involved, by his or her legal representative, or by the Child Welfare Council.

9. Gay discussion groups were founded by the PSP and the PvdA in 1978 and the PPR and the CPN in 1979.

10. Within the FNV, the Civil Servants' Union (ABVA/KABO) and the Dienstenbond both formed gay groups as did the Christian union, CNV. The Catholic and Protestant Teachers Unions (KOV and PCO) also organized their lesbian and gay members.

11. The first article of the 1983 constitution states explicitly, "All those resident in the Netherlands shall have equal treatment under equal circumstances. Discrimination on the basis of religion, philosophy of life, political view, race, sex, or any other basis whatsoever, is not permitted." When Parliament discussed the concept of this constitution, it explicitly stated that "any basis whatsoever" included homosexuality (*Tweede Kamer* (Minutes of the Dutch Parliament) 13872, no. 4 [1975–76]: 87).

12. Almost single-handedly she defused Christian opposition to the law when her anger over the issue confirmed her reputation as a lesbian. Upon her unexpected death within the year, she was surprisingly outed by Prime Minister Ruud Lubbers.

13. These are the European Convention for the Protection of Human Rights and Fundamental Freedoms (especially Article 14) and the International Covenant on Civil and Political Rights.

14. Roodnat.

15. Of the total circulation, *Gay-Krant* had 16,500, *SEK* had 10,000, *Homologie* had 6,000, *Diva* had 3,500, smaller lesbian magazines had 4,000, and mixed and gay magazines had 7,500.

16. *Homologie's* circulation was 4,000, *Gay-Krant's* was 30,500, *XL's* (the COC magazine) was 12,000, *Zij-aan-Zij's* was 5,500, and *Ma'dam's* was 2,000.

REFERENCES

Akker, A. van den. 1996. *Een hoorn des overvloeds zonder exotische vruchten: de stand van zaken rond seksuele voorlichting op scholen voor voortgezet onderwijs in Utrecht*. Utrecht: GG & GD.

Andeweg, R. B., Th. van der Tak, and J. J. A. Thomassen. 1980. "Government Formation in the Netherlands," in *The Economy and Politics in the Netherlands since 1945*. Ed. R. T. Griffiths. The Hague: Martinus Nijhoff.

Budge, I., D. Robertson, and D. Hearl, eds. 1989. *Ideology, Strategy and Party Change: Spatial Analysis of Post-War Election Programs in Nineteen Democracies*. Cambridge: Cambridge University Press.

Burgers, C., and J. Franssen. 1992. "Tussen verlangen en belangen. De homo- en lesbische beweging." In *Tussen verbeelding en macht: 25 jaar nieuwe sociale bewegingen in Nederland*. Ed. Jan Willem Duyvendak, Amsterdam: SUA.

Bussemaker J., and K. van Kersbergen. 1994 "Gender and Welfare States: Some Theoretical Reflections." In *Gendering Welfare States*. Ed. D. Sainsbury. London: Sage.

Daalder, H., ed. 1987. *Party systems in Denmark, Austria, Switzerland, the Netherlands and Belgium*. London: Pinter.

———. 1995. "Leiding en Lijdelijkheid in de Nederlandse Politiek." 1964. Reprinted in *Van oude en nieuwe regenten, politiek in Nederland*. H. Daalder. Amsterdam: Bert Bakker.

Dagevos, H. 1966. *Tolerance in the Netherlands*. Rotterdam, Netherlands: Institute for Sociological-Economic Research, Erasmus University.

Daudt, H. 1982. "Political Parties and Government Coalitions in the Netherlands since 1945." *Netherlands Journal of Sociology*, no. 18:1–23.

De Swaan, A. 1973. *Coalition Theory and Cabinet Formation*. Amsterdam: Elsevier Scientific Publishing.

Dobbeling, Marion, and Pieter Koenders. 1984. *Het topje van de ijsberg: Tien jaar homodiscriminatie in Nederland*. Utrecht, Netherlands: Homostudiesreeks.

Duberman, Martin 1993. *Stonewall*. New York: Dutton.

Duyvendak, Jan Willem. 1995. "De Hollandse aanpak van een epidemie: Of waarom ACT UP! in Nederland niet kon doorbreken." *Acta Politica* 30(2):189–214.

Esping-Andersen, G. 1987. "Institutional Accommodation to Full Employment: A Comparison of Policy Regimes." In *Coping with the Economic Crisis*. Ed. Hans Keman, Heikki Paloheimo, and Paul Whiteley. London: Sage.

———. 1990. *Three Worlds of Welfare Capitalism*. Princeton: Princeton University Press.

Ester, P., L. Halman, and R. de Moor. 1993. *The Individualizing Society: Value Change in Europe and North America*. Tilburg, Netherlands: Tilburg University Press.

European and World Value Surveys. 1981, 1990. Tilburg, Netherlands: Tilburg University Press.

Hekma, Gert, ed. 1992. *De roze rand van donker Amsterdam: De opkomst van een homoseksuele kroegcultuur 1930–1970*. Amsterdam: Van Gennep.

Ingelhart, Ronald. 1990. *Culture Shift in Advanced Industrial Society*. Princeton: Princeton University Press.

Irwin, G. A., and J. van Holsteyn. 1989. "Decline of the Structural Model of Competition." *West European Politics* 12:112–38.

Kersbergen, K. van. 1995. *Social Capitalism, Social Capitalism: A Study of Christian-Democracy and the Welfare State*. London: Routledge.

———. 1997. "Between Collectivism and Individualism: The Politics of the Centre." In *The Politics of Problem Solving in Postwar Democracies*. Ed. H. Keman. London: MacMillan.

Koenders, P. 1996. "Tussen christelijk reveil en seksuele revolutie: bestrijding van zedeloosheid in Nederland, met nadruk op de repressie van homoseksualiteit." Ph.D. diss. Leiden University, Netherlands.

Krouwel, André. 1993. "Het CDA als *catch-all* partij?" In *Geloven in macht, de christen democratie in Nederland*. Ed. Kees van Kersbergen, Paul Lucardie, and Hans Martien Napel. Amsterdam: Het Spinhuis.

———. 1994. "Nederland: Van potten en flikkers." In *De verzuiling van de homobeweging*. Ed. J. W. Duyvendak. Amsterdam: SUA.

———. 1996. "Partijverandering in Nederland: De teloorgang van de traditionele politieke partijen." In *Jaarboek DNPP 1995*. Ed. E. Voerman. Rijksuniversiteit Groningen.

———. 1998. The Development of the Catch-All Party in Western Europe, 1945–1990. PhD diss., Free University of Amsterdam.

Laver, M. 1995. "Party Policy and Cabinet Portfolios in the Netherlands, 1994: Results from an expert survey." *Acta Politica*. 30 (1):1–11.

Lijphart, Arend. 1968. *Verzuiling, pacificatie en kentering in de Nederlandse politiek*. Amsterdam: De Bussey.

OECD. 1994. *The OECD Jobs Study: Evidence and Explanations*. Paris.

———. 1995. *The OECD Jobs Study: Implementing the Strategy*. Paris.

Oosterhuis, H. 1992. "Homoseksualiteit in katholiek Nederland: Een sociale geschiedenis 1900–1970." PhD Thesis, SUA, Amsterdam.

Roodnat, Bas. 1960. *Amsterdam is een beetje gek*. Amsterdam: De Bezige BG.

Schmidt, M. G. 1991. *"Political and Social Aspects of Female and Male Labour Participation: The German-Speaking Family of Nations in Comparative Perspective."* Paper, RSSS/ANU, Canberra, Australia.

Schuyf, J. 1994. "Een stilzwijgende samenzwering: Lesbische vrouwen in Nederland 1920–1970." PhD Thesis, RUU, Interfacultaire Werkgroep Homostudies, Leiden, and IISG, Amsterdam.

Seidman, Steven. 1993. "Identity and Politics in a 'Postmodern' Gay Culture: Some Historical and Conceptual Notes." In *Fear of a Queer Planet: Queer Politics and Social Theory*. Ed. Michael Warner. Minneapolis: University of Minnesota Press.

Slob, M. 1996. "Het pingpong stadium te boven: De opkonst van de vrouwen in het COC." *Homologie XL* 5 (6).

Sociaal Culturele Planbureau (SCP). 1995. "Sociale en culturele Verkenningen. Nijmegen, Netherlands.

Steakley, James. 1975. *The Homosexual Emancipation Movement in Germany.* New York: Arno Press

Stolk, B. van. 1991. "De kracht van de moraal: De doorbraak in het emancipatieproces van Nederlandse homoseksuelen." *Amsterdams Sociologisch Tijdschrift* 18, no. 1 (May):3–34.

Tielman, R. A. P. 1982. *Homoseksualiteit in Nederland: Studie van een emancipatiebeweging.* Meppel, Netherlands: Boom.

Veen, E. van der. 1985. "De Nederlandse homo-pers: Historie, omvang en bereik." In *Homoseksualiteit en de media.* Ed. E. Bakker and J. Schuyf. Utrecht, Netherlands: Homostudiesreeks.

Wansink, H. 1985. "Verzuiling en homo-emancipatie." In *Homojaarboek 3.* Ed. J. Schuyf, Amsterdam: Van Gennep.

OLIVIER FILLIEULE
AND JAN WILLEM DUYVENDAK

8   Gay and Lesbian Activism in France

Between Integration and Community-Oriented Movements

OVER THE past decades we have witnessed the emergence of many identity-based movements in Western Europe and the United States. Having confronted the world with the slogan "Black is beautiful," the civil rights movement in the United States inspired oppressed groups all over the world to creep out of their shells. No longer asking for sympathy, these groups proudly and vehemently demanded equal treatment and recognition of their right to be different. The feminist movement was, of course, among the front-runners, sparking a process of cultural change that has reverberated to the present day. But there were other minorities, such as the disabled, immigrants, gay men, and lesbians, who also started to take action.

This wave of emerging identity movements has repeatedly been interpreted in terms of the concept of "new social movements"—so much so, in fact, that a new social movements (NSM) paradigm has even developed (Pizzorno 1978:277–98; Touraine 1978; Offe 1985; Melucci 1989). It contends that the prime objective of these movements is to bring about cultural, rather than political, change (Melucci 1980: 220), casting the NSMs as the champions of a new, postmaterialist world. This concept has, however, endured a torrent of criticism (Cohen 1985; Klandermans 1986; Kuechler and Dalton 1990; Rucht 1991: 355–84), mainly because many older movements, such as the trade unions with their flourishing workers' culture, were similarly characterized by a profound sense of identity (D'Anieri, Ernst and Kier 1990; Tucker 1991).

This objection does not wholly invalidate the NSM theory, however; it merely implies that these new movements are not new in terms of their compelling sense of collective identity. Instead, their novelty seems to lie in the specific constellation of movements dominated by (parts of) the new middle classes, whose goals are predominantly nonmaterialistic (Kriesi 1989; Duyvendak 1995a: 19).

A significant characteristic of some of these new movements, such as the peace and environmental movements, is that identity of the members is of only secondary significance (Nelles 1984). Within these instrumental movements, collective identity is little more than a (transient) product of collective action. It is not a fundamental mobilizing factor, and it is certainly not their raison d'être. In other new movements, however, the identity of members plays a vital role. These new, "exclusive" movements (Zald and Ash, 1966: 330–31) are characterized by a "politicization of personal identity." They include the feminist, gay, and many immigrant movements, which all advocate an identity-based political strategy (Duyvendak 1994).

It bears mentioning, however, that social movements based on the collective identity of a specific group do not have equal opportunities to develop in their respective countries. (Fillieule and Péchu 1993). France is especially interesting in this regard, because the prevailing republican tradition of egalitarianism and universalism conflicts with the pursuit of a specific group identity and the representation of particular desires and interests (Hoffmann 1963; Ambler 1971; Hazaseeringh 1994). In this chapter we discuss how this tradition has affected the development of the French gay and lesbian movement.

The gay and lesbian movement is an identity movement that combines elements of subculture and movement in an intriguing manner. It is a subcultural movement par excellence (Koopmans 1995). Gays and lesbians develop a positive self-identity through participation in the movement: the common sexual orientation serves as an incentive for individuals to mobilize and organize collectively. A subcultural movement that is the exclusive provider of the collective good its members need does not suffer from free-riders (Duyvendak 1995b: 167). But at a given moment the gay and lesbian movement may be confronted by free riders, especially if its efforts are successful. Although direct participation is an indispensable prerequisite for sharing any collective benefits at the start of the emancipation process, "parasitic" behavior may arise as an option later on. As subcultures become increasingly *commercialized,* people can share collective identities outside the movement. Under such circumstances, many gay organizations can survive only by becoming more pleasure oriented and less political. Gay journals in particular will show a tendency toward commercialization, by publishing more erotic material and less political information. In this chapter I assess the extent to which the shifting relationship between subculture and movement may be attributed to either endogenous dynamics or exogenous factors, such as the republican tradition.

OLD AND NEW SOCIAL MOVEMENTS IN FRANCE: THE STATUS OF "IDENTITY"

France is fairly similar to other Western European countries in terms of the quantitative aspects of political protest (that is, in terms of the sheer number of movements and activists). It does, however, deviate in a qualitative sense. For instance, the dynamics of protest are fundamentally different. In France, demonstrations are not organized by specific groups with numerous members who systematically take to the streets for a specific purpose. Instead, political action is the domain of individual citizens, most of whom are not members of any organization. For a brief period they are induced to participate in mass mobilization, formulating ever more general goals, as they move through the spiral of protest toward head-on confrontation (Fillieule 1997, 1998). Furthermore, "traditional" objectives remain predominant in the protest actions of social movements in France, leaving very little room for new objectives. Ideological permanence may be attributed to both the formal political structure and the informal political culture of the system. All new movements are confronted with this problem, whether they are instrument oriented (the environmental, peace, and solidarity movements) or identity oriented (the feminist, squatters, gay, and lesbian movements) (Duyvendak 1995a; Fillieule 1998).

Concerning the status of identities, there are lessons to be learned from the development of the dominant, *old* movements. First, we may conclude that France is not fundamentally opposed to all identity-based politics, because identity has been a key issue of the traditional conflicts. Corsicans and Bretons, farmers, Catholics, and workers (Fillieule 1993) all foster a deep-seated sense of collective identity. In fact, many of them even consider acknowledgment of their identity to be the prime objective of their struggle. In light of the aforesaid, it is easy to refute the contention that identity-based politics is primarily the domain of the new movements. It also seems logical—perhaps even more so than for other countries—that France should be confronted with political strife based on collective identities. A society that swears by egalitarianism offers disgruntled citizens a powerful discursive weapon that allows them to organize themselves as a group in order to demand equal rights. There is therefore no reason to draw the a priori conclusion that identity-based politics will be less common in a universalist political culture than it will be in a particularist culture. After all, any French minority group that feels slighted has the right to demand equality.

It is also instructive to note that the older movements pursue a specific type of identity-based strategy: movements based on particular collective identities demand *equal*, rather than *special* treatment. They demand the same rights as the majority. The groups in question are engaged in a struggle against disfranchisement; they too wish to become real French citizens.[1] Even those groups that are proud of their unique identity often formulate their pride in general, universal terms. For example, Catholics will state that they are true Frenchmen and -women, workers will state that they are real republicans. On one hand, the Jacobin, egalitarian tradition grants groups of citizens the freedom to unite temporarily and demand equal rights. On the other hand, this tradition makes it impossible for such groups to maintain their appeal for support and preservation of their specific group culture. One may conclude, therefore, that it is (and always has been) impracticable to pursue a multiculturalist policy (Gutmann 1992; Taylor 1992; Seidman 1993: 105–42) in France.

The degree of freedom granted to *new*, identity-based movements in France is thus limited for two reasons. First, the legitimacy of identity-based political action is always temporary and conditional. This implies that it is tolerated as long as it is directed toward eradicating inequality or toward erasing the societal discrepancies and disadvantages that fuel the group's discontent. Second, the available space for new movements is limited, because the political field is already occupied by the aforementioned traditional identities. In terms of the prevailing political logic, however, these traditional political identities should have been of a temporary nature. Instead, they have become highly stable entities, as a result of the stagnation of the political system. This constitutes an intriguing paradox: although the French political system makes no provision for the permanent accommodation of specific collective identities, these identities have proved extraordinarily persistent, because of the obstructive dynamics of the political system.

These circumstances force the new movements not only to formulate their demands in terms of the republican rhetoric of universalism and egalitarianism but also to forge alliances with the dominant discourse of the older movements. In concrete terms, this prompted many new movements to seek the shelter of traditional leftist parties and movements in order to learn to speak the language of the left-wing political family (Duyvendak 1995a: 203–9).

This assimilation of new issues by older movements contradicts the concept of a zero-sum relationship between old and new issues (Brand 1985a, 1985b: 306–34; Kriesi and Duyvendak 1995: 3–25). The concept therefore requires qualification. After all, even in France there is scope for new issues, despite the fact that they must be formulated in terms of the traditional antitheses. However, new organizations that did make an all-out solo bid to place their issues on the political agenda have failed, indeed, almost without exception.[2] An empirical account of the factors that forced the French gay and lesbian movement to present itself as a left-wing element illustrates the assimilation of "new" issues into "old" movements.

FROM REVOLUTION TO INVOLUTION, 1970–81

It is difficult to fix a precise date when the French homosexual movement was born. A tentative start was made with the publication of the journal *Futur* in the period after the Second World War. But this remained almost unknown to the outside world, as all publicity for it was forbidden by the state. Homosexuality had no place in French *political* life, in contrast to cultural life, in which it was, and is, a source of inspiration.[3] Contact between the authorities and gays was absolutely one-sided: the authorities initiated every interaction on the basis of repression.

This particularly difficult situation improved to some extent in 1954, when the *Arcadie* journal was established. Some authors consider this the starting point of the gay movement (Bach 1982, 1988; Cavailhes, Dutey, and Bach-Ignasse 1984); others (for instance, Girard 1981) consider that neither the journal nor CLESPALA (Club Littéraire et Scientifique des Pays Latins),[4] the social club that was affiliated with *Arcadie,* constitute a *movement.* Nevertheless, *Arcadie* is important in that it does constitute a reference point for all subsequent organizations. André Baudry, its leader from start to finish, dictated a(n) (a)political line[5] about the self-help nature of *Arcadie*[6] which stressed the *equality* of hetero- and homosexuals: *l'homosexuel est aussi un homme social.*[7] In the contact that developed slowly with the outside world, *Arcadie* followed a so-called key-figure policy. Public activities were absolutely impossible under the repressive conditions of the day, but, even when the political climate became a little less wintry after May 1968, *Arcadie* maintained its strategy: for the improvement of the homosexual condition, homophiles were advised to behave as "normally" as possible.

The highly confrontational style of the Comité d'Action Pédérastique Révolutionnaire (Committee for Revolutionary Homosexual Action), at the Sorbonne in May 1968 and, more important, that of the Front Homosexuel d'Action Révolutionnaire, or FHAR (Homosexual Front for Revolutionary Action) after 1971, were contrary to *Arcadie's* strategy. "Whereas *Arcadie* rejected the effeminates, the queens, the transvestites and the transsexuals, the FHAR in return gathered together a rich variety of behaviours" (Girard 1981: 91). It strongly opposed the *clandestinité digne et virile* (dignified and manly clandestineness) of *Arcadie* in an attempt to fight the stigmatized identification of homosexuals with a pathological condition. In contrast with *Arcadie,* it considered *la différence* as something positive. "Abnormal" sexuality was no longer something to be hidden; it was instead something to be shown in public. In that respect, the founding event of the FHAR is highly significant: the interruption of a radio broadcast on *"l'homosexualité, ce douloureux problème"* (the painful problem of homosexuality) on 10 March 1971. "That is not true; we are not suffering at all!" shouted the activists, and their first press communiqué declared that "homosexuals are fed up with being a 'painful problem.' "

Because the FHAR was born out of the turmoil of the 1968 movement, it was strongly linked to Marxist ideology: "In a world based on sexual repression and on such foul obscenities as work, all those who are unproductive, those who make love exclusively for pleasure and not for production of an industrial army reserve have no other alternative but to perish or revolt" (pamphlet cited in Hamon and Rotman 1982: 329). The FHAR stressed not only the political character of homosexuality but also its revolutionary potential. *Notre trou du cul est révolutionnaire* (Our assholes are revolutionary) as FHAR spokesman Guy Hocquenghem put it.[8]

This radical assertion is evidence of the fundamental ambiguity from which the movement could never escape: on one hand the strategy aimed to construct a new identity based on overturning the stigma associated with being homosexual and asserting gay pride;[9] on the other hand, the movement refused to limit its action to the building of communities, extending the struggle to highlight the economic and political exploitation of the capitalist order. Thus, there was, for example, the hostility of the organization to the commercial development of gay meeting places (bars, clubs, and saunas), which was not in accord with its harsh denunciation of capitalism.[10]

This ambiguity shows itself also in the FHAR slogan "*Le droit à la différence*," which added an entirely new element to French politics. After all, groups demanding "the right to be different" were something of a novelty within the political culture of egalitarian France, and such demands had certainly never been made in combination with an attack on dominant, heterosexual normality.[11] The FHAR clearly refused to bow to the republican logic, which held that minorities should strive to obtain the same rights as the majority. Instead, the FHAR turned this logic upside down: the minority not only demanded the right to be different but also argued that the majority should change. This countercultural trend, which also emerged in many other Western European countries at that time (Duyvendak 1991: 124–34; Adam 1995), was not likely to last very long in France. In the first place, the political establishment interpreted the emphasis on collective identity as an appeal for equality, because variety or pluriformity was (and is) not seen as a legitimite political objective in itself. Therefore, in contrast to the gay and lesbian minorities in the Netherlands and (even more so) the United States, which demanded to be recognized as minorities (Meijer, Duyvendak, and Van Kerkhof 1991; Seidman 1995), the dominant political culture in France forced the gay and lesbian movement to speak the language of egalitarianism. In order to achieve its political goals, the French gay and lesbian movement, therefore, had to join the majority, instead of turning against the dominant "normality." In concrete terms, this meant they had to join the left-wing family, which brings us to the second reason underlying the transience of the French movement's bid to be different. The coercive solidarity within the left-wing bloc forced the FHAR to generalize its demand for *"le droit à la difference."* This meant that the right to be different should be seen to apply not only to homosexuals (male and female) but to all minorities. Paradoxically, the generalization of *"le droit à la difference"* led to uniformity. In terms of the left-wing, *gauchist* ideology, all affiliated groups were different in the same way: they were all victims of capitalism. The FHAR consequently adopted the slogan "Their struggle is our struggle," effectively erasing any possible distinction between its own struggle and those of other groups.

In its ambiguity, the FHAR managed to balance pleasure with policy interest, organizing parties and meetings simultaneously at the same venue; its revues *Le Fléau Social* (The Social Plague) and *L'Antinorm* were interesting mixtures of anarchistic chaos and Trotskyist consistency.

New organizations became increasingly involved exclusively in political activism, aggravated by the fact that many entertainment institutions (bars, journals, and the like) were still repressed by the police and politics. The FHAR faded away in 1973, to be replaced by the Groupe de Libération Homosexuelle (GLH). Within this group a struggle developed between those who favored a political line in the "antinormality" tradition of homosexuality, GLH-Groupe de Base (GLH-Grassroots Group), or GB, and those who argued for more pragmatism GLH-Politique et Quotidien (GLH-Politics and Daily Life), or PQ. Of all these tendencies, GLH-PQ survived and even succeeded in building a network of local organizations. Besides organizing a great number of activities with other contemporary movements (prochoice, feminist, antimilitarist, anti–nuclear energy), it also organized the first massive demonstrations in the streets of Paris and ran gay candidates in local and national elections.

In its political discourse, GLH-PQ expressed strong sentiments against the PCF (the French Communist Party). As a matter of fact, if left-wing groups had, albeit reluctantly, taken on board gay and lesbian demands insofar as they were conceptualized in terms of class, the PCF remained opposed to gay liberation, even "disguised" in anticapitalist terms.[12] During the second half of the 1970s, the gay movement made inroads into the more moderate parties of the Left, which "deradicalized" the discourse of the movement: the total politicization of homosexuality faded away. Homosexuals moved away from a partly countercultural position toward a more *instrumental* approach.

At the end of the 1970s, an umbrella organization was established, comprising sixteen gay and lesbian organizations, with the exception of the *Arcadie* group. This so-called CUARH, or Comité d'Urgence Anti-Répression Homosexuelle (Emergency Committee against the Repression of Homosexuals), openly supported the candidacy of François Mitterrand for the presidential elections in 1981. On one hand, this showed a certain moderation in the political opinions shared by lesbian and gay activists; on the other hand, it clearly indicated that the movement was still highly politicized, which implied, in terms of the French political opportunity structure, that they were highly dependent on the Left and, more specifically, the Socialist Party. In some countries liberal parties also showed some sympathy toward lesbian and gay issues, at least to the extent that they were formulated in terms of equal rights (for example, in Germany and the Netherlands), but in France only the Socialist Party opened itself to the gay and lesbian movement at the end of the 1970s. Apart from this umbrella organization, some other new organizations and publications emerged, such as *Gai Pied*, providing structure and publicity for the subculture. Whereas in the CUARH, men and women cooperated in promoting their common interests, these new, subcultural organizations were nonmixed.

On the lesbian side, one of these organizations was Lesbia, whose journal paid at least as much attention to lifestyle issues as to the world of politics. *Lesbia-Magazine* is to date the most successful lesbian "organization." It can be considered the successor of many attempts to establish an independent journal for lesbians in France, attempts that failed because of the extremely marginal position of lesbians in French social and political life and because of the ideological fights between several groups of lesbians over politics, feminism, and (non)cooperation with gay men.

Whereas many lesbian women were strongly involved in the feminist movement during the 1970s, both the "heterosexualization" of French feminism at the end of the 1970s and the growing political opportunities for gays and lesbians at the start of the 1980s stimulated, on one hand, the development of a mixed, interest-oriented movement (CUARH) and, on the other, the growth of radical, countercultural lesbian groups—Lesbian Archives, autonomous projects, and so on (Mossuz-Lavau 1991; Gonnard 1997). After 1980, lesbians were no longer very eager to participate in a rather hostile, declining feminist movement. (Simone de Beauvoir wrote in 1980, "Lesbians are presenting their specific and limited group interests as the interests of feminists in general"[cited in Martel 1996: 417].) Their cooperation with gay men was not long lasting either, however. After the successes reached by the CUARH (discussed below), there did not seem to be a further reason for mixed organizations.

Moreover, any political organization seemed outdated after the realization of the goals of the movement at the start of the 1980s. Not only radical lesbian organizations disappeared during the 1980s but the more moderate as well. It was only after the resurgence of the gay movement at the end of this decade (as a result of AIDS) that lesbians manifested themselves publicly again. In particular the organization of the film festival Quand les Lesbiennes Se Font du Cinéma at the start of the 1990s showed the increasing visibility of lesbians and the tendency to organize non-mixed, cultural activities. A Coordination Nationale des Lesbiennes was established, providing a network for both political and social activities.

The more intense cooperation between lesbians and gays around 1980 can be understood from the perspective of changing political conditions in a climate that had been rather repressive until then. Two legal texts demonstrated the discrimination against homosexuals, in comparison to heterosexuals, in France. Article 331, paragraph 3, of the Code Pénal punished by fine and imprisonment any "indecent or unnatural act with an individual of one's own sex under the age of twenty-one years" (eighteen years after the age of adulthood was lowered), even though heterosexual relations were allowed from the age of fifteen years; Article 330 of the same code imposed higher penalties for an act of indecency when it concerned persons of the same sex. At the instigation of H. Cavaillet, the Sénat voted for the abrogation of these two clauses on 28 June 1978, but the bill was not submitted to the National Assembly for another two years. The provision abrogated Article 330 but refused to amend Article 331. On 4 April 1981, the CUARH organized a national demonstration in Paris in favor of the abrogation of the law in question. It was a tremendous success; ten thousand people, many of them women, attended the first mass demonstration of gays and lesbians in France. Soon after, Mitterrand adopted a campaign position in favor of abrogating the law, and on 20 December 1981, following his election on 10 May, the National Assembly repealed the law ("Homosexualités" 1981).

The success provided by the PS reinforced the instrumental wing of the gay and lesbian movement. This process was accelerated further by the foundation of homosexual groups either within or closely linked to political parties like Homosexualité et Socialisme and Gais pour la Liberté (both PS-oriented) and (right-wing) Mouvement des Gais Libéraux. However, the climate of *reform* was not particularly stimulating for mass mobilization. Although at the end of the 1970s and the beginning of the 1980s, French gay and lesbian movement mobilization was the strongest in Europe, the subsequent decline was indeed even more dramatic.

The rapid successes of the movement after Mitterrand's election, concurrent with both the dominance of the instrumental wing within the

CUARH and the flourishing gay commercial subculture, led to the rapid decline of CUARH. As a matter of fact, this wing had already become isolated because the gay community generally gave priority to social and cultural activities. This was so because the left-wing government itself looked after homosexual interests and had cleared away all judicial impediments to the development of the gay and lesbian subculture. CUARH's membership declined after 1982, and the regional groups disappeared. Its journal *Homophonies* survived until 1986 but faced strong competition from nonmixed magazines, which were better able to balance interests with pleasure.

The good relations that existed between the CUARH and mainstream politics precipitated the disappearance of *Arcadie* in 1982, which by that time found itself hopelessly outdated. *Arcadie*'s obsolete character came to the fore in June 1981, one month after Mitterrand was elected, when it protested against the closure of the police department that had specialized in the control of gays. *Arcadie* complained about the loss of the good contacts it had developed with some key figures in this (repressive!) corps: "*Arcadie* had not realized that the gay movement could count on nondiscriminatory attitudes from the police, even if this needed time and considerable action on the part of the movement" (Bach, 1982: 71). At the same time, *Arcadie* ceased to function as a meeting place, because the commercial circuit was booming and people were no longer forced to meet behind closed doors.

It is interesting to note that the commercial circuit was also too competitive for the meeting places developed in the early 1980s—subsidized by the Ministry of Culture[13]—which faded away during the second half of the decade. In addition, the rather intellectual journal *Masques*, which was neither commercial nor parliamentary-political, disappeared. The success of the CUARH's policy of "equal rights" outdated not only the antinormality discourse so eloquently formulated by the FHAR and its successors (Duyvendak 1991: 124–34), but also *each* normality and *all* collective sexual identities: "Even more fundamentally, the future of homosexuals rests in the disappearance of the very concept of homosexuality itself, which *ipso facto* implies an end to heterosexuality and, therefore, all sexual normality" ("Années 80" 1985: 31).

Apart from commercialization, the essential *subculture* was characterized by territorial concentration, especially in Paris, and a strong emphasis on sex: pleasure became an even greater binding element than it had been before, and all kinds of sexual substyles developed after the restrictions had disappeared. Although at the outset this newly acquired sexual freedom was still shown to the outside world, some years later it turned out that the drive to show just how "gay" gay life was no longer generated sufficient incentive for mobilization. This can be illustrated by the development of the Gay Pride Parade. The number of participants had declined from ten thousand at the start of the 1980s, to two or three thousand by the second half of that decade. The character of the march underwent both a quantitative and qualitative change: whereas in earlier days political demands were expressed, as time went by the element of fun became more important. In 1985, in a public letter in *Gai Pied*, David Girard, the most significant gay entrepreneur of the day, wrote: "Everyone to the demonstration! What is certain is that we are not going to demonstrate in the same spirit as the people of CUARH. They march in order to denounce anti-homo racism. That is their right. But allow me to say that taking up a banner and marching under it chanting, "No to anti-homo racism" will not change a thing, it will not even attract sympathy. It is sad. It is grey. All of us, we come to celebrate. And what we shall defend is the right to celebrate. It is surely more communicative (and communicating), more of a tonic for the participants, and consequently more impressive and attractive for onlookers and media."[14] The same development, from an external, rather political orientation toward a subcultural one, can be traced with regard to *Gai Pied* (Duyvendak and Duyves 1993). In 1979 this magazine was founded by former members of the GLH-PQ who had discovered the impact of media use by the gay movement. From its beginnings, however, tension existed between political purity and sexual pleasure, which resulted in several crises within the editorial board. The booming subculture, and the growing number of people who considered themselves openly homosexual, nevertheless provided a basis for a commercially viable project. A "price" had to be paid however: the magazine dealt increasingly with issues related to pleasure, as its readers were no longer very interested in politics.[15]

THE AIDS CRISIS: FROM FEAR TO SELF-HELP, 1981–89

At the beginning of the 1980s, then, one can say that if in part the French homosexual movement failed, as the other left-wing movements born of 1968 had failed, to revolutionize society and overturn the capitalist order, at least the demands specific to homosexuals themselves were satisfied. Gay people had asserted their right to live as they wished, and, in consequence, everyone set about testing this newfound freedom. This was the situation—with a relatively weak (because successful) instrumental movement and an increasingly inward-looking, sex-oriented subculture—when HIV started to circulate.

At the moment of the spread of the epidemic, the militant tendency of homosexual associations was limited to CUARH, with the monthly *Homophonies* and weekly *Gai Pied Hebdo (GPH)* and the Association des Médecins Gais (AMG), founded on 5 May 1981, five days before the election of François Mitterrand.[16] Among associations oriented rather more toward subculture, the range is somewhat richer, notably with the launch of the journal *Samouraï* in 1982 and the revue *GI,* which devoted themselves to lifestyles, to cultural matters, and to the commercial services offered to homosexuals. Homosexuals also began to appear on the airwaves, with the June to September 1981 launch of a pirate radio station, Fréquence Gaie, which obtained an official permit to broadcast from May 1982.[17]

It is in this context that the first doctors and researchers to tackle AIDS started to group together in an association (ARSIDA) and attempted to alert homosexual organizations to the risks being run. These organizations responded to the call in different ways, and it was the *subcultural* wing that launched the first initiative with the creation in 1983 of Vaincre le SIDA (VLS). (Information about the first years of the anti-AIDS movements is mostly derived from Busscher and Pinell 1996).

What brought this about? The first explanation that comes to mind is that the militant tendency was then in such a state of dereliction that it had become quite incapable of taking charge of the problem, whereas the subcultural associations were flourishing. This phenomenon without doubt played a part, but equally significant was the fact that the militant arm of the movement was not ideologically ready to recognize the threat of AIDS, precisely in defense of the normalization of homosexuality only recently obtained.

Also, perhaps, it was less through organizational weakness than deliberate choice that the CUARH, the AMG, and *GPH* resisted the diffusion of information on AIDS. Up to 1984, the AMG and *GPH* were trying in effect to play down, indeed deny, the significance of the illness. Persuaded that AIDS was being used to disturb and to weaken them, they counterattacked by refusing to take seriously what they considered to be "a paranoid panic . . . which allows homosexuals, by way of their specific illness, to go back on the list of social afflictions that they had begrudgingly left."[18] *GPH* popularized the (foolhardy) slogan "Fucking is dangerous? Isn't crossing the street?" This position, which was maintained long after medical research had categorically demonstrated that AIDS was indeed a contagious disease touching mainly homosexuals, is explained by the fact that for the most militant of the associations, the fight against discrimination had to take precedence over the dangers of the contagion.[19] This attitude, moreover, was not confined to France.

Therefore, as mentioned, the first reaction related to the epidemic came from the subcultural wing, with the creation of Vaincre Le SIDA (VLS) in 1983. The association focused on the provision of services and information to the gay community by setting up a telephone hot line. The most striking feature of this first initiative, which would characterize all associations involved in the fight against AIDS up until 1989, was the often obsessional will to put forward demands that were completely devoid of all reference to homosexuality, even though many members of these organizations, and the first people affected by the disease, were principally homosexuals. Once again, as with the more militant associations, fear of stigma and of a rising homophobia were at the root of the attempts to give the cause a broader base.[20]

From 1985, the anti-AIDS campaign, still mainly sustained by homosexual subcultural organizations, saw a major change of direction with the creation of AIDES, an association destined to have meteoric success, taking the lead, among the associations involved in the campaign at least until 1989.[21] From its foundation, and without any real deviation thereafter, AIDES adopted a hostile attitude toward any identification of the association as a homosexual movement, despite the fact that the chief contributors to publications such as *Masques* and *GPH*[22] could be found among its founders.

For the militant homosexual organizations, their involvement in the campaign came later, once the media, following the lead of the public authorities from the summer of 1985 onward, began to recognize that AIDS in fact affected everyone, not just homosexuals.[23] The belated realization that gay participation in the campaign was imperative is explained in part by this increasingly universal appeal of the AIDS campaign, which posed less of a threat to the emancipation of homosexuality. At the same time, internal rivalry among the multitude of organizations forming the gay movement had hindered collective action. Strong competition within the specialized gay press of which *GPH* and *Samouraï* were part, meant that *GPH*, and consequently AMG, found it difficult to establish links with VLS, supported from the beginning by *Samouraï* (Busscher and Pinell 1996). Nevertheless, by 1985 *Homophonies* and *GPH* had started to give out information on AIDS without trying to play down its importance, and in the same year *GPH* published the first booklet from AIDES with advice on AIDS prevention. It was also *GPH* that welcomed the inquiry (by Michael Pollak and Laurindo) launched by the Centre national de la recherche scientifique (CNRS) into the sexual behavior of homosexuals (Busscher and Pinell 1996).

From 1987 to 1988 the range of anti-AIDS associations spread; many new associations were created, notably after a schism within AIDES in March 1987. The common characteristic of these new groups was that they remained fundamentally faithful to the line adopted by AIDES con-

cerning the question of the *homosexualization* of AIDS—always except-
ing Santé et Plaisir Gay (SPG), which, born of an initiative of militants
within AIDES, introduced into France *les jack-off parties* and tried to
raise the question of homosexuality again in the debate.

In summary, during the years 1981–88 homosexual associations became involved belatedly, and often in a relatively hidden way, in the fight
against the AIDS epidemic. If all the campaign associations were created
and sustained at arms length by homosexuals, they persisted in regarding
their action as removed from any element of gay activism and, in good republican tradition, without any reference to a so-called homosexual identity. It was only after 1989, with the arrival of a new generation, that the
anti-AIDS movement began to come up against a new dynamism from homosexual activism.

AIDS and the Attempt to Found
a Gay Community, 1989–96

At the end of the 1980s, anti-AIDS associations underwent a dual process
of differentiation and institutionalization, with, on one side, the multipli-
cation of associations orientated toward specific groups of people (hemophiliacs, blood-transfusion patients, drug addicts, and children) and,
on the other, a newfound professionalization of which AIDES was undoubtedly the most striking example. This professionalization explains
why these associations were founded as neither a counterforce nor even a
pressure group. The administration constantly pushed to obtain subsidies
and integration with government bodies for managing the epidemic, such
as the Agence Nationale de la Recherche sur le SIDA (ANRS) and the Association Française de Lutte contre le Sida (AFLS). This desire to integrate
into the decision-making structures of the state and the diversification of
the groups of people under its charge had several effects. First, homosexual groups, inside and outside these associations, started to feel a sense of
dispossession, as much from the growing degaying within the associations
as from the fact that people with AIDS had been deprived of a direct voice
in deference to professionals speaking on their behalf (one starts to speak
of an "AIDS establishment" and of the "AIDS business"). Second, the
methods of managing the AIDS problem through associations go hand in
hand with a political neutrality, which prevented the adoption of any critical stance vis-à-vis the numerous and obvious deficiencies of governmental politics, especially in terms of prevention.

For these two reasons new associations were born in 1989, with the
objective of giving the sick their voice back, clearly establishing a link
between homosexuality and AIDS, and refusing to cooperate with the

political authorities when it was clear that they were not doing everything they could to fight against the epidemic. This regeneration of the associational setup thus had the effect of reactivating the old cleavages in the homosexual movement, opposing once again subcultural and political orientation, searching for recognition and political opposition. To these old divisions—which had led to the rupture at the beginning of the 1970s caused by the creation of the FHAR—was also added a new opposition: the opposition between a "general" model and a model based on identity and community, which, in the wake of movements on the other side of the Atlantic, defended the idea of the politics of minorities based on the claim to a specifically HIV-positive or homosexual identity. It was in this context that the associations Solidarité Plus, Positif, and AIDS Coalition to Unleash Power-Paris (ACT UP–Paris) were founded.

Created in May 1989, Positif saw itself as an "association of self-help and of solidarity, conceived for HIV-positive people, run by HIV-positive people," with the goal to defend "all HIV-positive people who suffer discrimination and to organize the defense of the HIV-positive consumer." The aim of the association was to think about the development of a new identity and to assert the association's own demands—demands neglected by medical specialists and the existing associations. The same is true of Solidarité Plus, which took from American parlance the notion of People with AIDS (PWA).[24]

Behind the problematic claim to an *"identité séropositive"* (an HIV-positive identity), in fact, lies the claim to a *singularization* of the AIDS cause, which is advanced in the name of a strong link with homosexuality.[25] From this point of view, the formation of ACT UP–Paris positively overturned the associational landscape, putting the homosexual movement as such back on the map.

The structure, the organization, and the strategy of ACT UP–Paris are based on the model put forward by the association created in New York in 1987. Defining itself above all as an association of people affected by AIDS, the group used intense lobbying and direct action (demonstrations, zaps, die-ins, and the like) to put pressure on the public authorities and the sectors that were charged, to varying degrees, with dealing with the illness[26] for a more effective and less discriminatory campaign against AIDS. More precisely, ACT UP–Paris's activity of denunciation articulates at once the search for greater *visibility* for AIDS and a fight against the *stigmatization* of affected people (principally homosexuals).[27] These two aspects are intimately tied to the struggle for a monopoly in scientific expertise, which combines simultaneously with a claim by people with HIV to take charge of AIDS themselves (what Michael Pollak [1990:84] calls "the transformation of the socio-medical assistance into a self-help movement") and a challenge to the medicalization of homosexuality.

In the same vein as ACT UP in the United States, the group aims to construct a homosexual identity and community. The justification for this path is simple: AIDS does not affect everyone in the same way, and it is the most oppressed minorities that were its first victims. This phenomenon calls for a political analysis of AIDS as revealing the multiple exclusions of our world:

> In industrialized countries, AIDS did not affect in the first place just any man or woman, but socially definite categories: homosexuals, drug addicts, ethnic minorities, prison inmates, now women, forgotten by medical research; the list is not exhaustive. In this sense, AIDS is not only a human or collective drama; today it is still a drama aimed at precise social categories, defined by their practices and their differences with relation to a dominant model: practices related to socially determined and politically significant human groups. To this extent . . . AIDS has nothing to do with the mythology of previous epidemics: "all equal before death." . . . AIDS spreads by conduits not by simple contact. So it attacks at root the very way we live our lives, and not simply our geographical situation. . . . In this way, to fight against AIDS is necessarily to call into question the founding model of our society, and to stand as a common front of minorities against the short-sightedness and cynicism of the do-gooders. (ACT UP–Paris 1994: 11–12)

However, extending beyond an attempt to widen the discourse on minorities to all minorities placed in the first line of the epidemic, it is the homosexual community that is central to the extent that the association seems, in the public eye, to be an association in defense of homosexuals rather than against AIDS:

> ACT UP is often reproached for the way in which we constantly affirm our link with the gay community. Under the pretext that AIDS today concerns everyone, it would be better that we hide the fact that all anti-AIDS associations were born of the gay community and that ACT UP has been the most assertive amongst them. . . . But the fundamental position of ACT UP has been that the point of view of minorities can be asserted only from within strong communities. We cannot today start relying, in the struggle against AIDS, on those who have played into its hands for years by waiting until the epidemic explicitly affected everyone before realizing its importance. . . . To fight for the gay community, which remains closest to us, is to fight as much against those who reckon that the homosexual question is solved now and that their battle is a rear-guard action (they confuse their own privileges with the state of the world) as against those who bolt the door, taking exception, for example, to the idea of a mixed homosexual community. (ACT UP–Paris 1994: 18–19)

From this point of view, the rhetoric employed by ACT UP–Paris is very near to that of the left-wing movements of the 1960s (in its denunciation of sexual repression), but at the same time it radically distinguishes itself by its call for the foundation of a homosexual *community,* something no other movement previously sought to defend:

> To set about a struggle against AIDS that aims at politically denouncing the abandonment of People with AIDS by the public authorities and by civil society, it is necessary that the queer community make of the gay movement a movement for the fight against AIDS and make of the anti-AIDS movement a gay movement. To fight against AIDS, one must therefore fight also for the thousands of shameful fools who live their sexuality badly. . . . From the point of view of the gay community, to survive, it is imperative to get out of the closet, to go out into the street asserting oneself as gay to fight against AIDS, not only because the virus is decimating its members but because AIDS threatens gay sexuality. . . . Right off AIDS has been set as the inescapable corollary to all sexuality that is not geared toward the family and reproduction, as the price to pay for pleasure: AIDS serves to orchestrate a great, repressive offensive not only against homosexuality but against sexuality pure and simple. (ACT UP–Paris 1994: 209–10)

From 1989, then, one can see that the anti-AIDS movement gave birth to a militant homosexual movement, of which ACT UP is at the vanguard. The most notable feature is that this homosexual identity shows itself not solely in the discourse held by the association but in its sociological composition as well. An unambiguous verification of this point is provided by a survey done by questionnaire to study militants in the organization (see Table 1), the results of which can be compared with those from a survey conducted by AIDES in its own grassroots support.[28]

In 1994, according to Table 1, more than one-quarter of ACT UP activists declared themselves directly affected by the disease. Comparing this percentage with the proportion of affected activists in AIDES (13 percent), one can deduce that ACT UP is the anti-AIDS association with a membership made up in greatest part of people with AIDS, even though the association does not provide them with direct support. However, intravenous drug users, as well as blood transfusion patients and hemophiliacs, are almost totally absent from ACT UP.[29] Moreover, the fact that more than two-thirds of militants declared themselves HIV-negative does not serve to place them into the classic form of *solidarity activism* stemming from some notion of altruism. When members were asked what made them join ACT UP, the primary reason put forward was closeness to the illness and to the suffering of others (32 percent in spontaneous statements). It is therefore true, as Michael Pollak highlighted, that "the veritable network which feeds [the associations] . . . was created by the

TABLE 1: *Comparison between Militants in AIDES and in ACT UP–Paris, 1994*

	ACT UP				AIDES
Constituents	Activists	Occasional Activists	Sympathizers	Total	Total
Men	76%	70%	62%	70%	57%
Homosexuals	68	62	57	62	44
Heterosexuals	21	25	34	27	45
Individuals who never used intra-venous drugs	94	96	96	96	72*
HIV-negative individuals	65	68	71	68	72
HIV-positive individuals or AIDS patients	26	27	26	26	13

*In the AIDES questionnaire there was no distinction between hard and soft drugs.

virus itself, through people affected physically and/or psychologically" (Pollak 1990: 83).

But above all, Table 1 indicates that those actively involved are essentially gays, and this, rather than the degree of engagement, reinforces it. The comparison with the results of the AIDES survey suggests, however, that this situation cannot be explained in the same way at the end of the 1980s, when homosexuals were indeed the sole supporters of the associations (Pollak and Schlitz 1991). If before 1987, 90 percent of volunteers in AIDES were male, the situation then started to change; in 1994, only 57 percent of activists were men. The rise in the number of women in AIDES translates logically into the proportionately smaller number of homosexual men and women in AIDES than in ACT UP (44 percent against 62 percent). Among the heterosexuals, 85% are women. This *hétérosexualisation de la cause* is explained at once by an altruistic commitment to AIDES and a sizable arrival of volunteers from the health and social services, a strongly feminine sector directly involved with the infirm.

Rather than being a sign of a manifest failure of an attempt at *de-singularization* of the cause (as it was a few years ago for AIDES), the preponderance of gay members of ACT UP highlights above all the highly visible homosexual identity of the association, the importance of which has already been stressed.[30]

The dual concerns adopted by ACT UP–Paris—politicization of AIDS and identity building—did not fit in well with the associational and political establishment, and after 1991 ACT UP became the object of fairly virulent attacks in both these areas in which one might say they highlighted the difficulty of building up a homosexual movement on a truly communitarian basis in France.

In part, ACT UP has been accused of seeking to politicize a problem that should not be political—nobody can be held responsible for an epidemic. This accusation rests at root on a debate about homophobia. Frédéric Edelmann, in *Le Journal du SIDA*, engaged in a polemic with the association on the basis of a refusal to admit that homophobic sentiments existed in France, implying the association's vague responsibility in the selective spread of the disease. For example, in December 1993 he wrote with regard to a film on the plague as a metaphor for fascism, "This film incites, constrains even, one to ask questions about the basis on a discourse which tends, today, to confer on AIDS the status of a political debate, by distinguishing the epidemic as revelatory of the sickness within the social fabric. . . . Without mentioning a much more radical discourse which has been raised and received a fairly large following, instituting the campaign against AIDS as being essentially a political struggle."[31] In the same way, an interview appeared in *Le Journal du SIDA* with Alain Finkielkraut, taking up this denunciation of the politicization of AIDS in the name of the myth of homophobia:

> AIDS is a catastrophe. It is not, as certain slogans from ACT UP, or as Tom Hanks, the hero of the film *Philadelphia,* say, a holocaust. This analogy contains a desire to negate fatality in the name of "everything is political," which I find dangerous. . . . We are waiting for the enemy that will allow us to exist. Here we must invoke once again Michel Foucault: homosexuals do not need homophobia in order to live. Some may need it to support the unsupportable and to give but a little sense to the absurdity of fate. Here again, I understand the movement but we cannot make out that AIDS is a homophobic conspiracy. The concept of homophobia has appeared in the West at the time when homophobic attitudes are in decline.[32]

In a similar vein, the desire by people with AIDS for a confrontation with the public authorities is analyzed in psychological terms as derived from fear of dying: "As for the militants, would we still dare today . . . to suggest that the appearance of AIDS was for some almost a stroke of luck, smited as they were, perhaps, that the practice of homosexuality would at last obtain . . . a (relative) right to exist?"[33] "Even to the extent that it designates objectives or those responsible, the politicization of the illness allows a release of anxiety and permits to escape the inevitable by action. If I were myself infected with AIDS, I would perhaps succumb to this paranoia. I believe however that it is demagogical to flatter it."[34] This violent stigmatization in fact finds its explanation in the very negative reaction on the part of most French associations to ACT UP's attempt to found a homosexual movement on the basis of the American identity/community model. The attachment of the French Left to the classic republican model, in which "minority politics" is not tolerated, is here contested in its own terms.[35] An analogy to this struggle can be found in the development, at the start of the 1980s, of movements like SOS-Racisme, which asserted (like the FHAR for gays and lesbians in the 1970s) a *"droit à la différence"* for French people of immigrant parents (Blatt 1995). Furthermore, it is because he had already taken a stance numerous times on the question of the right to be different that Alain Finkielkraut found himself once more solicited by *Le Journal du SIDA* in 1995 to denounce the "identity trap" into which ACT UP would like to draw gay associations and the anti-AIDS campaign:

> Gays today form . . . a community of destiny. . . . To this extent, I do not believe that it is necessary to encourage, as in the USA, a "gay culture." Let us remember the warning of Michel Foucault against the identity trap. It serves to fix into identities sexual behavior, whatever it is. . . . Discretion, ambiguity, indeterminacy, decency are not, as one often believes them to be, the remnants of a repressive order or signs of inhibition, but indispensable of the art of living. . . . What seems to me to be incontestable is the manifest desire of some in this movement to constitute what Paul Ricoeur calls a "narrative identity" in explicit reference to the Jewish model of identity.[36]

French political tradition has clearly had a far-reaching effect on the development of the gay and lesbian movement, especially in terms of the (limited) political opportunities for gays and lesbians to manifest themselves as a collective political identity. Because this new identity was granted only limited access to politics, many homosexuals took an apolitical view of their sexual orientation. French gays and lesbians found it difficult to develop a collective political identity and seldom took collective political action, because the political establishment refused to hear—let alone support—their appeal, particularly as long as other, traditional, *cleavages* remained predominant. This has resulted in a weak movement on one hand and an almost invisible, apolitical subculture on the other—a logical consequence of the immense divide between the state and the street in France.

The far-reaching effect of the universalist, republican tradition on the gay and lesbian movement was proved once more when AIDS reared its

ugly head (Favre 1992). Whereas most other Western countries soon realized the need to combat AIDS in a specific, focused manner, the French
government refused to develop prevention campaigns directed solely at
male homosexuals (Altman 1988; Duyvendak and Koopmans 1991;
Duyvendak 1995c). The development of a target-group policy proved to
be well nigh impossible in a republican country (Pollak 1988; Arnal 1993).
Even the organizations founded to assist HIV-infected people and AIDS
patients tried to avoid being labeled "homosexual," despite the fact that
almost all of their members and patients were homosexual, especially at
the start of the epidemic (Pollak and Rosman 1989; Hirsch 1991). Claire
Ernst analyzed the situation as follows: "The enduring influence of the
French republican model of citizenship and politics is evident in the gay
community's response to AIDS. The reluctance of AIDS organizations to
"own" the disease, and to interpret it as a civil rights issue, and to instead
view it as a health problem is testament of the degree to which identity-
based politics remain illegitimate in France. While French AIDS organizations certainly recognize the ways in which the disease poses a threat to
civil rights, this threat is viewed as a general one. AIDS poses a threat to
the universal human rights of all French citizens, not to the right of French
gays" (1995: 17). Even under these extremely difficult circumstances,
however, since the beginning of the 1990s, a series of indicators seem to
herald a renaissance in the homosexual movement in France—a renaissance centered on the identity/community model proposed by ACT UP-
Paris. A Gay and Lesbian Center has opened in Paris, a successful Gay and
Lesbian Film Festival has been organized since 1995, demonstrations commemorating the deportation of homosexuals during the Second World
War have taken place, the Gay Pride events of June 1995 and since have
proved to be spectacularly successful, a Gay Night is being broadcast on
the television channel Canal Plus—all these elements indicate the community slant of what can well be called a "gay and lesbian movement." Moreover, there have been efforts to have the New Left government pass a law
on gay marriage (the "Contrat d'Union Sociale et Civile"). A first bill was
promoted by a faction of the Socialist Party in 1990. After hesitations and
changing majorities, the New Left government, after its election in 1997,
decided to enact the law before the end of its term.

It is not certain, however, that a movement founded on the notion of community and of minority interests can maintain itself in France, as the failure
of the FHAR in the 1970s and the "differentialist" antiracism movement in
the 1980s demonstrated. The risk of failure is as great, whether for the anti-
AIDS movement that gave way to a resurgence of a homosexual movement
(and not the other way around) or for an association like ACT UP, which
must manage simultaneously a permanent tension between its homosexual

identity and its principal aim, the fight against AIDS. From this point of view, the homosexualization of AIDS as much as the "AIDSification" of homosexuality presents a problematic challenge to these movements today. The future of the gay and lesbian movement in France in the coming years depends on the political opportunities to manifest oneself as being different. "In contrast to the United States, which provides a rich substrate for group differentiation, and in contrast to the Dutch state, which recognizes specific groups as political actors, the French state often approaches specific groups with a view to privatizing them, repressing them, dispersing them, or subjecting them to centralized, hierarchical control. France may be a nation of individuals, but all these individuals are French men first and foremost; only in second instance are they men or women, bourgeois or working class, gay or heterosexual, Catholic or Muslim" (Seidman 1995: 72).

Notes

1. The exceptions are the few regionalist groups whose struggle reached such high levels of radicalization that they wished to dissociate themselves from France.

2. In fact, only one organization has been partly successful: the left-wing, Catholic trade union, the Confédération française du travail (CFDT) (Hamon and Rotman 1982). Since 1968, this union has criticized the dominant political culture, which makes it so difficult to broach new issues. Even the Parti Socialiste (Socialist Party), or PS, was unsuccessful in this regard, mainly because it strove to compete with the Communist Party by imitating it as much as possible. As a result, the PS was the most dogmatic socialist party in Western Europe until the early 1980s, thus obstructing the emergence of a New Left and granting hardly any latitude to the new social movements. The CFDT took a different approach. It tackled the dominant position of the Communist trade union, the Confédération generale du travail (CGT), by being "different." The CFDT broached various nontraditional trade union issues, such as *autogestion* (autonomy), environmental policy, women's rights, and the dangers of nuclear energy. The CFDT presented itself as a mouthpiece for the antistatist *deuxième gauche,* as "*le parti de la société civile*" ("La CFDT" 1980).

3. In France, famous authors and other artists have traditionally been able to deal relatively openly with issues related to homosexuality (Marcel Proust, André Gide, Marcel Jouhandeau, Jean Cocteau, Jean Genet, Michel Foucault, Colette, Dominique Fernandez, Michel Tournier, and Hervé Guibert). However, this openness has little bearing on the public's rather hostile attitude toward homosexuality. Researchers who overplay this cultural tradition neglect the fact that these extraordinary people have rather exceptional points of view, which are not generally shared by the broader society. Although their contribution may have been of support to the emancipation movement as a whole, most writers did not take an active part in it. This was because they had artistic freedom and were not directly confronted with discrimination and related problems in their work (which

is why the category of "gay literature" did not develop in France as it did in the United States, for instance).

4. The English translation is Literary and Scientific Club of the Latin Countries. As in many other countries, we see that under repressive circumstances homosexual organizations favor the use of labels with a high protection value, either suggesting literary groups (in the Netherlands: Shakespeare Club), or scientific organizations (Scientific-Humanitarian Committees in Germany and Holland prior to World War II).

5. The statement "*Arcadie* attempts to be apolitical: it does not believe that improvements in the fate of homosexuals should automatically be linked to the victory of such a party, or of such an economic doctrine" is repeated in every publication of *Arcadie*.

6. "*Arcadie* enables homosexuals to meet each other, to escape from their loneliness" (*Arcadie*, no. 273[1976]:12).

7. This translates as "The homosexual is also a social man" (*Arcadie*, no. 273 [1976]:12).

8. This visible manifestation of homosexuality on the street (the CGT's May Day demonstration was disrupted) meant a split within the movement in France between the radical *pédés* and the homophiles of *Arcadie*, whereas, for instance, in the Netherlands the main homosexual organization, Cultural and Recreational Center (COC), was capable of incorporating these opposition tendencies (Tielman 1982: 165; Warmerdam and Koenders 1987: 341).

9. "We are more than 343 sluts; we have been fucked by the Arabs. We are proud of it and would do it all again", and "One can never be too gay" are some of the slogans published in the twelfth issue of *Tout*, quoted in Girard (1981: 89).

10. To illustrate that point, suffice it to say that FHAR activists were the first to stigmatize the development of a gay subculture as creating a "homosexual ghetto."

11. The FHAR (1971) published the *Rapport contre la normalité*.

12. In the first half of the 1970s, Pierre Juquin, in those days spokesman for the PCF, formulated the party's position as follows: "I did not know that homosexuality, glorified in the left-wing movement, has an especially radical position. . . . But the cover of homosexuality or drugs never had anything to do with the workers movement. Each of them actually represented the opposite of the workers movement." (quoted in Girard 1981: 96–97). By 1977 the PCF's position had become somewhat more liberal: "We must revise legislation, not because homosexuality in itself would have either a liberalizing or revolutionary value (that would seem absurd to me), but because homosexuals have as much right to live in peace as any other citizens of our country" (Girard 1981: 138).

13. Whereas the more interest-oriented organizations, which desperately needed support for their survival, did not get much money, the entertainment side, which developed pretty well autonomously, was subsidized by the left-wing government. This shows that this government did not realize the value of *intermediary organizations*; only inwardly oriented organizations, such as the Fédération des Lieux Associatifs Gais, which were built on participation and not representation were, in fact, subsidized.

14. *Gai Pied*, no. 174 (1995):61.

15. Data from the annual readers research by *Gai Pied* in cooperation with Michael Pollak showed that in 1983, 25 percent of readers considered *Gai Pied* too political, 30 percent would have liked to see more erotic or pornographic pictures, and 36 percent wanted more "pictures" in general. The 1986 results indicated that the readers thought that attention given to politics—which had already diminished considerably—was still too much.

16. This association was founded on a militant ticket with the primary goals of encouraging positive representation of homosexuality in the medical field and struggling against venereal diseases. From this point of view, the militancy of the association goes hand in hand with an orientation tending toward a form of communitarian self-help in the same vein as the Gay Men's Health Crisis (GMHC) in the United States.

17. It was with the coming to power of the Left that the airwaves started to be liberalized and pirate radio stations received broadcasting licenses. Fréquence Gaie was taken over by *GPH* in 1987 with the idea of turning it into a profitable enterprise. It then became Futur Génération, until April 1990, when it again changed its name, to FG 98.2. Its commercial success was by this time assured.

18. "Gais toubibs en colloque" 1982. In March 1982 Dr. Lejeune wrote that "since the beginning of the year, barely a week has passed in which the press has not blasted out headlines on a disease which is now afflicting us, we poor gays. Worse than the plague and gangreen combined. . . . One thing is certain, homosexuality is good for business. We have become a consumer product. A French dermatologist announces four cases of Kaposi sarcoma. The plague? No, these cases have been diagnosed and treated over several years" (*Gai Pied Hebd. [GPH]*, no. 37 [March 1982]).

19. This attitude, which might seem surprising in retrospect, can be fairly well explained in the context of the day: in part, knowledge about AIDS was still vague, and homosexual militants have traditionally been suspicious of moralizing talk and reference to normalization in medical science; in part also, the manner in which the press represented AIDS in the early years of the epidemic tended toward a cautious attitude: one hears talk of the "gay cancer," and it was principally the "traumatizing" practices of homosexuals to which the cause of the disease was assigned (poppers, sodomy, and so on). (On the media coverage of AIDS in France, see Herlich and Pierret 1988, and Mercier 1993).

20. "It will be the pioneers of '68 who will be the first to mobilize, perhaps because they are also the first to be affected. These people undoubtedly have no need to assert their homosexuality high and wide. Confronted with AIDS, it is only natural for them to turn outwards, to put the experience of exclusion to good use to avoid others also becoming victims of it; not to shut themselves away once again avoiding latent pressure from those who are already pointing the finger at them and suggesting that they shut themselves back up in the closet. They are simply demanding that the law be respected, that discrimination should not be added to the worry of being ill. Departing from the principle that he no longer has any taste for the subtleties of his own homosexual identity, but wishes above all else to be considered as a "normal" ill person, with nothing—in the end—to distinguish him from others." (Ph. E., quoted in *SIDA*, no. 6, [July–August 1989]: 14).

21. If associations came to be formed after this date, it is undoubtedly due to the discovery, of HIV itself (1984) and to the development of a test for HIV (1985), which made tens of thousands of people aware of the deadly threat surrounding them. Previously, the only people really interested in the discovery of an effective treatment were those positively diagnosed as having AIDS, and many of these could not engage in the campaign because of the state of their health. Those diagnosed as HIV-positive but not yet showing symptoms of full-blown AIDS were obviously more strongly motivated to campaign.

22. "Daniel Defert, sociologist and companion of Michel Foucault, was the founder of the association. The hallmark of Foucauldian thought partly explains the refusal to homosexualise the cause—but without invalidating the hypothesis set out above with regard to *VLS*. *AIDES* relies in particular on the idea that the anti-AIDS movement must rely on AIDS-sufferers themselves, those who attest in the flesh to the disease, and not on those who are most susceptible to become victims (homosexuals). Questioning the position of AIDS-sufferers with regard to medicine and medical knowledge counts more than the question of a homosexual identity in Michel Foucault's philosophy" (see Busscher and Pinell 1996, 22).

23. Although since 1983, the French press, has referred to the 4 Hs (homosexuals, Haitians, hemophiliacs, and heroin addicts), no article has been dedicated to the last two categories. It was not until August 1985 that *Libération* dedicated its first article to drug addicts, followed by *Le Monde* in February 1986. And it was only very belatedly, in 1987—after Minister of Health Michèle Barzach made AIDS a "great national cause" and announced at a press conference that "among AIDS patients, in 32 percent of cases, the persons affected are heterosexual"— that the mainstream press started to examine the case of heterosexual AIDS sufferers (the February 1987 edition of *Libération* and the March 1987 editions of *Le Nouvel Observateur* and *Le Point,* for example).

24. It was during the same period that the project of the États-Généraux du SIDA was launched, allowing HIV-positive people to speak out and escape from the technocratic discourse of the associations. "There are some things that cannot be delegated, to understand how we stand on the things we are living through. One cannot ask people who, for a whole heap of reasons, remained detached from the illness to speak for us," declared Alain Vertadier, one of the committee leaders, during a demonstration on 17 and 18 March 1990 in Paris. Quotation on Positif from interview with Jean René Grisons, *Journal du SIDA,* no. 89 (1990).

25. "Today, while AIDS finds other footholds in society and hits the heterosexual population, homosexuals have little by little and almost unconsciously integrated the illness into their condition. Strangely, even they who vehemently denounce the slightest linking of AIDS with homosexuality today manifest a fairly paradoxical desire to appropriate it for themselves, as if it represented a coveted heritage, now that they have in some way domesticated it. Many speak of a new homosexual consciousness, a new identity; of an enrichment, indeed of the chance to set about organizing a new "militancy." . . . One moreover speaks of "profiting" from AIDS to make homosexuality something banal, to constrain the heterosexual authorities to take into account the homosexual reality, and to recognize it" (Ph. E., quoted in *SIDA,* no. 6 [July–August 1989]: 14).

26. I refer especially to government agencies, the hospital sector, the pharmaceutical sector, medical laboratories, associations of doctors and chemists, and insurance companies.

27. An exposé setting out the political manifesto of ACT UP can be found in ACT UP–Paris 1994.

28. This survey by questionnaire was undertaken by Olivier Fillieule in the framework of a working group on activism in France at the Paris Institut d'etuds politiques (IEP). All results are analyzed in Fillieule (forthcoming). The ACT UP questionnaire was distributed in 1994; 221 questionnaires were received or collected. By varying degrees of militant involvement, we have distinguished three categories among those responding: activists, who participate regularly in action or in commissions (33 percent of the total, or seventy-three people); occasional activists, who participate only in large-scale demonstrations and at weekly meetings (35 percent, or seventy-one individuals); and finally sympathizers, who participate rarely but subscribe to *Action* (32 percent, or seventy-one persons). Only 42 percent of sympathizers live in the Paris region, as opposed to 94 percent of activists and 80 percent of occasional activists. All respondents form the mobilizable potential of ACT UP.

29. It is important to note on this matter the chronic difficulties faced by the drug-addiction commission, particularly in being heard by the rest of the movement. From this point of view, the explanation of the quasi absence of drug addicts from ACT UP certainly does not stem solely from any disinterest in taking action that is generally and unfairly assigned to them (for an example, see Pollak, 1989: 83).

30. The communitarian tendency of ACT UP is also demonstrated in the editorial line of the monthly *Têtu*, clearly inspired by the American model, launched in July 1995 by Didier Lestrade, a founding father of the movement.

31. *Le Journal du SIDA* (December 1993): 3. See also the fairly violent reply of ACT UP in *Action*, the journal of the association (no. 21 [January 1994]: 9).

32. *Le Journal du SIDA*, no. 72 (April 1995): 39. See also ACT UP's response in the words of Agnès de Luna (*Le Journal du SIDA*, no. 73 [May 1995]: 42).

33: *Le Journal du SIDA* (December 1993).

34: *Le Journal du SIDA*, no. 72 (April 1995).

35. See also the editorial of Gérard Dupuy (1995) in *Libération*, an article by Pascal Bruckner (1995) in *Le Monde*, and the public debate started by Martel 1996 (see also "Les homosexuels" 1996; *Le Nouvel Observateur*, 25 April 1996). For an analysis of the reasons that France is fundamentally reticent about the communitarian model, in the tradition of the principles of the République, see also the sophisticated analysis in Ernst 1995.

36. *Le Journal du SIDA*, no. 72 (April 1995).

REFERENCES

ACT UP–Paris. 1994. *Le SIDA: Combien de devisions?* Paris: Dagorno.

Adam, Barry D. 1995. *The Rise of a Gay and Lesbian Movement.* Rev. ed. New York: Twayne.

Altman, Dennis. 1988. "Legitimation through Disaster: AIDS and the Gay Movement." In *AIDS, The Burdens of History.* Ed. Elizabeth Fee and Daniel M. Fox. Berkeley and Los Angeles: University of California Press.

Ambler, J. S. 1971. *The Government and Politics of France.* Boston: Houghton Mifflin.

"Années 80: Mythe ou Libération." 1985. *Masques.* 25–26.

Arnal, F. 1993. *Résister ou disparaître? Les homosexuels face au SIDA. Le prévention de 1982 à 1992.* Paris: L'Harmattan.

Bach, G. 1982. *Homosexualités, Expression, Répression.* Paris: Le Sycomore.

———. 1988. *Homosexualité: La Reconnaissance?* Boulogne-Billancourt, France: Espace Nuit.

Blatt, D. S. 1995. "Immigration Politics and Immigrant Collective Action in France, 1968–1993". Ph.D. diss., Cornell University, Ithaca.

Brand, K.-W., 1985a. *Neue soziale Bewegungen in Westeuropa und den USA. Ein internationaler Vergleich.* Frankfurt: Campus Verlag.

———. 1985b. "Vergleichendes Resümee" In *Neue soziale Bewegungen in Westeuropa und den USA: Ein internationaler Vergleich.* K.-W. Brand. Frankfurt: Campus Verlag.

Bruckner, Pascal. 1995. "La démagogie de la détresse." *Le Monde,* 23 June.

Busscher, P. O. de, and P. Pinell, 1996. "La création des associations de lutte contre le SIDA." In *Sida et vie psychique: Approche clinique et prise en charge.* Ed. S. Héfez. Paris: La Découverte.

Cavailhes, J., P. Dutey, and G. Bach-Ignasse. 1984. *Rapport Gai. Enquête sur les modes de vie homosexuels.* Paris: Persona.

"La CFDT et la crise du syndicalisme." 1980. *Esprit,* no. 4.

Cohen, Jean L. 1985. " 'Strategy or Identity': New Theoretical Paradigms and Contemporary Social Movements." *Social Research* 59, no. 4 (Winter): 663–717.

D'Anieri, P., C. Ernst, and E. Kier. 1990. "New Social Movements in Historical Perspective." *Comparative Politics,* 22 (July): 445–58.

DuPuy, Gérard. 1995. "Visibles." *Libération,* 24 June.

Duyvendak, Jan Willem 1991. "Hoe uitdagend is de homoseksuele subcultuur? De marges van de normaliteit en de normen van de marginaliteit." In *Over normaal gesproken: Hedendaagse homopolitiek.* I. C. Meijer, Jan Willem Duyvendak, and M. P. van Kerkhof. Amsterdam: Schorer.

———. 1994. *De verzuiling van de homobeweging.* Amsterdam: SUA.

———. 1995a. *The Power of Politics. New Social Movements in France.* Boulder, Colo.: Westview.

———. 1995b. "Gay Subcultures between Movement and Market." In *New Social Movements in Europe: A Comparative Analysis.* Hanspieter Kriesi, Ruud Koopmans; Jan Willem Duyvendak, and M. Giugni. Minneapolis: University of Minnesota Press.

———. 1995c. "From Revolution to Involution: The Disappearance of the French Gay Movement." *Journal of Homosexuality* 29(4):369–85.

Duyvendak, Jan Willem, and M. Duyves. 1993. "*Gai Pied,* Je T'aime. Ten Years of *Gai Pied*: Success or Moral Bankruptcy?" *Journal of Homosexuality,* no. 1–2.

Duyvendak, Jan Willem and Ruud Koopmans. 1991. "Weerstand bieden aan AIDS: De invloed van de homobeweging op de ontwikkeling van AIDS." *Beleid en Maatschappij,* no. 3.

Ernst, C. 1995. "AIDS and the French Gay Community: *Dédramatisation* and Gay Identity." Paper delivered at the 1995 Western Political Science Association Annual Meeting.

Favre, P., ed. 1992. *SIDA et politique. Les premiers affrontements (1981–1987).* Paris: L'Harmattan.

Fillieule, Olivier. 1997. *Stratégies de la rue.* Paris: Presses de Science Politique.

————. 1998. "Plus Ça Change, Moins Ça Change: Demonstrations in France during the 1980s. In *Acts of Dissent: New Developments in the Study of Protest.* Ed. D. Rucht and Ruud Koopmans. Berlin: Sigma Press.

————, ed. 1993. *Sociologie de la protestation: Les formes de l'action collective dans la France contemporaine.* Paris: L'Harmattan.

————, ed. Forthcoming. *Activisme et guerre contre le SIDA: Regards sur les ACT UP d'Europe et des USA.* Paris: L'Harmattan.

Fillieule, Olivier, and C. Péchu. 1993. *Lutter ensemble: Les théories de l'action collective.* Paris: Harmattan.

Front Homosexual d'Action Révolutionnaire (FHAR). 1971. *Rapport contre la normalité.* Paris: Champ Libre.

"Gais toubibs en colloque." 1982. *Gai Pied Hebdo (GPH),* no. 39 (June):12.

Girard, J. 1981. *Le mouvement homosexuel en France 1945–1980.* Paris: Syros.

Gonnard, C. 1997. "L'amante de la veuve du Soldat inconnu." *La Revue,* no. 5:23–26.

Gutmann, A. 1992. "Introduction." In *Multiculturalism and "The Politics of Recognition": An Essay by Charles Taylor.* Ed. A. Gutmann. Princeton: Princeton University Press.

Hamon, H., and P. Rotman. 1982. *La deuxième gauche: Histoire intellectuelle et politique de la CFDT.* Paris: Ramsay.

Hazaseeringh, S. 1994. *Political Traditions in Modern France.* Oxford: Oxford University Press.

Herlich, C., and J. Pierret. 1988. "Une maladie dans l'espace public: Le SIDA dans six quotidiens français" *Annales ESC,* no. 5, (September–October): 1109–34.

Hirsch, E. 1991. *Solidaires, AIDES.* Paris: Les éditions du Cerf.

Hoffmann, S. 1963. *A la recherche de la France.* Paris: Éditions du Seuil.

"Homosexualités 1971–1981." 1981. *Masques 9–10.*

"Les homosexuels se divisent sur la question du communautarisme." 1996. *Le Monde,* 15 April.

Klandermans, Bert. 1986. "New Social Movements and Resource Mobilization: The European and the American Approach." *International Journal of Mass Emergencies and Disasters* 4 (2):13–39.

Koopmans, Ruud. 1995. *Democracy from Below: New Social Movements and the Political System in West Germany.* Boulder, Colo.: Westview.

Kriesi, Hanspieter. 1989. "New Social Movements and the New Class in the Netherlands." *American Journal of Sociology* 95 (5):1078–116.

Kriesi, Hanspieter, and Jan Willem Duyvendak. 1995. "National Cleavage Structures." In *New Social Movements in Europe: A Comparative Analysis.* Ed. Hanspieter Kriesi, Ruud Koopmans, Jan Willem Duyvendak, and Marco Giugni. Minneapolis: University of Minnesota Press.

Kuechler, M., and R. J. Dalton. 1990. *Challenging the Political Order: New Social and Political Movements in Western Democracies.* Cambridge, Mass.: Polity.

Martel, Frédéric. 1996. *Le rose et le noir: Les homosexuels en France depuis 1968.* Paris: Éditions du Seuil.

Meijer, I. C., Jan Willem Duyvendak, and M. P. van Kerkhof. 1991. *Over normaal gesproken. Hedendaagse homopolitiek.* Amsterdam: Schorer.

Melucci, Alberto 1980. "The New Social Movements: A Theoretical Approach." *Social Science Information* 19(2):199–226.

———. 1989. *Nomads of the Present: Social Movements and Individual Needs in Contemporary Society.* Philadelphia: Temple University Press.

Mercier, A. 1993. "Les médias comme espace scénique: Information sur le SIDA et émergence dans le champ politique." In *SIDA et politique: Les premiers affrontements (1981–1987).* Ed. P. Favre. Paris: L'Harmattan.

Mossuz-Lavau, J. 1991. *Les lois de l'amour. Les politiques de sexualité en France 1950–1990.* Paris: Documents Payot.

Nelles, W. 1984. "Kollektive Identität und politisches Handeln in neuen sozialen bewegungen." *Politische Viertel-jahresschrift* 25:425–40.

Offe, Claus. 1985. "New Social Movements: Challenging the Boundaries of Institutional Politics." *Social Research* 52 (Winter): 817–68.

Pizzorno, A. 1978. "Political Exchange and Collective Identity in Industrial Conflict." in *The Resurgence of Class Conflict in Western Europe since 1968.* Ed. C. Crouch and A. Pizzorno. London: Macmillan.

Pollak, Michael. 1990. "Constitution, diversification et échec de la généralisation d'une grande cause: Le cas de la lutte contre le SIDA." *Politix* 16:80–90.

———. 1988. *Les homosexuels et le SIDA: Sociologie d'une épidémie.* Paris: Métaillié.

Pollak, Michael, and S. Rosman. 1989. *Les associations de lutte contre le SIDA: Éléments d'évaluation et de réflexion.* Paris: EHESS/CNRS.

Pollak, Michael, and Marie-Ange Schlitz. 1991. *Les homo- et bisexuals masculins face au SIDA: Six années d'enquête.* Paris: GSPM.

Rucht, D. 1991: "Sociological Theory as a Theory of Social Movements? A Critique of Alain Touraine." In *Research on Social Movements: The State of the Art in Western Europe and the USA.* Ed. D. Rucht. Frankfurt: Campus Verlag.

Seidman, Steven. 1993. "Identity and Politics in 'Postmodern' Gay Culture: Some Historical and Conceptual Notes." In *Fear of a Queer Planet: Queer Politics and Social Theory.* Ed. Michael Warner. Minneapolis: University of Minnesota Press.

———. 1995. "Verschil en democratie in het Westen: Conceptuele en vergelijkende observaties." *Krisis,* no. 60:60–74.

Taylor, Charles. 1992. "The Politics of Recognition." In *Multiculturalism and "The Politics of Recognition": An Essay by Charles Taylor.* Ed. A. Gutmann. Princeton: Princeton University Press.

Tielman, R.A.P. 1982. *Homoseksualiteit in Nederland: Studie van een emancipatiebeweging.* Amsterdam: Boom.

Touraine, A. 1978. *La voix et le regard.* Paris: Éditions du Seuil.

Tucker, K. H. 1991. "How New Are the New Social Movements?" *Theory, Culture and Society,* 8:75–98.

Warmerdam, H., and P. Koenders. 1987. *Cultuur en ontspanning: Het COC 1946–1966.* Amsterdam and Utrecht: NVIH COC/Rijksuniversiteit Utrecht.

Zald, Meyer N., and R. Ash. 1966. "Social Movement Organizations: Growth, Decay and Change." *Social Forces* 44:327–41.

RICARDO LLAMAS AND FEFA VILA
TRANSLATED FROM THE SPANISH BY
STEPHEN BROWN

9   Passion for Life

A History of the Lesbian and Gay Movement in Spain

THE INSTITUTIONAL ARTICULATION OF HOMOPHOBIA AND LESBIAN INVISIBILITY

IN THE struggles of lesbian and gay movements, "speaking out" has a special relevance as the sole act that allows new social subjects to construct their own history, their own identity. It permits them to distance themselves gradually from the identity that has been created by the "other" through denial, pathologization and prohibition, and, more recently, assimilation and normalization. Paradoxically, the effects of banishment and silence have sometimes been achieved through the naming of lesbians and especially gay men, and having been named by the law, medical science, and religion, they are subsequently punished by the institutions of power through a series of violent practices. The process of becoming distanced from this inflicted identity is especially relevant in the context of the Spanish state—an imposed union of several peoples, traditions, and cultures, under the shadow of an authoritarian, religiously based monarchy symbolically incarnated by Ferdinand and Isabella, the Catholic Monarchs.[1]

Even if the symbolic framework is, in general, exclusionary, since the nineteenth century, Spanish penal legislation follows the French tradition of refraining from establishing any legal provisions that explicitly condemn homosexuality. The authoritarian order set up by Franco after a bloody civil war (1936–39), which was won by a sector of the army that mutinied against the legitimate republican government, waited several years before breaking with this tradition that left lesbians and gay men more in silence or in popular ridicule than in the space of judicial condemnation. The reforms to the Penal Code in 1944 and 1963 did not address private relations between adults of the same sex. However, nonspecific institutional repression took place under the guise of the misdemeanors of "indecent abuse" (relations with minors under age twelve: Article 430), "corruption of minors" (relations with persons between ages twelve and twenty-three: Article 452 bis, paragraph b), and "public scandal" (Article 431).

Franco's regime returned to traditional Spanish values, which had been abandoned after the proclamation of the Second Spanish Republic in 1931: family, Catholicism, and patriotism were the elements that held the dictatorship together. Social cohesion was reestablished, based on the exclusion of any peculiarity. A silence (one that had barely begun to be challenged) was once again imposed by brutal repression, either through physical violence or the strangulation of any space for dissident signs. Only official discourse colonized the public sphere with authorized signs of heterosexual masculinity and femininity, along with approved symbols of national identity and the imposition of Castilian over the other languages spoken throughout the country.

In a context of generalized political and cultural repression, in addition to traditional homophobic hostility, there was little room for the constitution of free spaces or discourses of resistance. There is little information on the small and isolated communities of lesbians and gay men that preceded the dictatorship. According to Armand de Fluvià (1978), the first symbolic manifestations of community took place in Barcelona before the civil war. According to Jean Genet's (1985) account, the demonstration of Las Carolinas reached the spot where a public toilet had stood before being destroyed by a bomb. In 1934, if we are to believe Genet, a group of about thirty queens (*mariconas*) from Barcelona solemnly laid a branch of red roses tied with a black ribbon where the urinals had been. This was an homage that the most famous victim of Falangist homophobic violence would never receive: Federico García Lorca was killed by "a shot in the ass" in 1936, the same year as the military uprising, "because he was famous and because he was homosexual," according to José Bergamín (quoted in Sahuquillo 1991: 67–68).

Nonetheless, Franco's regime wound up codifying its homophobia with some precision. The Military Justice Code (Article 352) was the only one that punished those who engaged in "indecent acts with individuals of the same sex" with six months to six years in military prison. To that was added, on 15 July 1954, a law including "homosexuals" in the scope of the Vagrancy and Villainy Act enacted in 1933 (one of the few legal provisions from the republican period that the dictatorship had retained). One year after the Stonewall rebellion in New York (the symbolic trigger for a renewed movement that spread across the Western world), the Vagrancy and Villainy Act was replaced with a new law that sought to be more effective and that showed to what extent the reality of lesbians and gay men was removed from the processes that were elsewhere bringing together liberation movements.

The Social Menace and Rehabilitation Act (Ley de Peligrosidad y Rehabilitación Social, LPRS) was approved on 4, August 1970. It stipulated: "Article 2. . . . B) The following are deemed to constitute a social menace and are assumed to be endangering society. . . . 3. Those who carry out acts of homosexuality." Article 6 listed the security measures to which transgressors would be subjected: "internment in a reeducation establishment" (for a maximum of five years) and "prohibition from residing in a designated place or territory."

The spontaneous Las Carolinas mobilization, the murder of García Lorca, and four decades of a "peace" characterized by silence and repression (during the last ten years of which economic growth accelerated and the country was opened to foreign capital, tourism, and fashions) opened a path in the early 1970s toward a timid and risky articulation of organizational resources that were within the reach of a few gay men, who were the only ones designated by the legislation and were the objects of widespread stereotyping and prejudice. All sexual dissidence was defined as a symbolic space foreign to the values upon which the regime supported itself. As a result, the lesbian and gay movement built itself up on its opposition to these same values: opposition to the institutionalized family, the Catholic church, and the unity of the native land.

Though the misdemeanor of "public scandal" was most often used to repress gay men, lesbians, who (as women) were banished from the public sphere, were subjected to less codified repression. They were paradigms of the "silent and nonexistent beings" that the dictatorship had eradicated from public space. As elsewhere, but in an even more patent way, their voices were not heard, and (unlike for gay men) it was not particularly necessary for them to speak, be referred to, and be identified by the dominant discourses. For these reasons, there exist barely any data allowing us to affirm that lesbians were subjected to legal repression: the laws that punished homosexuality did not specifically name them, though indirectly and by extension they were affected by this regulation so restrictive of freedom.

No detailed studies exist that analyze the legal persecution of gay men either. There is little information: According to the data collected by the Instituto Lambda, in applying the LPRS between 1974 and 1975 in Madrid's two "special menace courts" alone, 152 people were tried for homosexuality.[2] The rehabilitation mandate of the act was also oriented toward this "masculine homosexuality": a Rehabilitation Center for Male Homosexuals was opened in Huelva, as ordered on 1 June 1971; on occasion, aversion therapies (electroshock, emetics) were administered. This center could house only a few of those condemned; the majority of the sentences were carried out in regular prisons (de Fluvià).[3]

At the end of the seventies, Spain underwent structural changes (economic modernization, the crisis of the authoritarian regime, growing internal protests) that allowed a history of repression to begin to give way to new narratives of liberation, integration, assimilation and revolt. In order to understand the lesbian and gay groups at the end of the seventies and their evolution over the following decade, however, it is important to take into account the continuing regime of homophobia after the dictator's death on 20 November 1975. The reprieve decreed on 25 November 1975 and the amnesty of 31 July 1976 (symbols of a few new freedoms that began to emerge) did not include any of those classified as "social menaces," because the deprivation of their liberty was not considered a punishment or a penalty but a security measure. In that year, the number of interned people reached 763, equivalent to 7.68 percent of the total prison population (Terradillos 1981: 63).

Because, among other factors, Franco's death was followed by an inability to identify a successor who would ensure the continuity of the regime (Carrero Blanco, the dictator's chosen successor, was assassinated in 1973), a process known as the Transition began: the gradual renewal of state institutions and organizational principles. Basing itself on a broad pact among the various newly legalized political forces (with the notable exclusion of trade unions and the Spanish Communist Party), this process ended with the approval of a new constitution that established a parliamentary democracy. In the first few years of this period, led by a centrist coalition of Liberals and Christian Democrats (the Unión de Centro Democrático), freedom of the press and freedom of association were restored. This progressive renewal and regeneration of public life spanned the period from 1975 to the first alternation of power, with the election of the Socialist Party in 1982.

In this context of public effervescence, the lesbian and gay movement burst onto the public scene (as did numerous other social movements that began as underground organizations). In addition to a cry of "Down with the Social Menace Act," demanding the repeal of the LPRS, which articulated homophobia directed at gay men, a specifically lesbian struggle was born: a struggle for its existence, its own voice. Not only was it necessary to repeal legislation and change structures; it was also important to cover, to fill the symbolic empty (sexual) space of women, recovering and reconstructing a history (of their own). The dykes and fags began to come out of the closet, to name for themselves their loves and desires that now constituted social and political relations. In March 1978 one of the first public manifestos issued by a lesbian collective, Col.lectiu de Lesbianes de Barcelona (Barcelona Lesbian Collective), stated, "Our voice must be heard to keep watch over and reveal the common aspects of our reality as women and assert *our difference* as lesbians."

THE EMERGENCE OF THE MOVEMENT: FROM GAY ORGANIZATIONAL FUROR TO LESBIAN AUTONOMY

"Together with [the 'respectable' demands of citizens' movements], with the same fundamental radicalism, 'shameful' aspirations and desires are made clear by the marginalized: crazy people, prisoners, women, young people, queers [*maricas*] and lesbians."

Agrupación Mercurio para La Liberación Homosexual
López Linage, *Grupos marginados y peligrosidad social*

"We queers [*maricas*] are somewhat fashionable among progressive people, and much is being said in the gay community about the apparition of 'the revolutionaries' of the FHAR [Frente Homosexual de Acción Revolucionaria], 'the reformists' of the MDH [Movimiento Democrático de Homosexuales], and the members of the 'Mercurio' group, whom nobody is too sure what they are about."

Ramón Linatza, "La homosexualidad tiene truco"

The public appearance of mixed gay and lesbian fronts that followed the dictator's death had a few historical precedents. In the context of the debate that surrounded the passing of the LPRS in 1970, Roger de Gaimon (Armand de Fluvià's pseudonym) and Mir Bellgai wrote to parliamentary representatives to pressure them to reject the proposal, succeeding only in having the expression "homosexuals" changed to "those who engage in homosexual acts." The first underground organization, the Homophile Group for Sexual Equality (Agrupación Homófila para la Igualdad Social, or AGHOIS), emerged in Barcelona in 1972. This group soon became known as the Spanish Movement for Homosexual Liberation (Movimiento Español de Liberación Homosexual, or MELH). The danger involved in publishing a magazine led this association to contact France's *Arcadie,* which since 1972 had been publishing and sending to Spain a Spanish supplement to the journal. In 1973, following objections raised by the Spanish ambassador in Paris, a Swedish publisher began printing the magazine and sending it to Catalonia (still clandestinely). The MELH met weekly until, faced with the risk of political repression, it decided to split into small cells. In addition to establishing a short-lived gay association in Madrid, its members participated actively in meetings at the European level (Paris in 1973; Edinburgh in 1974; Sheffield, England, in 1975).

At the end of 1975, the MELH, following an internal ideological evolution similar to that of other anti-Franco social movements, changed its name to the Gay Liberation Front of Catalonia (Front d'Alliberament Gai de Catalunya, or FAGC) and, along with the groups that emerged in the region of Valencia (the FAHPV in 1976) and the Balearic Islands (the FAGI), drafted its first political manifesto, the 1977 Manifest. In June 1977, Gay Pride Day, the first such demonstration in Spain, organized by the FAGC, was celebrated in Barcelona, and violently repressed by the police. The Basque country's gay liberation movement, Euskal Herriko Gay Askapen Mugimendua (EHGAM), was founded in Bilbao, which also organized a public protest in November; the death of a prostitute in Basauri, arrested under the LPRS, prompted the orgnization of a demonstration by the Coordination Committee of the Marginalized, of which EHGAM was a member. In 1978, EHGAM chapters were formed in San Sebastián, Pamplona, and Vitoria, although only the first of these maintained continuity.

In general, the lesbian and gay struggle was articulated alongside other marginalized social collectivities and other liberation movements (all the citizens' and revolutionary movements and trade unions that had come out of the closet kicking and screaming). Especially in Catalonia, the Valencian country, the Baleares, and the Basque country, the movement forged links with the struggle for national liberation and independence.

In 1977 in Madrid, far from the nationalist struggles but in the same context of social mobilization against the remainders of dictatorship, the Homosexual Front for Revolutionary Action (Frente Homosexual de Acción Revolucionaria, or FHAR), originating in the libertarian movement, was also founded. Two other groups soon joined it: the Mercurio Group for Homosexual Liberation, which started off reformist but became revolutionary, and the Homosexual Democratic Movement (Movimiento Democrático de Homosexuales, or MDH), founded by activists from the Spanish Communist Party. In mid-May 1977, the members of this organizational maelstrom joined together to form the Coordination Committee of Spanish Homosexual Liberation Fronts (Coordinadora de Frentes de Liberación Homosexual del Estado Español, or COFLHEE), which made itself known to the Madrid press in order to campaign against the LPRS.

COFLHEE's first public activities in Madrid in 1977 were the organization of the Week of Struggle against the LPRS at the Law School of the University of Madrid in March, the presentation of a manifesto against the law on behalf of the Coordination Committee of the Marginalized in April, and the collection of signatures against the LPRS in June.[4] In July, as Parliament opened, the Mercurio Group for Homosexual Liberation approached members of Parliament and senators to ask "that they intervene in establishing a complete amnesty, which would also include those convicted under repressive legislation regarding sexuality, and in abolishing the special tribunals and the judicial apparatus set up to apply it."[5]

These three collectives tried to form an Assembly of Madrid Homosexuals, which in turn spawned in 1978 the Homosexual Liberation Front of Castile (Frente de Liberación Homosexual de Castilla, or FLHOC). In June of that year FLHOC organized Madrid's first Gay Pride Day demonstration, with seven thousand participants. Demonstrations were also held that year in Barcelona, Bilbao, and Seville.[6]

Though lesbians were a minority within the main groups (FAGC, EHGAM, FHAR, and so on), they were active. Yet not long after joining these "mixed fronts," the lesbian activists left to incorporate into the feminist movement as lesbian feminist collectives. The 1978 presentation made by the FAGC Lesbian Collective in Barcelona, entitled "I Am Unfaithful to You with my Clitoris. What Is Said and Thought about Lesbians" (Enríquez 1978: 181), clarifies the reasons for the split:

> On February 12 the first session of the Fifth General Assembly of the Gay Liberation Front of Catalonia was held in Barcelona, during which the Lesbian Collective decided to separate from the Front. . . . This first phase of the Collective within the FAGC presupposed an expansion of the Collective, to make its existence known and to develop a feminist consciousness of the lesbian's struggle for her liberation. . . . This internal evolution of the Collective has sharpened inside the FAGC the contradiction between homosexual men and lesbians, a contradiction that is given because a lesbian's oppression originates in her being a woman. For that reason our struggle is a feminist one. From now on, the Lesbian Collective, asserting its independence from the FAGC, defines its revolutionary space, alongside women, within the Feminist Movement.

The joint struggle that had been articulated in the face of the urgent battle against the LPRS, after a process of internal political reflection, had to come to an end. Once the LPRS, the symbol of the oppression of gay men as well as lesbians, had disappeared, nothing could prevent the lesbian collectives that formed part of the mixed fronts from seeking their own concerns and articulating their struggles autonomously.

Indeed, the repressive legislation was about to disappear. This was not solely due to opposition from the lesbian and gay movement (which, though active, had very little impact compared to the destabilization caused by trade unions and nationalist struggles). Already by the end of 1976, twenty-four psychiatrists had signed a manifesto maintaining that "homosexual conduct cannot be modified by applying correctional measures to homosexual subjects, nor by depriving them of their freedom" and rejecting the supposed therapeutic goals of the LPRS (Soriano Gil 1978: 41). One of the special judges in charge of applying the law stated that it was necessary to repeal the famous Article 2.3 of the LPRS (Rico Lara 1978). The Socialist and Communist parliamentary groups included this article in their long list of those that had to be repealed before the new constitution was enacted. The entire spirit of the law (the concept of "menace" and especially its capacity for "rehabilitation") was put in doubt and deemed incompatible with democracy.

The main priority of lesbian and gay mobilization and the main cause of the emergence of many groups was the repeal of repressive legislation. The constitution, approved in a referendum on 6 December 1978, and the project of bringing the political order to European standards both made it impossible for the LPRS to continue to be applied. The urgent measures for legal reform proposed by the Spanish Socialist Workers' Party (Partido Socialista Obrero Español, or PSOE) in January 1979 eliminated many of the law's clauses, including the reference to "acts of homosexuality." This should not suggest that there existed any link between that party and the organized movement of gay men and lesbians. The democratic political forces were responding instead to claims that had come to seem obvious. Representatives of the lesbian and gay movement inside the party associations, where there were any, were in extraparliamentary groups of the Left.

That fact and the apparent subsequent democratic normalization marked a crisis in the Spanish gay and lesbian movement; some groups disappeared (the FLHOC, for example, dissolved in 1980), and others restructured themselves around new mobilizing elements. The process of forming independent lesbian organizations, which soon joined in the Coordinating Committee of Spanish Feminist Organizations (Coordinadora de Organizaciones Feministas del Estado Español, or COFEE), was initiated by Catalan women but was not an isolated occurrence. Lesbians organized alongside gay men in the Basque country, and Madrid immediately followed their lead after the first countrywide meeting of lesbians held in Madrid in June 1980. Gradually, different lesbian collectives organized within the feminist movement. In 1981 the Lesbian Feminist Collective of Madrid (Colectivo de Feministas Lesbianas de Madrid) was founded, in 1982 the Lesbian Feminist Group of Barcelona (Grup de Feministas Lesbianes de Barcelona), and in 1983 the Vizcaya Lesbian Feminist Collective (Bizkaiako Lesbiana Feministen Kolektiboa).

In addition to the discussions between lesbians and gay men within the mixed groups, the ideological differences of the various leftist factions (Trotskyist, Maoist, nihilist, and so on) and between these and social democratic and liberal positions caused the splintering or dissolution of many groups.

CRISIS AND DIVERSIFICATION, STRUGGLE AND PRIDE

"The revolutionary fags [*maricas*] still inspire in us an innocent optimism, as if it were a question of finding an acronym, running some manifestos off the printing press, and going in search of social support in the homosexual world on one side and on the Left on the other."

Ramón Linatza, "La homosexualidad tiene truco"

"We are very far from even being accepted and tolerated because we are not visible. But our objective goes beyond that. We want to change social organization so that there will be not only permissiveness but also recognition. We want to build a new political structure that will allow this recognition and create the bases required to bring new elements to our way of understanding the world."

Bizkaiako Lesbiana Feministen Kolektiboa, "Amor . . . deseo . . . seducción"

Throughout the eighties, gay men and lesbians moved in separate spheres. Along these independent paths new questions arose, while some old questions were temporarily put aside. One of the main pitfalls that lesbians had to face when organizing in mixed groups was misogynous attitudes and behavior on the part of gay men, an issue that largely disappeared as a concern of the movement. When they incorporated into the feminist struggles, organized lesbians found themselves in the unpleasant position of having to challenge internalized lesbophobia among women and question the heterocentrism that dominated their discourse. They assumed the task of raising the consciousness of feminist women so that they would assume an unprejudiced vision of sexuality that would finally defend "lesbianism" as just another sexual preference.

In honor of feminist unity, lesbians opened this door cautiously and, though progress was initially very slow, there was no turning back. In 1983 in Madrid they organized the first lesbian workshops on sexuality, where the collectives initiated a debate on the various contributions of feminism to understanding sexuality. The workshops not only won a physical space in which to exist but also conquered the feminist ideological space. This optimism was initially translated into a respect, apparently consensual, for "sexual freedom of choice." From that date on, there was an organized lesbian movement in Spain.

The creation of the first relatively open autonomous spaces had a significant influence on the gay communities in large cities. The repeal of the LPRS served as a sign that a new, nonrepressive reality was ready to be enjoyed. It was a precarious reality, which did not allow the assumption that discrimination and violence were things of the past. However, the

FAGC, noted a "very serious setback in the number of activists."[7] Paradoxically, though spaces of freedom were plain to see, gay men, who until that moment had been dispersed in parks and public toilets, made themselves at home in the narrowness and darkness of a "depoliticized ghetto," becoming frequently hostile to any glimpse of activism. Gay activism continued to reject the so-called commercial ghetto; for example, in 1982 the COFLHEE considered it necessary to do away with the homosexual ghetto. However, around this still narrow but growing ghetto a good part of the incipient "out" gay community started to come together. Throughout the eighties the gay communities of large cities were more attentive to their leisure than to the quarrels and crises inside a movement whose existence, at the national level, was testified to only by the survival of the COFLHEE.[8]

A sign of this crisis was the fact that, after the departure of the lesbian collectives, only representatives of EHGAM, FAGC, and MAG-PV attended the twenty-third meeting of the COFLHEE, held in Bilbao in January 1983. Despite the obvious crisis in activism, the coordination committee decided to engage in new activities at the national level and meet with the new socialist government, in power since 1982. The committee presented new demands, including the end of discrimination against gay teachers, the repeal of article 352 of the Military Justice Code (misdemeanor against honor), the repeal of articles referring to public scandal and the corruption of minors, the removal of "homosexuality" from the World Health Organization (WHO) catalogue of diseases, the end of police harassment of gay establishments, the destruction of police files—in short, demands that were gradually and partially taken into account more out of a desire to eliminate the remains of the dictatorship than as a response to the requirements of a weak movement.

The COFLHEE's fourth debate workshops, held in Moncofa (Castellón) in 1983, allowed the observation of "the ebbing of the Gay Movement as a consequence of the general demobilization of social movements in Spain and the development of tolerance of homosexual men and women within the commercial ghetto, and the priority that gay men and lesbians placed on personal matters."[9] About one hundred men and women attended these debates, coming from Catalonia, the Basque country, Andalusia, the Baleares, and Valencia. This meeting announced the need to draft an antidiscrimination law, similar to those existing in Norway, Quebec, the Netherlands, and Italy, which would extend identical lesbian and gay rights through a single legislative act.[10]

The presence of lesbians in the COFLHEE wound up being tokenistic. But the lesbian movement also diluted its specificity by participating actively in the major feminist struggles of the first half of the decade—that is to say, the struggles for divorce, contraception, and free abortion on demand.[11] Demonstrations and struggles on behalf of the rights or free existence of lesbians were much more sporadic. These issues were raised only in the "unitarian" demonstrations of 28 June (Liberation and Pride Day for Lesbians, Gays, and Transsexuals). Indeed, 28 June is an exception to this separation of lesbians and gay men, a day adopted by transsexual collectives to put forth their demands as well.[12]

However, the annual celebrations on 28 June had less impact in general than did specific campaigns organized around particular issues. Lesbian mobilization was less motivated by large projects of legislative renewal than by protest against a few attacks that, if they had not been addressed, would have wound up being merely incidental. In this manner, the incidental was converted into important political struggles, becoming milestones in the history of the lesbian movement. On 23 October 1986, the LPRS had already been repealed, though Article 431, which condemned "public scandals," had remained on the books. Arantxa and Esther were arrested by the police for kissing each other on the mouth while walking past the Directorate General of State Security in the Puerta del Sol square in Madrid. For two days, during which they were not informed of the reason for their arrest, they were continually mistreated and humiliated by the police.

This arrest alerted the lesbian movement and allowed it to bring to the public's attention two facts: the routine use of violence by police, who subjected people being detained to physical and psychological aggression with complete impunity; and the aggression against lesbians, gay men, or transsexuals for expressing their desire in public spaces, which had far from disappeared. Homophobia was more than a "social prejudice;" it was also manifested in the paralegal violence originating in the very structures of the state responsible for order.

The subsequent judicial process not only became a way of denouncing heterosexist institutions such as the judiciary (which took several years to admit that the aggression had taken place) but also allowed a good dose of provocation and public self-affirmation against a society that, on the whole, explicitly or implicitly represses and penalizes lesbians. On 23 January 1987, in many Spanish cities, hundreds of lesbians occupied plazas to protest the arrest of and police aggression against the freedom of the two lesbians. It also became a noisy demonstration of the existence of lesbians proud to be visible, one that had wide repercussions and good coverage in the media. This permitted not only debate over a specific act of violence but also, for the first time, broader debate on lesbianism, in the press and on television. Since then, public kissing has been the ritual that marks the visible, proud, and vocal existence of Spanish lesbians, defying the dominant moral constraints. This is recalled every 28 June and every time some type of aggression takes place.

The case of the Puerta del Sol kiss allowed the lesbian movement to articulate an analysis of the specificity of lesbophobic violence. Spanish lesbians brought attention to specific acts of aggression that result from living a sexuality that confronts and resists a single compulsory heterosexual model. The results of these reflections are expressed in the various presentations made by lesbian collectives during those years. The Vizcaya collective expressed it as follows: "Lesbians, unlike heterosexual women, are not normally battered wives, murdered girlfriends, mistreated lovers or whores exploited by their pimps" (BLFK 1988). The lesbians stated that they are systematically condemned when they enter heterosexual spaces. They agreed that, unlike heterosexual women, who are rarely attacked for their heterosexuality, lesbian women are attacked for their lesbianism—for loving and desiring women and for demonstrating it, or for simply refusing to hide it. This is the case when they are forced to live in a normative regime of compulsory heterosexuality that simply prohibits them from being who they are. Lesbian collectives deepened the debate on the political implications of this regime of compulsory heterosexuality for the everyday lives of lesbians.

The personal again became political in July 1987, when the judge of Family Court 17 in Barcelona, José Luis Sánchez Díaz, required in his ruling "the removal from Montserrat Garrart of her daughter's custody in favor of the father, due to her possible lesbianism." A team of "professional psychologists" released a detailed report mentioning "the suspicion of potential homosexuality with all that that would entail for the girl."

This ruling was appealed through all the strictly judicial channels. Organized lesbians immediately seized on it in their fight against judicial institutions and the sexist application of its laws. On the whole, they appealed against an oppressive, hypocritical, and puritanical morality, which supported a sociofamilial organization based on "good" and "bad" sexualities. Montserrat Garrart recovered custody of her daughter. The lesbian movement burst significantly onto the public scene in 1987, the moment of their greatest numerical strength and political cohesion.

Despite these mobilizations internal ideological debate was the predominant activity during the "insipid eighties": fighting over difference versus equality, the debate over pornography and the autonomy of the movement manifested itself from the beginning of the feminist movement. This was a prelude to the coming schisms among feminists and among lesbians themselves.[13] By the end of the eighties, the idea of a unified feminist movement—and, as a consequence, that of a single, unified lesbian movement—had been abandoned. The numerous internal struggles resulted in the appearance of many diverse feminisms but left the movements exhausted. For the still-weak lesbian movement, this was disastrous. Tiny groups remained in the large cities: Madrid, Barcelona, Gijón, and Bilbao.

While the strength of the lesbian movement was being diluted in transcendental debates, with little influence and only sporadic acts of visibility and public presence, the gay movement was preparing to knock on the doors of the highest state institutions. After many years of discussions, COFLHEE finally presented its antidiscrimination bill in 1989.[14] This project proposed amendments to the Civil, Penal, and Military Codes, as well as to labor and housing rental laws. The coordination committee alone struggled for the extension of full equality of legal rights to lesbians and gay men. New groups and federations that had arisen preferred to use their limited resources to defend what they saw as more realistic partial proposals.

After the repeal of LPRS, the subsequent legal changes, in spite of the gay movement's aspiration to influence legislation, had little to do with the existence of a strong social movement. Of the laws changed, it is worth mentioning the 1983 amendment of Aticle 431, the law on "public scandal," and the United Left's (Communist) 1987 proposal to repeal the article, approved the following year. Greater "legalist" pressure from the lesbian and gay movement did bear fruit in the nineties. The 1994 Urban Rental Act covers granting the continuation of a lease to the surviving member of an unmarried couple. The 1995 Penal Code deems illicit those associations that "promote discrimination, hate or violence against persons, groups or associations . . . based on their members' . . . sexual orientation" (Article 507) and mandates up to three years of prison for those who incite such behavior (Article 502). The principle that "there is no normality without juridical normality" (Col.lectiu Lambda 1994) is particularly salient in the Valencian country. The Valencian Community Parliament was the first legislature in the world to recognize the right of lesbian and gay couples to adopt. The Spanish adoption law grants this right only to individuals or heterosexual couples.

In the late eighties and early nineties, the lesbian and gay movement renewed itself and began to emerge from its crisis of activism, thanks to new modes of participation. New groups were founded, not only in large cities where associations had already existed, but also where there had never been a gay or lesbian movement. This second wave was characterized by two fundamental differences: (1) presence in the street was abandoned in favor of the establishment of social centers, where gay men often coexist with lesbians who have few links to the feminist movement and existing lesbian activism and (2) the provision of social services around AIDS prevention and information hot lines (requiring the institutionalization of the movements to obtain public financing) became the main goal of many new groups. Demands were also being made through the connections of the movement's elites (the new "homocracy" of efficient managers who are out and, furthermore, speak the bureaucratic language) with representatives of political parties and parliamentary groups.[15]

Within this new strategy of collaborating with institutions, the CGL began to launch campaigns at every election called the Pink Vote, in which it recommended voting for political parties that were sensitive to its demands. Faced with the stupor of a good part of the lesbian and gay movement, still imbued with revolutionary principles, the CGL repeatedly recommended voting for political parties represented in the Parliament whose commitment was considered lukewarm (as in the case of the United Left, of which the Communist Party is a member), merely symbolic (in the case of the PSOE, the party in power at many levels, from the central government to many city halls), or clearly hypocritical (in the case of centrist Liberals or Christian Democrats). The CGL also participated in the official Democracy Means Equality campaign, under the slogan "Respect for all."[16]

Just like the lesbian groups, those gay activists that maintained a street presence made the struggle against homophobic violence and discrimination at the workplace a fundamental element of their political activities. Over the years, and until the legalist strategy was imposed, some campaigns undertaken by member groups of the COFLHEE—such as the trial of the murderers of Sonia, a Barcelona transvestite, or attacks (specific or routine) in parks like La Taconera in Pamplona or El Retiro in Madrid— articulated discourses of condemnation or self-defense.

In 1992 the COFLHEE and a large part of the organized lesbian movement challenged discrimination at RENFE, the Spanish railway company, which had an internal rule intended to allow police or security services to harass, humiliate, arrest, threaten, and sometimes beat up gay men loitering on the premises. Demonstrations were held in several cities (including Pamplona, Bilbao, and Barcelona). In Madrid's Chamartín Station, for example, more than fifty people were arrested by the police. Demonstrations were held in several airports after an employee denounced Iberia airlines for discrimination in the workplace in 1994.

For no apparent reason, in the absence of a strong lesbian and gay movement, the mayor of Vitoria (a member of the moderate Basque Nationalist Party) opened a registry for common-law couples, beating the left-wing parties and unleashing the disorderly opening of similar registries in dozens of cities and in a few autonomous communities. Although these registries have no legal standing until a law is passed that defines them, their mere existence is often considered a victory. The early nineties were characterized mainly by demands for a law recognizing domestic partnerships, which became the latest banner of the movement.[17] Around the issue of legal regulation of partnerships, alliances and divergences were formed and dissolved within the lesbian and gay movement throughout these years. After years of debate, the proposed bill was finally drafted from COGAM's proposal, and the PSOE expressed its commitment to passing it. At this writing, it still remains to be approved, however, as much because of the socialist government's reservations as because of the lack of sufficient parliamentary support, pending the coming legislative elections.[18]

In the nineties, with a healthily diversified movement (lesbian feminists, lesbians in gay groups, gay men who flirt with bureaucracies and fight for minor grants, groups that help lesbians and gay men with psychological problems, lesbian separatists, queer movements, lesbians and gay men devoted to cultural renewal projects or who form groups and disappear under the umbrella of trade unions like Comisiones Obreras or a political party like the United Left, companies that target the lesbian and gay market and also want their voices to be heard, imported drag queens, and so on), Spanish society, seeking out new sensations, prepared to let certain types of lesbians and gay men into the press, television, and film.

Neither lesbian nor gay culture is as common or widespread in Spain as it may be in other countries. It is difficult to speak of lesbian or gay literature or cinema. Esther Tusquets, who never has defined herself as a lesbian author, has been recognized as one of the main representatives of lesbian literature. In her work, complicity between women forms the basis of the narrative. In 1994 an anonymous writer won a well-known erotic literature award, La Sonrisa Vertical (The Vertical Smile), awarded annually by a publishing house. Because of the lesbian content of her novel, she preferred to remain anonymous. Luis Antonio de Villena, Eduardo Mendicuti, and Leopoldo Alas are the current representatives of Spanish gay literature. Other authors, such as Antonio Gala and Terenci Moix, still present a "camp," sublimated, or pre-Stonewall version of sexual dissidence.

To date, Pedro Almodóvar, acclaimed by Vito Russo (1992) as "the openly gay Spanish director," has not come out of the closet. Even though he has clearly created many lesbian and gay characters, their stories have remained in the context of the depoliticized hedonism of the cultural renewal of the early eighties, known as La Movida. In this context, sadomasochistic lesbians and transvestite junkies were not subversive, but rather truly "modern," terribly "hip." The lesbian and gay characters who do not seem to be hallucinations are produced by and according to the vision of heterosexual men. They revolve around unfortunate stereo-types and live in social contexts that are far from what may be day-to-day reality for lesbians and gay men. *La Monja Alférez* and *Extramuros,* directed respectively by Javier Aguirre and Miguel Picazo, are good examples of this construction of lesbianism from the masculine viewpoint.

Since 1985, the International Women's Film Festival has been held annually in Madrid. Although this competition presents very few lesbian themes, a small space is reserved for the screening of a lesbian film (always foreign made). The first Spanish film to be directed by and feature lesbians, *Costa Brava,* was presented in 1995. Marta Balletbó-Coll was its director.

Nonetheless, especially around 28 June, the mass media periodically present a number of approximations of lesbian and gay realities. These do not reflect a shared feeling; instead, they (re)construct a specific image of what is publicly acceptable. Far from opening up spaces for self-representation, for the autonomous representation of lesbian and gay lives, these strategies deform or hijack them. They homogenize diversity in projects for integration and "normality" ("They want to get married and have children: they are Spanish lesbians"). The images of lesbians are exoticized for masculine lust. "The Other Love," "Modern Love," "The Mystery of Desire," "Fresh Meat," and "Lesbians on the Attack" are a few of the headlines of articles on "homosexuality."[19]

Thinking from the Body, from Denial to Prevention: Toward a Political Struggle against AIDS

"Speaking, touching, looking from the lesbian body is identifying oneself based on perversity and dissidence that puts up with making our bodies visible, showing them excited, wet, rubbing, panting. . . . Because only from our bodies can we exist, can we be lesbians."

Lesbianas Sexo Diferente (LSD), *Non-Grata* (1995)

"Here we are again. Visible as fags and as people with AIDS. Fernando and Cleews were like that. Both died between the last stroke of a pen and this one. They always made it clear that 'their' AIDS was part of a strategy to exterminate the margins of this well-intentioned society that wants us to stay locked up at home and threatens us with a horrible death if we step onto the street to have fun, to seduce each other, to tear down their conceptions of respectability. Be it HIV or fascist homophobia, all that we are struggling against joins to make us disappear from public space, from the world of the living, from the collective subconscious that obsesses over prohibitions. Here we are again. We are still alive and kicking. We are still using our asses."

La Radical Gai, *De un Plumazo* (1995)

The feminist struggles in which the organized lesbian movement participated actively throughout the eighties (not to mention the struggle against
sexist stereotypes in advertising and the incipient protest against of the
models of lesbianism constructed by the media) took place against the
background of demands for "the right to one's body." Throughout the
decade, the development of the AIDS epidemic also raised new political
issues, such as the construction and promotion of alienated bodies, im-
mune-deprived bodies, sick bodies. And in the nineties, the new lesbian
and gay activism of groups like LSD and La Radical Gai established a critical approximation of the mechanisms through which a homophobic system decides between the life and death, be it physical or social, of those
who incarnate dissidence. While most of the movement turned toward legal abstractions and ethical principles, a new current once again valued
social presence, visibility, the management of pleasure, the interchanges
of bodies. Knowledge, self-determination, and the diffusion of the body
as seat of our sexes/genders, as a geography where our pleasure and pain
are located and manifest themselves, acquired a decisive importance in
lesbian and gay struggles. The carnal dimension of lesbian and gay lives
became a place of resistance and subversion. "The personal is political"
was expanded into "The body is political."

However, while feminist struggles addressed the portrayal of women
as objects and raised issues relating to the body, the gay movement was
anxious to escape anatomical/medical determinisms without confronting
them, shirking the physical dimension to find refuge in the ethereal space
of a disembodied politics. It looked aside when, at the beginning of the
eighties, news of a "gay cancer" was first heard. Nonetheless to note the
delays and reticence of the gay and lesbian movement does not imply that
the much more decisive public responsibilities concerning the lack of
health protection for the entire population can be ignored.

The depoliticized hedonism that prevailed during the years of the socialist governments (1982–96) and the integration with Europe (1986)
meant that the first news about AIDS was seen by the communities (and
the surviving organizations) as antihomosexual propaganda. Caught between confusion, disbelief, and mistrust, organized gay men faced the homophobic backlash that accompanied the disease. "We now see that the
terror of prejudices, of the law, of religion to combat homosexuality are
no longer enough. Now science not only considers it a pathology, deviance or arrested normal development, but also, we are told, that intense
homosexual activity leads to immunological deficiency."[20]

A 1983 interview with the minister of health raised the need to launch
"a large information and prevention campaign on sexually transmitted diseases." The "bad faith and poorly hidden homophobia of certain media

that want to see homosexuality associated with horrible diseases" was continuously denounced.[21] Thus, the struggle against AIDS was built on the margin of the gay movement. The first associations were formed by gay activists who decided to fight the battle against HIV at the margin of already existing organizations. These former gay activists were joined by many other people who had participated in various types of organized movements, especially groups providing assistance to drug users. Eventually, these people all joined in a network of Anti-AIDS Citizens' Committees.

In Madrid, in 1984, concerned by the alarming spread of HIV, "faced with the lack of other initiatives and aware of the seriousness and urgency of the problem, [a] group of friends went into action. They published a booklet that explained what AIDS was and how to prevent being infected. They gave out their home telephone numbers and published them in order to make more detailed information available and thus (without intending to) became of one the first AIDS hotlines in Europe" (Comité Ciudadano Anti-SIDA de Madrid, n.d.). This first anti-AIDS committee was legally incorporated in 1986, though it had begun its operations two years earlier. Many more followed, totaling almost thirty in the mid-nineties.

In 1985, in spite of official figures that confirmed that the syndrome was already well established, the gay movement (which had promoted the formation of anti-AIDS committees) continued to spread mistrust: "We smell a new homophobic campaign by certain members of the press, harping on possible AIDS cases."[22] Shortly afterward, in October of the same year, EHGAM-Bilbao carried out the first safe-sex campaign in which the use of condoms was recommended. During its thirty-fourth meeting in Barcelona (December 1985), the COFLHEE confirmed that denial and condemnation were political strategies on AIDS. The lack of "minimally objective" information was decried. "The moral rearmament campaign" and "the new Puritanism . . . are revealed in the homophobic and intolerant reaction that is being spread, because of AIDS, in most mass media."[23] The gay movement was still more worried about the image of homosexuality in the media than about the promotion of safe sex or the effects of that same homophobia on the lives of those sick with AIDS.

The thirty-seventh COFLHEE meeting, held in Madrid in September 1986, expressed "its concern over the inertia and unproductiveness of the Central and autonomous Administrations with regard to AIDS prevention."[24] An article entitled "Prevention, Prevention, Prevention"[25] marked a change of direction in gay activism concurrent with a change of direction in government. From that moment on, the promotion of "safe sex" was a task that gay groups as well as health officials gradually assumed. All the back covers of the Basque magazine were henceforth devoted to AIDS prevention, with the slogan "Don't deprive yourself, but have safe sex." AIDS stopped being an antihomosexual campaign and became a risk that could be avoided. By 1987 more than 1,800 cases of AIDS had been recorded. Of these, 350 were homosexual or bisexual men and 79 were gay or bisexual men who also used drugs.

The reluctance took a long time to dissipate. COGAM, for example, waited until 1989 to publish a long article on AIDS in its magazine. The article, furthermore, was signed by someone who was not a member of the organization, the president of the Federation of Anti-AIDS Committees.[26] Only one year later, in the context of an internal debate on the need to provide services to gay men, which took place during the second conference, the Madrid-based group joined those that were already carrying out publicly funded prevention campaigns. From 1987, prevention slowly became a concern of the movement, yet no other form of struggle against AIDS was recognized. The large number of gay men who were HIV-positive or had AIDS and those who had died of AIDS continued to be invisible. Publicly, there were no HIV-positive people or PWAs (people with AIDS) in a movement that did not see the political dimension of the pandemic.[27]

The debate on AIDS, which throughout the eighties revolved around whether to get involved in the struggle or ignore it, was articulated in the nineties around the issue of whether to engage in a political struggle or to keep to prevention campaigns. In this debate, La Radical Gai played a fundamental role. Since the year it was founded, this Madrid-based group had condemned the inefficacy of the prevention campaigns that took for granted that everyone could have access to information and condoms. "A preventive vaccine and free and effective curative treatments are the only solutions that will stop our freedom and our lives from depending on pharmaceutical laboratories, from being the 'concern' of social security systems . . . and the businesses of rubber, morality, control, and fear" (La Radical Gai 1992). This claim had never before been formulated.

ACT UP-BCN (Barcelona) was founded in Barcelona in 1992, with strategies and objectives similar to those of other chapters: "We are going to raise consciousness, protest, condemn, pressure and demonstrate, defy prejudices and falsehood and the lack of information until we reach our objective: the end of AIDS."[28] In 1992, at the suggestion of La Radical Gai, the COFLHEE condemned "the public authorities' criminal silence, repressive vocation, negligence, inaction and criminal lies." In the same text appeared the first list of demands that includes issues pertaining not only to prevention but also to treatments, access to health care, and so on. (La Radical Gai 1992). From that moment on, many groups within the COFLHEE included AIDS as one of their struggles. The first of December became a day of public protest. La Radical Gai, which from

1992 on defined itself as a "seropositive movement," undertook in 1993 the first "political prevention" campaign, with messages like "Clean your works with bleach," "Use a condom and lubrication for all acts of penetration," "Use latex squares, especially during menstruation" and "Put on a condom, or else . . . forget it."[29] The first countrywide prevention campaign targeting gay men (but limited to gay locales) was carried out at the initiative of the CGL in 1994. A second campaign, which used drawings by Ralph König, was launched the following year with the slogan "Take care of yourself '95." During those two years, the first national meetings of HIV-positive gay men were held.[30]

Until the founding of LSD, the lesbian movement (like much of the gay movement) had left the struggle against AIDS to the Anti-AIDS Citizens' Committees. In 1994, at the national meeting of feminist organizations held in Madrid, L.S.D. organized an informational event at which, for the first time, lesbian sexual practices were linked to the possibility of HIV transmission. On that occasion, the group also distributed a guide entitled "Sexo seguro, caliente, bollero." Since then, LSD has actively participated in the demonstrations organized by La Radical Gai held on 1 December in front of the Ministry of Health in Madrid.

Of the more than 47,000 officially registered cases of AIDS in Spain, around 15 percent of infections were transmitted through homosexual contact. According to official figures as of 30 September 1997, there had been 6,675 cases of homosexual transmission and 805 of intravenous drug users who also had engaged in homosexuality. Official statistics still ignore the possibility of woman-to-woman HIV transmission. If it is taking place, it is surely being classified as "of unknown origin" or used to inflate the number of cases of heterosexual transmission.

A "MIXED" MOVEMENT?
A "QUEER" MOVEMENT?

The "mixed" character appears to be a dominant feature of the nineties movement.[31] Whereas the first organizations in the seventies were rapidly dissolved because of insurmountable political differences, the current organizations are characterized by a potentially durable cohabitation. This cohabitation, albeit desirable, is characterized nonetheless by a minority position being accorded to lesbians, not only numerically but also because they are encouraged in many cases to abandon their own discourse. The existence of a distinct lesbian entity—like the one that defines certain lesbian associations, such as LSD—would be lost in the development of discourses, goods, and services that define a movement that is almost always "mixed gay." The alliances between lesbians and gay men, according to this critique, might be possible if they also contained diversity of meaning and practice.

In recent years, the unstable processes that are allowing lesbians and gay men to come out of the closet and have a public presence are making it easier to recognize the differences that exist between "women" and "men." Thus, it is now beginning to be possible to recognize new bodies. The formerly unknown "lesbian body" is now being presented as heterogeneous; gay bodies go beyond the stereotype and for the first time are diversifying. In this manner, reinventing and claiming the existence of lesbian and gay bodies will form part of the strategies that reaffirm new identities in a corporeal reality that acquires social, erotic, and political dimensions. Reformist discourse avoids these dimensions to avert an important debate that problematizes the model that until now has been dominant and exclusionary: heterosexuality. Its most characteristic feature is sexual dissidence, but this factor does not exhaust all its significance and implications.

Doors are definitely being opened to a deconstruction of a body that tries to construct itself as legitimate and monolithic but that runs the risk of remaining stereotyped and reproducing the same exclusions that it claims to fight ("the homosexual," in which all lesbians and many gay men remain trapped). New, multiform identities are thus constituted in the context of a renewed political space. The new physical as well as symbolic bodies are the manifestation of new subjects that can no longer be ignored.[32]

Every year at the demonstrations on 28 June, there are more numerous and diverse multiple subjects. After almost twenty uninterrupted years (the first five were of exaltation and the next ten of decadence), these demonstrations have begun once again to constitute "massive" acts in the large cities. Gradually, 28 June is turning into a time of festive public celebration, showing not so much a unity of political action of indeterminate results, but rather a plural and diverse community, which articulates different political discourses and which carries out its struggles at different times and in different contexts from the official agenda. From the early nineties to the present, participation in the Madrid demonstration went from a few hundred to approximately six thousand in 1997. The first countrywide demonstration, held in Madrid on a cold and rainy afternoon on 25 November 1995, brought together about five thousand people. Simultaneously, in the nineties, various events began to be organized in smaller cities; including Santiago de Compostela, Seville, Gijón, and Vitoria.

This plurality suggests the existence (the possibility) of a "queer" movement in Spain. The English term "queer" (impossible to translate into Spanish and, for that reason, used in its original form) designates a posture and a theoretical reflection that emerged in the United States. For Teresa de Lauretis (1991: iii), it is "an agency of social process whose mode of functioning is both interactive and yet resistent, both participatory and yet distinct, claiming at once equality and difference, demanding political representation while insisting on its material and historical specificity."

Suggesting the existence of a "queer" movement in Spain makes sense only in the context of minority groups that swim in a sea of a historical and institutionally stabilized gay and lesbian movement, which occurs in spaces and dimensions where one does not necessarily tend to locate "the political." The "queer" movement takes place in the margins, and its goals are not limited to "relevant" issues, such as institutional negotiations, guidelines for Pink Consumption, or unquestioned presence in the media. The term "queer," referring to the activist practice of a group, first appeared in issue 3 of La Radical Gai's *De un Plamazo*, defined in 1993 as a "queerzine." In *Non-Grata* the following year, LSD used the expression "I am 'queer'; I am different."

"Queer" politics inserts itself into the "historical" debate on the question of identity in opposition to the traditional positions of dissolving fundamental categories into the Freudian terms of sexual polymorphism and universal bisexuality. These suppositions were virtually unquestioned within gay groups, yet they have never been at the core of lesbian activism. From the beginning, the COFLHEE opposed the construction of identities. Its 1979 manifesto reads, "We consider unrealistic the categories 'homosexual' and 'heterosexual.' . . . We favor the disappearance of male/female, masculine/feminine and active/passive roles."[33] Most groups are hostile to the use of terms like "dyke" and "fag" (among many others); they did not enter into the activist vocabulary until La Radical Gai and L.S.D. were formed. To avoid labels, including "gay," sometimes complicated paraphrases are used (going back to Alfred Kinsey), such as "those people who to a large or small extent feel homosexual desires."[34]

Underlying the importance of the term "queer" and the terminological renewal that has made "dyke" and "fag" vindicatory terms is the need to establish a distance from "lesbian" and "gay" political figures and especially from people "who engage in homosexual practices," categories that were used during the first twenty years of activism. Simultaneously, there was an attempt, in this process, to bring in related issues of social class, national identity, ethnicity and *"sidentidad"* (AIDS-related identity) (Llamas 1995). This is not the ruckus raised by lesbians and gay men who capitalize on a discourse that is less and less problematic for the sociosexual order. It is, on the contrary, a revolt of lezzies, fags, queens, diesel dykes, PWAs, and sadomasochists, faced with a social context that ignores and excludes possible transformative subjects. The social order thus becomes intolerable because it limits movements and the possibilities for action and the articulation of differences.

The construction of collective identities from "queer" reflection and practice not only allows the rewriting of the past and the enjoyment of the present. Furthermore, and more important, the unquestionable agents of social change that are generating and propelling this process are already building the future.

NOTES

Acknowledgments: Thanks to Maite and the women in the Bizkaiako Lesbiana Feministen Kolektibao, Angel (EHGAM-Iruña), Arantxa, Herme, Colectivo de Feministas Lesbianas de Madrid, Colectivo Gai de Compostela, Pepe and José Luis (Col.lectiu Lambda de Gais y Lesbianas del País Valencia), Colectivo Gai de Murcia, Maite (Comité Ciudadano Anti-SIDA de Madrid), SomoS (Plataforma Gai-Lesbiana de Sevilla), Susana and Pedro (COGAM), Sílvia (Casal Lambda de Barcelona), Serafín (T4-Bilbao), and all our friends at L.S.D. and La Radical Gai.

In addition to the sources cited in the References section, I consulted the following journals: *Amaranta, Andaina, Desde el Silencio con Amor, De SIDA, De un Plumazo, Eh, Tú, Mira!, Entiendes? Gaiceta, Gay Hotsa, Info Gai, Homosexualitats, Informa-LES, Non Grata, Nosotras, No Te Prives, Paper Gai, Por Ti, Sorginak,* and *Vida.*

1. The marriage of the king of Aragon and the queen of Castile was the origin of the unity of Spain. The Moorish kingdom of Granada was conquered, its population was forced to convert to Catholicism or leave the country, the Jewish population was exiled, and the pursuit of sodomy became more rigorous.

2. The Instituto Lambda's data mention the cases of two women, though details are not known. If lesbians were sentenced under the LPRS, they are not yet part of a documented history of lesbophobic repression. Of the people sentenced, according to the institute, two-thirds were either unemployed or working class. It would appear that repression has a class component.

3. The use of more radical therapies is also documented. For example, referring to lobotomies, prison physician Dr. López Ibor stated, "My last patient was a deviant. After surgery to the inferior lobe of his brain, he certainly suffers from confused memory and troubled vision, but he seems somewhat more attracted to women." These words were spoken at the same March 1973 San Remo Medical Conference at which the group FUORI! (Fronte Unitario Omosessuale Revoluzionario Italiano) made its protests heard (Lamo de Espinosa 1989: 84).

4. The April manifesto, promoted by the FHAR, was also signed by Acción Comunista (AC), Comités de Apoyo a COPEL (Coordinadora de Presos en

Lucha), Confederación Nacional del Trabajo (CNT), Frente de Liberación de la Mujer (FLM), Juventudes Comunistas Revolucionarias (JCR), Juventudes Socialists (JJSS), Liga Comunista Revolucionaria (LCR), Mujeres Libres, Organización de Izquierda Comunista (OIC), Seminario Colectivo Feminista, Colectivo de Psiquiatrizados en Lucha, Minusválidos Unidos, Colectivo Feminista, and Grupos de Educación Especial. Together, they formed the Madrid Coordination Committee of Marginalized Groups for the Abolition of the LPRS (Coordinadora de Grupos Marginados de Madrid por la Abolición de la LPRS).

   5. Quoted in *El País*, 26 July 1977.

   6. For the number of people attending the Madrid demonstration, see Linatza 1978. A short-lived group also formed in Málaga: the Democratic Union of Homosexuals (Unión Democrática de Homosexuales de Málaga, or UDHM). Later, the Andalusian Homosexual Liberation Front (Frente de Liberación Homosexual de Andalucía, or FLHA) was founded at the initiative of the Málaga group. By 1982 it had coordinated groups in Málaga, Seville, Granada, and La Línea. A group also emerged in Cordoba. The Aragonese Homosexual Movement (Movimiento Homosexual Aragonés, or MHA) and the Galician Homosexual Liberation Front (Frente de Liberación Homosexual Galego, or FLHG) completed the activist craze in 1977.

   7. Quoted in *Infugai*, no. 15 (1980).

   8. Of the groups founded at the end of the seventies, the only ones to survive were the FAGC in Barcelona and EHGAM in Bilbao. After the disappearance of the FLHOC, the Asamblea Gai de Madrid (AGAMA) was formed in Madrid in 1983. This collective also languished and was finally dissolved, giving way to the Colectivo Gai de Madrid (COGAM) in 1986. That same year after the dissolution of the Moviment d'Alliberament Sexual del País Valencià (MAS-PV) and the Moviment d'Al.liberament Gai del País Valencià (MAG-PV), founded in 1980, the Col.lectiu Lambda de Gais y Lesbianes del País Valencià was founded in the city of Valencia and eventually formed chapters in Alicante and Castellón. Other lesbian feminist groups were organized during the eighties in Granada, Valencia, Santiago de Compostela, San Sebastián, Gijón, Pamplona, Zaragoza, Alicante, Seville, and Salamanca. At their peak, the numerically strongest groups were those in Madrid and Barcelona, encompassing thirty to forty activists. During the second half of the eighties, many of these groups ceased to operate, and those that still existed saw their chances of transcendental activism cut back after the militant fervor of the beginning of the decade died down. The organized group in Salamanca (COGLES) is notable for being mixed from the beginning.

   9. *Gay Hotsa*, no. 18 (1983).

   10. In April 1984 similar workshops were held in Vitoria; 118 people from nine collectives, including two lesbian collectives, attended.

   11. Some gay groups (such as the FAGC) also included these "heterosexual" demands in their platforms.

   12. No politically organized transvestite movement has ever existed in Spain. However, in spite of the suspicion that transvestites raise in gay and lesbian groups for the "image they give the movement" or the "image they give women,"

they have made themselves visible in every 28 June demonstration, garnering the attention of the mass media through their provocativeness. Transsexuals organized at the beginning of the nineties in cities like Barcelona and Madrid for recognition of their specific gender identity. Their main demand was, and is, the coverage of sex-change operations by the social security system.

13. The debate among organized lesbians in the eighties was influenced by the works of Monique Wittig, Kate Millet, Shulamith Firestone, Adrienne Rich, and, to a lesser extent, Luce Irigaray. This debate, centered on the questioning of heterosexuality, led to two very distinct and well-defined schools of thought: radical lesbianism (Wittig [1992:]: "Lesbians are not women") and lesbian separatism (Rich [1989:]: the "lesbian continuum," under which women decided to reject and not collaborate with heteropatriarchal institutions). The Amazon Network (Red de Amazonas), founded in Barcelona, clearly aligned itself with Wittig's position and, generally speaking, was very critical of lesbian feminists' double activism and the development of feminism from a heterosexual perspective. This collective, still in existence, serves as a link between lesbians throughout Spain. Since the beginning, it has kept in constant contact with lesbian organizations in other countries. The lesbians in the feminist movement (which also includes autonomous lesbians and feminists) join forces on more or less eclectic proposals, but always in a more integrationist perspective.

14. At a meeting held in Madrid in December 1988, COFLHEE voted to follow COGAM's proposal: the definitive drafting and proposal of an antidiscrimination law. FAGC had proposed instead a Charter of Rights for the Free Expression of Homosexual Practice, which would not be aimed solely at the legislative level. Barcelona's hostility to contact with the large political parties in power was overruled by a new, joint political strategy (*Gay Hotsa*, no. 43 [1989]).

15. Throughout these years, as the fruit of innumerable initiatives, intrigues, quarrels, and conspiracies, many new groups formed (some of them mixed, such No Te Prives, which was founded in Murcia in 1985 and is a member of COFLHEE). In some cities, the movement became more diversified. In Barcelona, the Coordinadora Gai Lesbiana (CGL) and the Collectiu Gai de Barcelona (CGB) were formed. The Colectivo Reinvindicativo y Cultural de Lesbianas (CRECUL) was founded in Madrid in 1991. The CGL inspired the formation of groups in other cities and became another countrywide coordination committee. The Madrid-based COGAM left the COFLHEE in 1991 and wound up forming the Federación Estatal de Gais y Lesbianas. This coordination committee was joined by the Casal Lambda de Barcelona (inheritor of the Instituto Lambda) and the Col.lectiu Lambda de Gais y Lesbianas del País Valencià, which had been excluded from the COFLHEE. La Radical Gai was formed in Madrid in 1991, after a split in COGAM; it joined the COFLHEE, alongside the Gais Lliures del País Valencià, Liberación Gai de Córdoba, and the Colectivo Gai de Compostela, among others. Several other groups also founded in the nineties, such as Lesbianas y Gais de Aragón (LYGA) and Xente Gai Astur (XEGA), maintain their independence from the large coordination committees. In 1993, Lesbianas Se DiFunden (L.S.D.), a lesbian collective, was formed in Madrid.

16. This tolerance campaign used the images of Martin Luther King, Albert Einstein, Stephen Hawking, and Oscar Wilde to illustrate a "black," a "Jew," a "cripple," and a "fag." Lesbians, once again, were absent.

17. The COGAM, initially a proponent of the dissolution of the family, suspended that part of its program shortly before making the partnership law its main objective. The FAGC, on the contrary, advocated from the beginning "the suppression of the concepts of marriage, the couple and the family" ("Manifest," 1977) and did not participate in these campaigns. Most of the groups in the COFLHEE did not either, though the symbolic weight of the couple began to become apparent. The "Anti-Discrimination Guide for Gay Men and Lesbians," published by the EHGAM in Bilbao (1992) and based on the CGL's guide, entitled "What Rights Do We Have?" divides rights into "1. Couples" (nineteen pages) and "2. Individuals" (nine pages).

18. The whole "legalist" movement, which shortly before had been divided over the means and scope of the bill, finally supported it. Other lesbian and gay groups never consented to make the partnership law the primary goal of their struggle. The first demonstration of "Spanish gays, lesbians, and transsexuals," held on 25 November 1995, was sponsored by all the associations and attracted some five thousand participants. It was designed to be a show of support for the partnership law, but the COFLHEE and other groups predicated their participation on a broader claim that would incorporate the concerns of all associations. In the end, the official sign read, "For our rights."

19. Llamas 1997 analyzes the stereotypes that determine the public presentation of lesbians and gay men in the Spanish media.

20. Héctor Anabitarte, quoted in *Gay Hotsa*, no. 18 (1983). The information on AIDS that was made available in Spain during the first half of the eighties basically responded to the same stereotypes as in other Western countries. See Llamas 1995.

21. Quoted in *Gay Hotsa*, no. 19 (1983).

22. *Gay Hotsa*, no. 26 (1985). An article on anal sex and disease prevention published in the same issue stated that "any venereal disease treated in time is easily curable." It nonetheless recommended "hygiene, caution and reasonable judgement." In addition to enemas and lubricants, it recommended "trying to avoid sexual contact with people who cause the slightest suspicion of venereal disease. A rapid examination of your partner may reveal signs that s/he might not have noticed him- or herself." No mention is made in the article of AIDS or condoms. No preventive techniques were mentioned in the first detailed article on AIDS (*Gay Hotsa*, no. 27 [1985]), though it listed the symptoms that could be caused by immunodeficiency.

23. Quoted in *Gay Hotsa*, no. 30 (1986).

24. Quoted in *Gay Hotsa*, no. 33 (1986).

25. *Gay Hotsa*, no. 35 (1987).

26. *Entiendas*, no. 10 (1989).

27. The Anti-AIDS Citizens' Committees encouraged the formation of support groups, such as El Ciempiés (the Centipede) in Madrid or the T4 group in Bilbao, in which, gay men (and nongays) with HIV/AIDS began to organize for the first time. The message that the committees frequently repeated—that AIDS

"is everybody's problem"—and the struggle against talk of supposed "high-risk groups" both caused some gay men with HIV/AIDS to feel a lack of recognition in the committees' work. Starting in 1990, several gay HIV/AIDS groups were founded in Bilbao (*Gay Hotsa*, no. 46 [1990]): Gais Positius, part of the CGL in Barcelona; Entender en Positivo, within the COGAM in Madrid; and the Grup Positiu, of Valencia's Col.lectiu Lambda.

28. Most people who joined ACT UP-BCN were gay or lesbian, from old FAGC activists to American and French residents of Barcelona. Some members were (former) drug users; some were transsexuals. In Madrid, at the behest of La Radical Gai, several meetings were held in 1992 to attempt to found an ACT UP-Madrid. The heterogeneity of the people who heeded the call, the fact that most were seronegative, and the subsequent absence of a sense of urgency eventually aborted the initiative. The appropriateness of adopting a foreign name and the possibility that the triangle might exclude nongays, especially women, were discussed. In a special publication on AIDS entitled *Silence = Death*, La Radical Gai reclaimed and adopted the symbols and strategies of ACT UP chapters.

29. The general slogan of the campaign was "Someone will have to prevent it." Its political character was derived from the explicit representation of the practices that no one wanted to show—intravenous injection, anal penetration between two men, oral sex between two women—and its explanation of how to carry out the activities under safe conditions, without having to give them up. The following year, La Radical Gai published the first "Leatherman's Guide to Safe Sex" (*De un Plumazo*, no. 3 [1994]).

30. *De SIDA*, no. 18 (1995).

31. Mixed can sometimes reflect intention: "The Lambda Project is a project of men and women. Lesbian issues have elements that are without doubt common to male homosexuality, which make working together not only opportune but essential, as the Spanish lesbian movement has recognized. The project that defines Lambda Valencia will remain incomplete until it includes an (autonomous) sectoral group of women who meet, work together and create their own discourse and their own way of life and action, and they participate with men in all levels of Lambda's tasks. . . . Lambda, in all instances . . . , must do everything it can to promote and develop the active internal participation of women" (Col.lectiu Lambda 1994).

32. When the activists of L.S.D. openly show their sex under the slogan "Es-cultura Lesbiana" in the centerfold of the "dykezine" *Non-Grata*, vol. 1 (1995), they are not only saying that it is an enjoyable to be a lesbian but also that from the body it is possible to reorganize erotically, politically, and symbolically—that is to say that they have the opportunity to disobey the rules of the dominant culture.

33. Quoted in *Gay Hotsa*, no. 3 (1979). These questions have only recently been addressed by scholars. Among the first contributions in the new field of lesbian gay, and queer studies are Buxón (1997) and Llamas (1998).

34. Quoted in *Gay Hotsa*, no. 51 (1992).

REFERENCES

Bizkaiako Lesbiana Feministen Kolektiboa (BLFK). 1988. "Divagaciones pornográficas para el seso." Presentation. Jornadas Estatales de Lesbianas, Madrid.

Buxán, Xosé, ed. 1997. *Conciencia de un singular deseo: Estudios lesbianas y gays en el estado español.* Barcelona: Laertes.

Col.lectiu Lambda. 1994. "El papel del Lambda, hoy." Presentation. Valencia.

Comité Ciudadano Anti-SIDA de Madrid. n.d. "El Comité Ciudadano Anti-SIDA: Cómo surge, porqué, los objetivos y las actividades que lleva a cabo." Pamphlet.

De Fluvià, Armand. 1978. "El movimiento homosexual en el estado español." In *El homosexual ante la sociedad enferma.* Ed. José Ramón Enríquez. Barcelona: Tusquets.

———, 1979. *Aspectos jurídico-legales de la homosexualidad.* Barcelona: Instituto Lambda.

De Lauretis, Teresa. 1991. "Queer Theory: Lesbian and Gay Sexualities. An Introduction." *differences, A Journal of Feminist Cultural Studies* 3 (2), iii-xvii.

Enríquez, José Ramón, ed. 1978. *El homosexual ante la sociedad enferma.* Barcelona: Tusquets.

Genet, Jean. 1985. *Diario de un ladrón.* Barcelona: Planeta.

Lamo de Espinosa, Emilio. 1989. *Delitos sin víctimas: Orden social y ambivalencia moral.* Madrid: Alianza Universidad.

La Radical Gai. 1992. *Silencio = Muerte.* Mimeograph. Madrid.

Linatza, Ramón. 1978. "La homosexualidad tiene truco." *El Viejo Topo: Homosexualidad.* Special issue. 23–27.

Llamas, Ricardo, ed. 1995. *Construyendo sidentidades: Estudios desde el corazón de una pandemia.* Madrid: Siglo XXI.

———. 1997. Miss Media: *Una lectura perversa de la comunicación de masas.* Barcelona: Ediciones de la Tempestad.

——— 1998. *Teoría torcida Prejuicios y discursos en torno a "la homosexualidad."* Madrid: Siglo XXI.

López Linage, Javier, ed., 1977. *Grupos marginados y peligrosidad social.* Madrid: Campo Abierto.

Rich, Adrienne. 1989. "Compulsory Heterosexuality and Lesbian Existence." In *Feminist Frontiers II.* Ed. Laurel Richardson and Verta Taylor. New York: Random House.

Rico Lara, Manuel. 1978. "Los homosexuales y la ley." *El País,* 12 January.

Russo, Vito. 1992. "The Film Historian." In *Making History.* Ed. Eric Marcos. New York: HarperCollins.

Sahuquillo, Angel. 1991. *Federico García Lorca y la cultura de la homosexualidad masculina.* Alicante: Instituto de Cultural Juan Gil Albert.

Soriano Gil, Manuel. 1978. *Homosexualidad y represión.* Madrid: Zero.

Terradillos, Juan. 1981. *Peligrosidad social y estado de derecho.* Madrid: Akal.

Wittig, Monique. 1992. *The Straight Mind and Other Essays.* Boston: Beacon.

SCOTT LONG

10   Gay and Lesbian Movements in Eastern Europe

Romania, Hungary, and the Czech Republic

IN 1989, the words "gay and lesbian" were rarely heard in Eastern Europe. Seven years later—at the time of this writing—they (or the local equivalents) are used more often, but the term "Eastern Europe" is dying out. Its validity is denied by the prime minister of the Czech Republic,
who reminds listeners acerbically that Prague is west of Vienna. An entire
school of Hungarian historiography has devoted itself to picturing
Poland, Hungary, the former Czechoslovakia, and the Baltic states as an
arrière-boutique to Western Europe: as participants in Western Europe's
political and confessional traditions, but detached from the West's historical trajectory by several inconvenient accidents, those favored states
are strangers to the less modernized societies and meaner situations to the
south and east.[1] Budapest, Budapesters remind us, is *not* Bucharest.

This is, of course, true. This chapter deals with three gay and lesbian
movements of widely differing size and success. One has achieved national scope and real political significance; one is fragmented and confused; one, confronting an oppressive law, barely has space or freedom to
move at all. The Czech Republic is contiguous to Hungary, and Hungary
is contiguous to Romania, yet a lesbian Romanian visiting Prague might
well envision it on a different continent—or planet.

Both historical differences and the unequal development endemic to
contemporary capitalism impose their characteristic disparities. Yet in all
three countries the former factors underlie, and the latter forces build
upon, forty-five common years of authoritarian domination. And in all
three countries—as across four thousand miles of Eurasia—this domination operated through shared structures in broadly similar ways. In constructing an archeology of the present, one must remember that history is
sedimented differently from the soil: often the topmost layer is the most
resistant rock. The most recent past may be the hardest to break through.

Most powerfully, the weight of that recent past meant that in 1989
gays and lesbians in all three countries entered a suddenly created political sphere with few political experiences or preconceptions. In that dizzy-
ing yet enabling vacuum, I contend, movements searched collective mem-

ories and surroundings for two complementary tools: a *paradigm* to explain their purposes to themselves and a *discourse* to justify them to others. The varying paradigms found (or discarded), the discourses used (or dropped) are explored country by country in the first part of this chapter. Those tools were taken up to confront situations created largely since about 1950. The second part of the chapter attempts to identify that conditioning commonality.

I continue to use the term Eastern Europe here, but more as a *was* than an *is:* the term serves as a sign of that of history since 1950 and its traces in the present, not of present reality in itself. Eastern Europe is (to use the inevitable phrase) an imagined community that may not be fully imaginable much longer. The real question underlying this chapter is What sorts of communities—what living possibilities—will be imagined in its place?[2]

Romania: Constructing a Minority

Homosexual acts are illegal in Romania, but this has not been *entirely* bad for the gay and lesbian movement. Opponents of the law (and its victims) would call this a callous statement; the Romanian Orthodox Church would chant anathemas at the idea that righteousness rouses sin. Both would be correct. But the law—which can still destroy any gay group—has given the tiny gay movement focus, direction, and a *discourse*. This has been no negligible gift. Legislators in their airy deliberations do not always realize what they have wrought.

Article 200, paragraph 1, of the Romanian Penal Code punishes consensual, adult homosexual sex with one to five years in prison. It is one of three such laws left in Europe and the only one penalizing lesbians as well as gay men.[3] The law proved convenient for Nicolae Ceauşescu. Since no human rights organization in the world (before 1991) was willing to take on the case of a person imprisoned solely for his or her sexuality, it was a trouble-free way to jail and discredit dissidents in one stroke. It also furnished the most surveillance-centered government in the Soviet bloc with extra leverage over private life. All the same, very small gay male subcultures managed to develop in major cities. Unlike in adjacent countries, these revolved exclusively around public cruising areas rather than private parties: apartments were, or were believed to be, wire-tapped and watched. Yet gays elaborated a corpus of knowledge about preventing, or surviving, blackmail and arrest.[4]

Political expediency alone does not account for the law. A June 1993 survey asked Romanians to rate homosexuality on a scale from one, "never justified," to ten, "always justified": 85 percent chose a ranking of one.[5] Romanian homophobia is often explained by the total silence about sexuality during the Communist years. However, it is surely an oversimplification to trace these figures—coming after debates on the subject had already begun—to a paucity of discourse. Romanian nationalism, imposing conformity on a country riven by ethnic, regional, and cultural differences, certainly has also contributed to a terror of "otherness".[6] And images of masculine virility and familial security are regularly invoked to bind citizens emotionally to the embodied nation.[7]

Article 200, paragraph 1, remained on the books after Ceauşescu's fall. Faced with occasional queries from the West, the government alleged that it was no longer enforced.[8] Debate over the issue arose only in 1993, when—in response to clear evidence that the article *was* being enforced— rapporteurs from the Council of Europe (CoE) drew attention to the law in considering Romania's possible entry. The CoE Parliamentary Assembly voted to admit Romania, contingent on the Romanian government's commitment to repeal the law within six months.

Romania has a playful attitude toward international commitments. The "fun and games" have, at this writing, gone on for three years. In Parliament the government did indeed propose a modification to Article 200, punishing "homosexual acts that cause public scandal" with one to five years in jail.[9] The only definition of "public scandal" in Romanian jurisprudence is "an act that becomes known to more than two people who disapprove of it." The survey mentioned earlier—and the fact that, for a quarter of a century, the most popular evening activity in Romania has not been watching television but watching neighbors—suggests that these conditions would be easy to meet. Conservatives in Parliament have added to the language of the proposal—punishing "propaganda, associations, or any attempt to proselytize" for homosexuality, thus denying even freedom of speech and of assembly to lesbians and gays. However, even this one-step-forward-two-steps-back modification has not been adopted. The neocommunist ruling party governs with the bizarre support of three small nationalist, neofascist parties, which interpret as criminal the aspirations of Hungarians and Jews, not only the legalizing of homosexuality but also most other steps toward European integration. The opposition is led by a Christian Democratic Party, uneasily cohabited by Christians and Democrats. The Christians tend to regard the Council of Europe as the local government of Sodom. In the last two parliamentary sessions, all legal reform was stalled by moral and political posturing.[10] In 1994 an omnibus Penal Code reform bill was rejected when the government's coalition partners deserted, citing the liberalization of homosexuality as the cause. Parliament would rather leave a Ceauşescu-era Penal Code completely intact than change a lone provision criminalizing consensual adult sex.[11]

In the meantime, Romanian Orthodoxy has entered the fray. This church is probably no more intrinsically homophobic—or less replete with homosexuals—than many other Christian sects; indeed, one of its monasteries, well-known among Romanian gays, is nicknamed San Francisco.[12] However, the church, discredited by its collaboration with Ceauşescu, is wielding homophobia as a wedge to reassert its political influence.[13] Seminary students have held large demonstrations, and priests have collected signatures in churches, hospitals, and schools for a petition to *increase* penalties; religious programming on television and radio harps ceaselessly about the fate of the real sin-laden San Francisco.

With homosexuality now a focal point for nationalist fears of the alien West, and fundamentalist loathing of the twentieth century, it is hard to see much hope in the situation. Homophobia ensures that the movement will remain small, and expectations low, for the foreseeable future. Yet the extent of oppression has opened the possibility for gays and lesbians to find a *paradigm* for themselves, as a mistreated minority, and to mantle themselves in a *discourse,* that of human rights. Gays and lesbians have become an issue in and a marginal part of Romania's underdeveloped civil society, grafting themselves onto mainstream human rights groups.

These solutions were forced on them by the legal situation. In 1992 no human rights organization in Romania was willing to work with gays and lesbians, not even to the minimal degree of helping them obtain information to prove that Article 200 was still enforced. Activists were able to gain access to the most prestigious of these organizations, the Romanian Helsinki Committee, by casting themselves in the light of an ethnic minority and interpreting their oppressions after the model of the persecutions suffered by Roma (Gypsies) and the inequities undergone by Hungarians.[14] In 1993 the committee's Ethnic Minorities Program set up a subprogram for "sexual minorities." This has enthusiastically sponsored documentation visits to prisons and courts and has lobbied Parliament and the Ministry of Justice for repeal of the existing law.

The effect may be wonderful; the argument remains strange. In Romania, the definition of "sexual minorities" by analogy with ethnic counterparts is riddled with logical lacunae. It presents the spectacle of a minority with no historical consciousness, institutions, or extensive spectrum of shared behaviors, claiming, in effect, the right to create all those from a vacuum—to create itself. Few gays or lesbians in Romania are openly gay or lesbian for more than a minuscule proportion of their waking hours. It is a fragmentary and ephemeral identity, only intermittently suitable to broad description, with a limited collocation of common knowledge, mostly about avoiding detection. To take this experiential deprivation as itself establishing a claim on rights may indeed be, from our perspective, just; it is a demand for the first conditions for self-determination. From the perspective of established ethnic minorities, constituted by history and autonomous institutions, it might understandably seem peculiar. Yet in Romania—where ethnicity to a large degree dominates politics and shapes identity—it has proved persuasive.

Success in self-articulation through human rights discourse has not been matched by success in organization. There have been four gay groups in the last four years, all Bucharest based. The first, founded in 1992, was a social circle that soon fell apart. In 1993, activists set up Group 200, a human rights organization named after the law.[15] And another activist, again grafting onto an established organization, persuaded a mainstream human rights group to let him operate a Gay and Lesbian Human Rights Commission under its auspices.[16] This group and Group 200 also collapsed, amid corruption allegations against their leaders.

Indicative of the dependency on others that gay Romanians feel—to provide them with not only paradigm and discourse but also an example—the fourth group was largely organized by gay foreigners living in Bucharest and by straights working for the Romanian Helsinki Committee. Supported by the Dutch Embassy, they held a symposium, Homosexuality: A Human Right? in the summer of 1995, and a retreat in the resort of Sinaia the following winter. The retreat, attended by forty Romanian gays (all men) was a tremendously moving gathering, one even most of the participants had secretly believed impossible. The group, now called ACCEPT and at last led by *Romanian* gay men,[17] is applying for legal status as a human rights group, with no mention of sexuality. The discourse of rights serves as a binding credo among members. However, the tenuousness of this solidarity reflects an almost total lack of real community—and the degree to which present reality belies the minority paradigm they have chosen to embrace. The group will probably be unable to organize effectively against the law: that effort must come from abroad. Its real task is the gradual creation of the absent community that its rhetoric invokes.

THE CZECH REPUBLIC:
INTEGRATION VERSUS IMITATION

Integration and imitation are fighting words for those on the contemporary U.S. Left. They describe abjuring an identity, an act that in identity politics lies somewhere between Samson's pulling down the temple (from the Philistines' point of view) and Oedipus's relieving himself of his eyes. I mean something a bit different.

Integration stands here for the therapeutic attempt to reduce a minority's separation while (and by) affirming its dependency. *Imitation* stands for a response that nonetheless incorporates the former's terms: it asserts that no cure is needed because the subject of care is capable of reproducing, *in*dependently and *in* separation, the norms and forms desired. *Introjection* might be a clearer, if uglier, name. Imitation is therapy transcended by agency; that is one way of putting it.

Translated into political terms, this begins to explain certain differences between the vocabularies of gay and lesbian rights in the Romanian and Czech cases. The Romanian movement emerged from a punitive situation, a brutal attempt at rejection; it is now beginning to affirm a differentiated identity for gays and lesbians, modeled after ethnic minorities in a multicultural nation. Czech gays and lesbians emerged from a curative context, which tried to change and absorb them. They learned not to embrace difference defiantly but to find security through absorbing, in turn, a version of belonging—becoming an imitation nation, swallowing whole the structure of citizenship.

Gay male sex was decriminalized in Czechoslovakia in 1961, with a discriminatory age of consent set at eighteen. The main pressure for the change came from the medical profession, particularly from the flourishing field of sexology, which had developed some forty years earlier, influenced by German models. Sexology created the climate and furnished the discourse for the first discussions of homosexuality in Czechoslovakia, which were confined to medical journals.[18]

Between lobotomies, forced castrations, and Michel Foucault, medicalizing homosexuality enjoys an understandably bad name in the West. All the same, in Czechoslovakia it served as a preparatory room for politics. It gradually engendered an atmosphere where homosexuality could be sympathetically and seriously described in public—even, in the late eighties, by the state newspaper for youth. Most important, though, sexology offered a space, both discursive and literal, where a group could achieve a self-understanding outside the categories of politics and class imposed by the state. The Institute of Sexology at Charles University in Prague was a territory where gays and lesbians could actually exchange, and reflect on, their experiences—discovering commonalities and contemplating *non*-therapeutic forms of change. The first gay organization in the country presented itself in 1988 as a circle for professional counseling: a Sociotherapeutic Club, gathering in and guarded by the institute. Adopting a different face abroad, it registered with ILGA as Lambda Prague in 1989.

The Velvet Revolution came, crowds chanted "Havel to the Hrad" (Prague's seat of power), and Lambda Prague tossed off its hospital gown and checked out of the ward. The gay and lesbian movement expanded rapidly, with other groups forming around the country. Contacts were initiated with Civic Forum, and members of the new Parliament met with activists. In June 1990, Jiri Hromada, head of Lambda Prague, ran as an openly gay candidate for Parliament; though unsuccessful, his campaign still served as a catalyst for gay and lesbian involvement. In July 1990 the age of consent was equalized and male prostitution decriminalized (measures actually prepared by the Communist government).

Many factors no doubt conditioned this success. Czech pride in a tradition of tolerance is almost a cliche. The predominating Protestantism is not only strongly individualistic but also still tinged with a Hussite respect for difference and dissent. Czechoslovakia also retained the memory of a flourishing civil society before 1938, a memory that had been tranformed into slogan and vision by dissidents in the 1980s. This rhetoric perhaps had the strongest effect on the gay and lesbian movement: as it moved beyond therapy, it took up the language of citizenship. This did not simply mean claiming citizenship rights—though the nationwide umbrella organization SOHO (Association of Organizations of Homosexual Citizens), founded in 1991, incorporated that idea in its name. It meant imitating citizenship structures *within* the gay and lesbian movement. SOHO tries to prove—like a cured patient—that it has the rules of civil society inside itself down pat.

SOHO is the only genuinely national gay and lesbian network in the former Soviet bloc—and, arguably, one of the best organized in Europe. It now contains nineteen organizations around the country. Autonomy of local groups makes figuring overall membership difficult, but one to two thousand people must have regular contact with it[19]—not counting the monthly *SOHO Revue* magazine, with a circulation estimated at well over ten thousand. Lesbians are allotted a separate-but-subordinate arrangement, with a vice-president for women in the governing presidium. (Jiri Hromada remains the head; my own conversations with Czech activists give the impression that the presidency of SOHO is now perceived as a permanently male post.)[20] Ultimate power rests with a Parliament, which represents all member groups and meets four times per year.

Figure 1 shows SOHO as a miniature of the Czech government (with Hromada as Havel in the Hrad). SOHO's attempt to imagine a national gay power structure appears to translate a Czech sense of inhabiting a cohesive, centralized, more or less monoethnic country[21] into the self-image, and need for security, of a minority group. Most of the member societies are geographically defined; only two are distinguished by gender, none by profession, age,[22] ethnicity, hobby, fetish—a triumph of the spatial over the social imagination. The creation of a complex federal structure with a Parliament and a foreign affairs section—like the decision to sever formal unity with Slovak groups when the two countries separated—

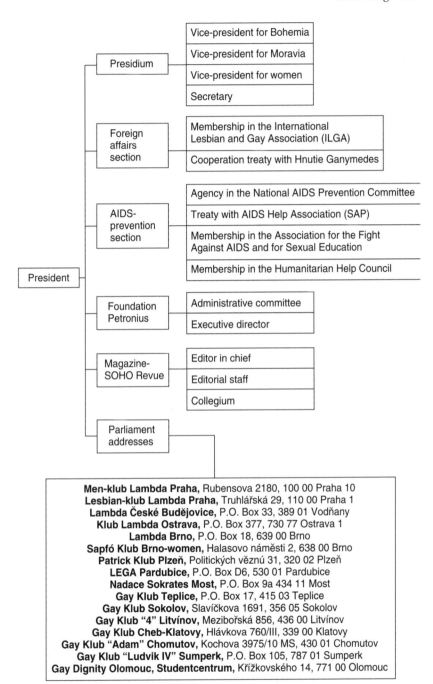

FIGURE 1. *Structure of SOHO, 1994. (Chart furnished by SOHO.)*

suggests a desire for the organization to replicate, both internally and externally, the contours of the national state. SOHO's "queer nation" seems built on the belief that the best way to influence the government is to flatter it by imitation.

The actual U.S. queer nation was *nationalist* in its imperial ideas of queer manifest destiny. SOHO, like Czechia, is not. Its notion is to make its nation liked, and in this it has had real success. Public opinion has shifted. Surveys by the Institute of Sexology showed that in 1988, only 23 percent of those asked endorsed the formation of gay and lesbian organizations; in 1993 the figure was 73 percent. In 1988, 25 percent agreed with legal recognition of same-sex partnerships; by 1993, the figure had risen to 60 percent. Interestingly, *personal* knowledge of homosexuals hardly increased during the period: those reporting that they had never known anyone who was lesbian or gay numbered 66 percent in 1988 and 61.4 percent five years later. This may suggest that coming out to friends and neighbors remains relatively uncommon in the Czech Republic; it surely indicates that the media have been the most important force in changing citizens' minds.[23]

Most of the groups in SOHO are still social organizations—perhaps an aftereffect of their birth in therapy. Political issues are the responsibility of the national leadership. In 1993 the organization began actively lobbying for registered partnership for same-sex couples. This was deliberately proposed as an amendment to the Family Law. "SOHO claims," the organization declared in a statement to ILGA in 1994, "neither a separate registered partnership law, which would single out the gay and lesbian minority from the society, nor the institute [sic] of marriage for same-sex couples." Politically, there may have been real ingenuity here. Polemically, though, it exemplifies the potential incoherences of an approach based on "imitation in separation": wanting the same (to be in the Family Law, to be recognized as a family), yet not wanting to lay claim to the *absolute* same (marriage), but refusing to settle for mere difference (a humiliating law of your own). You end up back where you started. In 1996 Parliament finally rejected the proposal.

HUNGARY: IN QUEST OF A PARADIGM

In Romania, a legal discourse criminalizing gays was met by a small gay movement armored in a discourse of minority rights. In Czechoslovakia, a therapeutic model of care meshed with and was succeeded by a paradigm of security found in citizenship. When we search for similar discourses in Hungary, we find a confusion of tongues. And yet, where Czechs failed, Magyars succeeded: in May 1996 Hungary became the only state in the world, outside Scandinavia and the Netherlands, to institute a form of domestic partnership for same-sex couples. The confusing part is that this took the Hungarian gay and lesbian movement virtually by surprise.

Like Czechoslovakia, Hungary decriminalized homosexuality in 1961, setting the age of consent at twenty for both gays and lesbians (as opposed to age fourteen for heterosexuals). The age was lowered to eighteen in 1978 and still remains on the books (as does a cryptic reference, in Section 199 of the Criminal Code, to "illicit sexual acts").

The few bars and cafes in Budapest quietly frequented by gay men—as well as cruising areas in parks and public baths—remained subject to police harassment. As elsewhere in Eastern Europe, gays met most often in private circles. Members of one of these, galvanized by awareness of AIDS, grew determined to organize and act.

The crisis of ideology, faith, and idolatry, the mass rending of the veil, which in the 1980s mobilized thousands of citizens on the streets of Gdansk, Leipzig, and Prague, materialized in Budapest as an immobilizing self-doubt in the corridors of the inner party. Hungarian Communism apologized itself to death between 1986 and 1989, in a phenomenon virtually unique within the bloc. Recantations of mistakes and reburials of executed victims became so frequent that the regime seemed to be staging its own show trial. As part of this obliging self-annihilation, in 1988 the government promulgated a Law on Associations to allow political parties.

One of the first groups to attempt to register under the law was a gay and lesbian organization, Homeros Lambda. A minor scandal was raised by those who opined that the law was meant for "politics, not perverts." The group was finally allowed to register, but only as an AIDS-prevention organization. This inauspicious entry into civil society was an omen: similar confrontations would characterize of the movement's future.

That future might also be summarized by an old Hungarian joke:

Q: What do you get when you lock three Hungarians in a room?

A: Four political parties.

Meiotic tendencies, amoebic splits have afflicted Hungarian groups. But I suspect we should see these divisions not as illustrations of some natural tendency to fragmentation, as though we were talking of tectonic plates, but as new turns in the search for a cohesive paradigm, which would explain to the Hungarian movement what it is actually trying to do. This search has been extensive. It is still going on.

Homeros Lambda opened the first fully gay bar and started, with the grudging permission of the Ministry of Health, an anonymous HIV-testing clinic. (Positive results at state clinics are still reported to the ministry.)

However, the head of the clinic was a psychiatrist whose paradigm was overwhelmingly medical: he still insisted at the time that homosexuality should be tolerated as an incurable disease. This model repelled more radical activists, as well as lesbian members. Lesbian departure from the group signaled a long period of lesbian invisibility within the movement.

In 1991 several of the younger men left Homeros to form Lambda Budapest, whose sole project was to publish a gay magazine. *Masok* (Others) still appears monthly, with a circulation of some three thousand. The seasoning of soft-core porn in its intelligent commentary ensures its exclusive appeal to men.[24]

The concentration on the magazine prevented Lambda from expanding its membership or establishing political ties. Pursuing these goals, in 1994 four or five activists, once again most of them young, founded an organization specifically couching itself in human rights terms, the Rainbow Coalition for the Rights of Gays (Szivarvany Tarsulas a Melegek Jogaiert). To many people's surprise, its application for legal registration was turned down by a local court on the following two grounds: that the use of the term *meleg* ("warm," the acceptable self-designation of gays and lesbians) for homosexuals in the organization's name was improper in Hungarian and that the group must specifically bar membership to those under the (discriminatory) eighteen-year age of consent. Refusing to change its name or charter, Szivarvany appealed. In 1995 the Supreme Court upheld the ruling, finding that, by not respecting the age of consent, the group disseminated a "threat to public morals." A campaign to enlist the support of liberal intellectuals generated press conferences but no change. Gays and lesbians were legally erased from both ethics and the lexicon. Szivarvany remains unregistered; and its small membership has drifted away.

The Supreme Court is Hungary's highest court of appeal, but only the newly created Constitutional Court has the power to review laws. At the time of Szivarvany's appeal, the Constitutional Court was considering a challenge to Hungary's marriage law, mounted by Lambda Budapest. Sources close to the court have reported that the justices first reacted to the appeal from gays with snickers. However, information on European models furnished by mainstream human rights organizations—as well as the European Parliament's 1994 Roth Resolution on nondiscrimination against homosexuals—slowly swayed them. The court has taken an activist stance on social rights, overturning parts of the government's austerity program on grounds of social welfare. In this case, it issued an altogether unexpected ruling in February 1995. It clearly affirmed that marriage itself "is the community of man and woman." The court insisted, however, that the benefits granted to *common-law* marriage[25] since the 1950s (including inheritance, pension rights, and immunity from spousal testimony, but not including adoption) be extended to same-sex couples.[26] It ordered Parliament to rewrite the law accordingly within one year.

The debate that ensued was relatively uneventful; the new law was passed.[27] The legislation leaves Hungarian gays and lesbians in a peculiar position. A crucial social right has been placed, almost unasked for, in their passive hands by a not entirely enthusiastic court. At the same time, they have been denied constitutive civil and political rights—the right to associate, even the right to—as *melegek* (gays)—exist.

This is not just a metaphor or a legal technicality. Community is the problem. Hungarian gays and lesbians have been unable to set up either a national organization or efficient, lasting local constituency groups. And this, too, seems tied to the inability to find a convincing paradigm for what the community should be or do. It is striking that the most successful groups have been social ones drawing on—almost parasitically on—other identities: gay Christian and Jewish circles[28] have drawn up to fifty participants at times, as has a gay student group at the University of Budapest. The contrast with SOHO's national/geographical form is striking: for Hungarians, engagement with other lived (not just *located*) identities provides models, meaning, and community that being "gay" alone now cannot. Lesbians too have channeled much energy into feminist organizations—though a lesbian group of ten to fifteen members began meeting in 1996.[29]

The Supreme Court's decision symbolically suggests one factor in the failure to capture a paradigm: if part of society is subtly prohibited even from *naming* itself, its self-representations will necessarily remain stuttering on a problematic level, a channel impaired by static. Still other causes probably reside in the broader confusions of contemporary Hungarian society itself. That society, always divided along certain fixed fault lines—between Catholic majority and Protestant minority, between Budapest and countryside—experienced the earthquake of the market and its dislocations earlier in the 1980s than did surrounding countries; income disparities and class differences increased, while ideological positions softened, and dissidents sometimes seemed more sympathetic to the decaying system than its own administrators did. It would be hard to expect too much clarity of purpose from those who witnessed the veteran Communist Party—which elsewhere in the region clung to power with all its geriatric might—voluntarily trade in its tin medals and sandpaper suits for the Emperor's New Clothes.

The present exception to the suffusive listlessness is an organization tellingly called Hatter ("Background"). It was formed in 1995 to organize a telephone help line for lesbians and gays. Small grants have enabled the group to start the line, which receives roughly ten calls nightly—from information seeking to crisis calls. The project is limited, the paradigm is therapeutic, but the purpose, for most of the thirty members,[30] is simple, animating, and clear: community building.

COMMUNITY, CIVIL SOCIETY, MARKET

All three movements—as in most of Eastern Europe—shared the same problem in 1989: to create a politics without an immediately usable past. They searched for models for action, and found—or failed to find—them in what could be scavenged from the local postsocialist vicinity: each society learned to see within itself a rag-and-bone shop of exigencies, examples, possibilities. Romanian gays slowly discovered a speakable similarity to the situation of minorities in a multiethnic state. The Czech movement instead took to duplicating the centralized look of the state itself. The prolonged confusions of the five-year Hungarian transition perhaps provided an embarassment of models but no clear criterion of need or choice.[31]

This problem of paradigms was not limited to gay and lesbian movements. In a sense it has been the problem of Eastern European societies in general, confronted with a "European" paradigm dangling with spangled incentives to conform. This, in turn, has had mixed consequences for lesbians and gays.

East European governments more or less look on European structures as a nephew might look on a rich eccentric uncle who is forever rewriting his will. The uncle's every crotchet must be humored if the nephew wants to get his hands on the inheritance, and if the uncle suddenly takes an interest in the shine on the nephew's shoes, or the cut of his hair, or the way he treats homosexuals or other nonexistent creatures, the nephew must put up a quick and busy show of improvement. When, in 1993, the Council of Europe politely reminded Romania that imprisoning gays and lesbians was an uncivil thing to do, every other polity in the region with similar laws raced to eliminate them, apologize, don sackcloth and ashes; only Romania itself, a particularly impenitent prodigal nephew, resisted (and got the inheritance anyway). The entirely unjustified impression created by the European Parliament's Roth Resolution, that homosexuality was a source of the highest interest to European institutions, was quickly refuted for Western European activists by their experiences of bureaucratic amnesia. But it remained with East European politicians as a reminder and a warning, and domestic partnership in Hungary is now the result. Many of the important advances for gay and lesbian rights have been imported from the West, *without* local gay and lesbian participation. The effect may be admirable, but the means reduce the mobilization. For lesbian and gay activism, Europe can be more an addiction than a model.

Phylogeny recapitulates ontogeny. The experience of movements mirrors the experiences of their members as well. The visionary expeditions that groups undertake in search of models to animate action are surely, if varyingly, bound up with the needs of the individuals within. And the identity of lesbians is especially illustrative.

In one Sir Arthur Conan Doyle story, Sherlock Holmes alludes to "the dog's curious behavior in the nighttime." Dr. Watson says, "The dog did nothing in the nighttime." Holmes replies, "That was the curious behavior."[32] Holmes knew: absence of evidence is evidence of a problem. The absence of lesbians from gay and lesbian movements—complete in Romania, conspicuous in Hungary, still clear in Czechia—evinces more absences than one. In part, there is the usual lack of willingness on the part of men to share power, create participatory structures, or surrender the floor. Gay men snort their contempt for feminism or women's concerns. I have twice heard Hungarian gay leaders explain that lesbians lead happier lives than do gay men, because it is easier for them to find lesbian pornography.

Probably none of this would surprise Western lesbians. Another absence, at the level of persons rather than groups, is more indigenous and more disabling: the absence—again—of *models* for lesbian identity. To link "lesbian" and "feminism," as I did above, would hardly seem automatic to many lesbians in the region. Feminist movements had no real strength anywhere in Eastern Europe in 1990, with the exception of what was then Yugoslavia.[33] Although in most places they have gained momentum since that time, for many lesbians outside the middle class or major urban centers, they are inaccessible (or unintelligible) as either sources or objects of identification. Or those movements may be unsympathetic to lesbians in turn. Lesbians are strongly involved in feminist organizations in Hungary, but I conclude a perceptible consensus persists that the movement must not become "identified" with sexual difference. Activist lesbians experience subtle pressures to suppress or subordinate lesbian issues or to keep themselves closeted—all for "the movement's" sake. Lesbians outside feminist movements, meanwhile, hover in a still obscurer void. Many mold their identities through attachments to gay men as the only available pattern for "deviance."[34]

Models, models: is this a fashion show? Are gay and lesbian groups in the region engaged in a politics of parody, all their paradigms generated by echoes and repetitions, busily reproducing the inherited and recycling the imported? Do these movements have a direction? Will they offer anything new?

Yes. Ethnicity and nation *have* proven powerful founding tropes to explain gay and lesbian community in Eastern Europe. Probably all inarticulate experience is originally made known through such tropes, which then harden into the heard, the familiar, and finally the known. But Eastern European experience still has an insistent, surplus quality of the unspoken about it, which accounts perhaps for this octopuslike groping for reference, comparison, contrast.

At the same time, this unspoken quality is not totally unquantifiable (see Table 1).

Ron Eyerman and Andrew Jamison have interpreted social movements not simply as actors but as producers of knowledge, of new ways to look at society and new perspectives from which to do it. "A social movement," they write,

> is not one organization or one particular special interest group. It is more like a cognitive territory, a new conceptual space that is filled by dynamic interaction between different groups and organizations. . . . And although movements usually involve the creation of organizations or the renovation of institutions, it is important not to mistake the one for the other. Organizations can be thought of as vehicles or instruments for carrying or transporting or even producing the movement's meaning. But the meaning, we hasten to add, should not be reduced to the medium. The meaning, or core identity, is rather the cognitive space that the movement creates, a space for new kinds of ideas and relationships to develop.[35]

Table 1 helps us contemplate the question of what knowledges East European social movements are likely to produce. In America, social movements—the civil rights movement, feminism, and lesbian and gay groups—have paradigmatically been concerned with reinvigorating our sense of what the public sphere is for. The slogan "The personal is political" has in different ways been central: it is the claim that supposedly inner feelings and experiences can be represented in the intersubjective world, that the passions and hurts of private life can claim equal rights to be heard in the open square.

The Eastern European experience of the public and private spheres has been radically different, though. The private has not been repressed, but invaded; not invisible, but vulnerable: it has been at the mercy of an arrogant public sphere claiming to regulate, speak for, punish, and inform it, driving it to the defensive. The Hungarian figures in Table 1 indicate the depth of this defensiveness—and of the countervailing rejection of the public sphere—as a realm of falsehood, ridiculous demands upon the self, untrustworthiness, and danger. The threats to privacy turn it into a

TABLE 1. *Individualism and Privatism in Ten European Countries: European Value Systems Study, 1982*

	England (%)	Ireland (%)	France (%)	Belgium (%)	Germany (%)	Holland (%)	Spain (%)	Denmark (%)	Italy (%)	Hungary (%)
You may trust people	43	40	22	25	26	38	32	46	25	32
Is there anything you would sacrifice yourself for outside your family?										
No!	60	55	64	61	52	54	38	49	45	85
Most important child-rearing principle:										
Respect for other people	62	56	59	45	52	53	44	58	43	31
Loyalty, faithfulness	36	19	36	23	22	24	29	24	43	10
How do you prefer to spend your leisure time?										
Alone	11	12	10	9	8	12	7	8	20	10
With family	48	39	47	51	52	49	53	53	36	72
With friends	27	27	22	18	27	15	23	12	29	10
Going out, seeing people	11	12	8	7	5	12	4	4	8	3

Source: Elemér Hánkiss, "In Search of a Paradigm," *Daedalus* (Winter 1990): 208.

fortress and a fountainhead of value. The "unspoken quality" is the refusal to speak.

Many writers have commented on the Biedermeier dedication to the inside, which Communism's mobilizations paradoxically fostered in its citizens: a commitment to cultivating one's garden, part "inner emigration," part interior decoration.[36] It is easy to interpret this as incapacitating, as a slow calcification of the power to act, and as a disabling obstacle for gay and lesbian movements. Indeed, it complicates political engagement. And when valorized privacy is identified with the heterosexual family, as "the source of dignity and creativity in a society characterized by alienated labor processes . . . a harmonious collectivity pitted against the difficulties and strife of coping with the shortcomings of daily life,"[37] then gays and lesbians are excluded from the center of values.

More basically, whereas in the consumer West, social movements have primarily produced forms of knowledge about the potential interrelatedness of public and private, the task in the East is different. Eastern movements must participate in producing two kinds of knowledge in a remarkably short time—two kinds, moreover, that can be seen as contradictory. The first is a founding and grounding knowledge about the differentiation of private and public, the division of the spheres: about how the fragile private sphere can be defined and protected.[38] The second is knowledge about the ways in which that differentiation can then be made porous, transgressed or transacted across, so that political action becomes possible. The complexity of this double task is daunting. It may give a sense of the peculiar difficulty these organizations face, and the time and effort needed to create a sense of the movement's paradigm and purpose. It may help account for the difficulty in building participation, when the knowledge needed to enable it is so intricate and Janus-faced.

But this task entails possibilities as well as losses: the *experience* of privacy should not just be identified with deprivation. Rather, I interpret the experimentation with paradigms that each of the three movements has undergone as a response to this problem: a creative effort to *build on* existing knowledges of identity, to find models that will help balance interiority against exteriority, autonomy against action. The Hungarian movement has shuffled and discarded various forms of identity, from victims of disease to agents of abstract rights. The Romanian movement has settled on an instrumental argument from minority rights. Most suggestively, though, in both cases this experimentation has ultimately produced a knowledge about the community itself. In both, a kind of return to the personal has taken place, with the disparity between paradigm(s) and reality revealing the need to root the community more firmly in the members' personal needs. Community building—relocating the political in the personal—is now the main agenda for both.

SOHO in the Czech Republic appears a grand exception, able to leap beyond the personal and identify itself imaginatively with the nation itself, the ur-form of public space. Concealed in its success, though, is a certain thinness to its structure. If one takes the model seriously, what is missing within SOHO's "nation" is exactly a simulacrum of civil society: the full variety of ways in which people can aggregate and affiliate *inside* an entity such as the nation-state. In SOHO's chart, the government is there; but the "citizens" beneath are bound together only by geographic ties. The movement does not yet engage with the range of other identities, experiences, needs that people may bring to bear on it. I suspect that a deepening of this "civil society within"—the construction of new intricacies, the recognition of new links and needs—is necessary before SOHO can be fully effective in the larger civil society without.

Invoking "civil society"—the realm where persons become political—was an almost sacred ritual for dissidents from the mid-1980s to the mid-1990s. Civil society and the creation of public spheres still dominated the goverment-building discourses of 1990. Meanwhile, though, another discourse has been extending its hegemony over the region: the market. The growth of civil society in the nineties and the market revolution have both been studied extensively, but no one as yet has thought intensively about the practical connection—or competition—between them. Yet the integration of the region into a market economy is now the most influential, and irresistible, factor both in political decisions and in daily life.[39] The gains by leftist parties throughout the former bloc since 1994 point to a popular rebellion against free-market rule, but the International Monetary Fund's control ensures that elections make gestures, not decisions. Poland and Hungary are well accustomed now to socialist governments carrying out Thatcherite agendas.

Western gay and lesbian movements developed in mature market economies. In the East, movement and market have grown up together. The effect on the movements is difficult to measure. A capitalist economy's individualist dislocation of old roles (and consumerism's eroticization of absolutely everything) have granted apparent new freedoms to personality and desire. But the market privatizes in a different way. In Hungary and the Czech Republic, most gays and many lesbians now meet exclusively in commercial spaces; and these reach a far greater constituency than any organization.

The first Hungarian gay group began with a circle of friends who took long hikes in the woods. These excursions represented a delicate balance between finding a safe and unseen place in which to be gay and reclaiming (even if in a subdued and secluded fashion) the outdoors as one's own. The Hungarian gay movement has retained a somewhat romantic relationship with the open sky; instead of a Pride march, it holds an annual Pink Picnic in a remote clearing, with hundreds of attendees. The substitution of nights in cellar discotheques for such activities is not entirely a gain as a symbolic appropriation of territory.[40]

What remains, amid these uncertainties, is a new version of an old vision: action rooted in the actuality of personal need. The intense cultivation of the personal in Eastern Europe may not survive the commodifications of the market. If it does, though, it may offer us a lesson. Activists in the West, despite our rhetoric of the personal and the political, still tend at heart to see the private as the privative, to believe that utopia must be imagined in an unrestricted openness, in the cleared spaces of Ceauşescu's leveled Bucharest rather than in the intimacy of furnished rooms. We must overcome this. What used to be Eastern Europe may begin to teach us how. "Utopia, not the past, is the foundation of autonomy," the dissident Gyorgy Konrad wrote. Precisely because it does not yet exist, utopia is always personal.

NOTES

1. This school, which implies unequal possibilities for the creation of civil society from historical precedents, is particularly associated with the revered name of Istvan Bibo. It divides Europe essentially between Western and Eastern Christianity, eliding confessional and cultural differences within Europe. See Jeno Szucs, "Three Historical Regions of Europe," and Mihaly Vajda, "East-Central European Perspectives," both in *Civil Society and the State: New European Perspectives,* ed. John Keane, (London: Verso, 1988).

2. Because I am neither a sociologist nor an anthropologist nor a political scientist, I am in those respects, reliant on others to do my work for me. Unfortunately, homophobia in the social sciences means that few empirical studies of lesbians and gays in the region have been undertaken. A body of documentation by sexologists in the Czech Republic largely reflects the medicalization of homosexuality there. Hungarian sociologist Laszlo Toth's *On Homosexuality (A homoszexualitasrol)* is the weightiest study published in the region, but it reflects a conservative and functionalist sociology of deviance and does not reflect lesbians at all. I have drawn on the work of a young Romanian sociologist, Catalin Stoica, who has attempted to study attitudes toward homosexuality in his country. I should note that all uncredited observations in this chapter are drawn from my own experience, which readers can take as they like—with a grain, or a pillar, of salt.

3. Bosnia and Macedonia still (in 1996) have sodomy laws. (Trouble also awaits gay men on the far Faeroe Islands.) The Romanian law does not include lesbians by name, referring neutrally (and neuteringly) to "persons of the same

sex." I know of no cases of women arrested under Article 200 either in the 1990s or before. Momentary and partial visibility in the legal text gives way again to invisibility in legal practice. Of course, the *symbolic* weight of the law contributes to lesbians' invisibility as well, intimidating lesbians from any kind of self-expression. See Ingrid Baciu, Vera Campeanu, and Mona Nicoara, "Romania," in *Unspoken Rules: Sexual Orientation and Women's Human Rights,* ed. Rachel Rosenbloom. (London: Cassell, 1995)

4. The fear of using indoor space no doubt especially inhibited lesbians. Interestingly, Ministry of Justice lists of persons convicted under *all* paragraphs of Article 200 show that in 1993 thirty-four of fifty-seven (male) prisoners were under age twenty-five; in 1994 twenty-one of forty-nine; and in 1995 thirty of sixty. One explanation for the high percentage is that young gay men just coming out may not have been integrated into those rudimentary communities long enough to have learned the available folk wisdom about avoiding getting caught. An ethnography of this surviving folk knowledge ought to be undertaken; the political situation, alas, suggests there is still ample time before it disappears.

5. These figures are taken from an unpublished paper by Catalin Stoica, "Homosexuals: Premises of Their Acceptance in Today's Romania," 1994.

6. In some Balkan countries (for example, Albania and Greece), there exists ethnographic documentation of traditional patterns of male/male sexual activity. I know of no such evidence for traditional Romanian culture. However, the violent (and very political) controversies about the origin of the "Daco-Romanian" people, and the related arguments over whether the roots of "Romanian culture" lie in transhumant shepherdry or the settled (probably highly heteronormative) life of the walled village—*fossatum, fsat*—make the "traditional Romanian" a difficult concept to discuss academically or, for that matter, sanely.

7. See Katherine Verdery, "From Parent-State to Family Patriarchs: Gender and Nation in Contemporary Eastern Europe," *East European Politics and Society* 8 (Spring 1994): 225–55.

8. This was the response, for example, to a delegation from the International Lesbian and Gay Association (ILGA), the International Gay and Lesbian Human Rights Commission (IGLHRC), and the World Health Organization visiting the country in 1992.

9. In 1991, Amnesty International (AI) changed its mandate to recognize as prisoners of conscience persons imprisoned for *private* homosexual acts between consenting adults. The government proposal was probably phrased with an eye to retaining the law while steering clear of infringing AI's guidelines. However, AI, has consistently condemned the dangerous vagueness of the new language.

10. I am not exaggerating. The tone of debates over homosexuality in Romanian politics lies somewhere between a pornographic novel and a Warner Brothers cartoon. In 1993 one senator urged that male homosexuals be put in women's prisons, and lesbians in men's prisons, to teach them the joys of the opposite sex by force (*Romania Libera,* 7 February 1993). Later the same year another senator demanded, "Where are those Romanians who conquered the world by using their organs properly?" (*Reuters,* 11 November 1994) Where indeed?

11. In November 1994 the Romanian Constitutional Court threw out the

existing language of Article 200, paragraph 1, while leaving a loophole for the "public scandal" language. Judicial review is ill-established in Romania, and a legal limbo now exists. The Romanian Helsinki Committee has documented that arrests have continued. I have seen one court document in which "public scandal" is established as follows: the accused is arrested; the police give the story to a newspaper, which publishes it; this is held to constitute "public scandal," thus justifying the arrest (Tribunal Militar Bucuresti, *sentinta penal* 149/1993).

12. I have stayed the night there; the nickname fits.

13. Banning abortion is probably an issue much dearer to priestly hearts. But the Ceauşescu pronatalist policies were so despised throughout the country that the church does not dare pursue the issue.

14. Emulating a minority is, of course, different from empathizing with one. In particular, most gays are as racist toward Roma as any other Romanians are.

15. Some members questioned whether the name would lose meaning if the law were repealed. It was decided that it would instead serve to memorialize the law. This debate showed a new awareness of a *need* for the historical consciousness that helps to constitute a "minority."

16. The name, borrowed from the organization for which I work—the International Gay and Lesbian Human Rights Commission in San Francisco—reflects yet another act of grafting.

17. A few lesbians are, in fact, in contact with the organization but are highly reluctant to participate.

18. Information on Czech sexology is drawn from an unpublished paper by Ivan Prochazka, of the Charles University Institute of Sexology, Prague, presented at the Organizing Sexualities Conference in Amsterdam, 1994. Czech activists have confirmed his insights to me.

19. This information is based on conversations with activists in Brno in January 1996.

20. This information is based on discussions with Czech activists in 1996.

21. Of course Bohemia and Moravia are not monoethnic and have never been. Substantial Roma and Slovak and small German minorities remain (the Germans reduced by forced population transfers at the end of World War II). Xenophobic Czech citizenship laws denying passports to Roma residents have recently caused international concern. But even this racist policy indicates what I suspect is a general Czech feeling since Slovakia's 1993 secession: that at last the Czechs have the room to themselves.

22. In early 1996 I visited a gay and lesbian student group in Brno that planned to join SOHO.

23. The same surveys showed that in 1988 nearly 90 percent wanted more information about homosexuality; in 1993 that figure was only 78 percent. SOHO has good relations with mainstream media and has collaborated on television and radio series that are sympathetic toward homosexuality.

24. In 1991, Budapest police found a copy of *Masok* in the apartment of a murdered man and used this as a pretext to detain the editors and demand their subscription files. After getting word to sympathetic mainstream media, the editors managed to secure their release, but not before officers had confirmed that

they wanted this information for their own Pink Lists. The police received considerable negative publicity, but no gay group has subsequently been able to maintain consistent contact with the force to establish whether lists are still maintained. (SOHO is certain that list keeping has ceased in the Czech Republic; it certainly exists in Romania.)

25. Common-law marriage is defined in Article 578/F (1) of the Hungarian Civil Code as "a man and a woman living together in a common household and in an emotional and economic community, outside a marriage."

26. The ruling makes it clear that—like the Supreme Court—this court was considering the protection of children as well as attempting to ensure that existing heterosexual marriages of same-sex partners would exert prior moral and legal claims. "The lasting communion of two persons can realize values such that—on the basis of the equal personal dignity of those involved—it can claim acknowledgment irrespective of the sex of those living together. [But] equal treatment must always be interpreted with respect to the life relations that are subject to the legal regulations—with special respect to whether children born in this communion have a role in the regulation, or previous or subsequent marriages, or whether the law evaluates the close personal relationship by itself. . . . If these exceptional cases do not apply, the regulation of partners in a common-law relationship, and that of the relatives, is arbitrary, and thus because of the violation of human dignity, it is in conflict with . . . the Constitution if we exclude from among persons living in a common household and in an emotional and economic community those who are of the same sex" (Decision 12/B/1993/8).

27. Gays were targeted by a popular, populist extremist politician, Jozsef Torgyan, who, during the debate, accused the government of "caring more for *buzik* [the ubiquitous national slang for faggots, used also for anything defective, for example, most telephones] than for Hungarian mothers" (*Heti Vilaggazdasag*, 23 March 1996). He was rebuked for using bad language on the floor of Parliament. Official notice of gays and lesbians has tended to focus on two issues: what to let them do (organize? work on AIDS? meet—or be—teenagers?) and what to call them. This certainly suggests the inability of gays and lesbians themselves to seize, or even contribute to, the discourse.

28. No doubt this is facilitated by the renaissance of minority life that took place in Hungary from the 1970s, particularly a cultural revival in the surviving Jewish community. Nothing comparable occurred in Czechoslovakia in the same period.

29. Even finding a gathering spot is difficult for lesbians: of seven gay bars now in Budapest, only one small lounge is truly women friendly. In 1994 a heterosexual-owned bar in a very distant Budapest suburb offered a lesbian night on Saturdays. It is characteristic of the particular economic problems lesbians face that getting back from the bar, given the cost of taxis and the absence of night transport, proved an almost insuperable difficulty. Finally women contracted with one taxi driver to carry customers from the bar to a spot in the city center, four at a time, for a fixed rate. Eventually, though, the bar canceled the women's night because of low earnings.

30. Almost a third are lesbians, unprecedented for a mixed group in Hungary.

31. I have given little attention to AIDS thus far, partly because it is not yet a *visible* reality for most gays and lesbians in the region. Men having sex with men still represents the largest transmission route in both the Czech Republic and Hungary; in Romania, where the virus initially circulated mainly through blood supplies, AIDS was initially identified with its pediatric victims, and attention only slowly shifted to the possibility of adult infection, with the continuing chaos in public health making reliable statistics difficult to obtain or to imagine. In general, throughout the region, both official figures and public perceptions of HIV infection are low, though certainly a serious underestimation of the actual extent. For the most part, HIV exists in relation to gay and lesbian *movements* in Czechia and Hungary as a potential source of both legitimation and funding. Funding, while irregular, has perhaps been more forthcoming than legitimation. In both Czechia and Hungary, gay publications have been partly supported by state or foundation funds for AIDS prevention. However, only in Czechia do gays have a real role in policy: SOHO has a seat on the Ministry of Health's National AIDS Prevention Committee. The comparable committee in Hungary has only one seat reserved for a National Gay Organization (NGO), out of nearly forty members; that seat has been assigned to a straight-dominated foundation. The prestige of doctors severely restricts the voices of patients, and although organizations of people with AIDS (PWAs)—largely composed of gay men—exist in both countries, they have little voice in deciding either policy or treatment. In Romania, of course, the criminalization of homosexual relations makes official gay or lesbian participation in AIDS organizations—governmental or NGO—impossible.

32. Sir Arthur Conan Doyle, "Silver Blaze."

33. As a result, lesbians in Croatia and Serbia have taken the leading role in gay and lesbian movements there—as well as in antiwar activism.

34. In 1994 an extremely popular Hungarian television talk show (hosted by an imperfectly closeted gay man) announced and organized a program about lesbians. The show featured a number of straight "experts"—psychologists and sociologists—and, adventurously enough, actual lesbians. Several of the lesbians were willing to have their names and faces shown on camera. They were told that they could not appear on the program *except* anonymously and in shadow. Lesbian invisibility lies far beyond the lesbian's own volition.

35. Ron Eyerman and Andrew Jamison, *Social Movements: A Cognitive Approach* (State College, Penn.: Pennsylvania State University Press, 1991), 55.

36. As particularly exact artistic representations of this self-protective sense of burying the self alive, I might cite two works from the former Yugoslavia, Borislav Pekic's excellent novel *The Houses of Belgrad* and the recent film *Underground*.

37. Barbara Einhorn, *Cinderella Goes to Market: Citizenship, Gender, and Women's Movements in Eastern Europe* (New York: Verso, 1993), 59.

38. This has been most obviously the case in Romania, where the argument over homosexuality has been a key testing ground for defining the right to privacy protected in Article 26 of the (1991) Romanian constitution.

39. Peter Gowan, in "Neo-liberal Theory and Practice for Eastern Europe," *New Left Review* 213 (September–October 1995), analyzes the West's instant re-

sponse to the revolutions in Eastern Europe: insistance on the immediate transparency of borders, the dissolution of regional, institutional, and traditional ties, the disappearance of every obstacle to the needs of capital. Processes that in the West had been accomplished over decades were imposed on the East overnight.

40. Compare Dennis Altman, *The Homosexualization of America* (Boston: Beacon, 1982), 85: "It is my hunch . . . that there has been a decline in street cruising, for example, with the growth of sex palaces. (The irony is underlined by the fact that many of the pornographic movies shown in such establishments are set out of doors, in woods, beaches, etc.) Much so-called sexual liberation has not, by and large, made for a genuine eroticism of everyday life as much as it has meant the creation of a set of specialized institutions within which people can, for a certain time that is quite consciously divorced from their everday lives, act out sexual fantasies."

MAI PALMBERG

11   Emerging Visibility of Gays and Lesbians in Southern Africa

Contrasting Contexts

BEFORE 1995, southern Africa experienced gay and lesbian visibility only in South Africa. But the so-called book fair dramas in Zimbabwe in 1995 and 1996 (discussed later in this chapter) put the issue of homosexuality onto the agenda of the whole subcontinent, at least in the countries that share English as the official language.[1] In Zimbabwe itself, the gay and lesbian movement began the transformation from merely providing informal social space to acquiring the characteristics and agenda of a rights movement. In Namibia, the homophobic attacks of Zimbabwean leader Robert Mugabe were somewhat later echoed by president Sam Nujoma, provoking the emergence of a new gay and lesbian movement in 1997. The history of the gay and lesbian movements in southern Africa, except for South Africa, is thus very short, and the following must be considered for further study.[2]

These countries share features that affect the development and success of their gay and lesbian movements and set them apart from other countries discussed in this volume, particularly those in the northern hemisphere:

1. Their societies and economies have been subordinated in the global world system. There is a political heritage of several decades of colonial or white minority rule and an economic heritage of dependence on foreign capital, trade outlets for raw materials, and, today, foreign aid.
2. These have been and to a large extent still are racially divided societies, where class and race have largely coincided. Power, influence, and wealth have been in the hands of the white minority, and in all countries there have been high social barriers, penetrated only by the presence of black domestic workers in the white households. There is a rising and growing black middle class, and the "political class" is largely black. This means that the once exclusive white residential areas and white schools are no longer all white. On the other end of the spectrum, however, in the growing army of unemployed in townships and squatter areas, there is hardly any racial mix.

3. These countries are led by movements that have waged many years of liberation struggle, guided by radical and emancipatory ideologies, with racism and oppression the declared enemy.

Given the last point, one might ask why the leadership of South Africa, on one hand, and the leaderships of Namibia and Zimbabwe, on the other hand, seem to move in opposite directions in their responses to the gay and lesbian community. After a sketch of the development of gay and lesbian visibility in these three countries, I venture some possible explanations.

A note on visibility is helpful here. Visibility presupposes a self-ascribed identity as gay or lesbian. A permanent homosexual identity—as opposed to same-sex relationships or experiences that do not preclude heterosexual relationships at the same time or later—is not easy to accept for many Africans because of the great importance attached to having children. In this respect the acceptance of homosexuality is concomitant with the changes from predominantly rural peasant society—where children are not only welcome but, in fact, necessary for survival and old-age care—to an urbanized society with a greater variety of household and family patterns. Homosexuality is far less frequent in Africa than are same-sex experiences, especially among men, although they are seldom spoken of in public.

When gays and lesbians form a community, it can emerge on two levels: as a space for social community and as an actor in the public arena. The purpose of the first level is to provide meeting places and to answer the psychological needs of insecure and harassed gays and lesbians. The second level mostly takes the form of lobbying for gay rights, but it can also take a more ostentatious form, giving the world a "here we are" message, through carnivals and other manifestations of visible existence.

When the social community form is prevalent, the self-definition is often not consistent. Males especially can take part in the gay community on some nights and, with a reluctance to define themselves as homosexuals, revert to heterosexual roles during day and on other nights. Moreover, in a repressive context there is hesitancy to come out as gay or lesbian. The visibility is thus fluid, and not something once and for all achieved.

In *Defiant Desire,* Mark Gevisser and Edwin Cameron stress that there is not one essential "gay identity." To them this means accepting and celebrating variety among homosexuals, from drag queens to "straight" queers. The insight could be applied to the writing of the gay and lesbian movement as well. The book aptly illustrates how the need for social community arises again and again and how it can never be superseded by the activist role. The fact that the political lobbying of gays and lesbians

emerged later than the formation of social communities does not mean
that they are evolutionary stages, one more primitive and the other more
advanced.

SOUTH AFRICA

Recognizing the inevitability of the variety of personal, social, and political needs, it seems rather pointless to contend, as do Gordon Isaacs and
Brian McKendrick, that "gay attempts at 'homosexual liberation' are
split."[3] The banal contention turns into a questionable theoretical construct when a reference is made to a parallel drawn between the development of the gay and lesbian movement and the individual's "identity
growth protocols."[4] We cannot understand gay and lesbian movements
as organisms but only as varieties of individual and collective experiences
in the complex and changing context of social forces.

South Africa was a racially divided society long before the apartheid
regime came to power in 1948, and it was not replaced by a government
based on universal suffrage until 1994. Yet the idea of territorially separate development for blacks and whites never really worked in practice.
Although millions of black people were forced to move to the scattered
homelands (later called Bantustans), about half the black population was
needed for labor in the white-dominated areas. Black farmworkers in the
rural areas were living an isolated and deprived life, under the foot of the
local white farmer. In the urban areas, rapidly growing since the 1930s,
black people working for white homes, mines, and factories were forced
to live in specified areas. Mine workers and many industrial workers
stayed in single-sex hostels, in areas surrounded by barbed-wire fences or
walls (compounds). General workers who settled more permanently in
the cities lived in the townships, which were planned for housing black
labor. One of the largest and the most famous black townships is Soweto
(South West Townships) near the financial and industrial capital, Johannesburg. Illegal settlements, squatter areas, grew with the explosive increase in urbanization when the pass laws restricting the movement of
blacks were removed in the mid-1980s.

The Afrikaans- and English-speaking whites, more than five million,
lived in suburbs and on farms. With a few rapidly diminishing exceptions
(Sophiatown in Johannesburg and District Six in Cape Town), there were
no mixed urban communities. Members of each designated race—whites,
Asians, coloreds (those of mixed origin), and blacks (increasingly called
Africans)—lived their own social lives. For this simple reason, the history
of gay and lesbian consciousness in South Africa should properly go into
each separate group.

In South Africa a gay community—that is, groups of people who saw themselves as having a homosexual identity—emerged on the public scene in 1968. It was apolitical, almost totally white, and predominantly male and English speaking.

A gay subculture, however, had emerged much earlier, most manifestly as the Cape "moffies" in the Cape Town colored community. The Cape moffies were indeed an important part of the culture of the colored community, with its hub in District Six in Cape Town. They also had a significant public presence in the annual Coon Carnival, organized from within the colored community of Cape Town and one of the major cultural events of the city. The carnival was led by a moffie, and one of its features was the playful mocking of conditions of gender and sexuality.[5]

Another nonwhite gay subculture of importance was the same-sex subculture among the migrant workers, particularly in the mining compounds. This has often been dismissed as "circumstantial" and not quite genuine homosexuality. Certainly it was bred by the single-sex living over a long period of time and was based, one might argue, on the feeling that for males access to sex is a natural right and a must. But who is the judge of what is genuine? Especially in societies and contexts with a strong heterosexual bias, many same-sex relationships are excluded if we can see sexuality only as lifelong identity, genuine only through coming out, rather than as lifelong experience.

If, indeed, the acquired same-sex behavior patterns are only a temporary and insignificant deviation from heterosexuality,[6] then same-sex relationionships in the mining compounds are perhaps peripheral for gay and lesbian identity history. That is an empirical question that could be researched. There are some indications that the accepted assumptions are worth testing. In Francis Wilson's classic study on migrant labor, same-sex relationships are mentioned as a prominent feature in the compounds.[7] A Protestant minister working in Soweto in the 1950s reported that he was approached almost every Sunday by migrant workers who wanted him to bless same-sex "marriages."[8] Hugh McLean and Linda Ngcobo tell of male-with-male sexuality in the mining communities, including the establishment of an all-gay *stokvel* (credit union) on the Reef in 1991.[9]

It is worth noting that there were many black gay and lesbian spaces, particularly in the townships, long before a gay and lesbian movement in South Africa emerged. These are only beginning to be documented. A fairly common notion among whites in South Africa and abroad is that gay and lesbian activity in the black townships was an imitation of and inspiration from whites. This has been rejected as condescending and paternalist by many black homosexuals.

Lesbians developed their own ways of creating space for social belonging. In most South African cities in the 1950s and 1960s there were lesbian circles of friends, often formed on the basis of profession—teachers, nurses, lawyers, and so on. This subculture was usually much more clandestine than its male counterparts. Sports became the arena into which lesbians emerged from the closet in big numbers. In the 1950s and 1960s, lesbian identity was largely concealed in soccer (among blacks) and hockey (among whites). But in the early 1990s women's softball league games in Johannesburg constituted perhaps the biggest lesbian outdoor gatherings ever.[10]

For various reasons it was more difficult for women to resolve the tension between the need for social space and the need for activism in the public space. Many lesbians belonged to service professions, pressure for marriage was greater, and economic autonomy was smaller. There are also special features to lesbian sexuality. The social space does not typically serve as a hunting ground for one-night sexual experiences, but as a place where women seek and sometimes find longtime partners. When relationships break up, lesbians find few other places to meet, and a tightly knit lesbian community can find itself torn apart over tensions from past relationships within the group.

In January 1966, police raided a large gay party in the Johannesburg suburb of Forest Town. The authorities achieved little through such clampdowns on private parties, since gay activities were statutory offenses only when committed in public. In 1967, therefore, a far-reaching law was proposed that would make both female and male homosexuality illegal. This sparked the first, though short-lived, gay human rights lobbying in South Africa. In early 1968 a group of gay professionals in Johannesburg founded a Homosexual Law Reform Fund (called the Law Reform), which soon established cells all over the country.[11] A new sense of community, with a new meaning, was forged by the threat of repression. As one activist put it, "You found that the latest subject of conversation was not likely to be the latest hairdo, but how you could get letters out in bulk."[12]

Both lesbians and gay men were involved, but the movement was all white, middle class, and directed only at forcing the ruling National Party to drop the antigay legislation. Wider politics were shunned, and no contacts were made with the small but existing white opposition. The proposed law was indeed dropped. Instead, the old law was amended to raise the age of consent for male homosexuality to nineteen, to outlaw dildos, and to forbid males to commit with another male "any act which is calculated to stimulate sexual passion or to give sexual gratification" at a party (ridiculously defined as any occasion with more than two persons present).[13] The Law Reform movement collapsed almost immediately after it successfully staved off the repressive law proposal. The reasons were many—Gevisser cites the lack of internal democracy; the absence of links to the broader, black-dominated liberation movement; and the limited and defensive agenda.[14]

After 1968, authorities seemed to accept the fact that homosexuality could not be eradicated, but they attempted to "move the subculture indoors,"[15] in part to keep it out of sight of conservative religious circles. Indoors, the gay and lesbian subculture thrived in a number of fairly secure places but at the cost of increased race and class segregation. In contrast to U.S. movement after Stonewall, the South African gay and lesbian movement, varied and growing as it was, was neither radical nor mass based. While the black masses in South Africa faced increasing marginalization in the 1970s, the white middle class thrived as never before. Gay venues and gay businesses flourished in the white urban areas, and Afrikaans-speaking gays and lesbians were drawn into the subculture in considerable numbers and with greater openness, because of the need to break radically with their closeted past.[16]

In 1979 a police raid was made on New Mandy's, a gay bar in Johannesburg. A few blacks who were there got the harshest treatment. Why the raid after the relative peace? Gevisser cites claims that it was "a more obvious and blatant" defiant sexuality that the government had to curb.[17] This raid has been called South Africa's Stonewall, because some people fought back and because it fostered a new awareness of the difficulty of combining an apolitical and nonmilitant stance with the growing refusal to be a silent minority.

But it took time before the gay and lesbian subculture (or parts of it) moved toward a liberation movement. Even in the mid-1980s, the gay establishment newspaper, *Exit,* devoted the bulk of its content to "bar and club round-ups, community news, hunk pictorial, and camp humour."[18] The newspaper did get into politics but in a revealingly restricted way. In the mid- and late 1980s, the townships of South Africa were exploding from anger and frustration with the government's harsh repression and President Pieter Botha's refusal to give black people the vote. While white boys organized in a refusal to serve with the army in the virtual occupation of the black township, *Exit* encouraged its readers not to forget to vote in the white 1987 election, listing political candidates who had indicated that they would support gay rights.[19] *Exit* was rightly criticized for turning its back on a large portion of the South African gays and lesbians through its intervention in the all-white election. Yet it is interesting that it was even possible to elicit support for sexual equality from candidates from all-white parties, ten of whom were from the National Party.

The conventional view of the National Party as a fundamentalist Christian advocate was no longer the whole truth. In fact the "modernization" of the ruling National Party ideology was already well underway. For the modernizing element, capitalism rather than Christian socialism needed to be saved, whether by increasing repression or by reform. In 1978, President Botha began with both but leaned more and more toward repression. There was enough reform for the most conservative elements to split from the National Party, which leaned more on electoral support from a large number of English-speaking whites than it had in the past.

For the government in 1987, the issue of homosexuality was more peripheral, and the very survival of the system more acute, than at the time of the 1966 Forest Town raid. Gevisser interprets this as a move in line with President Hendrik Verwoerd's attempt to consolidate the country under Afrikaner Christian Socialism and clamp down on anything threatening white civilization, from the liberation movement to nonconformist lifestyles.[20]

In the black community, gay (and, less often, lesbian) organizations with a militant character sprang up immediately after the Soweto revolt in 1976. Yet the need for social shelter and meeting places was great and in practice often overshadowed overt political activity. Gevisser notes an interesting point about black gay activism—it tended to be middle class, because human rights for gays meant rights to privacy, an irrelevant and impossible objective in the crowded housing of the townships and squatter areas.[21]

Toward the end of the eighties, there emerged in South Africa a number of gay and lesbian organizations that aligned themselves with the African National Congress's (ANC) Freedom Charter and asserted gay rights as human rights.[22] This process had started in Cape Town in 1986, with the formation of the first lesbian and gay organization, which placed itself as a political organization within the context of total liberation.[23] Under its final name, OLGA (Organisation for Lesbian and Gay Action), this organization then applied for and received membership in the ANC-aligned umbrella organization United Democratic Front (UDF). After the first hiccups, the UDF leaders opted for inclusiveness, moving to welcome OLGA also because some of its members were well-known antiapartheid activists. In 1991, after the ban on the ANC had been lifted and it started to build its own partylike structures, the UDF was disbanded. The umbrella organization had fulfilled its task. After much lobbying, the ANC formally recognized lesbian and gay rights at its policy conference in May 1992.[24] The policy was then included in the interim constitution adopted in December 1993.

With the text of the bill of rights enshrined in the new constitution, adopted on 8 May 1996, South Africa became the first country in the world to include in its constitution a reference to "sexual orientation" as one of the basic human rights to be protected against discrimination.

The bill of rights in South Africa's new constitution[25] states:

Rights

7. (1) This Bill of Rights is a cornerstone of democracy in South Africa. It enshrines the rights of all people in our country and affirms the democratic values of human dignity, equality and freedom.

(2) The state must respect, protect, promote, and fulfil the rights in the Bill of Rights. . . .

Equality

(3) The state may not unfairly discriminate directly or indirectly against anyone on one or more grounds, including race, gender, sex, pregnancy, marital status, ethnic or social origin, colour, sexual orientation, age, disability, religion, conscience, belief, culture, language, and birth.

(4) No person may unfairly discriminate directly or indirectly against anyone on one or more grounds in terms of subsection (3). National legislation must be enacted to prevent or prohibit unfair discrimination.[26]

There had been remarkably broad official political party support for the inclusion of the clause on sexual orientation. During the constitutional process for the interim constitution in 1993, all but one of the parliamentary parties proposed bills of rights including the rights of gays and lesbians for constitutional protection. The exception was the small fundamentalist African Christian Democratic Party (ACDP).

The process of adopting a new constitution in South Africa was unique in its popular participation. Hundreds of meetings were held at a grassroots level and in various organizations and sectors of society across the country. An intensive campaign was waged to encourage people to send or phone in their submissions to the Constitutional Assembly, both before the first draft was written and as comments on the working draft. The issues that caused the largest number of South Africans to voice their opinions in the first stage were the status of the Afrikaans language (half a million petitions), the secular character of the state, the death penalty, abortion, the right to self-defense and to own firearms, and, in seventh place, the sexual orientation clause. There were about as many submissions in favor of inclusion of this clause as there were against it. For the second stage, submissions invited on the working draft, four million copies of the draft had been circulated in December 1994 and January 1995. When the date for submissions closed on 20 February 1995, more than twenty thousand new submissions had been received. This time, the campaign against the inclusion of sexual orientation had subsided, with 564 petitions opposing and 7,032 petitions supporting the inclusion of the clause in the bill of rights.[27]

The fact that discrimination against homosexuals had been outlawed in the South African constitution did not, however, automatically win the battle. The interpretation of what constitutes "unfair discrimination" in section 7 (4) is not clear. There are still antigay laws on the books, which stand until explicitly repealed or tested and declared unconstitutional by the Constitutional Court.

How deeply committed is the ANC to the sexual orientation clause it has espoused? Gevisser writes that "official ANC support of gay issues has been at worst grudging, and at best half-hearted."[28] They point to the Winnie Mandela trial, and her largely unopposed Africanist homophobic defense for "protecting" Stompie and other boys from alleged homosexual "molestation," and the claim that "homosex is not in black culture."[29]

The success in South Africa is very much a result of an effective campaign by organized homosexuals—not least the National Coalition for Gay and Lesbian Equality—and the strong feelings against discrimination in the battle for liberation from apartheid. When I did research for Chris Dunton's and my "Human Rights and Homosexuality in Southern Africa," I recorded numerous speeches in which ANC leaders read the list of antidiscrimination clauses, including the sexual orientation clause, but not one explained it or elaborated on the reasons that the ANC wanted to include it. The only ideological stand that I found on the issue was one by Deputy Secretary General Cheryl Carolus of the ANC. At the March 1995 conference in which the National Coalition of Gay and Lesbian Equality was launched, Carolus said that she opposed homophobia for the same reason that she opposed racism and sexism.

In early 1997 I had an opportunity to ask Barney Pityana, chairman of the government-appointed National Commission for Human Rights, about popular support for the sexual orientation clause. He claimed there was very little. He said that people had to be educated about it but that because homosexuals did that so well themselves, the human rights commission could devote its energy to other things.

A considerable victory was won in South Africa with the new constitution, but the struggle is far from over. As Cheryl Carolus said, "Many people that we love dearly—our parents, our brothers and sisters, our priests, our teachers—are themselves quite often prejudiced when it comes to the issue of homosexuality. We must accept that we are not just confronting bigots, people with horns, but that we need to take on this debate with our families and those closest to us. Only then can we begin to shift the position in society."[30]

The ANC will not necessarily move fast, and there are signs that it may even backtrack. On 15 September 1997, Minister of Justice Dullah Omar announced that he opposed the decriminalization of same-sex acts between consenting adult men, which had been filed in court. "The rights of gays and lesbians and those of the public have to be balanced, he said."[31] Once again there had to be a call for lobbying and protests. And once again the Gay Pride March in Johannesburg, a yearly event since 1990 and a triumph of visibility, was planned as a combination of the celebration of varieties of homosexual existence (with drag queens always attracting media attention) and a rallying around political demands.

Who are the supporters of gay and lesbian liberation in new South Africa? Within the African National Congress much has happened since the antiapartheid movements in England and Holland felt they had to protest against an ANC spokeswoman's dismissal of the gay issue as something concerning only a small segment of well-to-do whites.[32] Cyril Ramaphosa, secretary general of the ANC at that time, even sent a greeting to the Gay Pride March in 1991.[33]

The vigorous campaign for gay rights has not only swayed the drafters of the constitution but has also contributed to increased acceptance and respect, at least among the urbanites, both black and white. One sign of this trend is the fact that Edwin Cameron, an openly gay human rights lawyer, was appointed as one of the judges in the Constitutional Court in 1994 and became a judge of the Labour Appeal Court in 1997.

Yet the human rights campaign for gay rights has been borne almost exclusively by homosexuals themselves. In the churches, Anglican Archbishop Desmond Tutu, now retired, is almost alone in placing gay rights high on the agenda. "If the church, after victory over apartheid, is looking for a worthy moral crusade, then this is it: the fight against homophobia and heterosexism," he writes in a foreward to a recent book on homosexuality and Christianity in South Africa.[34] In the lobbying for the new constitution, few churches supported gay rights. There are a few churches, among them some Quaker, that marry same-sex couples, although there is no legal provision for such marriages.

The gay and lesbian lobby in South Africa cannot rest on its laurels. The legal battle is far from over, and there is much to be done before there is a widespread acceptance of the existence of gays and lesbians. In fact, surrounded by countries with homophobic leaderships and government policies, the gay and lesbian movement feels locked into a new kind of laager.

THE BOOK FAIR DRAMAS IN ZIMBABWE

From its founding in 1989,[35] Gays and Lesbians of Zimbabwe (GALZ) had led a quiet existence as a support group and social club for Zimbabwe's small but growing gay and lesbian community. But when, in

January 1994, the group advertised its counseling services in the *Daily Gazette*, a public debate on homosexuality ensued. This debate raged during the first half of 1994, when suddenly all media fell quiet. Rumor had it that the government had placed an embargo on all gay related subjects.[36] Thanks to President Mugabe, the silence would not last.

Gays and lesbians in Zimbabwe were forced into visibility in July 1995, when the annual Zimbabwe International Book Fair (ZIBF) was about to open in the city gardens of Harare. By government order, GALZ, one of the smallest of the 240 exhibitors, was barred from taking part. The group wanted to exhibit and advertise its literature on the legal and constitutional aspects of gay rights. A GALZ sticker with the words "Don't hate! Tolerate" made an appeal to the general public—hardly a provocative self-assertion. But earlier in the year the Minister of Home Affairs Dumiso Dabengwa had declared that homosexuality was abnormal and would not be allowed in Zimbabwe.[37] News of the book fair ban and President Mugabe's subsequent outburst against homosexuals was broadcast throughout southern Africa and all over the world.

In March, at a meeting in Johannesburg to solicit South African publishers' support for the fair, Trish Mbanga, executive director of ZIBF, reported that security forces had intimidated GALZ after ZIBF had accepted the group's application and payment for a stand. She intimated that the ZIBF trustees were inclined to withdraw the application to avert disruption of the fair. The South African publishers at the meeting, who felt strongly that this would compromise their participation, wrote a letter supporting the acceptance of GALZ participation.[38]

One week before the opening, book fair organizers received a letter from Zimbabwe Director of Information Bornwell Chakaodza: "Whilst acknowledging the dynamic nature of culture, the fact still remains that both Zimbabwean society and government do not accept the public display of homosexual literature and material. The Trustees of the Book Fair should not, therefore, force the values of gays and lesbians onto the Zimbabwean culture."[39]

The ZIBF felt compelled to announce that "with the greatest regret" it had to withdraw its permission for GALZ to participate. There were some immediate protests, but these were mainly from visitors and from abroad. Writers who had been invited to An *Indaba* (conference) on Human Rights and Freedom of Expression preceding the book fair, including South African author Nadine Gordimer and Nigerian author Wole Soyinka, asked that the ban be withdrawn "and that the human rights principle on which we accepted to participate in this Indaba be honoured."[40]

Andrew Morrison, a university lecturer and member of GALZ, pointed out in vain that "freedom of expression is tolerating things we don't really like."[41] The Zimbabwean protests were generally weak, and few of these were printed in the Zimbabwean media. The Zimbabwe Human Rights Organization (Zimrights) issued a statement, and ambivalent support for homosexuals was expressed by Edwin Sakala of the Catholic Commission for Justice and Peace in Zimbabwe, who apparently could not quite decide whether he should believe that the gays and lesbians would display their sexuality: "It is my right if I decide to walk naked in public. But such an act constitutes public indecency, and the law will have to take its course. Gays and lesbians have the right to privacy but if they display it [their sexuality] in public, it becomes public indecency. . . . The police are infringing homosexuals' rights when they invade their homes. Homosexuality is not a crime."[42]

GALZ's visibility could have ended with its withdrawal from the book fair. But the limelight was assured by President Mugabe's speech at the official opening of the book fair on 1 August. He said:

> Supporting persons who believe that the denial of their alleged rights to have sex in public is a violation of their human rights formed an association in defense and protection of it and proceeded to write booklets and other forms of literature on the subject of their rights. Is any sane government which is a protector of society's moral values expected to countenance their accessions?
>
> I find it extremely outrageous and repugnant to my human conscience that such immoral and repulsive organisations, like those of homosexuals who offend both against the law of nature and the morals of religious beliefs espoused by our society, should have any advocates in our midst and even elsewhere in the world.
>
> If we accept homosexuality as a right, as is being argued by the association of sodomists and sexual perverts, what moral fibre shall our society ever have to deny organised drug addicts, or even those given to bestiality, the rights they might claim and allege they possess under the rubrics of individual freedom and human rights, including the freedom of the Press to write, publish and publicise their literature on them?[43]

At a press conference after the opening, President Mugabe commented further on homosexuals, "I don't believe they should have any rights at all. I hope the time never will come when we all want to reverse nature and men bear children."[44]

The exhibition space that was to have been occupied by GALZ was left standing by ZIPF organizers, allowing statements protesting the government-ordered expulsion to be mounted on the walls. The booth became one of the most popular meeting and discussion places at the book fair, and GALZ found a more effective platform than it could ever have dreamed of.

Mugabe continued his attacks on gays in Zimbabwe after the book fair. In a subsequently infamous speech on Heroes' Day (11 August) he urged churches and others to ensure that society not be distracted from traditional values: "It degrades human dignity. It's unnatural and there is no question ever of allowing these people to behave worse than dogs and pigs."[45]

Two weeks later the Women's League organized a meeting of five hundred members of the ruling Zimbabwe African National Union–Patriotic Front (ZANU-PF) Party, with placards such as "God created Adam and Eve and not Adam and Steve." A statement was adopted at the meeting: We are Zimbabweans and we have a culture for Zimbabweans to preserve. As mothers and custodians of our heritage, we stand solidly behind our president and leader on his unflinching stand against homosexuality. Human rights should not be allowed to dehumanise us. Do not be deceived. Neither the sexually immoral nor idolaters nor adulterous nor male prostitutes nor homosexual offenders nor the greedy nor drunkards will inherit the kingdom of God."[46] The *Sunday News* praised President Mugabe's "bold denunciation of homosexuals as undesirable sodomites" and rejoiced that "university students and the ZANU-PF Women's League have at last found something in common to agree on."[47]

The harshest criticism of Mugabe in the region came from South Africa. On Friday 11 August about a hundred people demonstrated outside the Zimbabwe trade mission on Sauer Street in central Johannesburg in protest of Mugabe's views on homosexuals. "Vorster said blacks have no rights. Mugabe says gays have no rights" was the text of one of the placards. The organizer, the National Coalition for Gay and Lesbian Equality, reported that it had received messages of support from Lawyers for Human Rights, Black Sash, the AIDS consortium, the Women's National Coalition, and the Centre for Applied Legal Studies at the University of the Witwatersrand.[48] When President Mugabe arrived at the Jan Smuts Airport near Johannesburg on 26 August 1995, for a meeting of the Southern African Development Community (SADC), he was met by demonstrators. One placard slogan read, "Zimbabwe needs a queen."

Peter Vale, professor of Southern African Studies at the University of Western Cape, saw the protests as something new in southern African politics: "For the first time in the region's history, an interest group in another country has put pressure on the leader of a majority-ruled government. This is an entirely new development, and it holds enormous potential for the growth of civil society in southern Africa."[49] But this turn of events also forced gay men and lesbians to place themselves in the larger context of human rights, whether that had been their intention or not.

As a militant organization, GALZ had scared off many white homosexuals who wanted a semiclandestine social space only. But now many black gays and lesbians joined, and by the next book fair, in August 1996, there were many more black members than white. There are some paradoxes in this situation.

First, one might think that whites, with their acquired privileges, would have a more secure social position and would be able to withstand the president's threats. But it was clear that there was much more courage and experience of political confrontation among black Zimbabweans. Few whites had been involved in the struggle against the racist Ian Smith regime, a struggle that did not reach the cities of Zimbabwe but reached only those few whites who were in exile. In contrast to the liberation struggle in South Africa, where the urban revolts brought generations together and pulled a section of the white population into the battle, the liberation struggle in Zimbabwe was a military battle between the ZANU and (to a lesser extent) ZAPU armies and the security forces of the Ian Smith regime.

A second paradox is the fact that whites continued to dominate at least in part because they were "better connected" in the situation where external communication was paramount—the verbalization of demands and statements in English and access to communication technology (from telephone, fax, and e-mail to cars and international networks).

After the 1995 book fair, the international limelight and expressions of support brought an initial phase of euphoria. But the situation did not change for the better in Zimbabwe itself, and the organization went through an identity crisis. The 1996 book fair meant a new start. The book fair trust had pledged a tougher stand, promising to go to court if the government barred the trust from deciding who could participate.[50]

GALZ had overcome the crisis; it had been promised grants from Dutch and Canadian sources. It had put together a small book, *Sahwira,* with a unique collection of life stories on being homosexual in Zimbabwe.[51] It maintained contacts with lawyers concerning its rights. GALZ submitted an application for a double stand at the book fair just before deadline. As promised, it was accepted. But as soon as news broke in Harare about GALZ's participation in the 1996 book fair, a homophobic mass media campaign began.

The newly founded Christian Communication Association of Zimbabwe and an "affirmative action" student organization called Sangano Munhumutapa threatened havoc and violence if GALZ was allowed. The student representative council at the University of Zimbabwe announced that if GALZ participated, the students would definitely be there. Furthermore, they said, the ZIBF management should be aware "that their uncultural behaviour may prove detrimental to the book fair" and that they may see the gays and lesbians "face public genocide unceremoniously."[52]

During this tense time there was no statement from any Zimbabwean leader condemning violence. The president remained silent all through this book fair. There was clearly a rift here between the government and the system of justice, with the presidential leadership in a silent alliance with gay bashers with no diplomatic prestige and no foreign aid for him to fear losing. The alliance worked—I got into a heated discussion with a male student at the book fair who defended the right to violence and claimed that the courts and lawyers could be ignored: "They will permit anything. This is not a question of law; it is a question of culture," he told me.

Although the threat of violence was great, no physical violence actually took place.[53] But the politics of threat is, of course, a form of violence, which sanctions "spontaneous" physical violence. This was the nasty experience of at least two black lesbians after the book fair: they were intimidated and physically threatened and had to seek protection in Harare.

This time, however, the government line was not entirely consistent in its homophobia. Interviewed by the press, Minister of Information, Post and Telecommunication Joyce Mujuru said the government could not intervene if GALZ participated, whatever views the government held on the issue. But her subordinate, Director of Information Bornwell Chakaodza denied soon after that she had said any such thing, and he announced that a banning order would bar GALZ from renting a stand at the Zimbabwe International Book Fair and at all future book fairs: "Gays and lesbians have, like anyone else, a right to live, but they have absolutely no right to publicly display literature and material at a public and cultural event where hundreds of children visit to fulfil one of ZIBF's commitments, which is 'to uphold the right of the people of Africa' to have full access to books which are culturally and materially relevant to their reading needs."[54] On the eve of the book fair, a "notice of prohibition," based on the Censorship and Entertainment Control Act, was handed to the book fair director and to GALZ. Despite its promise, the book fair management did not go to court, but GALZ did. In a statement, GALZ condemned the actions of what it mistakenly spelled "the Ministry of Homoe Affairs."

The High Court declared invalid the government order prohibiting GALZ from putting up a stand and exhibiting material at the book fair. The court's president, Judge Sandura, said that it was unreasonable for the censorship board to ban material it had not seen and that the censorship board could not prohibit pieces of wood and canvas from being erected in the shape of a stand at a public fair. The government attempted to lodge a counterappeal against Judge Sandura's ruling, but it was dismissed by the High Court. A government appeal was then lodged with the Supreme Court, which did not handle the matter during the book fair. In the end the government withdrew its case, avoiding yet another loss of prestige.

The explicit domestic defenders of GALZ were again few. Only the three human rights organizations (this time with stronger voices), the small newspaper *The Independent,* and a former High Court judge were heard warning against homophobia. In the *Sunday Mail,* Judge John Manyarara was quoted as being highly critical of the journalists: "Justice Manyarara claimed homosexuality existed in traditional Zimbabwe. He said he had read this from an article published by a local magazine. 'The story was killed by not being republished by anybody else—I have the clipping. This is self-censorship,' he told participants who included journalists from Uganda, Tanzania, Kenya, Cameroon and South Africa."[55] Judge Manyarara commented that Zimbabwean journalists had not investigated the legality of the ban on GALZ. He said he personally knew that the ban was illegal. He challenged Zimbabweans to carry out a referendum on the matter. No journalists had any knowledge of what was going to be exhibited, he said, so how could they support the banning?

The Legal Resources Foundation was quoted in the press as criticizing the ban on grounds of international law: "Section 20 of the Constitution deals specifically with the protection of freedom of expression which includes the right to receive and impart ideas and information without interference. . . . Government has declared its adherence to constitutional rights and to the International Covenants to which Zimbabwe is a signatory and in which freedom of expression, assembly and association are pivotal. The dictatorial statement by the Director of Information that GALZ may not exhibit either at this or any future Book Fair in this country, brings this into question."[56]

David Chiminhi, executive director of the Zimbabwe Human Rights Organization, was quoted as saying that the banning of GALZ was an overreaction by the government, "which is not in harmony with the international thinking on the issue. Yes, Zimbabwe is a sovereign country and we should never give up our hard-won independence, but our practices must be seen to be just, by our own laws."[57]

The Catholic Commission for Justice and Peace in Zimbabwe gave a statement in which it condemned repression but refused to respect the right of gays and lesbians to their sexual orientation.

Despite little publicly voiced support, the attention proved to be effective advertising for GALZ. The group was again the talk of the town, and wherever GALZ did appear at the book fair (the threat of violence kept the group away about half of the time), dozens of people gathered to ask them questions, mostly in a curious and ignorant but not hostile way. And this was not just a Harare affair. Local community media, youth club magazines, women's newspapers, among other publications with nation-wide circulation, have all talked about homosexuality with an openness that shows that civil society in Zimbabwe is not swallowed up by the au-thoritarian power pyramid of the ruling party.

Various cultural initiatives have been set in motion, such as a docu-mentary film and community theater plays, which will treat homosexual-ity as a theme. A "budding author" (heterosexual) approached me at the book fair, saying he was going to write a novel about gays and lesbians. "I think there is a market for it now," he commented.

In 1997 GALZ did not have its own stand at the book fair. Instead, it displayed some material in a human rights stand. There was no big dis-cussion about the gays and lesbians this time.

That same year it was disclosed that the first president of Zimbabwe, Canaan Banana, had sexually exploited men in his employ. This did not exactly help clarify the issues.[58] Here was a case of abuse of power and rape. But these were not the issues raised. And the fact that all this had occurred without the intervention of Robert Mugabe, who was prime minister at the time, was not raised either.

Several donors of foreign aid to Zimbabwe, among them the European Community, Canada, Holland, and Sweden, have pledged to watch de-velopments on human rights and homosexuality in Zimbabwe closely. The issue is already a bone of contention for the World Council of Churches anniversary conference, which is scheduled to be held in Harare in 1998. The churches are wavering, as the government of Zimbabwe tries to prevent having the issue put on the agenda and, above all, having any criticism voiced against it.

Inside GALZ the cleavage in practice between black and white contin-ued. GALZ remained dominated by white homosexuals. Black gays re-portedly feel a strong identity as black Zimbabweans, even to the para-doxical point of taking pride in Mugabe's courage "to stand up against the West."

In mid-1997 an organization for black gays and lesbians was report-edly founded.[59] There is also an organization for gays and lesbians in Bu-lawayo, the second largest city in Zimbabwe: the Bulawayo Gays and Les-bians (BUGLE). I have no knowledge of the relationship between these organizations, but the absence of a national umbrella organization sug-gests that they are not prepared or able to act fully in the civil society as an agency pressuring the state.

NAMIBIA

One of the most significant effects of the Zimbabwe book fair dramas was that they suddenly put homosexuality on the agenda in all of southern Africa, on quite another scale than developments in South Africa had, thus paving the way for gays and lesbians to organize and become visible. The effects have already been seen in Namibia. After the book fair in Zimbabwe, which was widely reported in the Namibian press and supplemented by interviews with Namibian gays, the debate was raised to the ministerial level, as two ministers joined the crusade against homosexuals.

"Homosexuality is like cancer or AIDS and everything should be done to stop its spread in Namibia," said Deputy Minister for Lands, Resettlement and Rehabilitation Hadino Hishongwa (quoted in the weekly *New Era* in early October 1995). Homosexuality was alien to Namibian society, and those who engage in homosexual and lesbian relations should be "operated on to remove unnatural hormones," he said. "In an emphatic tone," the reporter records, "Hishongwa said he did not take up arms to fight for an immoral society, neither does he want his children to live in such a corrupt state."[60] The reporter had also solicited the opinion of Finance Minister Helmut Angula, who warned that homosexuality had infiltrated Namibian society and might "lead to social disorder." In his view, the practice should be fought through intensified campaigns and political mobilization.

Meanwhile, the Namibian press also gave coverage to gay and lesbian organizations. Even before President Mugabe's outburst at the book fair in Harare, *New Era* had carried a story about homosexuals and lesbians who planned to establish their own church to overcome the marginalization they routinely suffer in Christian and Muslim religions.[61]

The Sister Namibia Collective, an organization committed to the elimination of gender oppression, racism, and homophobia, also got into the debate. This group was the first in Namibia to count open lesbians among its members. It commented on the comparison of homosexuality with cancer and AIDS: "We fail to see any similarity. Cancer and AIDS are life-threatening diseases of the body, whereas lesbianism and homosexuality are alternative, life-enhancing, physical, emotional, and spiritual forms of love."[62]

Namibia has not yet altered old laws against certain homosexual acts, which were inherited from the time that the country was occupied by apartheid South Africa. The constitution of independent Namibia (1990) does not mention "sexual orientation," but in its preamble it guarantees "the right of the individual to life, liberty and the pursuit of happiness, regardless of colour, ethnic origin, sex, religion, creed or social or economic status." For the first time, these fundamental rights appear to come under attack. Wolfram Hartmann, Andre du Pisani and James Steakley wrote to *The Namibian*, "Traditional targets of derision—women, children and foreigners—have seemingly been replaced by gays and lesbians. Has homophobia superseded xenophobia as Namibia enters a new phase of gay bashing, verbal for now, physical in the future? Are we witnessing the advent of politics of ostracism and displacement?"[63]

Homophobia in general, and its southern African variant at present, constitutes a grave threat to both the integrity of the individual and more broadly to the entire citizenry of this region. This is so, because homophobia propagates hatred of the very being of homosexually loving citizens and thereby tears at the fabric of civil society. At bottom it rests on the same logic of contempt that prompts all misanthropic acts: wife battering, rape, child molestation, disregard for the elderly, and so on. For that reason it also diminishes the dignity of the majority that happens to love heterosexually. Ironically, the thesis that homosexuality is Western and therefore by definition decadent constitutes itself a peculiarly Western power discourse, because it denies the richness of cultural and human experience.

According to Hartmann, du Pisani, and Steakley, "Psychologically defined, homophobia serves to bolster a male identity, disintegrating in the face of rising demands from women and other marginal social groups.— We are concerned that the recent expressions of homophobia may close down social and political space in our nascent civil society."[64]

In December 1996 the issue surfaced again. In a departure from the official speech at a South West African People's Organization (SWAPO) women's council congress in Gobabis on 7 December, President Sam Nujoma is reported to have said that "all necessary steps must be taken to combat all influences that are influencing us and our children in a negative way. Homosexuals must be condemned and rejected in our society."[65] The remark was reported to the press by one of the foreign guests. In February 1997, in a statement by the secretary for information and publicity, SWAPO reaffirmed the stand, saying that gays were not only alien but also foreign: "Most of the ardent supporters of these perverts are Europeans who imagine themselves to be the bulwark of civilization and enlightenment. . . . We made sacrifices for the liberation of this country and we are not going to allow individuals with alien practices such as homosexuality to destroy the social fabric of our society."[66] The National Society for Human Rights in Windhoek saw the attack as an impending drive against the rapidly growing civil society in Namibia, as well as a sign of emergent totalitarianism. The Journalists' Association of Namibia also protested the SWAPO statement's goal of total uprooting homosexuality, calling it a total disregard for freedom of expression.[67]

Namibia's first organization for homosexuals, the Rainbow Nation, formed in the capital of Windhoek in an attempt to gain an audience with the president. In its statement the group pointed out that in 1990, following discussions with members of the gay community, Prime Minister Hage Geingob had assured homosexuals and lesbians of their rights in terms of Article 10.2 of the country's constitution. The Rainbow Nation activists felt that they had a very positive response and wide support from society as a whole. Even the church and state had toned down their homophobic statements from threats of uprooting the alien evil to requests that gays and lesbians keep their homosexuality private.

WHY THE DIFFERENCES?

Under Nelson Mandela new South Africa is the first country in the world to ban discrimination against homosexuals in its constitution. Zimbabwe's leader, Robert Mugabe, has given his country a reputation as the most overtly homophobic country on the African continent, with Namibia's President Sam Nujoma trying hard to follow suit. Why did gays and lesbians reap so different a harvest from the liberation struggle?

On one level the answer lies in the saying that you reap what you sow. The organizational strength of the gays and lesbians, and their ability to unite for very effective lobbying in the constitutional debate, is the single most significant reason for the achievement of this world-first in gay rights. But this, of course, raises the question What made it possible for the South African gays and lesbians to organize early, lobby effectively, and find alliances?

In explaining the obstacles and opportunities faced by gays and lesbians in these three countries, three factors are relevant: social history, political history, and the contemporary political arena.

Social History

When new South Africa came into being, there was already a strong and diverse gay and lesbian movement. Its growth benefited from a relatively high degree of freedom in white society and a press that did not altogether toe the government line (even though it had to be silent on the liberation movement). The white gay and lesbian community had many contacts with gay and lesbian organizations and communities in Western Europe (and North America) and followed the developments in the world gay and lesbian community.

The exceptionally high degree of urbanization in South Africa helped gay and lesbian social spaces to come into being, both in white and black locales. Life in the black townships had very little resemblance to rural traditions, which encouraged tolerance for other lifestyles. In the 1970s a black middle class with an ideology of individualism started to emerge in South Africa.

The situation was quite different in Zimbabwe and Namibia, where the white settlers were a small group with a laager mentality and urbanization came later and did not produce such a vibrant township culture. In Namibia and Zimbabwe an African middle class, of much smaller size and with less autonomy, was found only among the conformist petite bourgeoisie of teachers and preachers.

The degree of urbanization and the key role of the urban centers in the liberation is perhaps the most important reason for the high degree of individualism as ideology in South Africa. The key internal basis for the liberation struggle in Zimbabwe and Namibia were the peasants and the rural structures. In South Africa the ANC continues to have its most important base in the cities, as witnessed in the Kwazulu/Natal provincial elections in 1996, where the ANC got a clear majority in the cities and traditionalist Inkatha won the countryside. The ANC stands for modernity as a positive value, but the leaders in Namibia and Zimbabwe try hard to foster its traditionalist basis. It is not insignificant that gay bashers are typically young men. As in many places in Africa, changing times hit men's traditional roles particularly severely. The anger and energy of such young men have been directed against apartheid, which was not abolished until 1994.

In the name of "indigenous culture," both Mugabe and Nujoma try to appeal to traditional leaders for whom modernity is a threat. This language, used by Chigwedere, one of President Mugabe's supporters in Parliament, could not have been used successfully in South Africa (where even Inkatha supported the sexual orientation clause). What is at issue in cultural terms is a conflict of interest between the whole body, which is the Zimbabwean community, and part of that body, represented by individuals or groups of individuals. Chigwedere said, "The whole body is far more important than any single dispensable part. When your finger starts festering and becomes a danger to the body you cut it off. . . . The homosexuals are the festering finger."[68]

But much of the abhorrence of homosexuality springs from the Christian churches rather than from indigenous culture. The old traditions of missionary teaching in combination with modern fundamentalism make for a strong brew of prejudice.

Political History

The fact that many gays and lesbians were activists in the antiapartheid movement gave gay rights in South Africa a legitimacy and brought the issue to the attention of the leaders of the ANC. As we have seen, homophobic statements by ANC leaders were uncritically passed as ANC policy as late as 1987. But five years later, as a result of successful lobbying, the ANC offered at least verbal support for gay rights.

A distinct characteristic of South Africa is the strength of its civil society, in general, but especially in nonwhite communities. South African civil society exploded into being after the Soweto revolt in 1976 and developed an enormous strength and breadth from the early 1980s. The umbrella organization, the UDF, rallied together all kinds of organizations, which united under the banner of the 1955 Freedom Charter. As we have seen, one member organization was a gay and lesbian organization in Western Cape.

From 1976 on, the ANC itself and its liberation army received tens of thousands of new recruits, mainly young people from the townships. They had not come from sheltered church-inspired sermons of the good and decent life. In any case the primary arena of liberation in South Africa's case was the cities inside the country. This organizational pluralism had no equivalent in the liberation struggles of Zimbabwe and Namibia. The primary and only important organizations here were the liberation movements themselves: ZANU and the Zimbabwe People's Union ZAPU in Zimbabwe, SWAPO in Namibia.

Because of the forms of struggle in South Africa, the issue of discrimination was on the top of the agenda, and it was the rallying point for a mass movement inside the country. Including gay rights on the civil and human rights agenda did not constitute a big step. The armed liberation struggles in Zimbabwe and Namibia were much more clearly battles for black liberation and were waged in the spirit of one-party rule, where the liberation movement saw itself as representing the people. A vibrant civil society was never the goal in Zimbabwe and Namibia; as far it has developed, it is an incidental result of circumstances.

In addition in all three countries a multiparty system is functioning, but the systems function differently. In Zimbabwe and Namibia the dominant parties (ZANU-PF and SWAPO) are authoritarian, resembling one-party states, and there is relatively weak opposition in the country. If the ANC in South Africa ever dreamed of one-party rule after a victory like that of Mozambique, this was ruled out with Nelson Mandela's reconciliation and compromise line from the mid-1980s. A strong opposition to the dominant parties does not in itself mean support for gay and lesbian liberation, but it increases the chances for having a recognized public space and freedom of expression and association, which can be used by groups outside the mainstream.

In South Africa there is still (in 1998) a euphoria after the liberation from apartheid and the first free elections in 1994. President Mandela has been true to his promise to be a leader of every single South African, and there have been enough small improvements to stave off massive discontent like Zimbabwe's. If moral issues come on the agenda, the increasing crime rate and violence, including rape, are those that are given precedence in South Africa. New South Africa was born as a very pluralist society, with the ANC as the indisputable election winner but far from having a monopoly on power and opinion.

In Namibia and Zimbabwe this pluralism has not had much play. The legal system in Zimbabwe is fairly independent, and there is some freedom of press. But the ruling party is a dominant and authoritarian opinion leader. Both Mugabe and Nujoma draw on Christian doctrine. It is typical of the conservative Christian ideological climate in Zimbabwe that homosexuality, rather than rape, is given precedence as a "morality" issue.

Both in Zimbabwe and Namibia the euphoria of liberation has evaporated, and in both countries social and economic problems plague the government. In Zimbabwe the GALZ issue was clearly used as a scapegoat. When I was in Harare in 1996 I heard many Zimbabweans, in high places and low, ask rhetorical questions about Mugabe like: "What is wrong with the man?" and "Why does he talk about this small group when we can hardly afford food?" One might reply: That is exactly why.

In Namibia, President Nujoma started gay bashing before there was any gay organization to bash. It could not be scapegoating in this case, since the goat had not yet appeared on the scene. But it was, as in Zimbabwe, an effort by the president to rally the nation around the leader, against a horrific "external" enemy, an Other that, he hoped, could not hit back.

Both Zimbabwe and Namibia are dependent on the Western world. Despite political independence, they rely heavily on foreign assistance, a humiliation that is symbolically retaliated against by painting homosexuality as a Western devil. For the gay and lesbian movements, this poses a problem, since the question of representation and race (the position and presence of white and black members) puts itself painfully on the agenda.

The question is how much support there really is for Mugabe's and Nujoma's homophobia and, conversely, for the ANC's antidiscrimination stand. In August 1995 Mugabe said, "What we are being persuaded to accept is sub-animal behaviour and we will never allow it here. If you see people parading themselves as lesbians and gays, arrest them and hand them over to the police."[69] Zimbabwean law is, in fact, unclear about the status of homosexuals, but under common law "unnatural sexual acts" are illegal, with penalties of up to ten years' imprisonment.

Given President Mugabe's persistent efforts to raise homosexuality to the level of a prime national issue, the only reasonable conclusion is that we have in Zimbabwe a case of massive civil disobedience. It is bad enough that the Youth League and the Women's League of the ruling party give governmental sanction to gay bashing. But the general climate is tolerance rather than animosity, as witnessed by the fact that there have been very few assaults. In Namibia, despite ministerial and presidential outbursts, there seems to be little suppression of homosexuals.

In South Africa the constitutional process was an open, transparent, and popular process, in which organizations and individuals were encouraged to take part. It gave gays and lesbians a platform and a reason for uniting. That was not the case in Zimbabwe or Namibia, where (as in most countries) the constitution writing was a matter for lawyers and politicians, without very much public debate.

In South Africa, the constitutional battle was won, but the legal battle remains. Much has been done to raise public awareness and acceptance, and the variety of gay and lesbian movements ensures their continuation as both providers of social space and, when necessary, agitators.

It is difficult to predict the future in any of these countries. What seems certain is that gay and lesbian movements best develop without harassment as part of a wider civil and human rights movement. At the same time, the need for social space will always remain. The dialectics between community and politics will have to be relived again and again.

NOTES

1. Although the debates in Zimbabwe and South Africa have had some effect on Portuguese-speaking Angola and Mozambique, these countries have not had any open debate on homosexuality. In Angola and Mozambique issues of national reconstruction after the apartheid-fueled civil wars have overshadowed most human rights issues, but the introduction of multiparty systems in the beginning of the 1990s opened up possibilities for a more varied and free public debate.

2. For South Africa, an unsurpassed source for the history of the movement is Mark Gevisser and Edwin Cameron, eds., *Defiant Desire: Gay and Lesbian Lives in South Africa* (Johannesburg: Ravan Press, 1994; London: Routledge, 1997). It sketches the history not only of the white gay and lesbian movement but of experiences and organization among nonwhites as well. The following summary account draws heavily on this source. For Zimbabwe I have used Chris Dunton's and my report "Human Rights and Homosexuality in Southern Africa," *Current African Issues* 19 (1996), published by the Nordic Africa Institute, Uppsala, Sweden, as well as information gathered during my visit to Harare in July–August 1996. I have benefited (through personal communication) from insights by Norwegian anthropologist Margrete Aarmo, who stayed with black gays and lesbians during nine months in 1995–96. During six different visits to South Africa (1993–97), I had contact with several gay and lesbian organizations and

individuals and some individual open homosexuals, and I discussed homosexuality with various politicians, among others.

I have also used a variety of news sources, such as dispatches from the Pan-African News Agency (PANA) and other news agencies and newspapers from the whole subregion, particularly the *Weekly Mail and Guardian* (Johannesburg) and the *Independent* (Harare). I have used bulletins from the International Lesbian and Gay Association and the International Gay and Lesbian Human Rights Commission, as well as direct contact with some of the organizations mentioned in this chapter.

Given the short history of gay and lesbian visibility in southern Africa (apart from South Africa), this chapter presents notes and reflections rather than a comprehensive analysis.

3. Gordon Isaacs and Brian McKendrick, *Male Homosexuality in South Africa: Identity, Formation, Culture, and Crisis* (Cape Town: Oxford University Press, 1992), 158.

4. Ibid., 159–60. The reference is to John Alan Lee, "Going Public: A Study in the Sociology of Homosexual Liberation," *Journal of Homosexuality* 3, no. 1(1977): 49–78.

5. On Cape moffie life in the 1950s and 1960s, see Dhiannaraj Chetty, "A Drug at Madame Costello's: Cape Moffie Life in the 1950s and 1960s," in Gevisser and Cameron, *Defiant Desire*, 115–127.

6. The prevailing thinking in the gay and lesbian movement today seems to be that "real" gay and lesbian identity is always innate. I tend to think that the possibility for both heterosexual and homosexual preferences are innate in each individual, a variety of circumstantial and other factors influencing the actual choices.

7. Francis Wilson, *Labor in the South African Gold Mine, 1911–1969* (Cambridge: Cambridge University Press, 1972).

8. The minister, who now resides in Sweden, disclosed this at a seminar at the Nordic Africa Institute in Uppsala, Sweden, in early 1997.

9. Hugh McLean and Linda Ngcobo, "'Abangibhamayo bathi ngimnandi,'" in Gevisser and Cameron, *Defiant Desire*, 158–85.

10. Marc Gevisser, "A Different Fight for Freedom. A History of South African Lesbian and Gay Organization from the 1950s to the 1990s," in Gevisser and Cameron, *Defiant Desire*, 65.

11. Ibid., 32ff.

12. Quoted in Gevisser, "A Different Fight," 33.

13. Ibid., 35.

14. Ibid., 36.

15. Ibid., 37.

16. Ibid., 38.

17. Ibid., 47. Relevant as background is the crisis in the National Party, as well as the need to appease the Calvinist Right while trying to contain the post-Soweto crisis by reforms in collaboration with capital.

18. Gerry Davidson and Ron Nerio, "Gay Publishing in South Africa," in Gevisser and Cameron, *Defiant Desire*, 227.

19. Ibid., 228.

20. Gevisser, "A Different Fight," 30–31.

21. Ibid., p. 79.

22. Ibid., 63.

23. Mary Armour and Sheila Lapinsky, "Lesbians in Love and Compromising Situations," in Gevisser and Cameron, *Defiant Desire*, 298. The original name of the organization was Lesbians and Gays against Oppression (LAGO).

24. "ANC Policy Guidelines for a Democratic South Africa," as adopted at the National Policy Conference, Johannesburg, 28–31 May 1992.

25. The final version of the South African constitution was adopted on 10 December 1996 after an obligatory review by the Constitutional Court.

26. South African Constitution, Chapter Two (as adopted by the Constitutional Assembly on 7 May and the Parliament on 8 May 1996).

27. Constitutional Assembly. Submissions Pack, 4th edition, 20 March 1996, 6.

28. Gevisser, "A Different Fight," 75–76.

29. This was the text of a poster outside the court. See Rachel Holmes, "White Rapists Made Coloureds (and Homosexuals): The Winnie Mandela Trial and the Politics of Race and Sexuality," in Gevisser and Cameron, *Defiant Desire*, 284–94.

30. *Equality* (Johannesburg), no. 2 (July–September 1995): 4–5.

31. Quoted in *Weekly Mail and Guardian*, 5 September 1997.

32. Gevisser and Cameron, *Defiant Desire*, 70.

33. Ibid., 76.

34. Foreword to *Aliens in the Household of God: Homosexuality and Christian Faith in South Africa*, ed. Paul Germond and Steve de Gruchy (Cape Town: David Philip, 1997).

35. This date is contested; 1990 and 1991 have been variously given by GALZ members as the founding year.

36. This information came from personal communication with Stephen van Breda, Harare.

37. *Mmegi/The Reporter* (Gaborone), 12, no. 32, 18–24 August 1995.

38. Stephen Johnson, Report to the PASA Executive, 16 August 1995.

39. Bornwell Chakaodza, director of information, Ministry of Information, Posts and Telecommunications. Letter to Trish Mbanga, executive director of the Zimbabwe International Book Fair, 24 July 1995.

40. Resolution passed at the book bair *indaba*, 28 July 1995.

41. Quoted in Lewis Macipisa, "Human Rights: President Lashes Out at Gays," *IPS [Inter-Press Service] Africa*, 18 August 1995.

42. Quoted in *Free Press* 5 (1995): 12, published by the Media Institute of Southern Africa, Windhoek.

43. Quoted in the *New York Times*, 2 August 1995.

44. South African News Agency (SAFA), in the British Broadcasting Corporation's (BBC) Summary of World Broadcasts, 3 August 1995.

45. Reuters News Agency. Published in the *Globe and Mail* (Toronto), 12 August 1995, and the *Herald* (Harare), 12 August 1995.

46. Quoted in *IPS Africa*, 18 August 1995.

47. *Sunday News,* 3 September 1995.

48. *Southscan* (London), 18 August 1995.

49. Peter Vale, "Gay People Changed the Region," *Mail and Guardian,* 6–12 October 1995.

50. ZIBF Trust statement, circulated to the Swedish International Development Authority (SIDA), Apnet, Sabdet, Norad, HIVOS, NOVIB, PASA, and the resigned trustees, 14 September 1995.

51. GALZ, *Sahwira: Being Gay and Lesbian in Zimbabwe,* 1996 (distributed by GALZ, Private Bag A 6131, Avondale, Harare).

52. *The Herald* 31 July 1996, 11.

53. Sensational international mass media reporting during the fair, speaking of "attacks" and the like, often gave the opposite impression. See my "Harare Reports," e-mailed from Harare daily during the 1996 fair, and the revised edition of Chris Dunton's and my "Human Rights and Homosexuality in Southern Africa" (both published by the Nordic Africa Institute, Uppsala, Sweden, 1996.

54. *The Herald,* 24 July 1996.

55. *Sunday Mail,* 28 July 1996.

56. *The Herald,* 29 July 1996.

57. *The Herald,* 25 July 1996.

58. The disclosure was made by lawyers defending a man accused of police murder, who was described as having been traumatized by President Banana's repeated sexual exploitation of him. Banana had chosen him as his aide when he watched football.

59. A previous black organization—Zimbabwe Indigenous Gay and Lesbian Association—is reported to have existed among the black bourgeoisie and higher civil servants. It is difficult to establish whether the group existed, since it was reportedly clandestine, with its members desperately protecting their invisibility as homosexuals.

60. Fred Mwilima, "Homosexuality Is like Cancer or the AIDS scourge: Hishongwa Blasts Gays," *New Era,* 5–11 October 1995.

61. Moses/Gowaseb, "Tired of Marginalisation, They Plan to Go It Alone: Lesbians, Gays to Erect Own Church," *New Era,* 13–19 July 1995.

62. "Sister Roars Back on Gay Rights," *The Namibian,* 10 October 1995.

63. Wolfram Hartmann, Andre du Pisani, and James Steakley, "The Politics of Ostracism," Opinion, *The Namibian,* 17 November 1995.

64. Ibid.

65. An unnamed "African guest" at the congress was quoted in the *Windhoek Adviser,* 12 December 1996, as having heard the remark.

66. *Mail and Guardian,* 14 February 1997.

67. Journalists' Association of Namibia, press release, 3 February 1997.

68. Mr. Chigdwedere (Anias-Wedza), Zimbabwe Parliamentary debate, 28 September 1995.

69. Quoted by Associated Press and Reuters News Service, as broadcast on "This Way Out," program 386, distributed 21 August 1995.

WIM LUNSING

12   Japan: Finding Its Way?

THE EARLY 1970s brought the first recorded attempts at lesbian and gay political organization in Japan, but the impact was limited. In the 1980s new organizations were founded, and by the 1990s their influence had become strong enough to make a major impact. From the early 1990s onward lesbian and gay groups and individuals gained much media attention and began to work with politicians and bureaucrats in matters concerning AIDS and discrimination against homosexuals. The political and cultural environment had long been thought to prohibit such activities, but the response was not the homophobic, violent reaction many lesbian and gay people had feared. It has been suggested that the considerable upheaval in parliamentary politics in the early 1990s created an environment of new possibilities. Foreign influence and the media also played their roles in promoting gay and lesbian activity. But we still might ask What prevented lesbian and gay people from coming out until recently, and what caused the changes in the attitudes of the mass media and the general public toward homosexuality?[1]

ATTITUDES TOWARD AND CONSTRUCTIONS OF HOMOSEXUALITY

Historical evidence of homosexuality in Japan has often been interpreted as indicating that Japanese culture has been tolerant of homosexuality (Leupp 1995). However, even during the Edo period (1603–1868), when homosexuality is thought to have flourished most abundantly, it met with prohibition from time to time, depending on the whim of the shogun in power. In these cases, homosexuality was cast as disruptive to the social order, similar to heterosexual activity outside marriage, particularly prostitution. In this context the appropriate place for sex was in marriage, with the goal of procreation—a goal that came to be stressed more at the end of the period, at the expense of sex for the sake of pleasure (LaFleur 1992). All other sexual activities could fall under the term of *asobi* (play), and although play was not necessarily seen as reprehensible, it could become so if it interfered with the duties of those involved: duties toward the family, the community, and the state. Homosexuality could be condoned as long as it remained either limited to clearly identifiable individuals or to clearly identified contexts, both of which would have to have little or no influence on the existing social order.

Two constructions that existed simultaneously during this period were men loving young men or boys and men loving feminine men, which is mirrored by the construction of female homosexuality as women loving masculine women. In both cases the cross-gender person—that is, the feminine man or the masculine woman—rather than those who loved them, was marked as being different.[2]

The general attitude toward homosexuality was that as long as people engaged in it discreetly, it need not interfere with the rest of their lives. This attitude is also reflected in gay magazines like *Barazoku,* in the writings of readers who state that they have fulfilled their duties—that is, that they have married and fathered children—and therefore are free to engage in homosexual activity. Homosexual activity was allowed as long as it remained a private entertainment and as long as those practicing it married properly. This is comparable to the tolerance toward married men who have affairs with women, which has only lately become a focus of criticism (Lunsing 1995, forthcoming b).

Children are taught at an early age that they should avoid being too different from others and that they must be cooperative within the family. Sanctions include denying them entry into the house (Hendry 1986), thus stressing the importance of group membership over individual difference and instilling the fear of ostracism. In kindergarten, children are taught to behave in accordance with each situation; learning that they may be wild and noisy in one context but must be subdued in another (Tobin 1992: 21–39) prepares them for a life of compartmentalization. In elementary schools, harmony and cooperation are key words in children's social education (White 1987). This, again, stresses that children should not be too different from others, since that could lead to disharmony. Notwithstanding efforts by the bureaucracy to change the system to allow for more individuality and creativity (Lock 1992: 98–125), in the high schools attention remains largely directed toward rote learning. Since entrance into one of Japan's highest-ranking universities is the path to a successful career, rote learning in preparation for the entrance examinations remains the priority for students. Space for discussion is nearly nonexistent (White 1987), which reinforces the idea that discussion is a manifestation of lack of harmony and is preferably avoided. Again, this emphasizes the idea of conformity. The exception is the difference between boys and girls or men and women, which is stressed throughout most of Japanese education to an extent rarely found elsewhere (Brinton 1993: 189–221).

Although Japanese education is certainly not designed to keep children from growing up to be gay or lesbian—this possibility being neglected altogether—the stress on harmony and cooperation and the lack of development of skills for discussion and creative thinking can be detrimental to people who are not in agreement with the general perception. Since being different is something that is to be avoided, homophobia is implicitly internalized, often at an age when children are not yet even aware of the existence of homosexuality. Belonging to a group, whether to one's family or one's place of employment, is stressed over expressing personal difference. The emphasis on cooperation and harmony is most likely to amount to an emphasis on conformity. In order to maintain the feeling of belonging (Lebra 1976), instilled so early in life, people tend to conform to the groups to which they wish to belong, foremost the family and the workplace. To be openly gay or lesbian in such contexts contradicts everything people have been educated to be.

Japanese indigenous psychiatry stresses cooperation over individuality. Contrary to the Freudian emphasis on discovering the psychological problems that may have led to mental disorder, the Naikan therapy stresses the need to be cooperative and refrain from causing problems for one's family or one's outside environment by behaving oddly. Mental disorder is treated by encouraging people to suppress feelings that disagree with social norms (Murase 1986: 388–98). The Morita therapy, rather than endeavoring to search for causes or fight symptoms, teaches patients to accept their disorder. This therapy seems to be little practiced today, but aspects of it have found their way into general psychiatric and psychological practices (Kasahara 1986). Western psychiatry has influenced Japan; in accordance with the American Psychiatric Association's 1973 decision to discontinue its characterization of homosexuality as a mental illness (Ueno 1992), people sent to a psychiatrist or psychologist because of their homosexuality have been told that they should be happy to be able to have interesting experiences that most people cannot have.

While in general, the structure of Japanese society denies gay and lesbian people the possibility to live gay and lesbian lifestyles, popular conceptions do not explicitly condemn or even criticize homosexuality as such. Instead, they ignore its very existence. Recovering from the silence surrounding homosexuality has been a major goal for lesbian and gay activists from the beginning. A condition fostering participation in gay and lesbian organization is certainly a positive evaluation of one's homosexuality. The Japanese situation, however, largely prevented this, because there was no concept of a lifestyle other than heterosexual marriage. Furthermore, the general emphasis on the importance of refraining from being different, which emanated from the value attached to harmony and cooperation, functioned to isolate people with homosexual desire.

Thus, it should be no surprise that there has been much fear that being openly gay or lesbian could be harmful. Fushimi Noriaki[3] was one of the first gay men, other than television personalities, to come out as gay on Japanese television. The publication of his first book, entitled *Private Gay Life* (Fushimi 1991), led to widespread reaction from young, often isolated, gay men throughout the country. Lesbian informants often pointed to the case of singer Sagara Naomi, who was outed as lesbian[4] by a former lover in the 1970s. As a result, her career was ruined, and until 1992 lesbians saw this incident as proof that coming out was "not possible" in Japan. In 1992, however, Kakefuda Hiroko published her book on being lesbian (Kakefuda 1992). Fearing negative and possibly violent reaction, she went into hiding. The book did not cause the uproar feared, and Kakefuda appears to have led the way for many lesbians, especially young ones, to come out in the mass media or their own environment. What seems to play a role here is the value of honesty and openness, also present in Japanese education; in Japanese it is represented by the words *sunao* (honest) and *honne* (true inner feelings). Although these values may not encourage people to be different, they can help people explain coming out as gay or lesbian in a positive way: that one is being honest and open about oneself.

Starting with a 1991 special feature by the women's magazine *Crea* on gay men's popularity with young women, and fueled by gay and lesbian people coming out, the visibility of homosexuality in Japan has increased enormously—with mainstream movies, books, and almost every magazine featuring articles, if not complete special theme issues, on homosexuality. The fact that women's magazines initiated this publicity is most likely related to the popularity of stories featuring gay male characters in *shōjo manga* (girls' comics) from the 1970s onward (Aoyama 1988: 186–204; Matsui 1993: 177–96; Lunsing 1997, forthcoming b). The commentary in this so-called gay boom is usually supportive toward homosexuality. It presents gay men and lesbians as very interesting and, especially in the case of men, good-looking. Notwithstanding criticism by gay and lesbian activists that these are misrepresentations, the boom has also given gays and lesbians the opportunity to express their ideas in mainstream media and to publish books (Lunsing 1997, forthcoming a, b).

In academic circles, homosexuality is generally ignored as a subject of investigation, but this arena seems to be changing as well. A book on homosexuality, based on a survey taken in the 1950s, showed that many respondents were having difficulty establishing a lifestyle other than heterosexual marriage and were experiencing feelings of loneliness (Ōta 1987).[5] Eexcept for some questionable material, mostly by psychologists who failed to note the bias in their samples or who apparently combined work straight from their imaginations with outdated western material, there was no further academic publishing on the subject for quite some time.[6]

There are no openly gay and lesbian scholars who work on gay and lesbian themes. Some heterosexual scholars, mainly of law, have lately become active in this field (Ninomiya 1991), providing some legitimation to the discussion of homosexuality as a serious subject. Until recently it was generally believed that if gay and lesbian scholars were active in gay and lesbian studies, a strong negative reaction would result. Not much of a reaction materialized when some gay professors came out, but those who wish to engage in gay studies fear that other scholars might not accept their work as academically valid for a subject in which they are personally involved. The fear is that others will not believe in their objectivity.[7] There has, however, been an increase in the number of people engaging in lesbian and gay studies, the number of courses on sexuality at Japanese universities, and the number of students who write theses on homosexuality.

Discrimination against lesbian and gay people is most clearly visible in the fields of housing and work. Two men wanting to live together beyond student age, although seen as an acceptable circumstance for financial reasons, are often rejected by landlords. In the case of two women wanting to live together, there is less of a problem. Because women are expected to have more difficulty making ends meet, their cohabitation for financial reasons is more readily accepted (Lunsing forthcoming a, b).

In employment, banking is often singled out as an occupation in which gay men do not fare well. The problem there is not so much homosexuality as the fact that gay people may not want to marry. An unmarried man may not be trusted to deal with large sums of money, because he is not tied down by obligations to a wife and children; therefore he is seen as someone who can, at any time, "take the money and run" (Lunsing 1995, forthcoming a). In other high corporate occupations, the picture is not much different. In Japan there are few occasions in which a male employee is expected to attend social meetings accompanied by his wife, as occurs more frequently in Western contexts. The prejudice is, instead, that someone who has not assumed the duties of taking (financial) care of a family cannot be trusted to be stable and that someone in a managerial position needs a wife who takes care of all household tasks and keeps him well-fed, well-dressed, and emotionally stable.

These problems play less of a role in the case of women, who are blatantly discriminated against in the labor market, regardless of whether they are married or not—notwithstanding the Equal Employment Opportunity Law, which took effect in 1986. The law led to a double career track for women: a subservient track in which they have no career but do

odd jobs like copying and making tea and are expected to retire upon
marriage or childbirth[8] and an elite track in which they are expected to
work like men, including overtime, transfers, and such. Most women end
up in the dead-end track (Lam 1992). Not being married may actually be
an advantage for women in the career track, because having a husband
and children could compromise their work life. I even came across the
case of a small company whose management reacted positively when a female employee divorced, because it meant that she would continue to
work (Lunsing forthcoming b).

Public and social condemnation of homosexuality remains largely limited to people who speak of it as repulsive in general terms. My experience, like that of many informants, is that such negative remarks do not
necessarily represent strong inner negative feelings about homosexuality.
It appears that speaking negatively of homosexuality is a habit that can
be easily broken, once knowledge replaces prejudice. If people know gay
or lesbian people in their own environment, they often start to take a genuine interest. Whereas they may join the general behavior of making jokes
about homosexuality when it is distant, which is the case when it appears
on television or in magazines, once they are confronted with homosexuality in daily life, their attitudes are likely to change for the positive, as all
surveys indicate (Hirosawa and Rezubian Ripōto Han 1991: 227;
Taniguchi 1992: 76–86; Ugoku Gei to Rezubian no Kai 1992: 336–338;
Lunsing forthcoming b).[9] Following Fushimi Noriaki and Kakefuda Hiroko, people started coming out in ever increasing numbers, not only in
the mass media but, more important, in their daily lives as well. Adverse
reactions remain limited. It appears that the example of two people who
dared to do what nobody thought feasible—come out—led the way for
many others and had a major influence in Japan.

RELIGION

Japan's major religion, Buddhism, is generally thought to be tolerant
and at times supportive of homosexuality. Historically, there are the
Chigo Monogatari (Stories of Novices) about beautiful adolescents or
boys who were loved by adult monks. It is not clear whether these stories were based on actually occurring behavior or whether they were
used as sermons (Childs 1980), but historians generally believe that homosexual activity was common among Buddhist monks (Watanabe and
Iwata 1987; Leupp 1995). The new Buddhist sect Sōka Gakkai, founded
in the late nineteenth century, even has a gay and lesbian network, condoned by its honorary president, Ikeda Daisaku (Lunsing forthcoming
b). Although the new sects are very active and, apart from the Sōka

Gakkai, usually very conservative, institutionalized Buddhism in general has little bearing on people's lives when it comes to providing moral or any other guidelines. It has come to occupy itself predominantly with services for the dead, which is the main source of income for the temples.[10] What remains of the influence of Buddhism is the provision of a general world view of people's lives as being directed by their karma, a view that sees people as having to put up with their lot and not rebel against it.

The new sects, in general, condemn homosexuality for reasons similar to those of many Christian groups in Western countries and because it conflicts with the high value they attach to heterosexual marriage as the pillar of society. They also tend to support the idea that a woman's place is in the home, as caretaker of her husband's basic needs and as educator of the children (Hardacre 1984), which obviously conflicts with women wishing to maintain an independent or lesbian lifestyle. The sect Seichōno Ie (House of Growth) has been politically influential because of links with conservative and nationalist elements of the ruling party, Jimintō—Liberal Democratic Party, or LDP (Buckley and Mackie 1986: 173–85)—which governed Japan during most of the postwar period. Other sects, such as Risshō Kōseikai (Resurrection Church) also have their connections to LDP factions or politicians.[11] Although they may oppose each other within the LDP, their common goal is to oppose Sōka Gakkai (Sone 1989: 259–95), which is closely related to the Kōmeitō (commonly rendered as Clean Government Party) a political party founded by its members.

In combination, the new sects and the LDP advocate Japanese nationalism in what seems to be a return to the prewar ideology of the state as one big family, with the emperor as the patriarch to whom all other households are related and subordinated.[12] This ideology is particularly detrimental to the position of women, who are cast in the role of providing all sorts of social services, including taking care of the sick and the needy, in particular their husbands' parents and more recently also their own.[13] The whole gamut of social problems, from juvenile delinquency to loneliness and suicide among the elderly, is attributed to a decrease in family values, which in particular refers to the failure of housewives to do their "duty" (Lock 1992: 98–125). Such rhetoric seems to have reached a pinnacle in the middle of the 1980s, when Nakasone Yasuhiro was prime minister (Buckley and Mackie 1986: 173–85). Reaction, however, was strong; the 1980s saw a surge in groups questioning the centrality of marriage to society[14] and a considerable increase in people who remained unmarried (Lunsing forthcoming b).

POLITICS

Japanese parliamentary politics is characterized by efforts to reach consensus as well as by factionalism. Many pressure groups feel free to alternately make behind-the-scenes shady deals with politicians in power and participate in street riots or demonstrations. This contradicts the common perception of Japanese politics as based on those in power harmoniously working together with little opposition (Stockwin 1982). The Japanese political system has been called a one-and-a-half party system (Baerwald 1979: 21–63), with the Jimintō always in power but nevertheless responsive to the demands of the major opposition party, the Shakaitō (Socialist Party, [of Japan], or SPJ), as well as to those of other parties, because failure to listen would lead the Jimintō to be criticized for misusing its powers and failing to cooperate (Baerwald 1979). Moreover, cooperation with opposition parties was necessary from the 1970s on, because the majority that the LDP commanded was not large enough to make major legislative changes (Curtis 1988).

In the early 1970s a progressive group broke off from the SPJ to found a new party, the Shamintō (Democratic Socialist Party, or DSP). This party provides a haven for intellectual voters whose numbers are small. The Kyōsantō (Communist Party, or CPJ) distanced itself from Marxist ideologies as employed in China and the Soviet Union (Curtis 1988) but, nevertheless, lost most of its voters after the Tiananmen massacre in Beijing in 1989. The third party of Japan, founded in the late 1960s, was the previously mentioned Kōmeitō. Founded by members of the Buddhist sect Sōka Gakkai, it later tried to distance itself from the sect in order to win greater support from the electorate. The separation had little effect. The party's base remained stable and, as the third party of Japan, the governing LDP listened to its demands, just as it did to those of the SPJ.

Apart from the major election victory of Nakasone in 1986, the LDP has been in decline since the 1960s, failing to gain more than 40 percent of the vote. It was able to hold onto a majority in both houses thanks to the district system, which gives an advantage to voters in rural areas (Curtis 1988). The Nakasone phenomenon was followed by a major upset of LDP power, when the Socialist Party's popular first-ever female leader, Doi Takako, led her party to a victory in the Upper House elections in 1989. This was, however, not repeated; after Doi quit her chairship, the SPJ went into a decline and everything seemed to be back to "normal" (Stockwin 1994). But this victory made it clear, that the Japanese electorate was displeased with the way it was governed, with the moral policies advocated by Nakasone, and probably most of all with the new 3 percent consumption tax, which was the major issue of the elections. Some informants reported that they did not want to pay more taxes because they did not see the money being put to good use. The SPJ was the major opponent of the tax.

In response to its loss, in 1989 the LDP, which was in disarray because of bribery scandals, selected a reformist prime minister, Kaifū Toshiki. He tried to reform the Japanese political system but because he lacked a power base in the form of a strong faction, his efforts were fruitless (Abe, Shidō, and Kawato 1994). In 1993 what nobody had thought possible happened. The LDP lost its majority in both houses, and for the first time since the 1940s a government was formed without it or its predecessors. Successive bribery scandals, in which most LDP and some SPJ members of Parliament were involved, thoroughly destroyed the image of the LDP and damaged the image of the SPJ (Iritani 1994). The Japanese electorate wanted something new, and that is what the people got, at least in name: a range of parties that called themselves "new" and promised to make a change won a considerable number of seats (Iwami 1995). Even before the elections, LDP members had left to found new parties and still other parties were founded in the run-up. Most notable of these was the Nihon Shintō (New Japan Party) founded in May 1992, which produced prime minister Hosokawa Morihiro of the cabinet that took office after elections including most other parties but excluding the Communists and the LDP.[15]

What followed were years of political turmoil, with coalitions following each other and new parties being founded and parties merging and splitting at a high pace. Every new coalition government promised to democratize the election system and to prevent more bribery scandals, but in the end little has been achieved. This has been attributed to the fact that changes are not in the interest of the majority of politicians (Jain 1995). In the autumn of 1996 the LDP returned to power under the new strong and popular leader, Hashimoto Ryūtarō, who is pushing for reform of the administration. Meanwhile, the newly formed Shinshintō (New Frontier Party) became the largest opposition party. The reforms the parties are proposing may eventually come about, but so far the major change in Japanese parliamentary politics seems to be the change from party factionalism to the founding of new parties when a faction lacks power. Most of the new parties were founded by former LDP members, making it look very much like old wine in new bottles. The Japanese public appears to have grown apathetic to party politics (Jain 1995) and to have lost faith that politicians will keep their election campaign promises. Politicians are widely seen as corrupt and distant from the population's needs. The general disarray of Japanese party politics leaves debates on social and moral matters largely to the media and the public.

MOVEMENTS

General attitudes toward movements and political activity in Japan are not very positive either. The concept of movement (*undō*) is unpopular. One gay informant, who agreed that something should be done to promote the position of gay and lesbian people, was adamant that this "something" should not be a movement. His image of the concept of movement stemmed from media coverage of the *buraku* movement, the movement that strives to improve the living circumstances of *burakumin*, a Japanese social outcast group.[16] He disagreed with the *buraku* movement's policy of attacking individuals for discriminating statements, which in some cases has ruined the lives of schoolteachers and others. As a result, the *buraku* problem has become something most Japanese avoid discussing, afraid that they might say something wrong (Pharr 1990).

Among lesbian informants, some had negative images of the concept of movement, stemming from images of the women's liberation movement of the 1970s. This is partly due to the way it was ridiculed by the press. Some of the movement's activities invited criticism, however. Two informants remembered, for instance, the New Year's Eve that Chūpiren, a radical group that advocated free use of the birth control pill, stormed the stage of "Kōhaku Uta Gassen," a popular live television show, and demanded equal rights for women. The strategy backfired enormously, and the leader of Chūpiren, who has been accused by other feminists of being an agent of the pharmaceutical industry because of her unconditional advocacy of the use of the pill, quit all her activities shortly thereafter (Akiyama 1991).

Probably Japan's best-known gay and lesbian organization—Occur: Ugoku Gei to Rezubian no Kai (Group of Moving Gays and Lesbians)—was refused access to the Fuchū Seinen no Ie, a youth hostel in suburban Tokyo, in 1988. The reason given was that heterosexual people were not allowed to share rooms with people they could have sex with—people of the opposite sex. Therefore gay people could not be accommodated, because they would all have to have separate rooms in order to eliminate the opportunity for them to have sex. When Occur had stayed in the Fuchū Seinen no Ie previously, the group had stated in the group leaders' meeting, in which groups introduce themselves to each other, that it was a gay organization.[17] This had caused problems with other groups and, apparently, with the staff of the youth hostel, which is under the auspices of the Tokyo Metropolitan Government. After a period of deliberation, considering whether it would make the group look vindictive and how the media would react, Occur took this case to court. It did not expect to win but hoped to gain supportive media attention. The trial took years, but in

1994 Occur won the case.[18] The Metropolitan Government of Tokyo appealed but lost again in a 1997 court ruling ("Gays Win Suit" 1997).

Although Occur won the—often tacit—support of many gay men and lesbians, others thought that the group was making much ado about nothing. This reflects the general attitude among the Japanese toward making use of the law to further one's goals (Hendry 1987). Disputes are preferably, and mostly, solved by reaching consensus between the parties before going to court (Upham 1987). Discrimination, especially, is not seen as something that can be solved by law, because it "is a matter of the heart".[19] The Equal Employment Opportunity Law condemns discrimination against hiring women but lacks sanctions, leaving them to companies and their employees (Lam 1992). Japan has no laws dealing with homosexuality in particular; for a brief period there was a law condemning homosexuality, but it was little used and abolished a short time later (Furukawa 1992). The absence of jurisprudence may reflect, on one side, the idea that homosexual activity is not considered a large enough danger to the social order to merit litigation and, on the other, the general Japanese attitude of dealing with complicated matters by neglecting them altogether. Many lesbian and gay people resign themselves to the niches that Japanese society provides for them, rather than risk the exposure and possible backlash that might result from political activity. The lesson that they should not stick out as different apparently had its effect.

GAY AND LESBIAN ORGANIZATIONS

The earliest evidence of gay organizations that I have come across, beyond circles of friends, stems from the 1950s. These groups were involved in social activities. One group, Adonisu no Kai (Adonis Group), is especially well documented, because many of its members participated in a survey.[20] In the late 1960s Tōgō Ken became an activist. He quit his job with his bank and deserted his wife, who refused to consent to a divorce.[21] Since 1971 Tōgō has participated in national elections as a gay candidate, but he has never won a seat. At present he is engaged in a court battle over the importation of pornography (the first round of which he won)[22] and in theatrical activities. His election platform, Zatsumin no Kai (Group of Miscellaneous People), is still in existence, but its activities are mostly social.

In the 1970s there were a number of groups of gay men, whose activities are rather obscure. A network of groups established through the first gay magazine, *Barazoku*, existed for some time but disappeared without making a lasting impression. The same is true for other groups of the 1970s, such as Furontoranā, or Frontrunners, and Puratonika, or Platonica (Kuia

Sutadiizu Henshū Iinkai 1996: 18–35). Informants who participated in the *Barazoku*-related network said that the main activity was drinking together. Individual activity also took place, with for instance, Ōtsuka Takashi hosting a weekly segment on homosexuality on a popular radio program in 1978 and 1979. According to Ōtsuka, who now runs a gay bar, writes for the gay magazine *Badi,* and recently published a book on his life in Shinjuku Nichōme (Ōtsuka 1995), the program had no impact whatsoever.

In 1984 the president of the International Lesbian and Gay Association (ILGA) traveled to Japan to meet Minami Teishirō, publisher of the gay magazine *Adon.* Minami had been married but somewhere along the way decided that he wished to be openly gay. After he started publishing his gay magazine, he wanted to become involved in political activities, but he did not know how. Minami, the president of ILGA, and a third man founded JILGA, which was set up as the Japanese branch of ILGA (Minami 1991: 124–32). Making use of his magazine, Minami assembled young people who were eager to engage in political activity. They proved too eager for some of JILGA's older members, however, and a split became inevitable. In 1986[23] Occur was founded by the young members. Minami tried to set up branches of JILGA in other parts of Japan, with mixed success. A branch was founded in Osaka, but, disagreeing with Minami and his authoritarian ways of communication, the Osaka people split off. In 1987, Osaka Gay Community (OGC) was founded.

A later effort by Minami to set up a group to counter the government policy on AIDS in Kobe, close to Osaka, ended in fights at the first meeting. Nevertheless, a gay social group was founded as a result. It later branched out into various groups, each with its own agenda. One engaged in outdoor activities, another in eating gourmet meals in restaurants. In 1985 the group Kamigata DJ Club,[24] was founded independently to make audio cassettes similar to radio programs, which are distributed to gay men throughout Japan. In 1989 the group Sākuru T (Circle T) was founded by students of Kansai University to discuss homosexuality on a personal level.

In 1991, because members of all these groups wished to become politically involved, Puapua was founded. Its first activity was to criticize the Osaka prefectural government for its new policy on pornography, which prohibited the sale of homosexual pornographic material in shops where it could be purchased by minors. The regulation was directed at lesbian pornography, which targets heterosexual male consumers, but because the regulation specifies homosexual pornography, it endangers the distribution of gay magazines. Another point of critique was that homosexuality was referred to as "unhealthy." The successor of Puapua, Gay Front

Kansai, saw victory in 1995, when the ruling was amended to comply with the group's wishes (Hattori 1996). Gay Front Kansai was founded by members of Puapua, Kamigata DJ Club, and Circle T in 1993, in order to streamline activities and improve the exchange of information and members' access to the various groups' activities.

In Tokyo, meanwhile, the situation was reversed. First Occur left JILGA, which thereupon assembled new members. Occur subsequently dismissed a number of its members who were not prepared to follow the leadership. Most of JILGA's new members in 1994 did not wish to work with Minami any longer and continued their activities separately. Activities include meetings in which personal matters are discussed (Together), the organization of a yearly gay and lesbian film festival, and the staging of theater shows (Flying Stage).

Minami again assembled young people around his JILGA. They organized the first Lesbian and Gay Parade in Tokyo on 28 August 1994. According to organizers, it drew 1,134 participants, many of them young lesbians (Satō 1994). The second parade, in 1995, drew 2,156 participants, according to an organizer. The organizers disagreed with Minami about the character of the parade: political with a stress on banners carrying political messages (Minami) versus more festive (the others). This battle was fought over the money the organizers received from a sponsor—the Seagram distillery, which in Japan was said to be a subsidiary of the huge corporation Kirin. For some time it seemed that there were going to be two separate parades in 1996, but this did not happen. A parade was organized by Minami's group and drew about 1,200 participants in August 1996, according to Ōtsuka Takashi (personal communication). A parade organized by Sapporo Meeting, a group related to JILGA, was also held for the first time in Sapporo in June 1996. Informants said that it drew about 300 participants. It has been reported that a fourth parade in Tokyo in August 1997 drew roughly 40 participants. Lesbians organized a Daiku no Hi (Dyke Day) on the national holiday Taiiku no Hi (Physical Education Day) on 10 October 1997; it drew about 200 participants and received much media attention.

The membership figures for the various groups are difficult to establish. Occur and JILGA claimed 200 people each in 1991, and by 1995 Occur claimed to have grown to about 350, but these figures must be viewed with caution. A member's involvement may be limited to donating money or reading the organization's publications. The general volatility of new groups being established and others disappearing and of groups splitting up and combining makes any figures tentative. A list of groups assembled in 1994 by Satō Masaki and others connected with *Kick Out*,[25] a small-scale noncommercial magazine—in Japanese called *minikomi*, as opposed to *masukomi* (mass media) lists thirty-three organizations. These vary from purely social groups to groups engaging mostly in the publication of a newsletter to groups with specific goals like organizing film festivals. It includes a group of deaf gay men, a group of Asian (that is, southeast Asian, Korean, and Chinese) gay men, and a private gay and lesbian library in Nagoya. Social groups usually do not have a membership system. They list the number of staff and the average number of participants per event.

Typically, the list does not include JILGA and Occur, both of which tend to see themselves as the major gay movement of Japan but relate little to the others. Some groups I am familiar with are also not listed. The proliferation of groups is so enormous that it is next to impossible to know them all.[26] Membership numbers in Kick Out's list vary from 5, for Hōsei Boys Club, a group of students from Hōsei University, to 390, the number on the mailing list for OGC. Gay Front Kansai was said to have 70 members, which by the beginning of 1996 had increased to about 100, according to that group's estimate. Largest are the computer networks, such as Lovin', with 400 members, and YB-Communication, with 550. Ultra-Camp Gays and Lesbians of Pleasure (UC-GALOP) did not provide a number (Satō et al. 1994), but its founder said that in 1996 about 2,000 people participated. Apart from providing its members with access to each other through the computer network, this group organizes parties and, occasionally, trips for members and others who are interested.

A feature of many of the groups discussed above is that they do not consist only of gay men; they usually include bisexual men, often lesbians, less commonly transsexuals and transvestites, and in quite a number of cases heterosexuals, particularly women. Women are most common in groups that have a political agenda.

Notwithstanding the prevalent idea that lesbians had little influence within Japanese feminist circles (Ueno 1991: 120–23), many lesbians have engaged in feminist activities. But even in the early 1990s some of them said that they did not think of coming out as lesbian in their feminist groups. They thought that the other women would not "understand" and would think that they were weird, which would weaken their position in their groups. Even in the most radical feminist group I investigated— Pāpuru: Sei Bōryoku o Yurusanai Onna no Kai (Purple: Women's Group against Sexual Violence)—sexuality was not discussed, despite the fact that the group's main project concerned sexual harassment (Lunsing forthcoming b).

The earliest lesbian organization known to me, Wakakusa no Kai (Group of Young Grass) was founded in the 1970s. A nationwide network of women who went hiking together, it tried to produce a newsletter, *Ibu &*

Ibu (Eve & Eve), but that was soon aborted because of a shortage of readers (Hirosawa 1991). Lesbian organizations may even be more volatile than male-dominated ones. Women of Regumi (Le [for "lesbian"] Group) said that it does not have members and that anyone who comes with an idea can use the name Regumi and its facilities. One of its major activities is publishing its newsletter, *Regumi Tsūshin*, started in 1985 (Hisada 1991). Regumi was founded by women of various backgrounds: some frequented the lesbian bars in Tokyo; others were involved in feminist activities.

In an Osaka coffeeshop called Furiiku (Freak), a group of women assembled in 1987 under the name Furiiku no Atsumari (Freak Meeting). From that group the YLP (Yancha [tomboy] Lesbian Power) eventually developed (Watanabe 1990: 184–89). In 1993 the YLP changed its name to OLP, with the "O" standing for *otona*, "adult"; for *ōki na*, "large"; for Osaka (OLP 1994), which is its main base; and for *ōpun na*, "open" (OLP 1997). OLP's activities include studying books on sexuality and providing information about being lesbian in relation to society, mainly at women's gatherings. In 1996 one of the group's central figures estimated membership at about 140 women.

Apart from these organizations, there is also the ALN (Asian Lesbian Network), which organized the Asian Lesbian Conference in 1993 in Japan. It is supported by people related to Regumi as well as to OLP and others. In addition there is an internationally oriented group called Kokusai Bian Renmei (International Bian [from "lesbian"] League), which is oriented toward social activities. Kakefuda Hiroko made a list of all lesbian organizations throughout Japan known to her. The total was twenty-nine, including a group of lesbian mothers, bisexual groups, and a group that organizes monthly parties at a club in Osaka (Kakefuda 1995). The last issue of Kakefuda's publication *Labrys* was sent to 1,657 people in all prefectures of Japan. Kakefuda decided to cease publication, believing that it had served its purpose of bringing lesbians into contact with each other, but others continued the service with a followup publication, *Labrys Dasshu*.

There has been a striking increase in lesbians who are involved in lesbian and gay activism. Kakefuda Hiroko even speaks of a "lesbian boom" in 1994, following the gay boom that started in 1991. Whereas Occur tends to keep its lesbian members out of the picture and Minami has little appeal for women, in other gay organizations throughout Japan, lesbians are commonly taking part in activities.

Although the combining and separating of groups may be similar to what is happening in Japanese politics, lately there seems to be a trend toward cooperating more and toward overcoming the power-oriented facets. In Tokyo a loose network, independent of JILGA and Occur, which interacts with groups in the Kansai area and elsewhere, has developed. It consists of not only lesbian and gay people but also all sorts of people who disagree with the general idea that heterosexual marriage and the family are the pillar of society and need to be protected against other lifestyles. People often visit other groups, and discussion is very open. One of the best-known places in this context is probably Artscape in Kyoto, a house given in use by a retired university professor to artists and others involved in activities concerning sexuality and AIDS. It has become a base for developing activities ranging from a gay and lesbian film festival to a prostitutes' union— well as AIDS-related activities, such as the AIDS Poster Project, which aims to provide useful information about AIDS and produce better posters than those produced by the national and local bureaucracies, which have been criticized for stressing risk groups over risk behavior.

AIDS was an important catalyst especially for gay men to come forward. Activities against the AIDS Protection Law, which is a shabby piece of work directed at isolating HIV-positive people (Ōhama 1988),[27] were and still are carried out by gay men and lesbian and feminist women. Heterosexual women also help organize the Gay and Lesbian Film Festivals in Tokyo and in the Kansai area and set up the commercial lesbian magazines *Phryne* and *Anyse*. The AIDS Candlelight Parades in May and the parades on International AIDS Day in December started in 1991, years before the Gay and Lesbian Parades, but most participants were nevertheless gay men and lesbians. AIDS provided a clear focus, about which there could not be much disagreement, making cooperation relatively easy.

The Japanese government and bureaucracy, lacking proper knowledge concerning AIDS, listen to pleas by gay organizations for policy improvement, even though gay organizations remain unsatisfied with what is actually being done. An informant reported that, in order to keep the dialogue going, Occur prevented AIDS Coalition to Unleash Power (ACT UP) from staging its usual antics of shouting abuse at official attendants at the Yokohama World AIDS Conference in the summer of 1994. During the conference, Occur member Ōishi Toshinori came out as a gay man living with HIV and shared the stage with the Japanese crown prince and princess (Ōishi 1995).

Apart from the groups, there are many people engaging individually in gay and lesbian activities, many of them writers. That there is an increase in overall participation in activities concerning homosexuality is without doubt. In relation to gay and lesbian politics, the word *undō* (movement) may not be a very appropriate description of what is happening. Groups like Occur and Gay Front Kansai can be called movements in the strict sense that they are organizations involved in trying to change Japanese society by addressing the authorities about particular issues: Occur with its court case about the Fuchū Seinen no Ie incident and Gay Front Kansai by questioning the Osaka prefectural government's policy concerning "homosexual" pornography.

Laws are, however, often not enforced in practice, as is shown by the AIDS Prevention Law. With the general attitude that law is a last resort, the use of which should be avoided if possible, the influence of law is much smaller than in Western countries. What matters more is what people in general think and do, and that is more easily influenced by talking with them than anything else. Providing information about homosexuality to all who ask for it is a prime activity of many groups. Requests for information meetings can come from a large variety of groups and organizations, including schools, voluntary groups assisting disabled people, and fire brigades.

The activities of other groups, such as Together, in Tokyo, are important because by participating in them people learn to discuss homosexuality, sexuality, and their personal problems in ways that have hitherto been impossible for most Japanese. Such groups also draw heterosexual people who are envious of the space for discussing personal matters available to gay men and lesbians. Fortunately for them, gay and lesbian groups are increasingly open toward heterosexuals, as long as they are prepared to discuss their own sexuality and show some degree of "queerness," a concept that gained currency at tremendous speed.

In Japanese gay and lesbian circles, interest in any other type of sex, sexuality, or gender—including transsexuality, transvestism, heterosexuality, bisexuality, and hermaphroditism—was apparent long before the word "queer" and its accompanying ideas were imported. Before the term "queer" came to be used in its present sense in the United States, in Japan "*hentai*," which translates perfectly as "queer," was used positively in a number of instances. It was used, for example, in the title of a publication on sexual variety: "Hentai San ga Iku" (There Goes Mr./Ms. Queer) (1991), in which queerness is presented as desirable to everyone (Lunsing 1995, forthcoming a, b). If one were to add up all the people who are involved in politics of sexuality and gender including homosexuality—from participating in group discussions to participating in political pressure activities—I believe that it would come to several thousand people, mostly gay and lesbian, but certainly many others.

GAY AND LESBIAN BUSINESS: PAVING THE WAY?

Gay magazines have been published continuously since 1971,[28] when the heterosexual publisher Itō Bungaku started *Barazoku* (The Rose Clan). It was followed by two other magazines, the politically oriented *Adon* (after Adonis), first published in 1972, and the sadomasochism-oriented *Sabu* (slang for "macho"), 1972. The early 1980s saw the introduction of the fat man–oriented *Samuson* (Samson) in 1982 and the sexually and politically radical *Za Gei* (The Gay) in 1980. In the 1990s two more magazines came to light: *Badi* (Buddy, connoting surfer and AIDS buddy) in 1994, which soon obtained the largest readership, and *G-Men* in 1995, focusing on a combination of bearlike men and sadomasochism.[29]

Total sales figures for these magazines are certainly well over 100,000, which was the rough estimate in the late 1980s (Domenig 1991: 506–25; Lunsing 1995). Exact figures are not available, but, after discussing the figures with five of the chief editors of the magazines and witnessing the increase in volume and availability, I would estimate sales at about 150,000. This figure may seem high compared with other countries, but the roughly 130 million Japanese buy more magazines and newspapers in general than do most other peoples. In Japan just about everything is printed, and many people buy large quantities of printed matter even though they may not read most of it.

Except for *Za Gei*, which censors itself less than the others,[30] the magazines can be bought in shops throughout Japan. Many closeted gay men feel awkward buying them in local shops, however, fearing recognition as gay by shop personnel (Lunsing forthcoming b). Gay magazines sell mainly on two features: pornography and personal advertisements. Most editors try to sandwich in some social, political, and cultural articles. In the autumn of 1995, when Minami Teishirō decided to stop publishing pornography in *Adon* and make it a lifestyle and political magazine, the sales figures plummeted, according to informants working in gay shops in Shinjuku in Tokyo (Lunsing forthcoming a). About a year later, the magazine closed.

Gay shops can be found in Shinjuku, Asakusa, and Ueno in Tokyo; in Doyama and Namba (also called Kita, or "North," and Minami, or "South"; in Osaka (Lunsing 1994); and in other major towns in Japan, including Kobe, Nagoya, Sendai, Hakata, Kyoto, and Sapporo. Typically they count as adult shops, and the largest part of their revenue is earned by selling pornographic videos and gay magazines. In addition, the assortment may include novels, comics, lingerie, and sex toys, as well as magazines for transvestites, transsexuals, and those who call themselves *nyū-hāfu* (new-half) or *shii-mēru* (she-male), people who were born physiologically male but have acquired breasts using hormones or implants.[31] Some shops, such as a chain called Amerikaya, offer facilities for watching videos in private cabins, with or without the possibility of seeing and sometimes touching people in adjacent cabins. They may also offer a service to contact men by telephone and in some cases a service to receive mail one may not want delivered at home.

Some attempts have been made to establish a commercial lesbian magazine. *Phryne* was aborted in 1995 after three issues. It was followed by *Aniisu Anysē* in May 1996, which was supported by the publisher of the successful gay magazine *Badi. Badi*'s chief editor, Ogura Tō, said that the aim was to reach a wider audience than only lesbians, an audience including gay men, heterosexual women, and other people with an interest in sexuality. It also failed, however. *Out in Japan* caters to both women and men. It consists of *Out in America,* accompanied by translations of some articles into Japanese and some Japanese articles.

A famous feature of homosexuality in Japan is the area of Shinjuku Nichōme, with more than two hundred gay bars. The bars are, however, generally small to tiny, which makes the presence of five or six patrons give them a filled feeling. Comparison demands that one look at the number of patrons rather than the number of bars. Based on a variety of experiences and discussions, I believe that the number of patrons who visit gay bars in the Kantō area, combining the metropolis of Tokyo and Yokohama (where thirty million people live), is definitely below five thousand on weekdays and fifteen thousand at most on weekends, if one includes gay nights at clubs. The number of bars is increasing and some newer bars are larger. Gay bars can be found throughout Japan in towns from about one hundred thousand inhabitants (Lunsing 1994, forthcoming a, b).

Lesbian bars exist only in Tokyo. According to Kakefuda Hiroko there are about eight lesbian bars in Shinjuku. In addition, there are lesbian nights in clubs in Tokyo and in Osaka. Clubs in various towns in Japan, such as Sendai, Sapporo, Niigata, and Hakata (Kitakyushu), also have gay and lesbian nights. There is an increase in the number of such social gatherings throughout Japan (Lunsing forthcoming a, b).

The extensive proliferation of gay venues and gay magazines is one of the reasons often given to explain why it is difficult to interest gay men in gay politics. Homosexuality can be engaged in freely by all who choose to do so, and therefore little need to engage in political activity is felt. However the bar circuit has made it possible for people to come into contact with each other. Social groups engaging in a large variety of activities, ranging from sports tournaments to travel and artistic pursuits, have developed from bar circuits.

CURRENT DISCUSSIONS: IDENTITY, SEXUALITY, GENDER, COMMUNITY

In August 1996, as mentioned, the third Gay and Lesbian Parade was held in Tokyo. About twelve hundred people participated, which was roughly one thousand fewer than the year before. Informants attributed this to the fact that many people did not wish to join under the conditions laid down by the organizing committee, which was supervised by Minami Teishirō. The conditions were, among others, that women were not allowed to expose their breasts and men were not allowed to expose their buttocks. Further, people who handed out leaflets would be dismissed from the parade. These measures were taken in order to provide an orderly and *majime* (straight, decent) image of gay and lesbian people to the Japanese public. At the end of the parade, Minami and his aides tried to have an appeal adopted by acclamation. He wanted to establish support for his plans to appeal to the Japanese government for an antidiscrimination law explicitly including sexual preference. Minami reasoned that, given the turmoil parliamentary politics was in, the times were favorable for politicians to listen to his pleas (Minami 1996: 172–81).

At this point some participants jumped onto the stage and vented their disagreement with the way the parade had been organized. No discussion had taken place about the appeal, even though there had been a conference of gay and lesbian groups from all over Japan before the parade. The protestors were from Project P and OLP, both Kansai-based groups. Project P had wanted to participate in the organization of the parade but was turned down by Minami. Apparently he was afraid of losing control, as had occurred the previous year, when organizers spent a sponsor's money without asking for Minami's approval. As a result of the protests, the appeal was not adopted.

This event highlights an opposition between two streams that exist among Japan's gay and lesbian activists. One is the stream of Minami Teishirō's JILGA and Occur, whose policies follow more or less those mainstream American gay policies stressing that gay men and lesbian women are "normal" and should be treated as equal to heterosexuals. This stream tries to achieve goals mostly by influencing politicians and changing laws. It presents gay and lesbian people as victims of discrimination in a hostile heterosexist society (Binsento, Kazama, and Kawaguchi 1997). In order to be accepted it stresses that gays and lesbians are *majime* and tries to present itself as "normal" and decent, almost denying sexual desire. Minami Teishirō's decision to quit publishing pornography in his magazine *Adon* fits in this effort to gain recognition. Similarly, Occur's Niimi Hiroshi's insistence that he is "perfectly male," or *kanzen na otoko* (Ida 1991) and Occur's presentation of its members as decent people in suits when they appear in public also can be seen in this light, as can the group's stress on gay men wishing lifetime relationships with male partners of the same age. All of this alienates considerable sections of the Japanese gay population who do not fit the model (Lunsing forthcoming a, b).

The other stream cares less about parliamentary politics and law and about being seen as *majime* and more about freedom of expression in a variety of contexts. And if its members' ways of expressing themselves are regarded as *fumajime*, then that is not their problem but that of those who hold this view. This faction's stance, although it is seldom expressed clearly, is that Occur and JILGA's efforts at being accepted by the mainstream establishment are self-suppressive. To demonstrate a lifestyle that denies lust and pleasure for the sake of gay liberation has its contradictions.

In a New Year's Day 1996 discussion concerning the desirability of the formation of a lesbian and gay community in Japan, Kansai people were generally opposed, and Tokyo people were in favor. The discussion was somewhat vague, because nobody explained what was meant by the Anglo-Japanese term *"konmyūniti"* (community). Proponents had been to San Francisco or Sydney and would like to have an area in Tokyo similar to the Castro street area in San Francisco. Opponents thought that having gay and lesbian people living in a concentrated gay/lesbian–dominated area would be detrimental to the acceptance of homosexuality in society, because it would deprive people elsewhere of opportunities to come into contact with gay and lesbian people in their everyday lives. Moreover, opponents did not want to live only with gay and lesbian people. They felt comfortable with straight and other friends and did not consider it an appealing prospect to share their lives only with gay and lesbian people.

One of Project P's critiques of Minami's appeal at the Gay and Lesbian Parade in 1996 was that it mentioned only lesbian and gay people, overlooking the fact that many other people whose sexuality or gender was equally at stake participated. The group thought that by not mentioning bisexuals, transsexuals, transvestites, drag queens, prostitutes, people living with AIDS, people with disabilities, or people with heterosexualities that do not agree with mainstream ideas of what is decent, a division was made within the large variety of people parading to question straight society rather than merely to ask for the acceptance of homosexuality. At the incident, Isogai Hiroshi, one of Minami's assistants, scolded a lesbian who jumped onto the stage. He said, *"Nani yo anta, rezu no kuse ni, nani shiyagaru no ka* (What do you think you're doing, being merely lesbian?),"* thus betraying that he did not even regard being lesbian as of much consequence. This was unacceptable to the majority of the participants.[32] As a result of these occurrences, and furthered by Minami's total neglect of efforts at discussing these matters, the parade Minami organized in 1997 failed to draw many people.

The next discussion centered on "identity," a term that is very vague in a Japanese context. Homosexuality had been problematic, because it was generally mixed up with femininity in men and masculinity in women. This seemed to especially provoke men, who, as in the situation of Niimi, stressed their masculinity at the expense of more feminine men (Lunsing forthcoming a, b). The politically correct word for male homosexual was "*gei*," obviously based on the American preference for the word "gay," which was an awkward choice because to most people it meant transvestite, transsexual, or *nyū-hāfu*. Increasingly, people feel unhappy with this term, not because of its feminine connotations, which have dispersed quite a lot by now as a result of the consequent use of "*gei*" by most groups. The problem is that its political significance is not clear. It is felt that the use of "*gei*" indicates a lack of full acceptance of one's homosexuality, because "*gei*" is a foreign term that can never adequately question Japanese prejudice against homosexuality (Onitsuka 1996: 124–39). Because "*okama*" is the word commonly used to speak of gay men in a derogatory manner, many originally felt awkward about applying it to themselves but later decided that using it was the only way to overcome the suppression of their sexualities, starting with self-suppression (Fukayuki 1996: 108–9).[33] As a result, "*okama*" is increasingly coming into use by people who use it in a self-liberating manner.

In the case of women, a similar problem exists. The term "*rezubian*" was never very popular, although it was presented as politically correct.[34] A term increasingly used is "*bian*," which is the last part of "*rezubian*." Further, the term "*onabe*" is gaining ground. Lesbian women have also come to the conclusion that introducing foreign terminology for themselves does not serve them well in the end. Increased aversion to the U.S. situation may be related to this. Informants who met with physically violent homophobia did so in the United States or Australia, and news about U.S. developments, such as states that introduce laws to forbid laws against discrimination on the ground of homosexuality, promote a trend toward reappreciation of the Japanese situation.

Many Japanese view the Japanese situation as progressive and the U.S. situation as increasingly regressive. Contrary to the situation in the United States, where much effort is put into changing laws, in Japan law is not seen as having much influence on daily life. A discussion among scholars in Japan about gay marriage registration (Ninomiya 1991; Ōmura 1995a, b) has only lately drawn some interest from gay and lesbian people.[35] What matters is daily life, and the absence of legal definitions of homosexuality is felt by some to allow for more freedom to develop and express sexualities in manifold ways. Although there is truth to Occur's insistence that gay identity in Japan is weak (Binsento, Kazama, and Kawaguchi 1997) the group's emphasis on strengthening it seems to be an attempt to Americanize,[36] which will not work. The trend is toward shifting identities, rather then having a rigidly set (*katamatta*) identity, and this trend fits perfectly with Japanese culture. Even Occur's suit against the Tokyo Metropolitan Government has been called problematic, because it led to a legal definition of homosexuality, and any legal definition is limiting.[37] Living and discovering one's life and sexuality as one pleases, without feeling victimized, is advocated by such critics (Hibino 1996: 203–6).

Notwithstanding his efforts to obtain a powerful and central position within the spectrum of gay and lesbian organizations in Japan, Minami Teishirō's influence has crumbled—even the relatively loyal group Sapporo Meeting joined the choir of people criticizing the organization of the Gay and Lesbian Parade and the appeal, Minami's magazine closed, and the last parade was a failure. Minami's position more and more has become that of someone who is honored for the good work he did in the past; after all he did assemble many gay men. Occur has largely remained outside discussions taking place within a gay and lesbian context in Japan, by failing to interact with other groups and individuals. I expect that the opposing stream will swell. And since it attracts not only gay and lesbian people but all sorts of people as well, it has the possibility of becoming an important force for sociocultural change—for changing *jōshiki* (common sense), the very basis of Japanese society (Lunsing forthcoming b).

Much is happening in the field of gay and lesbian politics in contemporary Japan. However, the occurrences in national politics of the late 1980s and early 1990s, which at times led to the belief that major changes were taking place, do not seem to have led to much of anything. Although some people have pointed out that the absence of centralized LDP power provided more opportunities for lesbian and gay people to come forward, gay and lesbian movements hardly seem to depend on that. Their voices were heard years before the LDP lost power in 1993. It seems rather that Japanese society and culture are developing in a direction that allows for more variation in lifestyles, of which lesbian and gay lifestyles are but a few. The increase in the number of people remaining single that started in the 1970s, the gay boom that started in 1991 but had its predecessors in girls' comics from the 1970s onward, and the idea that the 1980s was the decade of the woman—all these suggest that the present success of gay and lesbian groups and individuals in making their ideas heard is part of a larger sociocultural development, which also has its influence on the events in the parliamentary arena.

Parliamentary politics seems to be much more difficult to change than people's attitudes toward homosexuality. This may underscore the idea that sexuality is not thought of so much in terms of what is right or wrong, in terms of all-encompassing morals, as it is in Anglo-American contexts, but rather as play, something people may engage in if they wish to do so. Therefore, sexuality may not be easy to politicize by people who rally opponents of homosexuality in Western contexts. Since giving people the right and the opportunity to engage in alternative lifestyles does not necessarily cost the state any money, great opposition is not very likely to develop. The absence of a strong political opposition against homosexuality leaves Japanese gay and lesbian activists with the possibility of engaging in the major activity that produces clear results: discussions with each other and with the general public. Although there are many local differences, there is an open debate about a larger variety of lifestyles and how society can be adapted to give them more space. This debate does not change society overnight; it takes time. Contrary to Occur's political antagonism, personal discussions appear to hold much promise toward changing the Japanese situation—discussions in which positions far more radical than those of Occur can be and are taken. In Japan, when push comes to shove, not many people can say what is wrong with homosexuality, a fact that is being exploited successfully by lesbian, gay, and other groups and by individuals in contemporary Japan.

NOTES

Acknowledgments: This chapter is derived from research for a project on sexuality and gender in contemporary Japan, which was supported by grants from the Japanese Ministry of Education (Monbushō), the Japan Foundation Endowment Committee, the Austrian Ministry of Research and Science, Erasmus, and the Japan Society for the Promotion of Science. I am also indebted to Tik Ho Ong and my parents. Special thanks go to Okajima Katsuki and Tomioka Akemi and to the editors for their critique of earlier versions of this chapter. Some parts of this chapter are adapted from discussions in Lunsing (forthcoming a).

In addition to the sources cited in the References, I consulted various gay and lesbian magazines and *minikomishi,* including *Adon, Aniisu, Badi, Barazoku, Crea, G-Men, Ibu & Ibu, Kick Out, Labrys, Labrys Dasshu, Out in Japan, Phryne, Regumi Tsūshin, Sabu, Samuson,* and *Za Gei.*

1. Research for this chapter consisted mainly of fieldwork in Japan: participating in the activities of lesbian and gay groups, interviewing informants, and reading lesbian and gay publications. The most extensive fieldwork took place from 1991 to 1993. I also visited Japan in the summer of 1986, the autumn of 1988, the winter of 1993–1994, and the winter and spring of 1996. During and after my visits, I maintained contact with sources by fax, telephone, and e-mail and by meeting with them in Europe.

2. The *onnagata,* men who play women's roles in the Kabuki theater, are prototypical of men loving for feminine men. In particular, Buddhist monks and the war-

rior samurai class are thought to have been engaged in the love of young men or boys (Watanabe and Iwata 1987; Schalow 1989: 118–28; Furukawa 1994, 1996: 113–30). The greatest proof of of female homosexuality in history is believed to be the existence of *harigata* (dildos), the earliest of which stem from the Nara period (seventh century), and some rare *ukiyoe* (pictures of the floating world) showing women satisfying each other with or without dildos, in the context of the shoguns' harems in the Edo period (1603–1868) (Lunsing forthcoming a, b). In the case of male homosexuality, the perspective taken has been mostly that of the masculine or the older of the two men who have sexual contact. The younger or more feminine partner has been basically placed on a par with women. Homosexuality was called *danshoku* or *nanshoku* (male colors), and heterosexuality was called *joshoku* or *nyoshoku* (female colors) (Lunsing forthcoming a and b). This construction precludes the idea of an independent sexuality for women. In the nineteenth century the word *okama*, meaning "cooking pot," came into use for gay men, who were generally constructed as effeminate men who were sexually passive. Similarly, lesbian women were called *onabe* and were typically expected to be masculine (Robertson 1992; Lunsing forthcoming a, b). In the same period there was an idealization of special relationships between women, which are now generally likened to lesbian relationships. The women were called *shisutā*, (sister). These relationships were constructed as unrelated to sex (Robertson 1993) or as without necessarily including sex (Lunsing forthcoming a, b). After the Second World War, women emerged who identified with the idea of lesbian as understood in Western countries. But even in today's Japan, the idea of special friendships between women, characterized by romance, exists—as does Takarazuka, an all-women revue company whose members maintain special relationships. These relationships can be publicly discussed, but the management of Takarazuka would try to prevent publication of any "pollution" of the clean image of the revue (Robertson 1992), such as use of the word *rezubian* (lesbian), with its connotation of pornographic performance (Kakefuda 1992).

3. For Japanese names I use the Japanese order: first the surname name and then the given name.

4. I use "lesbian" only attributively when writing of women in a Japanese context, because the noun implies a significance of identity not generally found in Japan (Lunsing forthcoming b).

5. These problems are still common today (Lunsing 1995, forthcoming b).

6. The first is exemplified by the work of a psychologist who combined his (much quoted but also much criticized) idea of a type of dependency particular to Japanese culture with what he calls the pathology of homosexuality, featuring the Oedipus complex (Doi 1975); the second is exemplified by the work of a psychologist who treats his gay patients as if they were representative of homosexuality among frequenters of gay meeting places (Oikawa 1993).

7. This is an interesting argument if one compares it with women pursuing women's studies, which though a marginal field in Japan, is a field almost exclusively pursued by women.

8. The women in this track are called OL, which is short for Office Ladies. They have been dubbed flowers of the office. For more substantial descriptions of them and their position, see Carter and Dilatush 1976: 75–88; and Kelsky 1994.

9. My own research, and that of others, on the attitudes of straight people toward homosexuality in Japan may have a relatively progressive and liberal bias. However, research on attitudes toward homosexuality among Japanese employees at the Okura Hotel in Amsterdam—whose frame of reference can be expected to be close to mainstream thought—showed that many had a more positive impression after having been exposed to gay and lesbian people living openly as such in Amsterdam (Kraaipoel 1996). Most Japanese employees at the Okura Hotel work there for a couple of years before being transferred elsewhere. They do not usually speak Dutch and spend much of their time with their Japanese colleagues or the wider expatriate Japanese community in the Netherlands.

10. See LaFleur 1992 for a depiction of how Buddhism's influence declined to this point.

11. According to Ian Reader, expert on religions in Japan, there are more sects connected to LDP, than to any other, politicians although little about this phenomenon has been published (verbal communication, 1997).

12. There is abundant material about what was called the *ie seido* (the household system). The *ie* (household) is today still presented as central to Japanese social organization. And the theory that Japanese companies are organized like households or families in a vertical manner—with the patriarch at the top and others subordinate to him, as promulgated by the Japanese sociologist Nakane Chie (Nakane 1973)—is still much in vogue, notwithstanding many counterarguments (Kawamura 1989; 202–27).

13. This can mostly be attributed to the large number of one-child families today.

14. Most notable in this context are groups defending the rights of extramarital children and movements lobbying for legislation that will make it possible for spouses to keep their own names (Ninomiya 1991; Lunsing forthcoming b).

15. The new parties included the Nihon Shinseitō (Japan Renewal Party) and the Sakigake (New Harbinger), both founded by former LDP members, and the Mushokuzoku, a group of independents (Iwami 1995). In 1995 the Shinshintō (New Frontier Party) brought the Clean Government Party, the New Japan Party, and the Japan Renewal Party under one heading (Jain 1995).

16. A standard work on *burakumin* is DeVos and Wagatsuna 1966.

17. At the time, only men participated in the event.

18. It has been reported that the group received less in compensation than it had demanded, because the judge decided that the accused were not guilty of making defamatory remarks (this information comes from verbal communication).

19. Upham (1987: 208), quoting a minister of justice.

20. This survey was intended to obtain basic information about homosexual men. Results showed, among other things, that loneliness was a common problem and that many wished to marry, had been married, or were married (Ōta 1987), which is still the case today (Lunsing 1995, forthcoming b).

21. According to Japanese law it is not possible to divorce from someone who does not agree, unless that person has wronged one in clearly described ways, such as by having extramarital sex (Tsunoda 1992; Lunsing forthcoming b).

22. This case came about when Tōgō demanded the return of American

pornography that had been confiscated by Japanese customs officers upon his arrival in Tokyo. He won the case on the ground that he imported the material for personal use, not for commercial purposes. However, the Japanese state appealed this decision (Tōgō 1993).

23. Years that groups were founded are all from Kuia Sutadiizu Henshū Iinkai 1996: 18–35.

24. Kamigata refers to the Kansai area. It means upper side and, as such, refers to the supposedly higher cultural refinement of the Kansai area, compared with Tokyo.

25. The name of this magazine refers to the fact that its organizers were kicked out of Occur for disagreeing with the leadership's ideas.

26. Once at a railway station where I had gone to meet with another group, I unwittingly met people from a group that was until that time unknown to me.

27. Ohama Hōei, the man responsible for the law proposal, traveled the world to investigate AIDS policies in various countries. His book shows most sympathy for laws proposed by the French National Front of Le Pen and the Bavarian Christian Social Union, both of which count as extremely right-wing in Europe, voicing ideas such as the isolation of HIV-positive people from the major population. The point that Ōhama keeps making over and over in his book is that measures must be taken against HIV-positive prostitutes who continue working (Ōhama 1988). The only positive point I could see in this law is that it compels the Japanese authorities to inform the public about AIDS. Unfortunately, the Japanese government, which appears to understand little about AIDS, is violating the law on this point. Fortunately, the other points of the law are not carried out in practice either, making it a rather meaningless document.

28. Years are from Kuia Sutadiizu Henshū Iinkai 1996: 18–35.

29. The format of the magazines would make them look like books to most Western eyes. It is not uncommon for them to have four to five hundred pages. Extensive information on their content can be found in Lunsing 1995.

30. Japanese censorship laws state that no pubic hair may be shown. When producers of pornography, which in Japan is generally thought to include nude photography, took this literally and had their actors and models shave off their pubic hair, however, it became apparent that "pubic hair" was a euphemism for sexual organs. Policy is that the police buy suspect material to check whether it is transgressive according to their interpretation of the law, which changes over time. When a magazine is seen as transgressive, the publisher may be called in for interrogation and may be warned about the possibility of being closed down altogether. Usually the entire print run of that issue is confiscated. *Barazoku*'s Itō Bungaku said that he has experienced this several times, although it occurs less often than it used to. *Za Gei* can afford to censor itself less, because it is sold less widely than the other magazines and because its publisher, Tōgō Ken, is (according to his assistant) perceived as troublesome and argumentative by the police, who would rather not call him in. Gay magazines are under more scrutiny than most, so they censor art pictures (for instance, those of Robert Mapplethorpe) that appear uncensored in feminist magazines (for example, *Nyū Feminizumu Rebyū*). According to informants, censorship depends, to some degree, on context, which

in the case of gay magazines is considered pornography and in the case of feminist magazines is considered scholarship.

31. In Latin American context they called themselves *travestis* (Cornwall 1994: 111–32).

32. This quote and information about the incident comes from various pamphlets produced by members of Project P, which were signed by large numbers of people and organizations.

33. Shimōne (Simone) Fukayuki is the artist name of a gay drag queen singer from Osaka.

34. In relation to this, the most common word, "*rezu,*" was seen as politically incorrect, because of its strong connotation as "pornographic actress" (Kakefuda 1992).

35. It must be noted, though, that if gay men or lesbian women want a legal bond, they can achieve it by having one adopt the other. In Japan it is perfectly legal for adults to adopt each other, a remnant of the *ie* system that stressed the importance of continuing households, if necessary by adopting successors (Tsunoda 1992; Lunsing forthcoming b).

36. Significantly, the section of Binsento, Kazama, and Kawaguchi 1997 explaining Occur's position on this was written by an American, Keith Vincent.

37. This was discussed at the first gay studies seminar at Tokyo University in March 1996. Hino Masaaki, a Tokyo University Ph.D. student, raised the issue.

REFERENCES

Abe Hitoshi, Shindō Muneyoshi, and Kawato Sadafumi. 1994. *The Government and Politics of Japan.* Trans. James White. Tokyo: University of Tokyo Press.

Akiyama Yōko. 1991. Enoki Misako to Chūpiren: Ribu shishi nōto yori (Enoki Misako and Chūpiren: From the lib history notes). *Joseigaku Nenpō,* no. 12 (October): 109–15.

Aoyama, Tomoko. 1988. "Male Homosexuality as Treated by Japanese Writers." In *The Japanese Trajectory: Modernisation and Beyond.* Ed. Gavan McCormack and Yoshio Sugimoto. Cambridge: Cambridge University Press.

Baerwald, Hans H. 1979. "Parties, Factions, and the Diet." In *Politics and Economics in Contemporary Japan.* Ed. Murakami Hyoe and Johannes Hirschmeyer. Tokyo: Japan Culture Institute.

Binsento Kiisu (Keith Vincent), Kazama Takashi, and Kawaguchi Kazuya. 1997. *Gei sutadiizu* (Gay studies). Tokyo: Seidosha.

Brinton, Mary. 1993. *Women and the Economic Miracle: Gender and Work in Postwar Japan.* Berkeley and Los Angeles: University of California Press.

Buckley, Sandra, and Vera Mackie. 1986. "Women in the New Japanese State." In *Democracy in Contemporary Japan* Ed. Gavan McCormack and Yoshio Sugimoto. Sydney: Hale and Iremonger.

Carter, Rose, and Lois Dilatush. 1976. "Office Ladies." In *Women in Changing Japan.* Ed. Joyce Lebra, Joy Paulson, and Elizabeth Powers. Boulder: Westview.

Childs, Margaret H. 1980. Chigo Monogatari: Love Stories or Buddhist Sermons? *Monumenta Nipponica* 35 no. 2 (Summer): 127–31.

Cornwall, Andrea. 1994. Gendered Identities and Gender Ambiguity among *Travestis* in Salvador, Brazil. In *Dislocating Masculinity: Comparative Ethnographies.* Ed. Andrea Cornwall and Nancy Lindisfarne. London: Routledge.

Curtis, Gerald L. 1988. *The Japanese Way of Politics.* New York: Columbia University Press.

DeVos, George, and Wagatsuna Hiroshi. 1966. *Japan's Invisible Race: Caste in Culture and Personality.* Berkeley and Los Angeles: University of California Press.

Doi, Takeo. 1975. *The Anatomy of Dependence.* Tokyo: Kōdansha.

Domenig, Roland. 1991. "Aids in Japan." In *Beiträge zur Japanologie: Japan von Aids bis Zen.* Vol. 29-II. Ed. Eva Bachmayer, Wolfgang Herbert, and Sepp Linhart. Vienna: Institut für Japanologie.

Fukayuki Shimōne. 1996. Untitled. In *Kuia sutadiizu '96* (Queer studies '96). Ed. Kuia Sutadiizu Henshū Iinkai. Tokyo: Nanatsu Mori Shokan.

Furukawa Makoto. 1992. "Kindai Nihon ni okeru dōseiai no shakaishi" (A social history of homosexuality in modern Japan). *Za Gei* (May) 24–60.

———. 1994. "Sekushuariti no henyō: Kindai Nihon ni okeru dōseiai o meguru mittsu no kōdō" (The changing nature of sexuality: The three codes framing homosexuality in modern Japan). *Nichibei Josei Jānaru* (Japan-America Women's Journal) 17:29–55. In English in *US-Japan Women's Journal,* English supplement no. 7:98–127.

———. 1996. "Dōseiai no hikaku shakaigaku: Rezubian, gei sutadiizu no tenkai to danshoku gainen" (Comparative sociology of homosexuality: The development of lesbian and gay studies and the concept of *danshoku* [usually translated as "pederasty"]). In *Sekushuariti no shakaigaku* (The sociology of sexuality). Ed. Inoue Toshi, Ueno Chizuko, Ōzawa Masayuki, Mita Sōsuke, and Yoshiki Toshichika. Tokyo: Iwanami Shoten.

Fushimi Noriaki. 1991. *Puraibēto gei raifu: Posuto renairon* (Private gay life: Post-love theory).Tokyo: Gakuyō Shobō.

"Gays Win Suit against Tokyo." 1997. *Japan Times,* 17 September.

Hardacre, Helen. 1984. *Lay Buddhism in Contemporary Japan: Reiyūkai Kyōdan.* Princeton: Princeton University Press.

Hattori Kōichi (*sic;* should be Kōichirō). 1996. "Ōsakafu o utsu! Sabetsu jōrei e no torikumi: Ōsakafu jōrei o kaesaseta Hattori Kōichi-shi ni kiku" (Striking Osaka Prefecture! Questioning regulations that discriminate against homosexuality: listening to Hattori Kōichi who made the regulations of Osaka Prefecture change). *Adon* 2 (February): 19–26.

Hendry, Joy. 1986. *Becoming Japanese: The World of the Preschool Child.* Manchester: Manchester University Press.

———. 1987. *Understanding Japanese Society.* London: Croom Helm.

"*Hentai san ga iku*" (There goes Mr./Ms. queer). 1991. *Bessatsu Takarajima,* 141, published by JICC Shuppan, Tokyo.

Hibino Makoto. 1996. "Tasha to no deai no tanoshimi o saihakken" (Rediscovering the pleasure of meeting others). In *Kuia sutadiizu '96* (Queer studies '96) Ed. Kuia Sutadiizu Henshū Iinkai. Tokyo: Nanatsu Mori Shokan.

Hisada Megumi. 1991. "Genki no rezubian 'Regumi no gomame' tōjō!" (Lively lesbians "Regumi no gomame" takes the stage!). in *Onna o aisuru onnatachi no monogatari* (Stories of women who love women). *Bessatsu Takarajima* 64: 120–29, published by JICC Shuppan, Tokyo.

Hirosawa Yumi. 1991. "Nihonhatsu no rezubian sākuru: 'Wakakusa no Kai,' sono jūgonen no rekishi to genzai" (The first lesbian circle in Japan: "Group of Young Grass," its fifteen-year history and today). *Onna o aisuru onnatachi no monogatari* (Stories of women who love women). *Bessatsu Takarajima* 64: 111–19, published by JICC Shuppan, Tokyo.

Hirosawa Yumi and Rezubian Ripōto Han. 1991. "Rezubian ripōto" (Lesbian report). *Onna o aisuru onnatachi no monogatari* (Stories of women who love women). *Bessatsu Takarajima* 64: 149–285, published by JICC Shuppan, Tokyo.

Ida Makiko. 1991. "Tōkyō dōseiai saiban" (Tokyo gay trial). *Josei Sebun* (Woman Seven), 31 October.

Iritani, Toshio. 1994. "The Emergence of the Hosokawa Coalition: A Significant Break in the Continuity of Japanese Politics." *Japan Forum* 6, no. 1 (April): 1–7.

Iwami, Takao. 1995. "Behind the Growth of the 'No Party' Camp." *Japan Echo* 22, no. 3 (Autumn): 10–14. First published in Japanese in *Chūō Kōron* (June 1995): 106–10.

Jain, Purnendra C. 1995. "Electoral Reform in Japan: Its Process and Implications for Party Politics." *The Journal of East Asian Affairs* 9, no. 2 (Summer–Fall): 402–27.

Kakefuda Hiroko. 1992. *"Rezubian" de aru, to iu koto* (Being "lesbian"). Tokyo: Kawade Shobō Shinsha.

———. 1995. "Gurūpu, ibento, minikomi annai" (Guide of groups, events, and small-scale publications). *Labrys*, no. 10, 12 December, 49–57.

Kasahara, Yomishi. 1986. "Fear of Eye-to-Eye Confrontation among Neurotic Patients." In *Japanese Culture and Behavior: Selected Readings*. Rev. Ed. Ed. Takie Sugiyama Lebra and William P. Lebra. Honolulu: University of Hawaii Press.

Kawamura, Nozomu. 1989. "The Transition of the Household System in Japan's Modernization." In *Constructs for Understanding Japanese Society*. Ed. Ross Mouer and Yoshio Sugimoto. London: Kegan Paul.

Kelsky, Karen. 1994. "Postcards from the Edge: The 'Office Ladies' of Tokyo." *US/Japan Women's Journal* (English Supplement) 6:3–26.

Kraaipoel, Jascha. 1996. "Ontkenning of erkenning: Houdingen ten opzichte van homosexualiteit in Japan" (Denial or recognition: Attitudes toward homosexuality in Japan). Master's thesis, University of Leiden, Netherlands.

Kuia Sutadiizu Henshū Iinkai. 1996. "Kuia historii" (Queer history). In *Kuia sutadiizu '96* (Queer studies '96). Ed. Kuia Sutadiizu Henshū Iinkai. Tokyo: Nanatsu Mori Shokan.

LaFleur, William R. 1992. *Liquid Life: Abortion and Buddhism in Japan*. Princeton: Princeton University Press.

Lam, Alice. 1992. *Women and Japanese Management: Discrimination and Reform*. London: Routledge.

Lebra, Takie Sugiyama. 1976. *Japanese Patterns of Behavior*. Honolulu: University of Hawaii Press.

Leupp, Gary P. 1995. *Male Colors: The Construction of Homosexuality in Tokugawa Japan.* Berkeley and Los Angeles: University of California Press.

Lock, Margaret. 1992. "The Fragile Japanese Family: Narratives about Individualism and the Postmodern State." In *Paths to Asian Medical Knowledge.* Ed. Charles Leslie and Allan Young. Berkeley and Los Angeles: University of California Press.

Lunsing, Wim. 1994. "Kono Sekai: Functions of Places for Gay Men in Japan." Paper presented at the BSA conference, Preston, U.K., March.

———. 1995. "Japanese Gay Magazines and Marriage Advertisements." *Journal of Gay and Lesbian Social Services* 3 (3): 71–87. Also in *Gays and Lesbians in Asia and the Pacific: Social and Human Services.* Ed. Gerard Sullivan and Laurence Wai-Teng Leong. New York: Harrington Park.

———. 1997. "Gay Boom" in Japan: changing Views of Homosexuality?" *Thamyris: Mythmaking from Past to Present* 4(2):276–93.

———. Forthcoming a. "Lesbian and Gay Movements: Between Hard and Soft." In *Soziale Bewegungen in Japan* (Social movements in Japan). Ed. Claudia Derichs and Anja Osiander. Hamburg: Gesellschaft für Natur- und Völkerkunde Ostasiens (OAG).

———. Forthcoming b. *Beyond Common Sense: Negotiating Constructions of Sexuality and Gender in Contemporary Japan.* London: Kegan Paul.

Matsui, Midori. 1993. "Little Girls Were Little Boys: Displaced Femininity in the Representation of Homosexuality in Japanese Girls' Comics." In *Feminism and the Politics of Difference.* Ed. Sneja Gunew and Anna Yeatman. St. Leonards, New South Wales, Australia: Allen and Unwin.

Minami, Teishirō. 1991. "Sengo Nihon no gei mūbumento" (The gay movement in post-war Japan). In *Inpakushon* (Impaction). No. 71. Gei riberēshon (Gay liberation). Ed. Occur: Ugoku Gei to Rezubian no Kai. Tokyo: Inpakuto Shuppankai.

———. 1996. "Nihon no rezubian/gei mōbumento no rekishi to senryaku" (The history and strategy of the Japanese lesbian and gay movement). In *Kuia sutadiizu '96* (Queer studies '96). Ed. Kuia Sutadiizu Henshū Iinkai. Tokyo: Nanatsu Mori Shokan.

Murase, Takao. 1986. "Naikan Therapy." In *Japanese Culture and Behavior: Selected Readings.* Rev. ed. Ed. Takie Sugiyama Lebra and William P. Lebra. Honolulu: University of Hawaii Press.

Nakane, Chie. 1973. *Japanese Society.* Harmondsworth: Penguin.

Ninomiya Shūhei. 1991. *Jijitsukon o kangaeru: Mōhitotsu no sentaku* (Thinking about common-law marriage: Another choice). Tokyo: Nihon Hyōronsha.

Ōhama Hōei. 1988. *Nihon no eizu: Sekaiteki shibyō to no tatakai* (AIDS in Japan: The struggle with a global "lethal disease"). Tokyo: Saimaru Shuppankai.

Oikawa Taku. 1993. "Nichōmebyō: Gei sekkusu no otoshiana" (Nichōme disease: A pitfall of gay sex). *Imago* 4 (12):165–77.

Ōishi Toshinori. 1995. *Sekando kamingu auto: Dōseiaisha to shite, eizu to tomo ni ikiru* (Second coming out: Living with AIDS as a homosexual). Tokyo: Asahi Shuppansha.

OLP. 1994. "Onna o aisuru onnatachi no tame no akutibiti: OLP e no sasoi" (Activities for women who love women: An invitation to OLP). *OLP no Newsletter*, no. 1 (September): 2–3.

———. 1997. "OLP for Active Lesbians" and "Ochiya Kumiko." *Tsunagari no tame no kamingu auto* (Coming out in order to relate). (Two articles from *OLP no Newsletter* [January and February], published in a separate pamphlet.)

Ōmura Atsushi. 1995a. "Sei tenkan, dōseiai to minpō, jō" (Sex change, homosexuality, and the civil law. part 1). *Jurisuto,* no. 1080, 1 December, 68–74.

———. 1995b. "Sei tenkan, dōseiai to minpō, ge" (Sex change, homosexuality, and the civil law part 2). *Jurisuto,* no. 1081, 15 December, 61–69.

Onitsuka Tetsurō. 1996. "Gei ribu to eizu akutibizumu" (Gay lib and AIDS activism). In *Kuia Sutadiizu '96* (Queer studies '96). Ed. Kuia Sutadiizu Henshū Iinkai. Tokyo: Nanatsu Mori Shokan.

Ōta Tenrei. 1987. *Daisan no sei: Sei wa hōkai suru no ka* (The third sex: Is sex breaking down?). Tokyo: Ningen no Kagakusha. (Reprint of *Daisan no sei: sei no hōkai?* [The third sex: The destructions of sex?] [Tokyo: Myōgi Shuppan, 1957].)

Ōtsuka Takashi. 1995. *Nichōme kara uroko: Shinjuku gei sutoriito zakkichō* (The scales from my eye of Nichōme: A notebook on the gay streets of Shinjuku). Tokyo: Shōheisha.

Pharr, Susan. 1990. *Losing Face: Status Politics in Japan.* Berkeley and Los Angeles: University of California Press.

Robertson, Jennifer. 1992. Doing and Undoing "Female" and "Male" in Japan: The Takarazuka Revue. In *Japanese Social Organization.* Ed. Takie Sugiyama Lebra. Honolulu: University of Hawaii Press.

———. (Jenifā Robātoson). 1993. "'Dōseiai' no butaijō, butaigai ni okeru hyōgen." (Expression of "homosexuality" on and off stage). *Mugendai,* no. 94 (August): 165–93.

Satō Masaki. 1994. "Daiikkai rezubian and gei parēdo" (The first lesbian and gay parade). *Kick Out,* no. 12:16–17.

Satō Masaki, ed. 1994. "Gei gurūpu gaidobukku 1994" (Gay groups guidebook 1994). *Kick Out* no. 12:1–6, 10–15, 25–31, 34–39.

Schalow, Paul Gordon. 1989. "Male Love in Early Modern Japan: A Literary Depiction of the 'Youth.'" In *Hidden from History: Reclaiming the Gay and Lesbian Past.* Ed. Martin Bauml Duberman, Martha Vicinus, and George Chauncy. New York: New American Library.

Sone, Yasunori. 1989. "Interest Groups and the Process of Political Decision Making in Japan." In *Constructs for Understanding Japan.* Ed. Yoshio Sugimoto and Ross Mouer. London: Kegan Paul.

Stockwin, J. A. A. 1982. *Japan: Divided Politics in a Growth Economy.* 2d ed. London: Weidenfield and Nicolson.

———. 1994. "On Trying to Move Mountains: The Political Career of Doi Takako." *Japan Forum* 6, no. 1 (April): 21–34.

Taniguchi Shōko. 1992. "Tasha e no kamu auto to sabetsu, henken" (Coming out toward others and discrimination, prejudice). In *Dōseiai kenkyū josetsu:*

dōseiaisha to iseiaisha no hikaku chōsa yori (An introduction to the study of homosexuality: From a comparative investigation of homosexuals and hetero-sexuals). Ed. Yajima Zemi. Tokyo: Chūō Daigaku Bungakuba Shakaigakka, Chūō Daigaku.

Tobin, Joseph. 1992. "Japanese Preschool and the Pedagogy of Selfhood." In *Japanese Sense of Self*. Ed. Nancy Rosenberger. Cambridge: Cambridge University Press.

Tōgō Ken. 1993. "Futatabi waisetsu o tou" (For the second time questioning what obscenity is). *Za Gei*, no. 131 (April): 39–62.

Tsunoda Yukiko. 1992. *Sei no hōritsugaku* (The jurisprudence on sex and sexuality). Tokyo: Yūhikaku Sensho.

Ueno Chizuko. 1991. *Onna to iu kairaku* (The pleasure of being a woman). Tokyo: Keisō Shobō.

———. 1992. "Sekushuariti wa shizen ka" (Is sexuality nature?). *Bungei* (Autumn): 323–30.

Ugoku Gei to Rezubian no Kai (Akā/Occur), ed. 1992. *Gei ripōto: Dōseiaisha wa kōgen suru* (Gay Report: Homosexuals speak out). Tokyo: Tottori Shinsha.

Upham, Frank K. 1987. *Law and Social Change in Postwar Japan*. Cambridge: Harvard University Press.

Watanabe Mieko. 1990. "Nihon ni okeru josei dōseiai no nagare: Atogaki ni kaette" (The flow of female homosexuality in Japan: Epilogue). In *Ūman rabingu: Rezubian ron sōsei ni mukete* (Loving women: Toward founding lesbian theory). Translation of six articles from a lesbian issue of *Signs: Journal of Women in Culture and Society* (1985). Tokyo: Gendai Shokan.

Watanabe, Tsuneo, and Junichi Iwata. 1987. *La voie des éphèbes: Histoire et histoires des homosexualités au Japon*. Paris: Editions Trismégiste.

White, Merry. 1987. *The Japanese Educational Challenge: A Commitment to Children*. New York: Free Press.

Geoffrey Woolcock
and Dennis Altman

13   The Largest Street Party in the World
The Gay and Lesbian Movement in Australia

A GAY peer educator from the Queensland AIDS Council was explaining some of the background of the epidemic in Australia to a group
of Filipino visitors. Asked why he thought the gay community had played
such a prominent role in the Australian response, he replied: "I really
don't know; we just seemed to come from nowhere." The development
of the gay and lesbian movement in Australia shows a gap between practice and theory, a trait mirrored in the largely untheorized development
of other social movements in Australia. (Note that from this point on, we
use gay movements to describe both gay and lesbian movements, except
where it is appropriate to differentiate between them.)

Despite some excellent descriptive historical accounts, there are few attempts to develop a theoretical framework capable of addressing the
movement as a whole. Certainly greater discussion of sexuality and, more
recently, the impact of HIV/AIDS has focused attention on the activities
of gay and lesbian identities and communities. However there is little systematic attempt to theoretically underpin the social and the movement in
the evolution of this social movement. This is partly due to the Australian
tendency to separate political commentary and theory. Much analysis of
formal institutional political life has reduced the impact of social movements to intermittent minor interest or pressure groups. Where theoriza-
tion has been undertaken, efforts have concentrated on the space sought
by collective action with respect to the more formal political players
rather than vice versa. Only recently has this analysis begun to change,
perhaps because of disenchantment with major political parties at recent
state and federal elections. Even here, movements are commonly reduced
to terms such as the "green lobby" or, in this case, the "gay lobby."

The history of Australian gay and lesbian movements has been largely
neglected by both social sciences and the movements themselves. Where
it has been written, it is largely in narrative personal histories, community
bulletins, and fiction.[1] What work has been done was often written with
very little support and rarely taken seriously. Not until the 1990s did gay
and lesbian research become acceptable in mainstream university depart-

ments, and only now can one speak of the beginning of "queer" studies in Australia.[2]

AUSTRALIAN POLITICAL CULTURE

Settled as a series of British colonies from the end of the eighteenth century on, Australia inherited British attitudes toward and legislative prohibitions against homosexuality. The nature of settlement resulted in colonies that were less marked by class distinctions than was England but possibly with even more rigid gender division. Thus, while homosexual behavior was undoubtedly widespread, it was barely spoken of and in the convict colonies was punished with extraordinary severity.[3] Unlike in some European countries, there was no lesbian and gay movement in the interwar years, and only very guarded references exist in pre-1970s literature.

This may seem to echo the U.S. experience, but Australia has a far smaller and until recently largely homogeneous population, heavily concentrated in the five mainland state capital cities. Australia is a federal system, with the states processing control over almost all criminal law. Thus, there is a commonwealth government in Canberra, six states, and two territory governments, all with relevant legal powers.

Unlike in the United States, there is relatively little tradition of fervent religiosity, which partially explains the rapidity with which contemporary Australia has come to accept homosexuality. The major churches are divided over the issue, with some support for gay issues coming from the Protestant Uniting Church and most antipathy existing within fundamentalist and High Anglican circles. The Catholic Church, nominally the largest in Australia, has been largely hostile to moves toward acceptance of homosexuality.

It is generally agreed that Australia has undergone significant social and cultural change since the late 1960s, the period Donald Horne termed the "the time of hope."[4] In Western societies in general this was the period that led to the creation of "new social movement theory," in an attempt to explain a new revolutionary politics that seemed to be emerging without the participation of, indeed sometimes in opposition to, working-class organizations. Most of those active in the first wave of the gay movement had been involved in other forms of activism, particularly the antiwar and feminist movements.

Three changes are particularly significant for understanding the emergence and relative success of the gay movement: the impact of second-wave feminism; the impact of large-scale and diverse immigration; and the growing integration into a global world order, strongly influenced by the United States but now looking increasingly for contact with the booming economies of east and southeast Asia.

It is perhaps symbolic that one of the most prominent second-wave feminists, Germaine Greer, was Australian, and feminism began to change the shape of Australian life from the early 1970s on. Anne Summers has recorded the extent to which feminism was institutionalized in social and political practices far more successfully in Australia than the United States,[5] and the impact of challenging assumptions about the gender order made it much easier to challenge related assumptions about the inherent "naturalness" of heterosexuality.

"Multiculturalism" was a term adopted by successive Australian governments from the mid-1970s to characterize a society that included a greater percentage of foreign-born inhabitants than any other country except Israel. We would argue that the stress on cultural diversity and official support for diverse communities became an important element in legitimizing the recognition of lesbian and gay communities.[6] Since the election of the John Howard government in 1996 and the emergence of Pauline Hanson's One Nation Party, there has been something of a backlash against multiculturalism, which could well threaten the extent to which Australia's overall tolerance of difference is established.

While Australian television seemed far ahead of U.S. television in its willingness to include gay characters in popular series (most notably the very popular soap opera of the early 1970s, "Number 96"), there has been a growing impact of American culture since the 1960s, when Australians turned from London to New York as the arbiter of fashion and ideas. Ironically, in some ways this may have slowed the willingness to allow positive depictions of homosexuality in mass media.

THE EMERGENCE OF A GAY MOVEMENT

As Craig and Robert Johnston have noted, the history of homosexuality in Australia "is mostly a history of sexual practice."[7] It was only after the First World War that identifiable homosexual networks began to emerge in Sydney; these began to flourish after the Second World War. Even here, though, "It remained an underground network, with members actively trying to keep things quiet."[8] Nevertheless, extensive social and gossip networks, an acute awareness of its own illegality and vulnerability (for example, passing on information about police activities), and even male prostitution were all signs of an emergent subculture. This was most obvious in Sydney, and, perhaps in response, in 1955 acts of indecency with a male and procuring and soliciting a male were deemed to be offenses by amendments to the New South Wales Crimes Act. The attorney general of the time proclaimed, "The government has acted because it considers that the homosexual wave that has struck this country—though not to the extent of continental countries—must be eradicated."[9]

Over a decade later the first gay political organizations in Australia emerged, with the founding of Homosexual Law Reform Societies in Sydney and Canberra in 1969 and the Daughters of Bilitis (named after the United States lesbian organization) in 1970. In mid-1970, the Campaign against Moral Persecution (CAMP) was established as a cosexual group in Sydney, and there were soon similar groups in all mainland capital cities, though only the Sydney group attracted large membership and real media coverage. (Note that "camp" was the common term for "homosexual," though it was quickly replaced by the U.S. word "gay.") Gay liberation groups followed very quickly in the major cities.[10]

Ralph Turner and Louis Killian's definition of social movements as "a collectivity acting with some continuity to promote or resist a change in the society or organization of which it is a part"[11] helps capture the disposition of the homosexual community in Australia at this time. Inspired by the empowering ideas of gay liberation and sexual revolution, the first demonstrations and marches were organized, the first in 1971 outside Liberal Party headquarters in Sydney. The beginnings of a gay press came with the short-lived journal *William and John* and the publication *Camp Ink*. By now some homosexuals were beginning to speak publically and to question the ways in which homosexuality was stigmatized in Australian society. "In questioning something that had been taken as a given for so long, they were similar to so many other young people in the society of the time who were aware of the emergence of new ideas, and of new social movements, and of the changes that were taking place in political culture."[12]

Lesbians were active in the early stages of both the women's and the gay movements; one activist saw lesbianism in feminist politics as "a really good political move. If you can lose your dependency on guys, you strengthen women as a group."[13] Lesbians fought the dominance of heterosexual women's concerns within the evolving feminist movement. Meanwhile, the perception of gay male patriarchy and an emphasis on lifestyle at the expense of activism were perceived as a major problem for maintaining a cosexual gay movement during the 1970s.

For a brief period in the mid- to late 1970s, post-Marxism was the favored model for activism in the Australian Left. This period coincided with the development of a gay male commercial world and the associated growth of a macho style among gay men, most prominently in inner Sydney. These developments remained quite distinct from the political movements associated with the Left, and political activism was not always welcomed by large sections of the gay subculture. In fact, Australia saw few expressions of mass political mobilization around gay issues, and relations with the state tended to be occasional and limited to an increasingly experienced activist core. There was little noticeable growth in attendance at the annual national gay conferences between 1975 and 1985, even though significant networks among gay activists were established during this period.

In the lesbian movement, post-Marxism's stress on the diverse spheres of activity across social movements was reflected in the rapid appearance of lesbian collectives and social groups in the mid- to late 1970s. By the early 1980s, lesbian separatism was moving to embrace these disparate elements. An issue of *Lesbian Network* proclaimed, "We want to promote attitudes that are pro-LESBIAN and anti-racist, non-classist, non-ageist and supportive of Aboriginal and disabled people's struggles."[14] Despite the rhetoric of post-Marxism, however, many of these objectives were overridden by a commitment to separatism often based on a sentimental essentialism, which argued for inherent "women's" (sometimes spelled "wymyn's") qualities.

Post-Marxist theory was in a poor position to explore the next stage of evolution, as the gay movement became more capable of combining direct political activism and social diversity. Some of the expressed and repressed tensions between the activist arm of the gay movement and the social and commercial networks gave way to a more cooperative synergy. A Gay Business Association was founded in Sydney, and avowedly gay candidates began to enter the political arena. Yet as Craig Johnston, an openly gay Sydney alderman, stated, "The fact is that most people in the sub-culture have few (if any) ties with the movement, do not accept the movement's claim to represent their interests and possibly wish it would stop making waves."[15]

This gap was to some extent already being bridged, although often at the expense of exacerbating the split between men and women. The advent of the Gay Mardi Gras (later the Gay and Lesbian Mardi Gras) in 1978 was a critical step in reconciling the community and the movement—by crystallizing the perceived achievements of law reform and community diversity, it enabled the community and movement sectors to identify with an effective common bond.[16]

The Sydney Gay and Lesbian Mardi Gras has, in many respects, come to be a public recognition of sexual diversity, but its origins were overtly political. An initiative of the activist arm of the movement, the street battles with police in its first year threatened many homosexuals unwilling to engage in politics. Since, in celebration of Stonewall, it was moved from winter to the end of the summer, it has become a mass celebration, drawing hundreds of thousands of spectators and considerable mainstream media and political support.[17] It is arguably the largest gay/lesbian street party in the world.

POLITICAL MOVEMENT VERSUS COMMERCIAL CULTURE

By the late 1970s, the gay movement had shown itself to be capable of sustaining an ongoing political project. The task now became reaching the diverse homosexual world, including the majority of women and men who rejected association with too "political" a movement. This was further tested in the clash between activist men and women, exemplified in the decision made by the Gay Publications Collective in Melbourne to change the style of the magazine *Outrage* (formerly *Gay Community News*) to attract more male readers and hence more advertising. All the women in the collective departed, but *Outrage* survived and continues as one of two monthly glossy gay publications. (In addition there are free bar papers in all mainland capitals, carrying extensive advertising, and several magazines aimed directly at women.)

For many lesbians in the mixed gay movement, this marked a defining point in the masculinization of the movement, which seemed more concerned with reaching the commercial world than maintaining a cosexual alliance. Partly in response, lesbian separatists developed their own political activism, free of male agendas. Unlike the development of peak gay/lesbian organizations in the United States—such as the National Gay and Lesbian Task Force (NGLTF)—relatively few lesbians opted to continue working alongside gay men.

In the late 1970s, the progress of the politically motivated arm of the gay movement seemed to have reached a plateau. The gay commercial world grew rapidly, attracting many former activists. But it would be a mistake to see this as other than a shift in emphasis—indeed, the less overtly political sense of community that was developing in the gay commercial and cultural world was to be critical in the impact that the movement would have in the 1980s and 1990s.

The growing gay world did not go unrecognized in the parliamentary arena. Tentative acceptance of the gay movement in mainstream politics came in both major parties during the 1970s, most notably from Gough Whitlam (prime minister from 1972 to 1975) and Don Dunstan (premier of South Australia for ten of the fourteen years between 1965 and 1979) within the Labour Party and Gorton (prime minister from 1969 to 1971) and Rupert Hamer (premier of Victoria from 1972 to 1981) within the Liberals. Their commitment to encouraging diverse ways of thinking, although not fully embraced by their own parties, was important in opening up debate around homosexuality alongside concerns about the acceptance of other marginal communities (Aboriginal, non-English speaking) into a multicultural Australia.

Certainly there were growing indications that Australia was becoming a more tolerant society, which were reflected in stances toward homosexuality. Comments from puritanical traditionalists, such as the Reverend Fred Nile, became the object of public derision; they represented only a small minority of the population and were viewed popularly as "morally prescriptive and authoritarian."[18] (Nile established the Call to Australia Party and had benefited from proportional representation to win two seats in the New South Wales Upper House. He has regularly called for the banning of Mardi Gras.) By contrast Burgmann argues that the gay movement could be seen as truly liberal, seeking no more than "the removal of restrictions without attempting to direct the sexual actions of anyone else."[19]

The decriminalization of (male) homosexual behavior had more to do with attitudes among mainstream politicians than with direct pressure from the gay movement. The South Australian government was the first to push through law reform in 1972, followed by the Australian Capital Territory a year later, Victoria in 1980, the Northern Territory in 1983, and New South Wales (NSW) in 1984. Only in NSW was there any significant pressure from the movement, although some individuals played an important lobbying role in Victoria. Queensland and Western Australia decriminalized homosexuality in 1990, leaving Tasmania as the last jurisdiction to resist decriminalization. The Tasmanian Gay and Lesbian Rights Group took its case to the United Nations Human Rights Committee, which ruled in the group's favor.[20] In response the federal government introduced the 1994 Human Rights (Sexual Conduct Act), which was intended to overrule Tasmania's remaining sodomy laws and certainly played a role in forcing change through the very conservative Tasmanian Upper House. Under considerable pressure Tasmania finally decriminalized homosexuality in 1997.

Nevertheless, support from senior political figures seemed tokenistic while the movement remained unrepresented in formal politics. Garry Wotherspoon has described the ascension of members of the gay community into public office as marking the difference between tolerance and acceptance.[21] Several candidates had received publicity for gay issues by standing as independents in the 1970s, but larger "success" came when Max Pearce won Labour preselection, albeit in a safe Liberal seat in Sydney. Further breakthroughs came with the elections of several gay aldermen in inner Sydney and Melbourne in the early 1980s, followed by a significant result in the seat of Bligh in the 1988 NSW state election, when Independent Clover Moore defeated a Liberal incumbent largely on the basis of her strong support for—and from—the gay community. In the 1995 state election, the Labour Party endorsed a high profile lesbian for Bligh, and the gay community was split very bitterly. Moore retained the seat.

Influence in the political sphere increased through some ties with other social movements, but the Tasmanian case meant that, even in the 1990s, the existence of criminal sanctions against male homosexual behavior concentrated efforts on law reform, making the activist agenda appear narrow in comparison with other movements. Though moves for de-criminalization were unifying achievements for the gay movement, inter-action with the state was in most cases seen as a necessary evil.

This changed to some extent as activists began lobbying for legal pro-tection under antidiscrimination laws. The first success came, again, in South Australia in 1972. Elsewhere there was some success in including homosexuals in antidiscrimination statutes.[22] At the time of this writing, there is protection in the statutes of all Australian jurisdictions bar Tas-mania and Western Australia. (In some cases, however, there are exemp-tions on the basis of religious beliefs or "care of children.") New South Wales presented the anomaly of including homosexuals in its antidis-crimination laws some years before decriminalization of homosexual be-havior.[23] In the second largest state, Victoria, the conservative state gov-ernment, which had previously opposed such inclusion, amended the Equal Opportunity Act in 1995 to include protection on the basis of "law-ful sexual activity," a phrase that lesbian and gay activists found dubious.

Because of the federal division of powers, the Commonwealth has lim-ited ability to legislate to protect homosexual rights. The federal Human Rights and Equal Opportunity Commission has the power to investigate and conciliate complaints of any breach of human rights; has recognized homosexual partnerships for certain limited purposes, most noticeably immigration; and, under its control of international relations, can over-rule state laws that are clearly inconsistent with treaties to which Aus-tralia is a signatory.

By the mid-1980s, the shift to the right in most liberal democracies led many social scientists to concentrate on the cultural and social spaces con-tested by increasingly global social movements. There was a growing in-terest in individual and social identities, particularly in the growth of fem-inist, environmental, and peace movements. Such theorists had difficulty explaining the representation of these movements in electoral politics, fo-cusing on the expressive and cultural arms of movements.

In Australia, some movements resembled their overseas counterparts, but the 1983 election of a Labour government advocating social change via consensus corporatism[24] offered a somewhat different challenge.

Many of the movement activists of the 1960s and 1970s had crossed into the bureaucracy, and they rose to senior positions with the change of government. Some critics saw these developments as a co-optation of social movements, particularly the women's and labor movements.[25] By the 1990s, the Australian gay community was perceived to be an influential voting bloc by all the major parties, with the small Australian Democrats most notable in nominating openly gay candidates but the Labour Party willing to court gay votes at least in inner-city constituencies. (There is currently one openly gay senator—a Tasmanian Green—and at least one openly lesbian state member in Western Australia.)

In the 1990s there were clear signs of rapprochement between gay men and lesbians, symbolized by the change of name to Gay and Lesbian Mardi Gras. Similarly, the annual Midsumma Festival in Melbourne involves both men and women, and there was a growing move to re-create cosexual political groups in the 1990s. In the early part of the decade, in the major debates in Sydney gay communities around the use of the term "queer," its opponents, both men and women, argued that this would again render lesbians invisible.

SOCIAL MOVEMENT THEORY AND THE AUSTRALIAN GAY MOVEMENT

In examining the gay movement in Australia, various theories of social movements can be applied. In some respects, the chronology of social movement theory can be matched to the shifts within the movement itself.

As argued above, the formation of CAMP marked the transition from subculture to social movement. Its aims of going beyond law reform, acting on liberationist ideas about the restructuring of society, and developing a politics around a homosexual identity all fit well into theoretical characterizations of collective action groups. The advent of gay liberation in the early 1970s similarly seemed to fit collective behaviorist models prominent at the time. It might also be argued that "relative deprivation" theory—focusing on the relative deprivation of group members in response to perceived grievances in relation to the state—offered an additional, if only partial answer to the question of what sort of Australian gay movement was emerging during this period. Its emphasis on symbolic structural disorder appeared particularly applicable to the lesbian movement of the 1970s, as it oscillated between attempts to seek structural change alongside gay men, straight women, or, in its more radical forms, the creation of separatist lesbian collectives.

"Collective behavior" theory followed the populist growth of social psychology in the 1950s and 1960s and disenchantment with pluralism's institutionalized view of movements as made up of disruptive and irrational malcontents. Although it did not clearly differentiate between collective behavior and social movements, collective behaviorism's essential focus on the measurable output of social movements tended to limit concepts of movements to intermittent interest and lobby groups. Collective action theorists neglected the structural preconditions of movements; that is, they focused too much on the "how" of social movements and not enough on the "why."[26]

Thus, by the 1980s, it was obvious that relative deprivation theory's overly developed focus on state relations came at the cost of exploring other critical social and cultural factors. A similar problem limited the applicability of the extremely popular "resource mobilization approach" (RMA) to the Australian gay movement. RMA originated from a project that sought to understand the 1970s institutionalization of 1960s social movements and to partially explain the plateau in numerical growth of popular movements. In so doing, it imposed a highly rational analytical framework, but again its accent on instrumental, institutionally driven political activity had limited use in explaining the evolution of the gay movement.

Moreover, available theories did not fully explain the gay movement's expansion into other cultural and social spaces. The problem was reinforced in Australia, where the failure of the gay movement to be recognized as part of the general community of progressive movements meant there was rarely recognition of the movement in general appeals for social movements across the broad Left.

However, the absence of a strong theoretical tradition in Australia provides room to proceed unfettered by entrenched European and North American social movement discourses. These approaches are often typecast as the one presenting the instrumental (North American) versus the other presenting the expressive (European) elements of social movements: the collision between the "core practical political theme" of movements and the poststructuralism that emerged as the theoretical discourse of choice[27] for many activists and academics.

The Australian gay movement had already exhibited many of the dual traits of expressive and instrumental politics. Indeed, its very durability had been partly due to its capacity to harness and nourish this dualism simultaneously. Much social movement theory had struggled to cope with these seemingly divergent and sometimes opposing dynamics within movements. However, by the mid-1980s, an exhaustion of the old social movement theories had led to a body of "new social movement" (NSM) theory, inspired by the German and French schools of philosophy.[28] The essence of new social movement theory, particularly these most recent adaptations, still offers the best prospects for explaining the contemporary gay movement in Australia.

THE GAY MOVEMENT AND AIDS: A NEW SOCIAL MOVEMENT?

In some respects the Australian gay movement of the late 1970s and early 1980s was similar to the new social movements blossoming in Europe. Social movement theorists argue that such movements do not want to be perceived as merely conventional and bureaucratized political actors,[29] and they may be reluctant to negotiate with the state, because they consider that political compromise will mean imperiling their overall goals.

All this was to change with the advent of AIDS. As in a few northern European countries, AIDS began as and has remained very heavily concentrated among male homosexuals. The latest epidemiological figures suggest there have been about eighteen thousand cases of HIV in Australia, well over 80 percent the result of homosexual transmission. Between 1983 and 1985 AIDS Councils, run by volunteers and elected boards, were established in all states and territories, almost always with a strong base among existing gay activists.

Thus, in an extremely short space of time, the gay movement was required to mobilize its own resources and simultaneously forge a cooperative relationship with the state to meet a new and serious health crisis. The urgency of the epidemic required a collective response perhaps without precedent for Australian social movements. It was a development that, in the short run, further increased gaps between lesbians and gay men; unlike in the United States there were very few lesbians involved in the leadership of AIDS organizations, and even today those women who have played leadership roles have most often been heterosexual.

Many gay men who had never seen themselves as activists were galvanized to belong to something tangible and immediate. The divide between "community" and "movement" rapidly blurred as gay groups across the nation developed relationships with government and other community agencies. A National Advisory Committee, established by Federal Health Minister Dr. Neal Blewett, included gay community representatives, as have its successors. The same government also financed the Australian Federation of AIDS Organisations (AFAO), and all state governments but Queensland accepted a cost-sharing arrangement with the federal government to help fund state-based AIDS Councils. It is beyond the scope of this chapter to suggest why Australia responded so efficiently and why the state has been willing both to fund community organizations generously and to condone some of the most confronting and explicit HIV-prevention campaigns devised.[30]

The AIDS Councils grew. Today the largest, the AIDS Council of New South Wales (ACON), has a paid full-time staff of ninety and a budget of over six million dollars. Consequently, many activists took AIDS-related paid employment, thus becoming responsible jointly to state and community. At the same time, the proliferation of government committees overseeing the AIDS area strengthened the legitimacy of the gay community, as a small group of organizational leaders became involved in these committees.

There is a risk of neglecting the development of a diverse gay movement since the mid-1980s, despite the devastating grief and loss caused by the epidemic. The AIDS leadership was an authoritative but nevertheless only partial voice for an ongoing social movement. New social movement theory would suggest that the advent of AIDS did not create a separate movement but rather that AIDS organizations became an instrumentally oriented arm of the original gay movement. Indeed, the spotlight AIDS threw on the gay community seemed to generate more interest and support for gay issues within the larger society. This did not occur without strong challenges from moral and political conservatives, but this opposition served only to strengthen the resolve of the movement and in most cases had only a marginal effect on government policies.

At the same time, a new generation of younger gay men and lesbians was shaping different boundaries and claiming new identities. The past decade has seen a nationwide trend toward defining identifiable groups as communities, as Australian society became more comfortable with its multicultural definition. Public dialogue in Australia shifted markedly from the use of the individualistic label "homosexual" to the term "gay community." This shift has occurred even as postmodern influences have led some to question the notion of "gay community," positing it as a misleading aggregation of a range of imprecise and fluid identities. Some have attempted to broaden definitions of the community; others have wanted to discard the term altogether (thus some campus groups have opted for names like Queer Tribes).

New social movement theory's tendency to reduce interactions with the state to periodic episodes understates the integral relationship between the gay movement and AIDS politics in Australia. It was clear that by the end of the 1980s, AIDS was to be a permanent feature of the Australian political landscape and the gay community a central player.[31] The state itself has helped foster a particular idea of "a gay community," one that is more institutionalized than social movement theory suggests is viable. With the establishment of peak bodies in the HIV/AIDS community sector, key government agencies appear content to label these bodies "the voice" of affected communities, especially "the gay community."

A necessary but inevitable tension between the expressive and the instrumental aims of social movements has been visible in the politics of representation surrounding HIV/AIDS. Although the overlap between gay and AIDS organizations is still substantial, the distinction is important. The membership of AIDS Councils originally consisted overwhelmingly of gay men working as volunteer educators and carers, and although the proportion is still high, the decline is attributed to everything from fatigue to bureaucratization. In any event, the HIV/AIDS community sector's role as a vanguard for the gay movement has noticeably diminished.

To a large extent, the impetus and energy that drove the initial AIDS organizations has given way to more traditional pressure group and service delivery agencies. Although it was not always acknowledged, early AIDS activism was often driven by a sense that AIDS was a demanding but short-term problem.[32] As prospects for a quick cure or vaccine have rapidly diminished, and as thousands of gay men have died, the nature of the organizations has changed substantially. What appeared originally as a seemingly organic bond between those working in AIDS and the gay community had begun to disentangle by 1990. This became evident in the growth of demands for leadership by people living with HIV/AIDS (PLWH/As), as well as in some direct activism in the form of a chapter of AIDS Coalition to Unleash Power (ACT UP), which denounced the lack of attention given to people living with AIDS (PLWAs) and the alleged bureaucratization of the AIDS Councils. Although ACT UP lasted only a few years and was heavily American influenced, the anger and alienation it expressed remains in some sections.

At the same time there has been a dramatic increase in other community-based gay organizations. In Melbourne alone, more than forty gay community groups advertise weekly in the community classifieds of the gay press. Beyond the community itself, relationships between the state and the gay movement are less straightforward than those observed by Adam Carr in 1988: "For the first time, [AIDS has] forced gay men and the government into a working relationship that compels each side to deal with the other as it really is rather than as rhetorical abstractions."[33]

In many policy forums, PLWH/As have come to represent affected communities, often replacing HIV-negative gay men. With the rise of an empowered PLWH/A movement in Australia, some tension has arisen within AIDS organizations where PLWH/As have been required to encapsulate both communities' viewpoints. This was clearly demonstrated in the 1995 Victorian AIDS Council/Gay Men's Health Centre elections. A bitter struggle between an activist gay faction and volunteers of its support programs and PLWH/A programs deeply divided the organization, each side accusing the other of attempting to "own" the epidemic.[34]

Attempts to close this rift have appealed to a sense of gay community, suggesting that at some levels AIDS has facilitated the strengthening of a gay social movement. It is clear that the gay movement in Australia continues both despite and because of the specter of AIDS, and this shows not only the movement's diversity but also its durability. Where the gay and AIDS movements have clashed, the arguments have been more of style than of substance, both fully aware of their mutual and reciprocal relationship. As the end of the twentieth century approaches, the more instrumentally oriented arm of the gay movement will continue to invest considerable resources in AIDS organizations, while the more expressive elements proceed to embrace an increasingly heterogeneous constituency.

The general acceptance of efforts to prevent the spread of AIDS among homosexually active men can be seen as a significant marker of a more tolerant society. During the 1990s gay and lesbian themes and images increasingly influenced Australian popular culture, leading to less reliance on American representations of being gay. Indeed, gay images and culture have rapidly become desirable and fashionable in Australian urban life. Gay dance parties are increasingly patronized by eager young heterosexuals,[35] and the gay market is now seen as the premier medium for pioneering fashion trends. The Pink Dollar thrives, courting national and international corporations for mass advertising exposure.[36] Lucrative films (for example, The Sum of Us, Priscilla), whatever their limitations, and national television broadcasts of Mardi Gras all suggest growing acceptance—though in the latter case there was considerable pressure on the Australian Broadcasting Corporation to schedule the Mardi Gras broadcasts after 9:00 P.M.

We do not wish to overstate the extent to which it is "okay to be gay" in contemporary Australia. Antigay violence and prejudice continues,[37] and in some parts of Australia, there has been censorship of gay HIV-education material. There are particular difficulties for those living outside the large cities, for indigenous and immigrant Australians. Still, in some areas AIDS has enabled significant community organizing—the first National Aboriginal Gay Men's Conference in Alice Springs was sponsored in 1994 by the Federal Health Department's HIV/AIDS unit.

Acceptance is a particular challenge in many immigrant communities, particularly those with strong religious traditions. Lesbians and gay men of non-Anglo origin often complain that they feel excluded from both mainstream gay life and their own ethnic communities.[38] One recent study of homosexual men in Darwin, the capital of the Northern Territory and often thought of as "the Australian frontier," captures the breadth of modern gay sexual identities through extensive interviews with rural, Aboriginal, and Asian homosexual men.[39] Issues of class have been considered in a large study of Australian urban working-class gay men,[40] further expanding notions of a heterogeneous gay community.

Among women, new lesbian groups are developing, even as coalition-ist politics has enjoyed a resurgence. Despite clear signs that the lesbian movement embraces of both the "lipstick lesbian" and the "butch dyke," its activists are still identified with the latter, often leading to externally imposed tensions. In some cities this has had demographic implications. In Brisbane, the inner-city suburb New Farm is readily identified as hip, glossy, and commercial, whereas across the river, West End is the politi-cal activist's enclave.

The contemporary Australian gay movement is neither principally dri-ven by expressive interests based on community and identity building nor limited to a series of instrumental engagements with the state. Rather, there is a persistent fluidity that characterizes the instrumental/expressive interplay within the movement and begins to blur some of the assumptions of NSM theory. This interplay has not been without its tensions, but nei-ther has it caused the disruption that most NSM theorists would assert.

Perhaps the greatest tension for the contemporary gay movement in Australia is the need to combine recognition of individual diversity with collective political and social empowerment. Postmodern theory illus-trates the capacity for social movements to adopt a range of quite com-plex, interweaving identities and offers considerable possibilities for the future shape of gay and lesbian movements. But the current fetish for de-constructionism may undermine the concept of effective social move-ments if it focuses only on diversity at the cost of commonalties. The ac-ceptance of sexual "lifestyles" within the marketplace pointed to by postmodern critics, obsessed as they are with media and consumption, does not mean we should ignore the discrimination and prejudice that re-main in many areas of institutional life.

THE PARADOX OF GLOBALIZATION

The Australian gay movement was, in its origins, very derivative of the movement in the United States.[41] As a gay movement and community has developed, and Australia has increasingly interacted with the Asian re-gion, there is evidence that Australia is, in turn, having some influence on the emergence of gay communities and movements in the countries to its north and west.

Again, AIDS has been the major impetus. AIDS opened up both inter-est and resources for contact between AIDS and gay movements in Australia and their counterparts in the region, such as Pink Triangle in Malaysia, KKLGN in Indonesia, and the Library Foundation in the Philippines. Although the epidemic is far less concentrated among homosexual men in Asian countries than it is in Australia, gay groups have been crucial in developing community-based responses in countries such as Malaysia, the Philippines, Singapore, and Indonesia.[42]

Growing Asian migration and ever expanding Asian student numbers are increasing the links between Australia and its region, and there is evidence that Australia is becoming a gay tourist attraction for middle-class Asian homosexuals. One Singaporean novel, Johann Lee's *Peculiar Chris*,[43] describes the narrator as traveling to Sydney to "come out," just as an earlier generation of Australians went to London and the United States in search of sexual freedom. Although a few Australians have participated in meetings of the International Lesbian and Gay Association, and Australian lesbians have been active in international women's forums, it is only very recently that there has been larger recognition of the international dimensions of the gay and lesbian movement.

Australia still looks to the United States as the arbiter of style and intellectual fashion, despite the growing rhetoric that Australia is "part of Asia." The challenge for the Australian gay and lesbian movement will be to develop real links with the fast-growing communities to the north, which in time will suggest new possibilities for being "gay" in an increasingly complex and globalized world.

NOTES

Acknowledgment: We thank Robert Reynolds for his helpful reading of this chapter.

1. Notable exceptions include Robert Aldrich and Garry Wotherspoon, eds., *Gay Perspectives I and II: Essays in Australian Gay Culture* (Sydney: Department of Economic History, 1992 and 1994); Garry Wotherspoon, *City of the Plain: History of a Gay Sub-Culture* (Sydney: Hale and Iremonger, 1991); Craig Johnston and Robert Johnston, "The Making of Homosexual Men," and Liz Ross, "Escaping the Well of Loneliness," in *Staining the Wattle: A People's History of Australia since 1788,* ed. Verity Burgmann and Jenny Lee. Melbourne: Penguin, 1988; Verity Burgmann, " 'Out and Proudly Out': The Lesbian and Gay Movements," in *Power and Protest: Movements for Change in Australian Society,* ed. Verity Burgmann (Sydney: Allen and Unwin, 1993); Dennis Altman, "The Emergence of Gay Identity in the USA and Australia," in *Politics of the Future: The Role of Social Movements,* ed. Christine Jennett and Randal Steward (Melbourne: Longman Cheshire, 1990); and Dennis Altman, *The Comfort of Men* (Melbourne: Heinemann, 1993).

2. See Annamarie Jagose and Chris Berry, eds. *Meanjin* 1 (February 1996), the "queer" issue of *Meanjin.*

3. See Robert Hughes, *The Fatal Shore: A History of the Transportation of Convicts to Australia 1787–1868* (London: Collins Harvill, 1987).

4. Donald Horne, *Time of Hope* (Sydney: Angus and Robertson, 1980).

5. Anne Summers, "Sisters Out of Step" *Independent Monthly* (July 1990): 17–19.

6. See Dennis Altman, "Homosexuality," in *Australian Civilisation* ed. Richard Nile (Sydney: Oxford University Press, 1994).

7. Johnston and Johnston, "The Making of Homosexual Men," 88.

8. Ibid., 93.

9. Ibid., 94.

10. Denise Thompson, *Flaws in the Social Fabric: Homosexuals and Society in Sydney* (Sydney: Allen and Unwin, 1985).

11. Ralph Turner and Louis Killian, *Collective Behavior* (Englewood Cliffs, N.J.: Prentice Hall, 1987), 223.

12. Wotherspoon, *City of the Plain,* 161.

13. Jenny Brown, "The Howling in the Liberation Tree," *William and John* 1, no. 8 (1972): 33.

14. "Collectively Speaking," *Lesbian Network* 1, (Spring 1984): 2.

15. Craig Johnston, "From Gay Movement to Gay 'Community,'" *Gay Information* 5, no. 6–9 (1981): 33.

16. See Graham Carbery, *A History of the Sydney Gay and Lesbian Mardi Gras* (Melbourne: Australian Lesbian and Gay Archives, 1995).

17. Ian Marsh and Larry Galbraith, "The Political Impact of the Sydney Gay and Lesbian Mardi Gras," *Australian Journal of Political Science* 30 (1995): 300–20.

18. Burgmann, *Power and Protest,* 147.

19. Ibid.

20. See Miranda Morris, *The Pink Triangle: Struggle for Gay Law Reform in Tasmania* (Sydney: University of New South Wales Press, 1995); Tim Tenbensel, "International Human Rights Conventions and Australian Political Debates," *Australian Journal of Political Science* 31 (1):7–23.

21. Wotherspoon, *City of the Plain,* 206.

22. As outlined in Shane Ostenfield, "Interactive Movements: Gay Lib, Trade Unions, Women, and Youth." Paper presented to the Australian Gay History Project, University of Sydney, 1995.

23. See Lex Watson, "Gay Rights Legislation," *Current Affairs Bulletin,* 1 July 1979), 19–25.

24. For more in this area, see Peter Beilharz, *Transforming Labor: Labour Tradition and the Labor Decade in Australia* (Melbourne: Cambridge University Press, 1994).

25. Suzanne Franzway, Dianne Court, and R. W. Connell, *Staking a Claim: Feminism, Bureaucracy and the State* (Sydney: Allen and Unwin, 1989).

26. This is an observation shared by Bert Klandermans and Sidney Tarrow, in "Mobilization into Social Movements: Synthesizing European and American Approaches," *International Social Movement Research* 1 (1988): 9.

27. This argument is developed further by Pauline Vaillancourt Rosenau,

"Health Politics Meets Post-Modernism: Its Meaning and Implications for Community Health Organizing," *Journal of Health Politics, Policy and Law* 19, no. 2 (1994): 303–33.

28. A considerable number of prominent NSM theorists have emerged during the 1980s and 1990s, the more notable including Alaine Touraine and Alberto Melucci.

29. Bronislaw Misztal, "New Social Movements: Plurality of the Forms of Struggle," *Social Alternatives* 6, no. 3 (1987): 13.

30. See John Ballard, "The Politics of AIDS in Australia," in *The Politics of Health: The Australian Experience* 2 ed. Heather Gardner. Melbourne: Churchill Livingstone, 1989.

31. This is outlined in "Slowing the Epidemic—the Education and Prevention Program," in *Valuing the Past . . . Investing in the Future: Evaluation of the National AIDS Strategy 1993–94 to 1995–96* (Canberra: Australian Government Publishing Service, 1995).

32. Dennis Altman and Kim Humphrey, "Breaking Boundaries: AIDS and Social Justice in Australia," *Social Justice* 16, no. 3 (1989): 158–66.

33. Adam Carr, "Victorian AIDS Council—Making a New Start?" *National AIDS Bulletin* 9, no. 6 (1995): 6

34. Ibid.

35. Lynette A. Lewis and Michael W. Ross, "The Gay Dance Party Culture in Sydney: A Qualitative Analysis," *Journal of Homosexuality* 29, no. 1 (1995): 41–70.

36. In the eighty-page December 1995 edition of *Outrage*, over twenty full pages were devoted to advertisements, including some for large corporations such as Telstra and Jim Beam.

37. Gail Mason, "Violence against Lesbians and Gay Men: Crime and Violence Prevention Unit Series," Paper No. 2, Australian Institute of Criminology, Canberra; 1993.

38. For a dramatic example of this, see Christos Tsiolkas, *Loaded* (Sydney: Vintage, 1995).

39. Dino Hodge, *Did You Meet Any Malagas? A Homosexual History of Australia's Tropical Capital* (Darwin, Australia: Little Gem, 1993).

40.. Gary Dowsett, Mark Davis, and Bob Connell, "Gay Lifestyles of the Not-so-Rich and Quite Unfamous," in Aldrich and Wotherspoon, *Gay Perspectives I,* 131–46.

41. Dennis Altman, "The Creation of Sexual Politics in Australia," *Journal of Australian Studies* 20 (1987): 76–82.

42. See Dennis Altman, *Power and Community: Organizational and Cultural Responses to AIDS* (London: Falmer, 1994).

43. Johann Lee, *Peculiar Chris* (Singapore: Cannon, 1992).

Barry D Adam,
Jan Willem Duyvendak,
and André Krouwel

14 Gay and Lesbian Movements beyond Borders?

National Imprints of a Worldwide Movement

WE BEGIN in this concluding chapter by summarizing the empirical results of this book, particularly taking into consideration those elements that all authors deal with in their country chapters. Since parallels in the development of gay and lesbian movements are striking, at least at first glance, we start by outlining similarities across countries. Closer scrutiny shows, however, that these similarities are sometimes misleading, and superficial analogies may hide fundamental disparities. In the second part of this chapter, we therefore try to explain both the cross-national similarities and the differences in the development of gay and lesbian movements. By comparing countries that are comparable in many aspects but divergent in others, we are able to present an "opportunities model" of movement emergence and development. By distinguishing between essential prerequisites as well as facilitative or accommodating conditions presented in the rich empirical material of this book, we deduce some fundamental principles underpinning the development of gay and lesbian movements.

A clear trajectory of factors can be distilled from the different national contexts. As a basic prerequisite for the emergence of a lesbian and gay organization, individuals must be able to find a social space where they can develop lesbian and gay identities, and they must be able to construct a rudimentary organization beyond private circles of friends. Once this space is carved out, lesbians and gays can start making political demands. This politicization of the social group seems to be facilitated, rather than hampered, when political repression is evident but not too strong. Several chapters show that the authorities' reaction to this politicization is crucial for the subsequent development of the movement. Movement leaders can seize opportunities only if and when they are available. It is evident, however, that the type and scope of political organization in different countries is very much influenced by developments elsewhere in the world. A process of transnational diffusion is discernible; all around the world gay and lesbian movements influence and learn from each other.

Still, we cannot speak of *the* gay and lesbian movement in the singular. Movements are strongly affected by local, national, or regional political and social structures; all movements show a clear national or regional imprint, reflecting a national "paradigm."

SIMILARITIES AMONG GAY AND LESBIAN MOVEMENTS AROUND THE WORLD

Compared with other social movements, "identity" movements, such as the homosexual movement, seem to be less influenced by national political opportunities and therefore might be expected to be more similar across countries (Duyvendak 1995). At first sight, similarities are indeed striking in both the phases of movement development and the issues that are politicized by the movement. In this part of the chapter, we deal with these similarities, particularly concerning issues, action patterns, strategies, and organized events; the development of social movement organizations; and, last but not least, the question of gender differences in movements.

First we found similarities in issue emphasis among movements all over the world. Since homosexual men and women suffer from discrimination virtually everywhere, it is not surprising that many of the topics their movements have dealt with in the last decades are fairly similar among countries. Everywhere movements pursue a double strategy of both fighting discrimination and establishing public spaces of their own. At the initial stage in the struggle against homophobia, laws prohibiting homosexual behavior in public and private are the main topic, often in combination with demands for legal recognition of the movement organization pursuing this goal. In the next phase, movements combat discrimination in other fields; they challenge unequal treatment in all areas, from the armed forces to the household. In the most recent phase of this antidiscrimination strategy—typical of northwestern Europe, the United States, Canada, and Australia—movements have directed their demands to the heart of heteronormative society: marriage should be opened for gay and lesbian couples and adoption no longer the exclusive privilege of heterosexuals.

The second strategy aims at establishing a space, in social terms as well as in terms of an actual physical area where homosexuals can meet. Depending on the phase of emancipation, this space strategy is directed either toward the creation of a place to hide from the homophobic outside world or toward a struggle for a free cultural place, a place to meet with each other. The social activities and group formation can ultimately result in commonalities in lifestyles and in the development of common identities. As is clearly illustrated in the previous chapters, the kind of identity "lived" by gays and lesbians, either imitating heterosexual role models or, on the contrary, emphasizing the right to be different, depends on the social and political context. Thus, struggles between more assimilationist or separatist tendencies within movements, implying differences between those gays and lesbians who are proud to be homosexual and those who want to hide their sexual orientation and who wish to be "normal," reflect the various conditions for the gay and lesbian movement in the respective countries. Both types usually coexist in all countries, and at different times each one can be dominant. Though an evolutionary model from repression to liberation is far from reality, we may conclude on the basis of the preceding chapters, that in many countries the movement has been able to win the first battles and to settle itself as a recognizable political and societal actor.

Significant cross-national similarities can also be found in the pattern of actions and events organized by movements in different countries. Following the dual strategy of both fighting for antidiscrimination and establishing gay and lesbian cultural space, movements use numerous forms of action. Mass demonstrations, consciousness-raising groups, sit-ins, and lobbying are among the tactics frequently mentioned in the preceding chapters. Among the countries, numerous parallels come to the fore. Almost everywhere, mass demonstrations became institutionalized as Gay and Lesbian Pride, celebrating the Stonewall riots of June 1969. The chapters also show, however, that mass participation is not limited to Gay and Lesbian Pride: in some countries (including the United States) mobilization was already occurring before Stonewall, and people took to the streets for many more reasons than simply celebrating Pride Day. As well, particular issues such as AIDS have provided a worldwide focus for mobilization.

The action repertoire of movement groups has additional cross-national characteristics. In many countries, mass mobilization occurs when the movement is already established and recognized and at a time when the main goals in the antidiscrimination struggle are already on the political agenda. This is very often the moment, as well, when radical tendencies come to the fore. Generally originating from student groups, radical activists no longer ask for compassion or equal treatment but fight for a radically different society and liberating sexuality. Interestingly, though, these radical aims are seldom accompanied by radical means: gays and lesbians rarely use violence or mass civil disobedience to reach their goals. Happy to be finally "accepted," movement leaders often work to remain on speaking terms with political authorities. Though grassroots participants dare to challenge conventional sexual wisdom, they do not risk the lives they have just secured.

The country chapters also show an impressive similarity in the stages of development among lesbian and gay movements. Everywhere the founding of organizations leads to the organization of some but not other constituencies of gay and lesbian communities. In particular the relation between gender-mixed or nonmixed social movement organizations was (and is) a hotly debated topic, as is the relation toward the broader public. Is a social movement organization oriented inward, strengthening the capacities of its members in a free space for identity formation, or does it pursue more "instrumental" goals, aiming to change or abolish laws? In some countries, social movement organizations are part and parcel of the "community." This is the case particularly in Anglo-Saxon countries, where political mobilization primarily originates from community efforts and is financially self-supporting. In some European countries, however, a gap developed between the commercial scene and the government-subsidized movement. In such countries a highly developed commercial scene competes with the political movement as a sphere where gays and lesbians socialize. In, for example, Eastern Europe and authoritarian political systems, a third model can be found in which there is little or no political activity, no community spirit, and at best a limited commercial infrastructure.

Interestingly, in many countries the movement "came out" as a result of a triggering event—a radio or television program dealing negatively with homosexuality, causing a storm of protest by those affected. Other forms of public attention, in politics or media, also offer opportunities for initiating mobilization. An "enemy" or "opponent" and a specific symbolic event may mobilize substantial numbers of lesbians and gays and galvanize movement organizations.

In most countries, the chapters show a gender conflict between gays and lesbians that splits the movement. In the beginning, internal division was muted in the dark days of severe repression. As societal repression diminished, gender differences came more to the fore. Political and theoretical currents within the women's movement often led to intense debates and changing viewpoints among lesbians. At times, the failure of many men to understand women's issues convinced lesbians to cast their lot with feminism. In other forums, women's, lesbian and gay organizations found areas of fundamental agreement and acted as firm allies. By the late 1970s and 1980s, a number of trends encouraged reconciliation: (1) the rise of the New Right, especially in the United States, drew various groups together into tactical alliances, (2) changes within feminist analysis and activism, in particular its central preoccupation with heterosexual relations, influenced some lesbians to look elsewhere for support, and (3) the politics of suppression that swirled around AIDS, primarily in the mid-1980s, called for a more united defense.

CROSS-NATIONAL DIFFERENCES AMONG LESBIAN AND GAY MOVEMENTS

The similarities in activities, styles, symbols, institutions, language, and so on observed above do not imply that the identities are the same. In particular, there are impressive differences in the way people experience their identities as being, or not being, politicized. The distinction between countries of British heritage with well-developed "communities" and northern European countries where movement and subculture are more separated is relevant here. There is perhaps more of a continuum between personal identity and community politics in the countries of British heritage, whereas the northern European countries are characterized by a split between a rather apolitical culture and formalized movement. Nonpoliticized identities and nonpolitical social interaction dominate in the Eastern European context, as well as in other parts of the world outside the Western hemisphere, where desire is not framed in terms of political interests.

An in-depth look at the country chapters shows that, in fact, it is not so much that movements look alike; it is more that cultural expressions resemble each other, perhaps through the borrowing or adoption of rhetoric from movements in other countries. In addition, even these similar cultural practices have quite different meanings in the various countries and in different settings within these countries. The worldwide use of similar symbols, language, dress styles, and so on shows commonalities among countries, but these apparent commonalities must not blind us to differences that exist in the meanings of these practices. Country-specific elements remain important, much more than is acknowledged by the postmodern rhetoric that celebrates globalization instead of emphasizing the local meanings of global tendencies. There are, for instance, surprising differences in strength among movements in countries with rather comparable subcultures (the United States, Canada, Australia) that illustrate the relevance of local parameters of global tendencies. Moreover, movements may change substantially in a single country over time, while the culture remains more or less unchanged during the same period (Britain, the Netherlands, France).

One of the more important findings in this study is that the trajectories and phases of the development of postwar gay and lesbian movements in Western capitalist countries (at least those that did not experience a democratic breakdown after World War II) are very similar: moderate movements in the 1950s, radicalization in the late 1960s and early 1970s, response to AIDS in 1980s, and broad, diversified movements in the 1990s. These superficial similarities camouflage underlying differences as well. In the first place, the development of movements of homosexual people around the world shows that the order given above follows neither a logical nor a necessary sequence. In addition, in many countries progress and backlash alternate. Moreover, the same phenomenon, for instance AIDS, causes strikingly different reactions in rather comparable countries. Whereas in many Western, capitalist countries a new more militant response—AIDS Coalition to Unleash Power (ACT UP), Outrage, AIDS Action Now—occurred around AIDS, in the Netherlands and some other European countries, radical organizations did not achieve a significant following. These differences show the limitations of an evolutionary model of movement development.

COUNTRY PARADIGMS AND NATIONAL IMPRINTS

Almost all of the authors in this volume show how national characteristics mold movements both in their aims and strategies: in Canada the struggle for autonomy in Quebec, in France the republican idea of universalism, in the Netherlands the heritage of pillarization, in the United States the quasi-ethnic community concept, in Japan the hegemonic traditional and conformist culture, in South Africa the fundamental right of nondiscrimination, in other postauthoritarian countries the democratic right of equal treatment, and so on. These contexts shape the country-specific path along which the gay and lesbian movement may progress. "The contemporary gay and lesbian movement has its own historical trajectory in each country," as Dennis Altman (1997:4) aptly put it. The gay and lesbian movement is not only dependent on the solidarity of social movements and other allies; it also has to "fit" into the emancipation model used by other groups in society and recognized by authorities as valid and justified. The way to a brighter future is carved out by the struggle in the past. In some countries gay and lesbian movements are "forced" to present themselves in terms of a cultural minority, in others as part of a broad movement for human rights and equality. All this depends on the country-specific political and cultural frames dominant in society and politics. Therefore, the main conclusion to be drawn from the country chapters is that national political and cultural characteristics play a crucial role in the development of national lesbian and gay movements. The next question then becomes Which characteristics are decisive for the emergence and development of lesbian and gay movements?

ESSENTIAL PREREQUISITES AND FACILITATIVE FACTORS

At the beginning of this book, the question of how to understand the development of an identity-based, "subcultural" movement was raised. In this concluding chapter, we refer to the different theoretical approaches to social movements dealt with herein: the difference between instrumental and identity movements used in the political process approach (see Duyvendak 1995, Kriesi et al. 1995), the effects of repression and facilitation on such movements, the relevance of chances of success, and so on. We have opted for a rather eclectic approach to understand movement development, taking into consideration the economic, cultural, and social contexts; the national political context; and the international context. Under these three headings we deal with aspects that prove to be relevant in the different national contexts. The country chapters lead to the conclusion that there are certain conditions (discussed in the next section of this chapter) that must be fulfilled for a gay and lesbian movement to emerge. In addition the contributors to this volume point to factors that prove vital for the development of the movement, yet these conditions differ considerably from country to country. In instances where these factors are not present or are weak, movements may still come about by finding strategies to overcome these deficiencies.

PREREQUISITES IN THE SOCIETAL CONTEXT

Whether or not a gay and lesbian movement develops depends on many factors. Some social factors influence the opportunities of a movement directly; some factors affect the opinions and attitudes of the public and thereby influence politics and, indirectly, movement opportunities. The very idea of a movement by homosexual people becomes imaginable only if people have sexual identities (Adam 1995). In other words, some cultural, social, and economic *prerequisites* have to be in place before other factors, such as political factors, become pertinent.

Meanings of Sexuality and Sexual Identity

There are enormous differences among countries in the meanings of sexuality and in the possibility of sexual identity in specific societies. Sexual identity, in the sense of a popular recognition or sense of commonality among people who share a sexual and affectional orientation, is a precondition for a gay and lesbian movement to develop, even if one of the aims of the movement is the deconstruction of these identities (see Gamson 1995:2). "Once homosexuality is transformed into a people, the idea of a gay movement found its place" (Adam 1995). In most of the countries researched, sexual identities in the modern sense of the word seem to exist today, though there remain impressive differences in the meanings of sexual identities in, for instance, Japan, Brazil, and the Netherlands. As well, all of these identity categories remain in flux, subject to continual negotiation and revision across generations and historical time. "Homophile," "gay," "lesbian," and "queer" all imply a different politics and sense of self. Whereas a modern "gay" and "lesbian" identity seems to be the most "unproblematic" basis for the construction of a social movement, other types of identities, other ways of experiencing sexuality, seem to be less conducive contexts for movement organization.

Sex/Gender Systems

Partly related to the issue of sexual identity are the various meanings of the sex/gender systems in the countries researched. Where gays are defined as passive or discredited men, they may not be permitted a place in civil society; where lesbians are not seen to exist, they can scarcely occupy a position as political actors. The chapters show that movements are somewhat weaker in countries where homosexual preference is constructed through the lens of gender (Brazil and Franco-era Spain). Patriarchal logic may reserve public and political agency for men, depriving all women and those men considered to be effeminate of civic participation. *Activo* men, in a gender-defined system of homosexuality, may escape a label and a sexual identity, thereby preserving their privileges as adult men. *Activos* are therefore not likely to feel a commonality with *pasivos*, any more than straight men do with feminists, thereby inhibiting solidarity and political organization among homosexually inclined men.

Development of Civil Society

One constructive factor for social movements is the national civic culture. As indicated in the Chapter 1 of this book, gay and lesbian movements are stronger and better organized where there are public, institutionally complex gay and lesbian communities (Kriesi and Duyvendak 1995: 3–25). Where gay and lesbian life is confined to "underground" or illicit niches, or private friendship networks, if movement organization can emerge at all, it is only under the cloak of scientific or cultural activity, such as the Wissenschaftlich-Humanitäres Komitee before the Second World War in Germany and the Netherlands or the Shakespeare Club, *Arcadie,* and several organizations in the 1950s and early 1960s. These groups are limited to a defensive posture in a hostile social climate and therefore have little ability to mobilize any kind of mass movement. Excluded from the mass media and silenced in the public sphere as "obscene" or as an affront to "public morals," these embryonic groups have few means of communicating with their potential constituency.

The country chapters reveal other differences pertinent to mobilization, with the recruitability of gays and lesbians in different cultural contexts varying from very limited to impressive. First, under certain circumstances the commercial infrastructure and political movement form one "community" (which implies that there is a manifest potential in the subculture that can be mobilized); under other circumstances, there is a split between a depoliticized, commercialized "subculture" and an often professionalized movement subsidized by local or national governments. Second, accessibility and visibility are vital to the recruitment and mobilizing potential of the movement. This potential is dependent on whether the (sub)culture is mixed or more exclusively homosocial, very much sex oriented or consisting of various social and cultural institutions, and concentrated in the larger cities or well dispersed throughout the country. And finally, it is also important whether the organization is legal or illegal.

There is no linear link between the makeup of a community and mobilization potential. The chapters show fundamental differences in the functioning of civil society and, consequently, in the space for gays and lesbians to organize, according to the characteristics of national political cultures and practices. An important aspect is the density of civil society in general—that is, the overall profusion of social organizations and associations (Putnam, Leonardi, and Nannetti 1993). In most of the advanced capitalist countries, civil society relies on a social fabric of trust and active cooperation on numerous levels. Where civil society has been largely eradicated by a totalitarian system, such as in the East European cases, widespread public distrust hinders the emergence of collective action. A high level of civic engagement creates more opportunities to master the political skills necessary for social organization and protest against repression and discrimination. A dense civic culture also creates the possibility for cross-cutting memberships among different organizations, making coalition building easier. Countries with a dense civil society are also more likely to be responsive to political claims by minority groups. The manner in which a society deals with minorities in general proves to be vital for the emergence and mobilization potential of lesbian and gay movements. In countries like Japan, where a homogeneous religious and political culture is dominant, "deviants" and minorities have considerable difficulty in finding a place for themselves on the public agenda. In immigrant countries or traditionally heterogeneous societies, such as Australia, the United States, Canada, and the Netherlands, there exists a certain extent of respect and tolerance for political demands from minority groups and cultures.

Organized Religion

The relation between organized religion and the state is of great significance to the rise of a gay and lesbian movement. Institutionalized religion plays a major role in policing public culture in many societies. When the church exerts state power through a dominant religious party and its ancillary organizations, the liberation of gays and lesbians is severely hampered. In the southern, eastern, and central regions of Europe and parts of Latin America, where politics and society remain heavily influenced by Roman Catholic or Orthodox churches, the level of acceptance of homosexuality tends to be considerably lower. The Roman Catholic Church contributes to this intolerance in Italy, Spain, Portugal, and Poland. Of course, the Catholic countries differ among themselves. In Italy, for example, the Communist (and its successor Party of the Democratic Left) counterculture provides an alternative for oppositional political organization outside the dominance of Catholicism. In Spain, the democratic fevor that emerged after the death of Franco diminished the power of the church, which had been guaranteed by dictatorship. And in Portugal, gay and lesbian community groups, movement organizations, and cultural expression burst forth in the mid-1990s. The legacy of revolution in Mexico and popular movements in Brazil have created secular spaces in civil society. The space that was opened for civil society in Sandinista Nicaragua (when the first gay and lesbian groups came about) gave way to a more repressive state when the conservative business-church alliance resumed power in 1990.

The Orthodox Church in Russia and Romania is even more homophobic. In countries where the influence of the church is not so strong, the general attitude of the population is more tolerant. In the Czech Republic, where 60 percent of the population does not adhere to a religion, public opinion on homosexuality has shifted significantly toward acceptance, between 1988 and 1993 and particularly since the fall of the Communist regime. In Romania and Poland, where church attendance is very high, the population remains highly intolerant of homosexuality (Ester, Halman, and de Moor 1993; Prochazka 1994).

Another example of the specific interrelation of national political power structures and organized religion is, for example, the evangelical Protestants in the United States, who are the most consistent opponents of gay and lesbian liberation. Elsewhere, Protestants adopted a more liberal and tolerant stance toward homosexuality, dependent on their relative political strength.

We may conclude, however, that in countries where organized religion plays a lesser role, gay and lesbian emancipation has progressed more. Canada, for instance, is less fundamentally religious than are many other countries; this and its heterogeneous culture foster a more tolerant social climate, despite the fact that English Canadians share a similar cultural heritage with their counterparts in the United States. And the Netherlands, having the lowest level of religious affiliation, is one of the most tolerant countries of the world with respect to gay and lesbian rights (Inglehart 1990).

The Capitalist World System

Another important—perhaps the most basic—condition for the emergence and development of a homosexual movement concerns the position of a country in the capitalist world system. As elaborated in Chapter 1, the historical development of capitalism is characterized by market society's subordination of traditional ties with families and the local community. This development, often summarized under broad labels like industrialization, urbanization, and the rise of individualism, provided homosexually interested people with opportunities to distance themselves from the control of their families of origin and to move into more urban settings, offering new possibilities for coming into contact with unattached people and space for the formation of gay and lesbian communities. In cities homosexual men and women discover that they are not alone, and they may become part of a "critical mass," empowering them both in their private lives and in politics.

Not all countries reviewed in this book experience capitalism in the same way, and a fully developed market society does not always result in the same type of social relations (see, for instance, Japan). Being a peripheral or core country in the capitalist system determines the wealth of nations and the opportunity to develop the public services of a welfare state. In addition to wealth, the organization and representation of the different social groups at the political level is important for the type and extent of welfare statism. The relation between the welfare state and the development of a gay and lesbian movement is complex. Welfare state regimes differ on various levels that determine the degree and scope of social security provided by the system.

First, welfare regimes differ with respect to the degree of decommodification or "the degree to which individuals, or families, can uphold a socially accepted standard of living independently of market participation" (Esping-Andersen 1990: 37). This decommodification is important, as it largely determines which and how many people are in a position to do voluntary work. Also, a certain degree of social security means that individuals can take the risk of losing their jobs when they "come out." This is also related to the second dimension, the dominant institution that guarantees social security, either the state, the market, or the family. In countries where the state provides universal and equal social rights (such as Scandinavia), governments familiarize people with social rights (housing, education, health) and may decrease their dependence on patriarchal structures for their income. In this type of welfare state, authorities become acquainted with negotiating and facilitating organized interests, generating a positive political culture for social movements. In more liberal welfare states, where social security is distributed mainly through the free market, provisions are usually very modest and dependent on labor market performance. Japan and the United States are cases in which the welfare state regime and capitalist production are closely associated, as social security is primarily arranged through private enterprises. Conservative welfare state regimes are oriented mainly toward protecting and privileging the traditional family. This results in status reproduction and dependency on the traditional familial economic structure. As the contributors to this book have shown, the conservative welfare state regime is less conducive to the development of a lesbian and gay movement. Movements, then, are related to the development and type of welfare state in capitalist democracies.

The 1950s were characterized in Western Europe and North America by a rapid process of state building, where governments took a hand in the management and regulation of economic growth, following the formula developed in the aftermath of the Great Depression and through wartime production. The 1950s were also characterized by the Cold War and "moral restoration," where states continued to invest in military hardware and to search for (and sometimes imagine) "enemies" both at home and abroad. This reconstruction of patriarchy entailed shifting employed women "back" into the domestic sphere and overtly suppressing gay and lesbian life.

In the 1960s, the "golden days" for socialist and social democratic parties, expansion of the welfare state and its related issues of redistribution had great appeal, particularly in Western Europe. The transformation of the economic and social structure of most Western societies was accompanied by more liberal attitudes toward moral issues. Gay and lesbian groups, along with a wide range of New Left movement organizations, rose to challenge social inequality and state repression both domestically and internationally.

In contrast, the late 1970s and early 1980s brought economic stagnation and fiscal crises in many parts of the world. Market philosophy reasserted its dominance, both in economics and in politics. In those countries in which the gay and lesbian movement was backed by government subsidies and other means of support, the economic crisis undermined this facilitation. The movements in many countries of the developed capitalist world therefore fell back on an "economic" strategy (the power of the gay consumer), and commercial subcultures became the exclusive backbone of political mobilization.

As theorists from Karl Marx to Karl Polanyi have observed, the expanding marketplace cleared away all sorts of traditional social formations in the eighteenth and nineteenth centuries, undercutting the once formidable powers of aristocracies, established churches, and agrarian kinship forms. The outcome was national populations that were bereft of traditional supports and rights but also faced with new freedoms and opportunities. For national minorities, women, Jews, and homosexual people, escape from subordination and the prospect of equal citizenship now seemed possible. In the late twentieth century, the resurgence of market dominance once again threatens to pull away a wide range of social supports and rights, this time guaranteed by the welfare state and including among its beneficiaries a series of vulnerable populations.

With Reaganism and Thatcherism, state and economic elites sought to "harvest" popular insecurity for their program of neoliberal economic restructuring and for the reconstruction of a conservative hegemony. Homophobia was again conscripted as an ideological weapon. Anna Marie Smith's (1994) *New Right Discourse on Race and Sexuality* follows on Stuart Hall's (1988) analysis of Thatcherism to demonstrate how the British elite wielded race and sexuality to try to mobilize people around an agenda of ethnic purification, family values, fundamentalism, and moral discipline. Along with the "specter" of the black immigrant, "queerness became one of the enemy elements which supported the phantasmatic construction of the family as the antagonism-free centre of the British nation" (Smith 1994: 196).

From a sociohistorical viewpoint, then, antihomosexual forces are part of a larger cultural conflict over tradition, family, and social status. One side of the conflict reads "homosexuality" as an assertion of personal autonomy in the erotic sphere; the other reads it as a sign of the abandonment of responsibility for the well-being of the family. The assertion of sexual and affectional preferences partakes of a larger disestablishment of church- and state-regulated family forms. Like the wars over religious and political orthodoxy that preceded it, the battle over homosexuality is part of the war between the enforcement of a single orthodoxy in family formation and an agenda of personal choice among plural options in personal relationships. For conservatives, homosexuality threatens to dismantle a "haven in a heartless world"; their critics point out that a great many people have already been "voting with their feet" by leaving families whose realities are abusive, repressive, or dissatisfying in favor of "havens" of their own making. "Homosexuality" has once again been freighted with a world of meanings that are not intrinsic to same-sex bonding but that give it both meaning and form inside the societies of which it is a part.

Boundaries of Public and Private

Related to many of the issues mentioned above is the degree to which sexuality and sexual identities are considered private or public. The chapters in this volume show that constructing community and experiencing collective sentiments are easier in countries in which sexuality is not absolutely privatized. The more visible and present is the gay and lesbian culture, the smaller is the step toward organizing collectively. Whereas in Japan and the Latin countries people can do a lot in private as long as they do not speak about it in public, in the truth-demanding Puritan countries, people are expected to confess what they do and, thus, what they are (thereby creating a foundation for collective identities). The chapter on Eastern Europe shows, however, that a minimum space free from state intervention and control is crucial for individuals to experience and live their homosexuality. In Eastern Europe decades of intervention and regulation of almost all aspects of an individual's personal affairs by the totalitarian regimes, extended state intervention to its absolute limits and minimized the private realm. This state control seems to have been somewhat less rigid in authoritarian systems such as Francoist Spain and during the military regimes in Brazil and Argentina. In these countries a minimal private sphere (and during the Brazilian Carnaval, even a public space) was retained. This proved crucial for the emergence of a lesbian and gay movement once there was a social and political opening.

Cultural Representations

A related, but nonetheless separate, topic is the way that culture and politics are conceptualized. In countries in which culture is relatively autonomous, homosexuality may flourish in the arts (as in France) without affecting politics and opportunities for gays and lesbians. In other countries, cultural expressions of homosexuality become immediately politicized. From the perspective of the gay and lesbian movement, the politiciation may stimulate mobilization, whereas a great divide between culture and politics may do little for its development.

Only a few of the contributors to this volume deal in depth with cultural products. The image of homosexuality in movies, books, theater, and popular music, as well as in newspapers and on television programs, is sure to affect public attitudes and the larger social and political climate for gay and lesbian people. In many countries in the 1970s, television programs appeared dedicated to homosexuality as a problem, and this public visibility fostered some mobilization by gays and lesbians. Moreover, in the 1980s and 1990s, the mainstream and gay and lesbian press played an important role in the mass mobilization of gays and lesbians in northwestern Europe, North America, Australia, and New Zealand. In this respect it is important whether the media, particularly television, is primarily under state control (as in Eastern Europe), a public service (as in France and the United Kingdom), or largely in the hands of commercial private enterprises (as in Brazil). Commercial broadcasting companies are more apt to portray, even if in a sensationalist manner, deviant patterns of social behavior, whereas state-controlled television tends to "educate" the general public. Publicly owned television in some countries, however, has provided a platform for minorities to present themselves and thereby increase their visibility. This aspect should be viewed from a dynamic perspective, in order to better understand the gay and lesbian movement, since the role of cultural products in general, and the press in particular, shifted in the course of the emancipation process. The chapters in this book show these differences across countries. The moment the gay and lesbian movement gains a degree of political legitimacy, the attention paid to gay and lesbian issues by the press increases significantly, reinforcing the emancipation process. In more repressive countries (such as Eastern Europe and other countries under dictatorships such as Francoist Spain), however, the press tries to silence gay and lesbian voices.

Sibling Movements

The contributors show that other, related social emancipation movements play an important role in the creation of an environment more conducive to the development of the gay and lesbian movement. In particular, the civil rights, women's, and student movements are significant. Countries lacking these movements lag behind in the development of gay and lesbian movements.

Science and Scholarship

For a long time, in almost all countries, both the natural and social sciences have had a negative influence on homosexuality. This is one of the reasons that, at least in some countries, science as such became a site for the struggle of the gay and lesbian movement, sometimes (for example, in the Netherlands and the United States) resulting ultimately in the scattered institutionalization of gay and lesbian studies. In these countries, the picture is quite complex. For instance in the Netherlands, science was quite supportive of homosexuals and their emancipation process. To what extent science could play an emancipatory role depends on the gay and lesbian movement's conception of homosexuality as well. If the movement embraces an essentialist idea of homosexuality, relating sexual orientation to brains, hormones, or genes, even the natural sciences in their ongoing search for a natural basis for (homo)sexuality may be welcomed as allies by the gay and lesbian movement.

Politics of AIDS

With regard to AIDS, two principal effects can be distinguished. First, AIDS increased the visibility of homosexuality in most countries and forced authorities to break through a conspiracy of silence to deal with it. AIDS meant that homosexuality was now discussed (if often negatively). Moreover, in some countries the gay "infrastructure" was used to implement policies of AIDS prevention. Funding and facilitation by the authorities in support of AIDS prevention strengthened some movements and allowed many activists to become professionalized. Some authorities allowed gays and lesbians to participate in official government bodies for the first time (for example, the United States, Australia, and Canada). But AIDS organizations often evolved in their own directions, sometimes denying their origins in gay activism and becoming well-financed social service agencies without little concern for a political agenda (Adam 1997: 23–38).

AIDS also weakened the movement, as the disease struck hard in the gay community and many activists died of its complications. Furthermore, AIDS often proved to be a convenient instrument for homophobic forces intent on using the state to harass or criminalize gay people. The result has been a "degaying" debate in several countries, where AIDS service organizations, gay and lesbian movement groups, and sometimes public health authorities sought to disconnect homosexuality from AIDS, pointing out that HIV transmission could affect "everyone." The consequence of this approach has sometimes been to invest considerable sums of public funds into AIDS campaigns directed to the "general public" to the neglect of those most at risk of infection.

In some countries the movement entered a new period as a result of AIDS, in particular the countries with the highest numbers of people with AIDS (the United States and France). In those countries, many new organizations were founded to combat the homophobic forces that chose AIDS as the new battleground. The new militance around AIDS, in turn, spawned a new queer politics around sexuality. In other countries, like the Netherlands, the recognition of the gay movement as an official counterpart for the government was strengthened by the epidemic, and radicalization did not occur (Duyvendak 1996: 421–38).

Popular Attitudes

All of these social, cultural, and economic tendencies result in and are expressed by the popular attitudes toward homosexuality. Findings (concerning postmaterialist values, support for repression and facilitation, and violence against gays and lesbians) by different contributors to this book illustrate substantial disparities among the countries. The general trend in Europe is for the population in the Nordic Protestant countries to be more accepting toward homosexual behavior than citizens in the southern Catholic belt of Europe. East European societies are even less supportive of homosexuality, and, with the exception of the Czech Republic, only a very small percentage of people in Eastern Europe find homosexuality an acceptable lifestyle. Canadian, Japanese, and Spanish citizens can be found in the mid-range of the distribution, with a significant proportion of the population considering homosexuality as an accepted lifestyle. Australia and the United Kingdom are relatively tolerant societies for lesbians and gay men, whereas parts of the United States are staunchly homophobic. Overall, the U.S. and the southern African populations rank among the least tolerant in the world (Inglehart 1990: 194).

Especially visible in the United States are social constituencies that actively oppose equal citizen rights for gay and lesbian people and that work to suppress any manifestation of homoeroticism. Studies of highly homophobic people show that their homophobia is associated with high scores on measures of racism and sexism (Adam 1978: 42–51; Larsen, Cate, and Reed 1983; Bierly 1985; Seltzer 1992). They are often connected to conservative Protestant denominations (Bouton et al. 1989: 892) that wrap together a set of contemporary social "ills," such as abortion, "increase in crime, drug addiction, family disintegration, sexual promiscuity and illegitimacy among teen-agers, rampant homosexuality, and widespread pornography" (Diamond 1995: 280) into a compendium of signs of social decline. Especially prevalent among people beleaguered by economic restructuring and anxious about family instability, the homophobic constituency has proven that it is available to be mobilized for a series of conservative political and corporate causes.

Empirical research has shown time and again that in most countries younger people are more tolerant toward homosexuality than are older generations, and an increasing proportion of the younger cohorts of the population now regard sexual freedom as more important than traditional sexual morality. This trend is visible in almost all advanced capitalist societies (though Steven Epstein—Chapter 3—notes a new contrary trend in the United States). In all Western countries acceptance of homosexuality increased between 1981 and 1990 (Ester, Halman, and de Moor 1993: 113).

Attitudes and values seem to represent intermediary factors in the development of lesbian and gay movements. Numerous elements discussed herein (gender, class, religion, age, and so on) influence the postures and viewpoints of citizens, which in turn exert their effect on the movement. It is precisely the "translation" of these attitudes and values of the population into a political context that we turn to now.

THE NATIONAL POLITICAL CONTEXT: FACILITATING CONDITIONS

If a certain configuration of the above mentioned prerequisites is not present, it is unlikely that a gay and lesbian movement can come into existence. In other words, these factors are necessary but insufficient conditions for the development of a gay and lesbian movement. Just whether and how a movement develops depend heavily on the national political context. "At least in rich liberal countries it is probably true that the sort of underlying social, economic and cultural shifts which allowed for the emergence of gay liberation, had strong parallels elsewhere. . . . But they only became significant where they could find local meanings" (Altman 1997: 4). The chapters point toward five political factors that determine these local meanings. First, the structure of social cleavages is important, as it determines the format of the party system and the "issue space." Second, the political structure of a country, in particular its electoral system, influences the chances of the movement. Third, variation can be explained by the dominant mechanisms of conflict regulation—in other words, political culture. Fourth, the national power configuration of political parties affects the prospects of gay and lesbian movements. Finally, the judicial situation surrounding homosexuality is relevant in two respects. A certain level of legal adversity facilitates political mobilization, as it provides a real or symbolic "enemy." In situations where legal repression is backed by harsh and regular violence from the police or other entities, it triggers different reactions from the movement and determines whether a movement radicalizes or adopts a more instrumental emancipation strategy. Too much repression, however, is lethal for social movements (see also Kriesi et al. 1992, 1995; Koopmans 1995).

Social Cleavages

When a single dimension of conflict is dominant, all political issues are politicized along the lines of this dimension, leaving little room for new issues to become salient. France is a clear case in point. Multiple cleavages generate multiple issue spaces and cross-cutting interests. In these cases, political elites become experienced in accommodating a multitude of interests, as for instance, in the Netherlands. The rise and fall of issue saliency is not unstructured; shifts in the saliency of issues are the result of changes in the social structure and the political representation of social interests. Political parties, whose origin can usually be traced back to specific social cleavages and conflicts, are crucial in the politicization of issues. As a rule, the political space for new social movements, such as the gay and lesbian movement, depends on the salience of old cleavages.

One of the most dominant cleavages in (at least) Western societies is the state/religion cleavage. The strength of this cleavage, in addition to the restrictive impact of a strong church on the opportunities for the gay and lesbian movement as described above, is dependent upon the extent to which the relation between the state and the church(es) is settled, or at least pacified. In countries where the church still opposes the authority and legitimacy of the state in moral affairs, value systems other than the dominant religious ones will have difficulty in their claim for recognition. In those countries, considerable political energy is spent on the struggle between state and church, hindering other, new topics from entering the political arena, unless the gay and lesbian movement succeeds in becoming a recognized member of a secular front. For instance, France shows that a tense relation between state and church is partly favorable, partly unfavorable for gays and lesbians entering the political arena.

Movement development also depends on the strength of ethnic, national, and linguistic cleavages. In general the occupation of political space by a nationalist, regionalist, or language struggle is not favorable for the gay and lesbian movement, as these issues are usually too dominant to allow other conflict any political saliency (see LaPalombara and Weiner 1966). Nationalist conflicts, for example, may create a social and political atmosphere in which all deviance is rejected as treason. When one conflict or issue dominates to the extent that it threatens the main political institutions, as for example in Ireland until very recently, the political system allows very little space for other issues to become salient. However, the chapters show some contrary examples. Rivalry among nationalist elements can lead to a search for allies and an opening for new political players. As well, nationalist political organization and resistance against repression in general can function as a model for successful contestation for other (minority) groups. Although the political arena may be dominated by these topics, the gay and lesbian movement can ally with these minorities, claiming comparable minority rights, as is evident in Québécois nationalism in Canada and Catalan and Basque nationalism in Spain.

Moreover, the development of the movement depends on the strength of the class struggle. In general we can state that the more class relations are polarized and politicized, the less space there will be for new social movements. Again, this rule needs qualification; a strong labor movement (with the accompanying tradition of political struggle and working-class emancipation) sets an example and creates a historical precedent of liberation, which can function as a model for other "resistance movements." When this historical precedent and potential ally is not available, the emancipation and liberation process is more problematic.

There is also more openness to new social movements in left-wing parties than in center or right-wing political parties. Though in Britain, France, Spain, and Brazil, left-wing political parties and, in particular, Communists were once rather hostile toward gay and lesbian issues, over time the left-wing parties and some unions became considerably more supportive than did right-wing parties. In France, the gay and lesbian movement developed as a new political force, by learning to speak the language of class struggle.

More directly, left-wing political and labor organizations can also become allies in the struggle against discrimination (as was the case with women's and ethnic minority movements), considering that some trade unions related to left-wing parties have to deal with discrimination and harassment in the workplace. In Canada and the United States, labor unions have played an important part in initiating and gaining sexual-orientation protection—and, subsequently, same-sex spousal benefits—in collective agreements, thereby making the extension of similar protections to all citizens less risky for politicians.

Political Structures

The political space for social movements in general, and the gay and lesbian movement in particular, also depends on the political structure. In countries where the political system allows very little room for social and political organization, as in the case of authoritarian regimes, lesbian and gay movements have sought to connect with other liberation or revolutionary movements. The chances of movements' emanating from authoritarian situations seem to depend on the social space prior to the democratic transition. The Institute for Sexology in the Czech Republic and the relative freedom during the period of Carnaval in Brazil are examples of these small niches for expression and organization. Furthermore, it is important whether allies can be identified and a coalition can be constructed with other liberation or emancipatory movements. When gay and lesbian movements face forms of exclusion and opponents similar to other movements around them, they may participate in common analyses and provide mutual support with other subordinated populations—as is evident in the inclusion of the South African movement under the umbrella of the African National Congress, the participation of gay liberation in New Left common fronts in the early 1970s, and the formation of nationalist alliances (as discussed above).

Additionally, the political institutions for the regulation of conflict are important to the development of the gay and lesbian movement. Comparative analysis shows significant differences between majoritarian party systems and multiparty systems with proportional representation. When political institutions are designed to pacify and depoliticize social conflict (consensus democracies), the culture of negotiation and compromise creates possibilities for success. Furthermore, consensus democracies are designed to represent all minorities, which makes the entry of new political actors easier. In majoritarian party systems, where institutions are designed to politicize conflict and generate clear majorities and strong executives, the outcome of the gay and lesbian struggle is dependent on the incumbent party. When opposed to "permissiveness" (like the Conservatives in the United Kingdom and the Republicans in United States), the movement is usually stalemated. When the incumbent is supportive (like the socialist parties in France and Spain), rapid success is possible. In multiparty systems (with coalition governments), parties cannot monopolize the state apparatuses. This usually leaves more room for the gay and lesbian movement to seek political allies within different political groupings and over a longer period of time.

Another dissimilarity between majoritarian and multiparty democracies is the political representation of lesbians and gays within the political institutions. In majoritarian situations, where seats in local and national parliaments have to be won in each constituency, it is difficult for a representative of a minority group to be granted the opportunity to run for office. The list system with proportional representation allows parties to select multiple candidates, which results in wider representation of minorities.

Another meaningful characteristic of the political structure is the level of centralization and decentralization of political authority within a country. What is relevant for the development of gay and lesbian movements is whether or not sufficient autonomy exists for local and regional authorities to deviate from national politics. If there is local or regional autonomy, lesbian and gay movements can create political openings at these levels without necessarily having a strong national political organization. As government entails the monopolization of legitimate coercion over a particular geographical area, the size of the geographical area is important. In decentralized federal states, such as the United States, Canada, and Australia, the local authorities have considerable autonomy in their decision making when compared with unitary states. The degree to which this favors the gay and lesbian movement depends, then, on local power configurations.

As a rule, the chapters in this book show that political opportunities for the gay and lesbian movement increase where there are more points of entry into the political system. Centralization normally obstructs access to the political arena for new political groups, though in some centralized countries this effect is mitigated by the attitude of the authorities toward those who challenge their legitimacy (for instance, in the Netherlands). Britain, under the leadership of Margaret Thatcher, however, was clear evidence that a more centralized system effectively blocks opportunities for gay and lesbian organizations to mobilize at a lower level. The British government introduced Section 28 of the Local Authorities Act to forbid local municipalities, dominated by the so-called socialist "Loony Left," to "promote" homosexuality as an accepted form of family life.

Political Culture

Political structures do not materialize out of thin air; they are the result of the dominant political culture (the system of subjective cognitive, affective, and evaluative predispositions toward processes and institutions of collective decision making). Countries marked by a more participatory political culture allow more social and political space for groups that feel deprived or discriminated against (Almond and Verba 1963). In the countries in our study, the authorities have distinct traditions of exclusion or inclusion of challengers, independent of their political color and social composition. Some of the national political systems have a tradition of facilitation, support, subsidization, and participation of social movements in official governmental bodies, whereas for others repression, censorship, and marginalization are the order of the day (see Kriesi et al. 1995). If, for example, a history of accommodation of minority groups exists (as in the Netherlands in the form of pillarization or in Australia and Canada in the form of multiculturalism), the behavior of the population and the authorities will differ from the behavior in situations where there is a republican tradition rejecting any kind of stable group identity (as is the case in France). In political science this aspect of political culture has been neglected until recently, in part because of a one-sided focus on instrumental movements in which group identities play a less important role. To understand the differences in movement development among, for instance, the United States, Canada, Australia, Japan, France, and the Netherlands, this factor turns out to have a strong explanatory power. Whereas in some countries group identities have a self-evident place and legitimacy in politics, in other countries political ideology hinders the recognition of the reality of a multicultural and multisexual society. In France, a country with a republican tradition, any development of an *identity-based* movement (and subculture) is attacked, from both the left and the right, as at odds with the revolutionary, universalist tradition. This shows again that the broader political culture influences the manner in which minorities are dealt with in different national contexts.

Power Configuration

Cross-national analysis shows unequivocally that the political space for social movements depends on the national power configuration. Support from left-wing parties, primarily of social democratic or liberal origin, is widely associated with movement success. The electoral strength and representation of left-wing parties in government has substantial explanatory power of movement success. Even without political pressure from a strong lesbian and gay movement, left-wing parties in power are responsible for the decriminalization of homosexuality and the implementation of antidiscrimination policies. In most West European countries, left-wing socialist and social democratic parties dominated the political scene in the late 1960s and 1970s, a period that coincides with the emergence and successes of lesbian and gay movements. The decline in political power of the Left in the 1980s (in the Netherlands in 1982, in Germany in 1982, in the United Kingdom in 1979, and in Belgium in 1981) has hindered the homosexual emancipation movements in these countries. Exactly at the moment that support was urgently needed, in order to confront the AIDS epidemic, the political situation became less favorable. The absence of a strong and united left-wing movement may go a long way in explaining the situation in the United States. The rise to power of the New Right, with Ronald Reagan as its mentor, made even liberal politicians reluctant to react to the menace of AIDS in a constructive manner. The strong gay and lesbian movement and community, which had developed in the 1970s, had to deal with the epidemic largely on its own. In southern Europe, the opposite picture emerges: left-wing parties were weak during the 1970s but gained power in the 1980s. Socialists gained control of the executive during the 1980s in France (François Mitterrand became president in 1981) and in Spain in 1982. Again, socialist parties in France and Spain have played a crucial role in the facilitation of lesbian and gay movements. As a paradoxical result of this immediate success, the movement declined. Consequently, the few remaining gay and lesbian organizations were not ready to deal with the AIDS crisis either. It took a long time before an adequate community answer to counter the epidemic developed. In Australia, both Labour and the Liberal Party were supportive, yet only the minor Democratic Party nominated openly gay candidates. In Canada, the small New Democratic Party can be regarded as the most supportive party of the lesbian and gay movement, while in Britain the movement has also leaned strongly to the left in search of support.

One main conclusion that can be drawn from many of the cases is that a negative change in the power configuration is often the principal trigger for mass mobilization. Facilitation by the Left is important to the chances and development of the movement, but the decisive factor seems to be the threat that the situation may worsen. The actions of the main opponents of gay and lesbian emancipation, not facilitation by its allies, provoke large-scale mobilization and activity (for example, Anita Bryant in the United States and the Netherlands, Clause 28 in Britain, and Article 200 and the Orthodox members of Romanian Parliament). This leads to the following conclusions: (1) A movement's strength is largely dependent on the saliency of an issue. (2) The saliency of political issues is not primarily determined by social movements themselves but by their enemies/opponents and, thus, the political configuration. (3) Since sexuality seems to be one of the core issues in late modernity, the saliency of homosexuality in politics will increase and, consequently, so will the need for the gay and lesbian movement to mobilize.

The Judiciary

In addition to the fact that legal repression plays one of the most important roles in the mobilization of lesbian and gay movements, the political space of the movement directly depends on the judicial status of homosexuality. Lesbian and gay groups almost universally direct their activities toward achieving the abolition of criminal penalties for homosexuality and other discriminatory legislation that marginalizes lesbians and gay men.

Apart from the direct and real threat on the quality of the lives of lesbians and gays, discriminatory laws also provide a symbolic focus for the movement, particularly where special laws and stipulations exist regarding homosexual activities and organizations. A clandestine movement may first focus on legalization through negotiation (as was the dominant strategy in northern Europe) or take to the streets and challenge the authorities directly. Where official repression is severe and backed by political violence (as is the case in Eastern Europe) or random violence is backed by homophobic opponents (as is the case in Latin America and South Africa), both strategies are more problematic to implement. The combination of legal and social repression is almost lethal to any social movement while the repression is maintained. However, as soon as legal and violent repression declines and a social opening is created, and perhaps even allies can be found among the "revolutionary" or liberating forces, lesbian and gay movements become visible and mobile. In cases of national repression, processes of international diffusion play a significant role; foreign examples of liberation provide a source of inspiration and imitation. Movements emerging around the world do not "invent the wheel" again. This brings us to our argument that the emergence and development of lesbian and gay movements are not unrelated and unconnected. A distinct and manifest process of transnational diffusion is discernible; gay and lesbian movements all around the world influence and imitate each other.

The International Context: Facilitating Conditions

The various chapters in this book show that it is difficult to write a history of the gay and lesbian movement restricted to a single country. In fact, the question is whether we should still speak of national histories, or whether the international context has become so important that we might talk of a global movement. National factors, nevertheless, do remain striking and weighty; it is better to speak of national imprints of a global movement. Moreover, similarities in movement development across countries do not necessarily imply international diffusion. We should not overlook the possibility that some countries share characteristics and these common characteristics color the national movements in the same direction. Nevertheless, the international context was and is of importance in understanding the emergence and development of lesbian and gay movements. Transnational diffusion is an important facilitating condition for movement development.

As elaborated in the respective country chapters, international organizations such as the International Lesbian and Gay Association (ILGA) actively diffuse ideas and models, stimulating movements to learn from each other in terms of goals, action repertoires, and strategies. The chapters show that representatives of national and international organizations have crossed many borders with the explicit idea of garnering international support for movements that have to work under difficult circumstances. The role of ILGA and of national movements is important in many of the countries researched (for instance, in Spain, South Africa, Brazil, Japan, and East European countries).

Imitation is not a modern phenomenon among homosexual emancipation movements. Even the early movements—for example, the Nederlands Wetenschappelijk-Humanitair Komitee, or NWHK (Dutch Scientific-Humanitarian Committee), which was a complete copy of the German original (Wissenchaftlich-Humanitäres Komitee)—followed a similar pattern. The Spanish movement, to mention just one example, followed almost entirely the French movement and action patterns. These examples illustrate that the impact of international diffusion is most impressive in the situation of a sudden change in political opportunities, such as the opening of the political system in the transition from dictatorship to democracy in which a movement must start from scratch.

Clearly, there is one movement that has been dominant in the world scene: the U.S. movement. Although it is inaccurate to speak of a single national U.S. movement, the worldwide wave of gay and lesbian movements since the late 1960s is attributed to the Stonewall riots in New York. More recently, mobilization around AIDS, for instance ACT UP, started in the United States and was taken over in many countries. These are clear examples of how events and organizations in one country may inspire people all over the world. The fact that the U.S. movement often functions as an example does not imply, however, that U.S. citizens intentionally diffuse their ideas and organizations via such international organizations as ILGA. "The American g/l/b movement has played a relatively small role in attempts to create an international g/l movement. . . . Most U.S. groups are far less interested in relations with their counterparts overseas than, say, groups in Scandinavia or the Netherlands, who have been the major forces backing the development of the International Gay and Lesbian Association (ILGA)," Dennis Altman (1997:4) correctly stated. The U.S. influence runs the risk of being overestimated, or more precisely, the Americanization of the gay and lesbian subculture is sometimes inaccurately extrapolated to the movement. Many European countries figure as examples for movements in Eastern Europe and Latin America.

Many chapters in this book show in detail how international diffusion actually works. Travel and emigration have inspired many people to start groups in their own country or in their newly established domicile. The two Dutch former members of the Cultural and Recreational Center (COC) who founded the Association for Social Knowledge in Canada are a case in point. Of course, these imitations and "transplantations" rarely work out in the same way as in the country of origin. What happens to the gay and lesbian movement in one country upon the development of the gay and lesbian movement in another country? Or to ask the question more precisely, What is the impact of the *perception* of the development of the gay and lesbian movement in one country on its development in another country? Similar names, symbols, issues (gay marriage, antidiscrimination laws), action methods, and so on show that movements learn from each other across borders. There are impressive parallels in the names of organizations: many countries have known "gay liberation fronts," "revolutionary leagues," and so on, indicating that movements follow more or less comparable paths, pass through the same phases, and draw names from other social and political movements with which there is some resemblance in terms of ideology, goals, or methods of resistance.

In an era when queer theory seeks to throw gay and lesbian identity into question, it is interesting to see that gays and lesbians very often feel themselves to be "a people," considering an attack on their brothers and sisters in another country as an assault on themselves (for instance, the Dutch solidarity movement with the U.S. struggle against Anita Bryant). These strong ties of solidarity should be understood in the context of an identity movement, in which the gap between "their" and "our" struggle is rather small. Still, even this international orientation does not necessary imply a smaller relevance of the national context. Many imported goals and strategies that were very successful abroad ultimately did not fit in another context. Consequently, they were altered in order to be applicable and successful in the local situation. Perhaps the most telling example was the transfer of Gay Pride in Australia from the winter (the official commemoration of Stonewall was traditionally in June) to the summer, which transformed a marginal event into a massive celebration of lesbian and gay visibility.

The national context is still of great importance in explaining movement development in a specific country—concerning both the societal context of the "essential prerequisites" for movement emergence and development and regarding the "facilitating conditions" of the political opportunity structure. These factors create impressive cross-national differences among movements; gay and lesbian movements show articulate national imprints, even in a globalizing world.

REFERENCES

Adam, Barry D. 1978. *The Survival of Domination.* New York: Elsevier.
———. 1995. *The Rise of a Gay and Lesbian Movement.* Rev. ed. New York: Twayne.
———. 1997. "Mobilizing around AIDS." In *In Changing Times.* Ed. Martin Levine, Peter Nardi, and John Gagnon. Chicago: University of Chicago Press.
Almond, G. A., and Sidney Verba. 1963. *The Civic Culture: Political Attitudes and Democracy in Five Nations.* Princeton: Princeton University Press.
Altman, Dennis. 1997. "The US G/L/B Movement as a Model: Learning the Limits." *Newsletter of the Gay, Lesbian and Bisexual Caucus of the American Political Science Association* 3(1):4–5.
Bierly, Margaret. 1985. "Prejudice toward Contemporary Outgroups as a Generalized Attitude." *Journal of Applied Social Psychology* 15 (2):189–99.
Bouton, Richard, Peggy Gallaher, Paul Garlinghouse, Terri Leal, et al. 1989.

"Demographic Variables Associated with Fear of AIDS and Homophobia." *Journal of Applied Social Psychology* 19 (11):885–901.

Diamond, Sara. 1995. *Roads to Dominion.* New York: Guilford.

Duyvendak, Jan Willem. 1995. *The Power of Politics: New Social Movements in France.* Boulder Colo.: Westview.

———. 1996. "The Depoliticization of the Dutch Gay Identity, or Why Dutch Gays Aren't Queer." In *Queer Theory/Sociology.* Ed. Stephen Seidman. Cambridge, Mass.: Blackwell.

Esping-Andersen, Gosta 1990. *Three Worlds of Welfare Capitalism.* Cambridge, England: Polity.

Ester, Peter, Loek Halman, and Ruud de Moor. 1993. *The Individualizing Society: Value Change in Europe and North America.* Tilburg, Netherlands: Tilburg University Press.

Gamson, Joshua. 1995. "Must Identity Movements Self-destruct? A Queer Dilemma." *Social Problems* 42 no. 3 (August):390–407.

Hall, Stuart. 1988. *The Hard Road to Renewal.* London: Verso.

Inglehart, Ronald. 1990. *Culture Shift in Advanced Industrial Society.* Princeton: Princeton University Press.

Koopmans, Ruud 1995. *Democracy from Below: New Social Movements and the Political System in West Germany.* Boulder, Colo.: Westview.

Kriesi, Hanspieter, and Jan Willem Duyvendak. 1995. "National Cleavage Structures." In *New Social Movements in Europe. A Comparative Analysis.* Ed. Hanspieter Kriesi, Ruud Koopmans, Jan Willem Duyvendak, and Marco Giugni. Minneapolis: University of Minnesota Press.

Kriesi, Hanspieter, Ruud Koopmans, Jan Willem Duyvendak, and Marco Giugni. 1992. "New Social Movements and Political Opportunities in Western Europe." *European Journal for Political Research* 22.

———, eds. 1995. *New Social Movements in Europe: A Comparative Analysis.* Minneapolis: University of Minnesota Press.

LaPalombara, Joseph, and Myron Weiner, eds. 1966. *Political Parties and Political Development.* Princeton: Princeton University Press.

Larsen, Knud, Rodney Cate, and Michael Reed. 1983. "Anti-black Attitudes, Religious Orthodoxy, Permissiveness, and Sexual Information." *Journal of Sex Research* 19:105–18.

Prochazka, Ivo. 1994. "Sexuality in the Czech Republic." Paper presented at the Organizing Sexuality. Conference, Amsterdam.

Putnam, Robert, Robert Leonardi, and Raffaelle Nannetti. 1993. *Making Democracy Work: Civic Traditions in Modern Italy.* Princeton: Princeton University Press.

Seltzer, Richard. 1992. "The Social Location of Those Holding Antihomosexual Attitudes." *Sex Roles* 26, no. 9–10:391–398.

Smith, Anna Marie. 1994. *New Right Discourse on Race and Sexuality.* New York: Cambridge University Press.

About the Contributors

BARRY D ADAM is professor of sociology at the University of Windsor, Ontario, and author of *The Survival of Domination* (Elsevier, 1978), *The Rise of a Gay and Lesbian Movement* (Twayne, 1995), and *Experiencing HIV* (with Alan Sears; Columbia University Press, 1996). He has also published articles on new social movement theory, on Sandinista Defense Committees and news coverage of Nicaragua, on gay and lesbian issues, and on social aspects of AIDS. Website: http://www.cs.uwindsor.ca/users/a/adam/index. htm.

DENNIS ALTMAN is professor of politics at LaTrobe University, Melbourne, and the author of nine books, including *Homosexual: Oppression and Liberation, Power and Community: Organisational and Cultural Responses to AIDS* (Taylor and Francis, 1994) and, most recently, *Defying Gravity: A Political Life* (Allen and Unwin, 1997). He has served on a number of community and government AIDS bodies.

STEPHEN BROWN, a native of Montréal, is currently working on his Ph.D. in political science at New York University. His dissertation will analyze the role of foreign aid in democratic transitions and consolidation in Africa. Brown's interest in Argentina's campier side can be traced to his days as a student of Latin American politics at the London School of Economics, when he came across a kitschy secondhand book on Evita Perón.

JAN WILLEM DUYVENDAK is professor of community development at the Erasmus University of Rotterdam and author, *The Power of Politics: New Social Movements in France* (Westview Press, 1995), *The Pillarization of the Gay Movement* (in Dutch, SUA, 1994), and numerous articles on gay and social movement issues. He is also the co-author, with Hanspieter Kriesi, Ruud Koopman, and Marco Giugni, of *New Social Movements in Western Europe* (University of Minnesota Press, 1995). He is former assistant professor of gay studies at the University of Nijmegen.

STEVEN EPSTEIN is associate professor of sociology at the University of California at San Diego. He is also affiliated with the Science Studies Program there. His recent book, *Impure Science: AIDS, Activism, and the Politics of Knowledge* (University of California Press 1996), received the C. Wright Mills Award of the Society for the Study of Social Problems.

He has written articles on topics such as AIDS activism, gay politics, and gay identity.

OLIVIER FILLIEULE is a researcher at the CNRS-CRESAL (Centre national de la recherche scientifique) and assistant professor at the Fondation nationale des sciences politiques, in Paris, France. His main areas of research include social movements, political violence, public order policies and AIDS activism. Among his publication are *Stratégies de la rue: Les manifestations en France* (Presses de science po, 1997).

JAMES N. GREEN is assistant professor of Latin American history at California State University at Long Beach and an editor of *Latin American Perspectives*. He was a cofounding member of Brazil's first gay and lesbian rights group, SOMOS: Grupo de Afirmação Homossexual, and currently coordinates the Gay and Lesbian Caucus of the Brazilian Studies Association (BRASA). A revised version of his doctoral dissertation from the University of California at Los Angeles, entitled "Beyond Carnival: Homosexuality in Twentieth-Century Brazil," is being published by the University of Chicago Press.

ANDRÉ KROUWEL is assistant professor of comparative political science at the Vrije Universiteit of Amsterdam, the Netherlands, and author of several articles on Western European politics and on gay and social movement issues.

RICARDO LLAMAS holds a Ph.D. in political science and sociology from Complutense University of Madrid (1995) and is the editor of the book *Construyendo sidentidades* [Constructing AIDS-related identities]: Estudios desde el corazón de una pandemia (Siglo XXI, 1995). He is also the author of *Miss Media: Una lectura perversa de la comunicación de masas* (Ediciones de la Tempestad, 1997), a critical study of representations of homosexuality in the Spanish mass media (see http://www.teclata.es/index/nou/missmedia/miss.html), and of the forthcoming book *Teoría torcida* (Twisted theory) (Siglo XXI). He was cofounder of the Madrid-based group La Radical Gai and was active in the group from 1991 to 1996.

SCOTT LONG is advocacy coordinator with the International Gay and Lesbian Human Rights Commission in San Francisco.

WIM LUNSING is associate research professor in the Department of Asian Studies at the University of Copenhagen. He received his master's degree in Japanese studies from the University of Leiden (Netherlands) in 1988 and conducted research at the University of Vienna in 1989 and 1994 and fieldwork in Japan, based at Osaka University of Foreign Studies and at Kyoto Seika University, from 1991 to 1993. This led to his dissertation, for which he received his doctorate in social anthropology from Oxford

Brookes University (England) in 1995. In 1996 he was a research fellow at the University of Tokyo.

MAI PALMBERG is a Finnish political scientist, journalist, and author. She is a coordinator of the research project Cultural Images in and of Africa at the Nordic Africa Institute in Uppsala, Sweden. Together with Chris Dunton, she wrote "Human Rights and Homosexuality in Southern Africa" (Nordic Africa Institute, 1996). Her e-mail address is mai.palmberg@nai.uu.se.

KEN PLUMMER is professor of sociology at the University of Essex (England). He has written widely on lesbian and gay issues; his major books in this area are *Sexual Stigma* (Routledge and Kegan Paul, 1975), *The Making of the Modern Homosexual* (editor; Hutchinson, 1981), *Modern Homosexualities: Fragments of Lesbian and Gay Experience* (editor; Routledge, 1992), and *Telling Sexual Stories: Power, Change, and Social Worlds* (Routledge, 1995). He has also written on symbolic interactionist theory and life stories and is currently editing a new journal, *Sexualities,* and coauthoring an introductory sociology textbook, *Sociology: A Global Perspective.*

JUDITH SCHUYF is senior researcher at the Information Centre for War Victims (ICODO) in the Netherlands. She studied history and prehistory at Leiden University (Netherlands) and is a founder of the Homostudies Department at the University of Utrecht (Netherlands). Recent publications include "A Conspiracy of Silence" (Amsterdam: Institute for Social History, 1994) on the history of lesbians in the Netherlands, and *Gevoelsgenoten van een zekere leeftijd* (Same-Sex Companions of a Certain Age, Amsterdam: Schorer-van Gennip, 1996).

FEFA VILA is a doctoral candidate in sociology at the Complutense University of Madrid finishing a dissertation entitled "Gender Divisions and Technological Change." She is the author of several articles on the ways that lesbians are represented in so-called dominant discourses, on the articulation of counterdiscourses, and on the expression of political practices from a queer standpoint. She has taught feminist studies at the University of Utrecht (Netherlands), the University of Manchester (United Kingdom), and the University of California at Santa Cruz. Fefa Vila is an activist in the Madrid group Lesbianas Sobretodo Diferentes and is coeditor of the queerzine *Non-Grata.*

GEOFFREY WOOLCOCK is a graduate student in the School of Politics at LaTrobe University in Melbourne. He was formerly the education manager of the Queensland AIDS Council and a researcher at the National Centre for HIV Social Research. He has also written a report for the United Nations Development Program (UNDP) on transitions from HIV to AIDS.

Index

Aarmo, Margrete, 289n. 2
Aboriginal people, 21, 26, 54, 332, 339–40
Abzug, Bella, 45
ACT-UP, 55–57, 60, 129n. 7, 138, 145, 147, 198–204, 209nn. 28–30, 232, 240n. 28, 308, 338, 349, 369
Adair, Casey, 46
Adair, Nancy, 46
Adam, Barry, 3–5, 70, 350
African people: in the Americas, 20, 37–38, 40–41, 44–45, 47, 50, 54, 56, 59, 65, 97; in United Kingdom, 138, 150. *See also* Namibia; South Africa; Zimbabwe
Age of consent, 13, 59, 142, 144–45, 164, 180n. 8, 192, 214–15, 247–48, 251–52, 270. *See also* Man-boy relationships
AIDS, 7, 15, 52–57, 59, 67, 80n. 27, 99–100, 103–4, 116, 121, 124, 133–34, 140, 142–43, 169–70, 194–204, 229–33, 249, 251, 264n. 31, 283, 304, 308–9, 313, 319n. 27, 336–41, 348–49, 359, 366
Alas, Leopoldo, 228
Almodóvar, Pedro, 228
Altman, Dennis, 2, 40, 43, 53, 55, 265n. 40, 349, 361, 369
Amsterdam, 1, 162, 165, 173–74
Anabitarte, Héctor, 230, 239n. 20
Anzaldúa, Gloria, 50
Apuzzo, Virginia, 72
Arcadie, 188, 191, 193, 206nn. 5–8, 218, 351
Argentina, 91–92, 110–30, 357
Asian people, in diaspora, 20, 54, 65, 138, 306, 340–41. *See also* Japan
Australia, 314, 326–43, 359–60, 366

Balletbó-Coll, Marta, 229
Barcelona, 215, 217–20, 226–27, 231–32, 237n. 8, 238n. 15

Baudry, André, 188
Beauvoir, Simone de, 191
Bergamín, José, 215
Berridge, Virginia, 142
Bilbao, 219, 223, 227, 231, 237n. 8
Bisexuality, 40, 50, 61–62, 68, 80n. 31, 99–100, 101, 105, 121, 125, 139, 149–50, 232, 306–7, 313
Brazil, 91–109, 353, 357
Brodie, Janine, 24
Britt, Harry, 46
Bryant, Anita, 46, 165, 367
Bryant, Gigi, 106
Buenos Aires, 110, 114, 127
Burgmann, Verity, 332

Cameron, Edwin, 267, 275
Canada, 12–27, 279, 282, 349, 352, 354, 359–60, 362–363, 367
Cape Town, 268–269, 272
Capitalism, 3, 5, 25–26, 42, 118, 124, 149, 189, 259, 268, 272, 339
Carolus, Cheryl, 274
Carr, Adam, 338
Censorship, 18, 51, 96, 141, 143, 149, 276–81, 319n. 30, 339
Chakaodza, Bornwell, 276, 280
Chiminhi, David, 281
COC (Cultural and Recreational Center), Vancouver, 12, 161–64, 169, 172–77
Cohen, Jean, 117, 122
Colorado, 6, 16, 68
Communism, 35, 178, 190, 206n. 12, 217, 219, 221, 226–27, 244, 248, 251, 253, 258, 300–301, 353, 363
Conservatism, 13, 15–16, 18, 23–26, 41, 49, 55, 67, 134–37, 145, 153n. 15, 159–60, 244, 272, 299–301
Cooper, Davina, 136
Corrigan, Philip, 5, 20, 24
Czech Republic, 246–50, 254–55, 259, 353, 360